The
CAT

A Black and white Longhaired Domestic.

A Golden Persian.

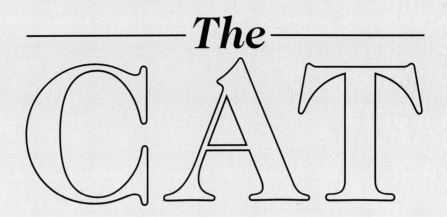

The
CAT

First edition by
Dorothy Silkstone Richards

Revised by
Phil Maggitti

Editorial Consultant (Revised edition)
Richard Gebhardt

Illustrated by
John Francis

TIGER BOOKS INTERNATIONAL
LONDON

A Salamander Book

This edition published in 1995 by
Tiger Books International PLC, Twickenham

© Salamander Books 1993

ISBN 1-85501-762-8

Credits

Editor: Will Steeds
Designer: John Heritage
Colour reproduction: Scantrans PTE Ltd., Singapore
Filmset: The Old Mill, London
Printed in Singapore

An Oriental Brown-spotted Shorthair.

Author (First edition)

Dorothy Silkstone Richards B.Sc. writes about cats from practical experience, for until recently Mrs. Richards bred Burmese at her home in Bedford, in the United Kingdom. Her cats have won many prizes at shows. Dorothy has written two books on cat breeding and co-authored one on her favourite breed, the Burmese. Many years serving on the committees of various cat clubs and the Pet Trade Association, first-hand experience of boarding all breeds and wide-ranging travels have given Dorothy a valuable insight into the problems and temperaments of all breeds of cats; an insight put to excellent purpose in this book.

Author (Revised edition)

Phil Maggitti has written extensively on cats and cat-related matters. He is a regular contributor to *Cats* magazine, edited the *Cat Fanciers' Association Yearbook* for several years, and has authored two books: *Scottish Fold Cats: A Complete Pet Owner's Manual* and *Show Animals on Parade*, which was published in the United States in 1989. He also edited Editorial Consultant Richard H. Gebhardt's *The Complete Cat Book*, which was published in 1991.

Editorial Consultant (Revised edition)

Richard H. Gebhardt became a Cat Fanciers' Association judge in 1953, and has since judged in Europe and Japan as well as in the United States. He was Guest Judge at the Centennial National Cat Show in London in 1971, and was President of the CFA from 1968 through to 1980. He has written extensively on cats. His latest book, *The Complete Cat Book*, was published in 1991.

Publisher's note

The British and the American cat fancies are two hobbies divided by a common language. Just as the appearance of some breeds varies between the United Kingdom and the United States, so, too, the conventions regarding the spelling and capitalization of breed names and colours. In this volume we have attempted to adhere to British conventions as regards capitalization of breed names and colours. Where breed names and/or colours differ according to American usage, the American version is given in brackets, following the name and/or colour used in the United Kingdom.

Contents

Part One
PROFILE SECTION
Detailed profiles of all major breeds, arranged in longhaired and shorthaired sections.

A Silver Tabby British Shorthair.

Part Two
PRACTICAL SECTION
Essential information for everyone who owns a cat or is thinking of buying one.

INTRODUCTION

There are more than 40 breeds of cats accepted for championship competition among the six independent cat registries in North America and the two cat associations in the United Kingdom. To the person used to thinking of cats in terms of only two breeds — the Siamese and the Persian — 40 might seem like an excessively large number of distinctions to make in a small animal such as the cat. Nevertheless, the cat fancy is built on such distinctions.

Although the cat fancy is more than 120 years old, the majority of the breeds eligible to compete at shows today have been accepted during the last 40 years. As recently as the mid-1950s, seven breeds were represented at shows: Persian, Siamese, Burmese, Abyssinian, American Shorthair, Manx and Russian Blue. Many of the breeds that have been accepted in the meantime are simply variations on these themes. The Colourpoint (Himalayan) and the Exotic Shorthair owe their facial type and body conformation to the Persian. The Balinese, Oriental Shorthair, Oriental Longhair and Havana (Havana Brown) owe the same debt to the Siamese. The Tonkinese is a hybrid creation of Siamese-Burmese ancestry; the Bombay is a hybrid whose components are Burmese and Black American Shorthairs; and there are some cat fanciers who believe that the Singapura, allegedly discovered on the streets of Singapore, may have been created from crosses between Burmese and Abyssinians instead.

Two of the original magnificent seven breeds — the Abyssinian and the Manx — are now available in longhaired versions: the Somali, which is a longhaired Aby, and the Cymric, which is a longhaired Manx. And one of the original seven breeds, the American Shorthair, has a wire-coated, distant relative called the American Wirehair, which sprang from a mutation in a domestic shorthaired cat, and a curl-eared distant relative called the American Curl that was inspired by a mutation of its own.

Many of the new breeds that were not created from traditional stock borrow several traditional characteristics. The Birman, Ragdoll and Snowshoe are pointed breeds, which means that their faces, ears, legs and tails are a different colour from their bodies.

Similarities are also found between 'sets' of new breeds: spots mark the bodies of the Egyptian Mau, Bengal and Ocicat; the Scottish Fold began life as a British Shorthair with folded ears; there are two Rex-coated breeds — the Devon and the Cornish; and two additional all-blue cats — the Korat and the Chartreuse (Chartreux) — have joined the Russian Blue on the show bench.

People who prefer longer noses on their longhaired cats may admire the Maine Coon Cat, the Norwegian Forest Cat, the Angora (known in America as the Turkish Angora) or the Turkish Van.

Cat fanciers for whom regular tails are too much and tailless cats are too little will find a new twist on tails in the Japanese Bobtail, while persons who believe that less is more might find the Sphynx, which is virtually hairless, to their liking.

Part One

PROFILE SECTION

Detailed profiles of all recognized breeds, divided into longhaired and shorthaired sections.

Part One of this book aims to provide the potential cat owner with a comprehensive guide to choosing the most suitable cat. Beautiful, full-colour illustrations present typical examples of each breed, and detailed drawings show the distinctive shape of the head in each case. Alternative coat colours and patterns are featured in accompanying colour photographs.

There are two basic body types in cats: the substantial, cobby, round-headed Persian (Longhair) and the svelte, tubular Siamese with its wedge-shaped head. All other breeds, regardless of coat length, occupy intermediate points on a continuum anchored by these two types. The Exotic Shorthair, for example, is close to the Persian body type while the Somali approximates to the Siamese type.

Coat length also comes in two basic varieties: long and short. Curly, crimped and near-hairless coats are all variations on the shorthair theme.

Colour is the cat's most variable resource. Whereas cats appear to lack the genetic malleability — *vis-a-vis* size — displayed by dogs, cat breeders have tended to develop new colours instead of new breeds. There are, accordingly, scores of different colours and patterns among cats.

In the Profile Section, each breed, and sometimes each colour, of cat is considered individually. Cats' virtues are listed under *Good points* and their liabilities, if any, are listed under *Take heed*.

As a rule, any discussion of breed personalities is fraught with generalities, and whenever someone makes bold to say what a breed is like, that person is most likely summarizing the characteristics of his or her cats. There are more than 40 breeds of cats, and it would be splitting hairs to assert that each has a distinct personality. Expect, therefore, to find some adjectives being recycled in the *Good points* lists.

The *Grooming* requirements of each breed are outlined: it is foolish to choose a Persian unless 15 or 20 minutes are set aside for grooming its long coat (at least three times a week). For people with less time there are other lovely cats that need little grooming to keep them looking smart.

The paragraphs devoted to *Origin and history* attempt to sort fact from fiction in discussing the development of each breed. The *Breeding* and *Kittens* sections present a glimpse of the difficulties involved in working with particular breeds.

The *Show standard* lists the details of each breed under headings such as Coat, Body and Tail. This description outlines what is expected of a top-show specimen. Each breed profile is concluded by a list of *Colours* and coat patterns available within the breed.

No animal has suffered more extremes of fortune than the cat, which still remains misunderstood for being so frequently misrepresented. Neither devil nor demigod, the cat deserves a fair interpretation.

Persons considering a cat would do well to reflect on this observation by Lloyd Alexander, author of *The Black Cauldron* and other books: 'Perhaps a small part of the cat's notorious reserve and aloofness is something like whistling in the dark. A cat's life can be as difficult as our own. And it may be that we comfort them for being cats as much as they comfort us for being human.'

COLOURS AND COAT PATTERNS

With the exception of lime green and canary yellow, cats come in virtually every colour imaginable. These colours are categorized according to two variables: the longitudinal amount of space they occupy on the hair shaft of the cat and the pattern in which they are deployed on the cat's body.

Self (or solid) colours

The most elementary colours are the solid colours, which are sometimes known as self colours. These occupy the entire hair shaft from its tip to its root. No matter the shade preferred, the most desirable trait is soundness and uniformity of colour.

Black Dense, coal black. Free from any tinge of rust on the tips of the hairs or any wisps of smoky undercoat. Ebony, which is black's mirror image, is a synonym for black in the Oriental Shorthair and Oriental Longhair breeds.

Blue An even, pale blue from nose to tail. Ideally the blue coat should be sound to the roots. A light shade of blue is preferred, but a sound, darker shade is more acceptable than a lighter shade that is uneven.

Red A deep, rich, brilliant red, unblemished by shading, markings or ticking.

Cream One level shade of buff cream from the tip of each hair to its roots. No tabby markings please. Lighter shades of cream are preferred but, as with the blue, an even, darker shade is more acceptable than an uneven light one.

White Pure, glistening unsullied white — different varieties of which occur in cats, including glacial, eggshell or a soft, glowing white. Any yellow tinge is objectionable.

Chocolate A rich, flavourful colour that is deep and sound throughout. Related colours are chestnut, which is chocolate's first cousin, and cinnamon and caramel, which are dilute variations of chocolate.

Lilac A frosty-grey colour with a pinkish cast. Sometimes known as lavender, frost or platinum.

Fawn Pale, pinkish fawn. Sound throughout. Lighter shades preferred. This colour is found in Abyssinians and Somalis and, as fawn cream, in Oriental Shorthairs and Oriental Longhairs.

The bicolour pattern A bicolour is a white cat with unbrindled patches of one of the following solid colours: black, blue, red or cream. Bicolours may also combine white with one of the tabby patterns. In bicolours, white should be distributed on the feet, legs, undersides, chest and muzzle.

The Van pattern A pattern displayed by cats that are mostly white with patches of colour occuring on the head, tail, legs and — in one or two small dabs — on the body as well.

Cats with more than two or three spots of colour on their bodies should be shown in the bicolour, not the van, class in the US.

Tipped cats

The hair shafts on some cats are tinted to varying degrees from the end of the shaft inwards. The remainder of the hair shaft, right down to the cat's body, is white or cream. These cats are called shell,

Black
American Shorthair

Red
Cornish Rex

Blue
Persian (Longhair)

Cream
British Shorthair

shaded or smoke, depending on how much of the hair shaft is occupied by colour and how much is given over to white.

Shell This is the most lightly coloured of the tipped varieties. When the colour at the tips of the hair shafts (the tipping colour) is red, this colour is known as shell cameo or red chinchilla. The undercoat is white. The coat on the back, flanks, head and tail is sufficiently tipped with red to give a characteristic, sparkling appearance to cats of this kind. Face and legs may be very slightly shaded with tipping. Chin, ear tufts, stomach and chest are white. (In the Devon Rex and Oriental Shorthair breeds this shading is called silver, which is not the same as the colour chinchilla silver that is found in the Exotic Shorthair and the Persian.)

Chinchilla silver The undercoat is pure white. The coat on the back, flanks, head and tail is sufficiently tipped with black to give a characteristic, sparkling-silver appearance. Legs may be slightly shaded with tipping colour. Chin, ear tufts, stomach and chest are pure white. Rims of eyes, lips and nose are outlined with black.

Chinchilla golden The undercoat of the goldens, both Chinchilla and Shaded, unlike that of the other shell, shaded and smoke cats, is a rich, warm cream. The coat on the back, flanks, head and tail is sufficiently tipped with black to give a golden appearance. Legs may be slightly shaded with tipping colour. Chin, ear tufts, stomach and chest, are cream. Rims of eyes, lips and nose are outlined with black.

Shaded This is the intermediate tipped colour, halfway in tone between the subtle shells and the solid-looking smokes. When their basic colour is red, cats with tipping are known as shaded cameo or red shaded. The undercoat is white with a mantle of red tipping that shades down from the sides, face and tail from a deep hue on the ridge to white on the chin, chest, stomach and under the tail. Legs are the same tone as the face. The general effect is much darker than a shell shading. Eye colour among shaded cats varies from copper in the shaded cameo (red shaded) cats to blue or blue-green in all other shaded colours.

Shaded silver The undercoat is white with a mantle of black tipping that shades down from the sides, face and tail from a deep hue on the ridge to white on the chin, chest, stomach and under the tail.

Legs are the same tone as the face. The general effect is much darker than a chinchilla. Rims of eyes, lips and nose are outlined with black.

Pewter Similar to the shaded silver but with copper instead of green or hazel eyes. This colour is recognized in the UK only.

Shaded golden The undercoat is a rich, warm cream with a mantle of black tipping that shades down from the sides, face and tail from dark on the ridge to cream on the chin, chest, stomach and under the tail. Legs are the same tone as the face. The general effect is much darker than a chinchilla. Rims of eyes, lips and nose are outlined with black.

Smoke The smoke is the most heavily coloured of the tipped varieties. Indeed, the best smokes

Chocolate
Havana (UK)

White
Oriental (Foreign)
Shorthair

Lilac
Angora

Bicolour
Black-and-white Maine Coon

Piebald
Black-and-white
Household pet

look like solid-coloured cats until they move, and their white undercoat comes peeking through. The undercoat is white, deeply tipped with the cat's basic colour.

Particolour cats

These are essentially patched cats in the US, and mingled in the UK; when combined with white, the colours are patched.

Tortoiseshell A cat with unbrindled patches of red and cream combined with some other colour such as black or chestnut. The patches are clearly defined and well broken on the body and extremities (US), or mingled (UK). A blaze of red or cream on the face is desirable.

Kittens may not display the colour attributes required in the breed standard. Young torties with greying in their black or chestnut fur should not be penalized by the judges for this temporary shortcoming.

Blue-cream In the United States a blue cat with patches of solid cream. The patches are clearly defined and well broken on the body and extremities. In the UK a cat on which the blue and cream colours are mingled together softly. In either country a blaze — one side blue, the other cream — down the centre of the forehead and the face is desirable, especially when the colours are reversed on the chin.

Lilac-cream The dilute form of chocolate tortoiseshell, this colour combines lilac with patches of solid cream (in the US), or lilac with cream hairs intermingled (in the UK).

Calico A white cat with unbrindled patches of black and red. White predominates on the underparts. Among many cat fanciers and geneticists, calicos are known by the far less sprightly and far more obvious term 'tortoiseshell-and-white'.

Dilute Calico A white cat with unbrindled patches of blue and cream. White predominates on the underparts. Serious cat admirers call this colour 'dilute tortoiseshell-and-white' or 'blue tortoiseshell-and-white'. But a Dilute Calico by any name is a fetching and oftentimes ethereal-looking cat.

The tabby pattern

There are five varieties of tabbies: Classic, Mackerel, Patched, Ticked and Spotted. The Classic Tabby has markings that are dense, clearly defined and broad. Its legs are evenly barred with bracelets coming up to meet its body markings. The tail is evenly ringed. There are several unbroken necklaces on the neck and upper chest, the more the better. There are frown marks on the forehead that form an intricate letter 'M'. An

unbroken line runs backwards from the outer corner of the eye. There are swirls on the cheeks, and vertical lines over the back of the head that extend to the shoulder markings. The latter are in the shape of a butterfly with both the upper and lower wings distinctly outlined and marked with dots inside the outline. Back markings consist of a vertical line down the spine from butterfly to tail with a vertical stripe paralleling it on each side. These three stripes are well separated by stripes of the ground colour. There is a large, solid blotch on each side of the cat, encircled by one or more unbroken rings. The configuration, known as a 'bullseye', is the distinguishing feature of the Classic Tabby cat. The side markings are the same on both sides. There is a double, vertical row of buttons on the chest and stomach. The hocks are the same colour as the markings.

The Mackerel Tabby has markings

Light Tipping
*Chinchilla Cymric
(Longhaired Manx)*

Medium Tipping
*Shaded Red
American Shorthair*

Heavy Tipping
Blue Smoke Persian (Longhair)

Tortoiseshell
*Brown Tortoiseshell British
Shorthair*

that are dense and clearly defined. Narrow pencillings decorate the body, starting at the spine and extending down both sides of the cat. The effect resembles a fish skeleton, hence the name mackerel tabby. The legs are evenly barred with narrow bracelets coming up to meet the body markings. The tail is barred. There are distinct necklaces on the neck and chest. The head is barred with an 'M' on the forehead. Unbroken lines run back from the eyes. Lines run down the head to meet the shoulders. Spine lines run together to form a narrow saddle. The hocks are the same colour as the markings.

The Patched Tabby (US) is also called a torbie or a Tortie Tabby. This is a brown, silver or blue tabby that has patches of red and/or cream in its coat.

The Ticked Tabby has body hairs that are ticked with various shades of marking colour and ground colour. The body, when viewed from the top, is free from noticeable spots, stripes or blotches, except for a darker, dorsal shading. The lighter underside may show tabby markings. The face, legs and tail must show distinct tabby striping, and the cat must have at least one distinct necklace.

The Spotted Tabby has spotted markings on its body. They may vary in size and shape, but round, evenly distributed spots are preferred. The spots should not run together in a broken mackerel pattern. A dorsal stripe runs the length of the body from the shoulders to the tip of the tail. This stripe is ideally composed of spots. The markings on the face and forehead shall be typical tabby markings: a well-formed letter 'M' on the forehead, an unbroken line running backwards from the outer corners of the eyes, and swirls on the cheeks. The underside of the body has 'vest buttons'. The legs and tail are barred.

Where tabbies get their stripes
The tabby is an intricate pattern, derived from two separate component patterns, one superimposed upon the other. These patterns are governed by two different sets of genes.

The underlying pattern, called the agouti, is a grey, camouflaging pattern found in the great majority of mammals, most notably in the rabbit. Hairs marked by the agouti pattern are blue at the base, black at the tip and have a band of yellow in between. Because the hairs of a cat slope naturally backwards, the yellow band of the agouti pattern appears grey between the tabby's darker stripes. (In solid or self coloured cats, the presence of a non-agouti gene eliminates the yellow band, thus making the hair shaft all one colour.)

Because the agouti pattern is produced by a dominant gene, a cat needs to inherit only one copy of that gene in order to develop a tabby coat. It is possible, also, for two tabbies to produce black, non-agouti offspring.

The second tabby pattern, which is superimposed over the agouti pattern, is responsible for the stripes and spots that decorate tabby cats. Stripes have been seen on cats from the time that cats were first seen by humans. Both the African and the European wild cats are striped, and these cats most likely bequeathed their stripes to the domestic Mackerel Tabby cat.

In the mackerel pattern, narrow, gently curving stripes running perpendicular to the spine encircle both sides of the cat. This pattern occurs in cats of any body type and coat length. The gene responsible for the mackerel tabby pattern is represented by the letter T.

There are two mutant alleles (or different forms) of the T gene. One of these alleles produces the blotched (or classic) tabby pattern. The other allele produces the ticked

Chocolate Tortoiseshell
Persian (Longhair)

Lilac-cream
Lilac Tortie
Burmese

Blue-cream
Scottish Fold

Tortoiseshell-and-white (Calico)
American Wirehair

(or Abyssinian) tabby pattern. In the hierarchy of tabbies, the ticked pattern is dominant to the mackerel, which is dominant to the blotched pattern. While each of the tabbies is attractive in its own right, the classic pattern is most striking, especially in short-haired varieties that have vivid, dense black markings and a rich, brown or silver ground colour.

Many novices are surprised to learn that the ticked (or Abyssinian) tabby pattern can appear on other breeds as well. What's more, if one looks closely enough, it becomes apparent that Abyssinians have tabby markings on their faces and, oftentimes, on their legs and tails. In the best Abyssinians virtually every hair is agouti with no overlay of a second tabby pattern.

In reality, all the colours that occur in Mackerel, Classic and Spotted Tabbies can occur also in Abyssinians. The basic Abyssinian colour — known in the United Kingdom as the 'usual' and in the

United States as the 'ruddy' — is described in the UK standard as a 'rich, golden brown, ticked with black'. The Sorrel (Red) Abyssinian is a lustrous copper, ticked with chocolate and the base hair [is] deep apricot'. Chocolate, Blue and Lilac Abyssinians also have been bred. In addition, Silver Abys incorporating the inhibitor gene have appeared. These cats may seem to be at some remove from the fundamental striped tabby cat, but they are more closely related than one might think at first.

Some breeders believe that a third mutation of the tabby gene is responsible for the spotted patterns on breeds such as the Egyptian Mau, the Bengal, the Ocicat, the California Spangled Cat and the Spotted Oriental Shorthair. The presence of spotted patterns in several wild cat species lends support to this theory. Most geneticists believe, however, that the spotted pattern on domestic cats is

actually a broken mackerel tabby pattern. The existence of a variety of tabbies — from mackerel to half-spotted to fully spotted — supports this view. Indeed, breeders working to produce Spotted Tabby cats must use only the most distinctly marked Spotted Tabbies in their breeding programmes or else the spots will eventually (re)unite into a mackerel tabby pattern. Moreover, tabby bars on the legs and chest may be found in some cats with the most clearly defined spots. Conversely, Mackerel Tabby breeders are challenged to maintain unbroken stripes on the cats they produce: all of which suggests that the spotted tabby pattern is not a monogenic trait (controlled by a single allele), but is polygenic (controlled by a number of alleles) instead.

Tabby colours

The basic tabby is a black cat genetically and possesses the same colour genes as the solid or

self black. Breeders of pedigree tabbies, however, have selected cats that exhibit the maximum expression of the rufous polygenes. These are responsible for modifying the ground colour of the garden variety tabby over generations of selective breeding so that its pedigree relative emerges with a rich brown rather than a drab grey colour between its stripes. In the same manner, selective breeding is responsible for transforming the ginger colour of the alley cat into the deep mahogany red of the pedigree Red Tabby — even though both varieties owe their colour to the same orange gene.

While different classes are provided at cat shows for solid red and red tabby cats, all red (or orange) cats are tabbies. Breeders working with solid reds select cats with little — or hopefully no — residual tabby markings.

Brown and Red Tabbies are the best-known tabby varieties, but

Mackerel Tabby
Cream Persian (Longhair)

Ticked Tabby
Blue Abyssinian

Classic Tabby
Silver Tabby
British Shorthair

Spotted Tabby
Cameo Tabby
Oriental Shorthair

tabbies can occur also in any of the other solid colours. Blue Tabbies derive from action of the dilution gene; Chocolate Tabbies derive from the brown gene; Cinnamon Tabbies from the light-brown gene; Lilac Tabbies from a combination of the dilution gene and either of the brown genes; and Cream Tabbies from the dilution gene working in consort with the orange gene. The most common expressions of these colours in pedigree circles are found in the spotted tabby pattern, especially in cats of the foreign (oriental) body type.

Pointed cats
These are cats on which the basic colour is confined to the points: face, ears, legs and tail. The best-known pointed cats are the Siamese and Colourpoint (Himalayan), but the pointed pattern also occurs in other breeds.

The body is usually pale cream, fawn or white. The latter may have a bluish, creamy, ivory or glacial overtone. Body colour and point colour are welded together in the pointed cat. For example, a Blue point must have a bluish white, not a cream or a fawn, body.

The solid-pointed Colourpoint colours are blue, chocolate, flame (red), lilac and seal. Particolour-pointed colours are tortoiseshell, blue-cream, chocolate tortoiseshell and lilac cream. Tabby-pointed colours are blue lynx, blue-cream lynx, chocolate lynx, chocolate tortie lynx, cream lynx, lilac lynx, lilac cream lynx, red lynx, seal lynx and seal tortie lynx.

How new colours are accepted
Before cats of a new colour can be allowed to compete for various championship titles and awards in the US, that colour must meet certain requirements to qualify for championship competition. First, cats that bear that colour must achieve registration status. This status is generally conferred after a specified number of breeders, from six to 12, depending on the association, has certified that they are working with the new colour. Those breeders or a committee or group that has been empowered to represent them must submit a proposed standard — along with several photos of typical representatives of the new colour — to an association's executive office. The association may also request that breeders bring cats of the new colour to a board meeting. If the board of directors is satisfied that the proposed colour is sufficiently distinct from existing colours and is free from genetic complications and any factors that would not be conducive to a cat's good health, then the board will grant registration status to cats of the proposed new colour. Achieving registration status does not guarantee that the new colour will some day be accepted for championship competition, for there are additional requirements that have to be met before a cat advances to that level.

After a new colour has been granted registration status, most cat associations will allow cats of that colour to compete in new breed and colour classes (at US shows) or in assessment classes (at UK shows). This allows judges to become familiar with the new colour, and it affords breeders a chance to present (and promote) their cats to the public.

Finally, after a minimum number of persons (a number that varies from one association to the next) is working with the new colour, and a sufficient number of cats representing that colour has been registered and the required number of cats has been shown, the colour is advanced, with board approval, to championship status. This process takes, on average, from four to seven years, depending on the association.

Himalayan Pattern
Seal point Siamese

Combination Coat
Japanese Bobtail

Patched Tabby (Torbie)
Brown Torbie
Exotic Shorthair

Himalayan Combination
Lilac point Birman

LONGHAIRED CATS

Longhaired cats are beautiful creatures, but some of them do need a lot of attention. If you favour a longhaired cat, make sure, in advance, that you or someone in your household will groom it properly. In particular, the show-quality Persians with their profuse coats need a good grooming session every two or three days without fail; not only to keep them looking beautiful but to prevent them swallowing their fur or getting the coat knotted up, with painful consequences.

Some of the other longhaired breeds, such as the beautiful Balinese or the rugged Maine Coon, are easier to groom than are Persians, and I would make this one of the deciding factors when choosing a kitten. You will find many lovely cats to choose from in this section and there may be one that is just right for you.

The Persians are firm favourites. They are available in more than 30 colour varieties in the United Kingdom and in more than 60 colours in the United States. You may also consider the stately Birman, the adaptable and graceful Angora, or the distinctively marked Colourpoints (Himalayans). Perhaps the tailless Cymric or the charming Somali is more to your taste. Whichever breed you choose, make sure that its temperament and personality are exactly what you are looking for; do not judge a cat by its looks alone.

Left: A beautiful (but non-pedigree) Shaded Silver Persian longhair.

PERSIAN

Good points
- Beautiful and elegant
- Affectionate
- Companionable
- Undemanding
- Quiet
- Docile

Take heed
- Needs frequent grooming
- Moults heavily

The Persian makes an attractive, sweet and undemanding pet. It is docile, quiet, companionable and elegant. It likes being with people and is generally even-tempered.

The Persian's main disadvantage is that it *must* be groomed often. The cat will moult all year, but especially in the summer months, and if it swallows large quantities of hair, fur balls may form and cause an obstruction in the stomach that, in extreme cases, would have to be removed surgically. For this reason, many Persian breeders in the United States prefer to clip their Persians down in the spring.

Owning a Persian is quite a responsibility, but if you have plenty of time to look after one, you will be sure to find it an excellent, loving and devoted companion.

Grooming

Frequent grooming with a metal comb or a brush with wire or natural bristles helps to remove dead hair from the coat and to stimulate the cat's circulation. Periodic bathing also helps a cat to look its best, a requirement whenever a cat is going to a show.

British cat fanciers are somewhat less convinced of the benefit of bathing their cats as frequently as Americans are inclined to do. Indeed, many British fanciers do not believe that a longhaired cat needs to be bathed before every show. Whatever your cultural preference might be, when you bath your showbound cat, do so one to three days before the show, depending on the amount of time the cat's coat requires to regain its lustre after a bath.

Fuller's Earth, talcum powder or a proprietary non-toxic grooming powder may be applied to Whites, Blues, Creams, Blue-Creams and other pale colours to aerate their coats. Be sure to rub the powder well into the coat and remember to comb all powder out before a show. Pre-show preparation for Blacks, Reds, Brown Tabbies and other dark colours involves a thorough bath and a subsequent rinse if you prefer. Some breeders, particularly in the United Kingdom, apply bay rum to the coat in order to bring out the gloss in the hair.

While the purpose of grooming most longhairs is to make the fur stand out from the body, the object of grooming a tabby is to accentuate the contrast between its markings and its base colour. Therefore, the coat on a tabby is always slicked down, whereas the coats on other breeds are whipped up. The latter effect is achieved by combing (or brushing) with the lie of the coat for a 1in. (2.5cm) distance, then rotating the comb or brush in the opposite direction, lifting it up and out of the coat as you do so.

A kitten that has been reared properly should not be a stranger to a comb or brush. But if you acquire a kitten that is not comfortable being groomed, initiate grooming lessons as soon as the kitten is settled in its new abode. Groom for five to ten minutes every second or third day until the kitten is used to being handled. (For a complete discussion of grooming requirements and techniques, see page 121.)

Origin and history

The Italian traveller Pietro della Valle (1586-1652) is believed to have brought the first Persian cats to Europe. According to della Valle, there was 'a species of cats (in Persia) that properly belong to the province of Chorazan'. The beauty of these cats, said della Valle, 'consists in the colour of their hair, which is grey, soft as silk and so long that . . . it forms ringlets in some parts and particularly under the throat'.

Count de Buffon (1707-1778), the French naturalist, observed that 'the Persian cats resemble, in colour, those we call Chartreux cats; and except in colour, they have a perfect resemblance to the cat of the Angora'. It is probable, thought de Buffon, that these three cats 'constitute but one race, whose beauty proceeds from the particular influence of the climate'.

While de Buffon believed that climate had created 'the most beautiful and longest hair' on the Persians and Angoras, their coats probably resulted from a spontaneous mutation preserved through inter-breeding in the enclosed mountain areas of Turkey and Persia.

By the time the cat fancy had been founded in the UK in the 1870s, there were some noticeable differences between Persian and Angora cats. The Angora had a smaller, more narrow, less rounded head, less rounded eyes and finer bone than the Persian. The Angora's tail was more fanlike and pointed at the tip; and the Angora's coat — frilly on the chest and longer on the under parts — was not so heavy nor profuse as the Persian's.

Despite these differences, the two types were bred interchangeably and their offspring were classified and judged as longhairs. Gradually the Angora faded from prominence. By 1903 Frances Simpson, an English cat breeder, author and judge, declared, 'There are two distinctive breeds, viz., the *Long-haired* or Persian Cats and *Short-haired* or English and Foreign Cats'.

The Governing Council of the Cat Fancy (GCCF), organized in the UK in 1910, decided that Persians should continue to be called longhairs and that each longhair colour should be allocated a separate breed number. This scheme acknowledges the slight differences in type and conformation among Persian colours.

The cat fancy in the US was established by the turn of the century, and Americans had been importing Persians and other cats from the UK for several years before that. Until the 1900s the Maine Coon Cat had been the ruling longhair at the majority of shows in the US, but the Persian eventually claimed that title.

When Frances Simpson wrote *Cats and All About Them* in 1903, there were already separate standards in the US for Blue Persians, Orange Persians (both self-coloured and tabby), Creams (also known as Fawns), and orange-and-white cats (longhaired and short). White Persians were being judged in two classes — one for Blue-eyed whites, the other for Golden-eyed whites; and there were separate standards for Shaded Silvers, Chinchillas, and Tortoiseshells.

In longhairs, as in all other breeds, imported cats set the pace in the US during the first decades of this century. In 1930 the Cat Fanciers' Association (CFA) established the rank of grand champion — the highest, show-ring title a cat could attain at that time. The first cat to 'grand' was Eastbury Trigo, a Red Tabby Persian male imported from England. Not until World War II had left craters in breeding programmes in the UK did American cat breeders at long last begin to assert their independence from British sovereignty.

SHOW STANDARD

General appearance. The show Persian is a sturdy cat of gently curving lines. It is a medium to large cat with a long, flowing coat, an ethereal look and a pretty face.

Coat. Long and thick (up to 6in. (15cm) in length), but fine, soft and silky, standing away from the body, ideally with every hair separate. The coat should shine with glowing good health. There is a very full ruff forming a halo around the head, and a long frill between the front legs.

Body. Cobby, solid and rounded, with short legs. Deep in the chest; massive across the shoulders and rump. Legs thick and strong with straight forelegs. Feet large, firm, rounded and well tufted.

Tail. Short and full, especially at the base. No kinks.

Head. Broad, round and massive on a short, thick neck. Face round and pretty with no hint of wedginess. Jaw broad. Chin strong, not undershot. Cheeks full. Nose snub, short and broad with a good break or stop where it meets the forehead. The stop is particularly pronounced in American Persians. Ears tiny, rounded at the tips, set wide apart and tilted forward, set low on the head with long ear tufts.

Eyes. Large, round and set wide apart. Full, brilliant and wide-awake with a sweet expression. Slanted, oval or deep-set eyes are faults. Eye colour may fade with age.

PERSIAN COLOURS

There are nearly 60 colour varieties of Persian at present, although not all are recognized for competition in all countries. In the UK, each colour variety is accorded a separate breed number, and classified by the name 'Longhair' rather than Persian; in the US, on the other hand, colours are listed simply as varieties of Persian.

BLACK PERSIAN

Like other longhaired cats, Blacks were known in Europe by the seventeenth century, but no one knows exactly where they came from, as there are no reliable early records. It can be said with certainty, however, that they first appeared on the British show bench in 1871. The early black cats were more like Angoras than Persians, with long noses and big ears, but these features have long since been bred out.

Breeding

Black kittens can appear in a litter if the parents of that litter meet one of two criteria: either the sire or the dam has black in its genetic makeup; or the dam has blue in its genetic makeup and was mated to a cat with a red gene.

Mating two Blacks together will not necessarily produce an all-black litter. If both Blacks are carrying the recessive blue gene, one-quarter of the kittens produced — on the average — will be blue.

Kittens

Black kittens are born with blue eyes, which gradually change to copper. Black kittens often have rusty coats or some white hairs until the full adult coat appears. In fact, the worst kitten coats at six months often become the densest black coats at 12 to 18 months.

SHOW STANDARD

The coat must be a solid even black all over, and each hair must be black from its tip down to its root. Jet black is required, with no tinge of rustiness, no white hairs and no tabby markings. Nose leather and paw pads black. Eyes brilliant orange or deep copper.

WHITE PERSIAN

White cats, among the first varieties exhibited in the United Kingdom, began to attract a following in the late 1800s. They were regarded as status symbols in smart London drawing rooms at the turn of the century.

Today there are three varieties — Blue-eyed White, Orange-eyed White and Odd-eyed White (one of each colour). It seems difficult to breed the best Persian type with blue eyes, and the Blue-eyed Whites on the show bench still have slightly longer ears and faces, although they often have better coats than Orange-eyed Whites.

One disadvantage of white cats is that many of the Blue-eyed Whites are deaf from birth. Deafness may be difficult to detect at first because

Persian
(Longhair)

Black Persian

Blue-eyed White Persian

the cat's other senses may compensate. It is quite a responsibility to own a deaf cat, and it is best to confine such a cat to your house to avoid any unforeseen accidents.

Breeding

The 'colour' white is produced by the effect of the 'W' gene, which masks the expression of all genes that produce other colours. Thus, a white cat is not 'white' genetically, but may be red or black or any of a number of colours. A white's 'true' colour can only be determined by breeding it to several non-white cats and deducing the white's colour from the colour(s) of its mates and their offspring.

Many Blue-eyed Whites — and some Orange-eyed and Odd-eyed Whites as well — suffer an inability to hear. Their deafness, which may affect one or both ears, is caused by an irreversible degeneration of the cochlea, the fluid-filled, spiral-shaped part of the inner ear. This degeneration begins when kittens are four to six days old; and, some breeders claim, the white cats with the deepest, sapphire-blue eyes — the most highly prized variety — are always the deaf ones. Breeders should eliminate deafness from their catteries by excluding deaf cats and their parents from future matings.

Kittens

All white kittens are born with blue eyes, and it may be some weeks before you can tell which are the blue-eyed, orange-eyed or odd-eyed kittens in the litter. The depth of the eye colour also takes some months to develop. Orange eyes should be deep orange or copper, and if a kitten does not have the deep eye colour by the time it is six or seven months old, then it is unlikely that the eye colour will intensify later in life. Some kittens are born with a smudge of black hairs on top of their heads. This spot disappears as the adult coat starts to grow at about nine months or sooner.

SHOW STANDARD

The coat must be pure white throughout, with no shadow markings or black hairs. Nose leather and paw pads are pink. Eyes deep blue, orange or copper — or one eye is orange or copper and the other one deep blue. Pale or green-tinged eyes are faults in show cats.

BLUE PERSIAN

Blues remain the most popular longhaired cats in the United Kingdom, though they have been supplanted now for some time by other Persians in the United States. From the 1930s through the 1950s in America, the Blue class always had the most Persian entries at shows. More advanced in type than other Persians at that time, Blues were more often than not the best cat and/or best kitten in show.

Blues have featured in artists' impressions for several centuries. They were certainly known in Italy

during the Renaissance and were prized in India. First bred principally in France and England, where they enjoyed the patronage of Queen Victoria, they were later exported to the US.

Breeding

One Blue bred to another will produce nothing but Blue kittens. For many years the *crème de la bleus* were the Colourbred Blues: cats that had three to five (or more) generations of nothing but Blues behind them.

Kittens

When born, blue kittens may have tabby markings, but these usually disappear as the adult coat develops. In fact, the more heavily marked kittens often become the cats with the best all-over blue coats. The kittens are born with blue eyes, which change to deep orange over the next few months.

SHOW STANDARD

The coat should be medium to pale blue all over, the same depth of colour from root to tip with no sign of a paler undercoat and no tabby markings or white hairs. Generally the paler blue coats are preferred. Nose leather and paw pads blue-grey. Eyes brilliant copper or deep orange with no green tinge.

RED PERSIAN

The Red Persian is an outstanding-looking cat with a flame-coloured, flowing coat. The name 'red' is misleading, as the coat colour is more orange than scarlet, more flame than crimson. Although red cats appeared at shows prior to the turn of the century, a really good specimen is still rare. In fact, it is almost impossible to produce a red without some tabby markings in its coat.

Breeding

It is unwise to mate Reds to Red Tabbies, as this will introduce or reinforce tabby markings. It is best to breed to other self-coloured cats.

Kittens

Red kittens are usually born with tabby markings, which they may or may not lose when the adult coat is grown. Often, therefore, it is difficult to tell whether there are Red or Red Tabby kittens in the litter, and breeding for Red Persians presents quite a challenge.

SHOW STANDARD

The coat should be a deep, rich red without markings of any kind or white hairs. Nose leather and paw pads brick red. Eyes copper or deep orange.

CREAM PERSIAN

Cream Persians are beautiful cats, quite ethereal-looking with their pale cream fur. The Cream was first recorded in the United Kingdom in 1890, but such cats were generally

regarded as Reds that were too pale to meet the show standard, and many were sold as pets. Others were exported to the United States, where breeders have always been more interested in Cream Persians. In the UK, serious breeding for Creams did not start until the 1920s.

Breeding

Continuous like-to-like matings between Cream Persians can produce gradual loss of type, and therefore outcrosses to other coloured varieties are necessary. Cream is genetically a dilution of the red colour and is, in fact, much easier to achieve than the solid red. Creams are produced most reliably from matings between Blues and Creams. A Cream female mated to a Blue male will produce Cream male and Blue-cream female kittens; a Cream male mated to a Blue female will produce Blue males and Blue-cream females.

Kittens

Cream kittens are often born with faint tabby markings, but these usually disappear when the adult coat starts to develop.

SHOW STANDARD

The cream coat should be sound throughout, without markings of any kind and without a darker area down the spine. A pale-to-medium colour is preferred in the UK; American associations prefer a paler buff cream; too red ('hot') a colour is a fault. There should be no sign of a paler undercoat; the hair should be the same colour from root to tip. The coat colour may be darker in older cats or just before moulting. Nose leather and paw pads pink. Eyes copper or deep orange.

CHOCOLATE PERSIAN

Colour. Medium to dark chocolate, warm in tone, sound and even in

---

Below: Cream Persian kittens; the faint tabby markings are likely to fade at about nine months, when the adult coat starts to develop.

colour. No shading, markings or white hairs. Nose leather, eye rims and paw pads chocolate.

LILAC PERSIAN

Colour. Lilac, warm in tone, sound and even in colour. No shading, markings or white hairs. Nose leather, eye rims and paw pads lilac.

BICOLOUR PERSIAN

Bicoloured cats have been known for a considerable length of time, but were excluded from the show bench because they were originally alley cats without registered parentage. Bicolours may be any solid, or tabby colour and white.

Breeding

For many years Tortoiseshells and Blue-creams were the only particoloured Persians on the show bench. But in the early 1950s a New Jersey breeder began working to develop a Calico American Shorthair, a colour that was not recognized in American Shorthairs at that time. As a result of using Persian cats to improve type in her Calicos, she managed to produce the occasional Calico Longhairs, which she registered as such according to then current open-registration rules.

Other breeders liked the picture-postcard look of these cats and began crossing them to Persians. This interest eventually resulted in the acceptance of Calico Persians in June 1955, the same month that Calico American Shorthairs were accepted. From these cats the earliest bicolours were developed.

Kittens

Bicoloured kittens may be obtained from matings in which at least one of the parents is a Bicolour. Though Bicolours in the United States have become quite extreme, outcrosses to solid and particoloured Persians are still recommended in the interest of maintaining type.

Persian
(Longhair)

Blue Persian

Black-and-white
Bicolour Persian

Cream Persian kitten

Red Persian

SHOW STANDARD

Popular additions to many breeding programmes, Bicolours can produce a fetching variety of flashy colours. For this reason their popularity increased by near-quantum leaps and bounds in the US during the 1980s.

At the least, a Bicolour should have white feet, legs, underside, chest and muzzle (US standard). The show bicolour Persian must have a patched coat with not more than two-thirds of the body coloured and not more than one-half white (UK standard). The pattern should be symmetrical with patches of colour on the face, head, back, flanks and tail. Nose leather and paw pads generally pink, otherwise in keeping with the coat colour. Eyes deep, brilliant copper to orange.

CHINCHILLA & SHELL CAMEO PERSIAN

The Persian Chinchillas and Cameos belong to a group that contains some of the most beautiful of all longhaired cats. They can conveniently be described as having a 'tipped' coat pattern. The undercoat is one colour (usually white, but sometimes cream), and the guard hairs are tipped to varying extents with a different, contrasting colour. These cats are classified further according to whether the colour tipping is light (Chinchillas and Shell Cameos), medium (Shaded Silvers and Shaded Cameos) or heavy (Smokes).

In the Chinchillas and Shell Cameos, the undercoats are usually pure white, and the ends of the guard hairs, for approximately one-eighth of the hair length, are lightly tipped with a contrasting colour, giving a shimmering, sparkling effect to the coat.

Chinchilla Persians have been so-named since the 1890s, although the early Chinchillas were much more heavily marked, and were probably more like today's Shaded Silvers. Chinchillas are believed to have been developed from cats with silver genes, probably Silver Tabbies whose markings were indistinct or almost absent, mated to Blue Persians or Smokes; further selective breeding used only the palest kittens or non-tabby kittens. Early Silver Tabbies would have had hazel or golden eyes, and the first Chinchillas also had hazel eyes.

After World War II there was a very severe shortage of all types of pedigree cats in Europe, and American Chinchillas were imported to improve stamina and eye colour. In Europe and Australia, Chinchillas are, and have always been, fairy tale cats, finer-boned than other Persians, but in the United States, they are larger and conform more closely to the general Persian standard.

Their delicate appearance belies their hardy nature; they are not in fact fragile cats, but very robust and healthy. Their sweet baby faces and ethereal looks have made Chinchillas among the most popular of cats. Patronized before World War II by Queen Victoria's grand-daughter, Princess Victoria, and being particularly photogenic, they are now known throughout the world. No doubt their popularity also benefited from their numerous appearances on television and in magazines.

Although the name Chinchilla traditionally conjures up a picture of a cat with a coat of black silk on white velvet, in recent years the name has been extended to cats of similar appearance and coat pattern but a different colour, notably the Chinchilla Golden, a lovely brown tipped variety.

The beautiful Shell Cameos are similar to the Chinchilla in coat pattern and were developed in the late 1950s, mostly in the US, by selective breeding of Silver Persians with Red cats. (In the United Kingdom, Creams were also used.) When Chinchillas were used, the kittens were green-eyed, which was not desired, so Smokes with copper eyes were then introduced. In general, tabbies of any colour are not used (except to produce the Cameo Tabby), so as not to reintroduce any tabby markings. Such mixed breeding produces a wide variety of coloured Cameos, from the Red to the Tortoiseshell and the Blue-cream.

Breeding

The expression of colour in Shell, Shaded, Smoke and Chinchilla cats is controlled by the 'I' (for inhibitor) gene. The effect of this dominant gene is the suppression of pigment in the hairs of a cat's coat. This suppression begins at the root of each hair and drives the colour outwards towards the end (or tip) of the hair shaft, leaving the portion of the hair shaft nearer the body either white or cream. The white or cream portion of the hair shaft is known as the base colour.

The greater the effect of the 'I' gene, the greater the length of the hair shaft occupied by the base colour. Thus, Shell Cameos and Chinchillas have a faint mantle of tipping on the outermost one-eighth (or less) of a hair shaft; Shadeds deploy their colour on the outermost one-quarter of a hair shaft; and Smokes have a heavy dose of colour occupying three-quarters of the shaft from the tip inwards.

Above: This Shaded Golden's undercoat is a rich, warm cream with a top coat tipped in dark brown. The given effect is of a beautiful golden overcoat.

Kittens

Chinchilla kittens are born with dark markings and tabby markings, particularly on the tail, but these disappear by the time the kittens are four to six weeks old. If a kitten still shows markings after 10 weeks of age, then it is probably not destined for showing. Cameo kittens are born white, the tipping gradually appearing.

SHOW STANDARD

Chinchilla. The undercoat is pure white. The coat on the back, flanks, head, ears and tail is lightly tipped with black. This tipping should be evenly distributed across these areas of the coat, thus providing the characteristic, sparkling silver appearance of the coat. The legs may be very slightly shaded with black tipping, but the chin, ear tufts, stomach and chest must all be pure white. Any tabby markings or cream tinge to the coat is a defect. The tip of the nose is brick red, and the visible skin on the eyelids and the paw pads is black or dark brown.

The eyes are large, round and most expressive. They should be emerald or blue-green in colour.

Chinchilla Golden. The undercoat should be a rich, warm cream to apricot. The coat on the back, flanks, head and tail is lightly tipped with dark brown to give a sparkling, golden appearance. The legs may be very lightly tipped. The chin, ear tufts, stomach and chest should be cream. The lips, nose and eyes should be outlined with dark brown. Nose leather deep rose. Paw pads dark brown. Eyes green or blue-green.

Shell Cameo (Red Chinchilla). The undercoat should be pure white with the coat on the back, flanks, legs and tail lightly tipped with red (and/or cream in the UK) to give a sparkling, pink-tinsel type of effect. The chin, ear tufts, stomach and chest are pure white. Tabby markings are a fault. Nose leather and paw pads rose. Eyes brilliant copper.

Shell Tortoiseshell. The undercoat should be pure white, lightly tipped with red, black and cream in well-defined patches, and well broken on the face. The chin, ear tufts, stomach and chest are white. A blaze of red or cream tipping on the face is desirable. Nose leather and paw pads black, pink or a combination of the two. Eyes brilliant copper.

Blue-cream Cameo. The undercoat should be pure white. The coat on the back, flanks, legs and tail is tipped with blue and cream that are softly intermingled. Tipping of any intensity acceptable in this colour. Nose leather and paw pads blue, pink or a combination of the two. Eyes deep copper.

Cameo Tabby. Undercoat should be off-white, lightly tipped with red in classic or mackerel tabby coat pattern. Nose leather and paw pads rose. Eyes brilliant copper.

SHADED PERSIAN

Similar to the Chinchillas and Shell Cameos, the Shaded Persians also have pale (usually white) undercoats, but approximately a quarter of the hair length is tipped with a contrasting colour to give the effect of a coloured mantle over the body.

Most people believe that the first Shaded cats, the silver-coloured Chinchillas, were produced in the early 1880s in the United Kingdom by breeders who crossed Silver Tabbies with unsound markings to Smokes with light tipping.

SHOW STANDARD

Shaded Silver. The undercoat should be pure white, the top coat tipped in black to give the effect of a black mantle overlying the undercoat on the back, flanks, face, legs and tail. Generally darker than the Chinchilla. Nose leather and paw pads brick red. Eyes green or blue-green, rimmed with black.

Shaded Cameo (Red Shaded). The undercoat should be pure white, with the top coat tipped in red to give the effect of a red mantle overlying the undercoat on the back, flanks, face, legs and tail. Generally darker than the Shell Cameo. Nose leather and paw pads pink. Eyes brilliant copper, rimmed with rose.

Shaded Golden. The undercoat should be a rich, warm cream, with the top coat tipped in brown to give the effect of a golden overcoat. Generally darker than the Chinchilla Golden. Nose leather deep rose. Paw pads dark brown. Eyes green or blue-green, rimmed in dark brown.

Shaded Tortoiseshell. The undercoat should be pure white, with the top coat tipped in black, red and cream in well-defined patches of the tortoishell pattern. Generally much darker than the Shell Tortoiseshell. A blaze of red or cream on the face is desirable but is not a requirement.

Cameo Mackerel Tabby Persian
(Shown in moult)

Shell Cameo Persian

Persian
(Longhair)

Chinchilla Persian

Nose leather and paw pads black, pink, or a combination of the two. Eyes brilliant copper.

Pewter. The undercoat should be white, with the top coat tipped in black, giving the effect of a black mantle overlying the undercoat. Generally darker than the Chinchilla, and similar to the Shaded Silver, except for eye colour. Lips, nose and eyes outlined in black. Nose leather brick red. Paw pads black. Eyes orange or copper, with no green tinge.

SMOKE PERSIAN

Like the Chinchillas and Shaded Persians, the Smokes are also characterized by their white undercoats and contrasting tipping. But their hairs are tipped for at least half their length with colour and, at first glance, Smoke Persians may look like solid-coloured cats until they move. Then the beautiful pale undercoat shows through. The ruff and ear tufts are generally of a paler colour, making these cats among the most striking of Persians.

Smoke-coloured cats have been recorded in the United Kingdom since the 1860s. Very good Smokes were shown in England in the first 20 years of this century, but then, oddly, their popularity declined, until interest was revived again in the 1960s.

In the United States, Smokes were originally part of the Shaded division, which they dominated because of their superior bone and head type. Thus, Silver breeders eventually convinced the Cat Fanciers' Association to create a Smoke division, thereby making the Silvers more competitive.

Breeding
Smokes must be outcrossed to solid or to particolour Persians to retain type. Since the inhibitor gene responsible for the Smoke coat is dominant, half the crosses between a Smoke and a Solid or a particolour should have tipped coats.

Kittens
At birth, Smoke kittens look as if they have cigarette ash on their noses and feet and smoke-tinted goggles around their eyes. The coat is often uneven during kittenhood.

SHOW STANDARD
Black Smoke. The undercoat should be white, heavily tipped on the back and flanks with black to give the effect of a solid-coloured cat until the animal moves. The coat shades to silver on the lower flanks. The face and feet are black, with no markings (colour solid to the roots in the UK; white at the roots in the US). The ruff and ear tufts are silver. Nose leather and paw pads black. Eyes brilliant copper or orange.

Blue Smoke. The above is also the standard for Blue Smokes, except that where the word 'Black' occurs, 'Blue' should be substituted.

Cameo Smoke (Red Smoke). The undercoat should be white, tipped with red on the back and flanks to give the appearance of a solid red cat until the animal moves. The face and feet are red without markings (colour solid to the roots in the UK; white at the roots in the US). The ruff and ear tufts are white. Nose leather and paw pads rose. Eyes brilliant orange or copper.

Cream Smoke. The above is also the standard for Cream Smokes, except that where 'Red' occurs, 'Cream' is substituted.

Smoke Tortoiseshell. The undercoat should be white, heavily tipped with black, red and cream in clearly defined patches on the back and flanks to give the appearance of a tortoiseshell cat when the animal moves. Face and feet solid red, black and cream, with preference given to a facial blaze of red or cream. (Colours solid to the roots in the UK; white at the roots in the US.) Ruff and ear tufts white. Nose leather and paw pads charcoal, rose, pink or a combination of these colours. Eyes brilliant copper.

Blue-cream Smoke. Same as Smoke Tortie, but tipping is blue and cream intermingled. Nose leather and pads are blue, pink or a combination of same.

TORTOISESHELL PERSIAN

Despite the fact that tortoiseshell shorthaired cats have been domesticated in Europe since the days of the Roman Empire, the longhaired Tortoiseshell was not recorded before the end of the

nineteenth century. Nevertheless, Tortoiseshells first appeared at cat shows in the early 1900s, and became popular on both sides of the Atlantic.

Breeding
Most Tortoiseshells are females because the Tortie pattern depends, among others things, on the presence of two 'X' genes in a cat, and the fair sex is the one with two 'X's. Male Torties are rare, and functioning male Torties are rarer still.

Most breeders produce Tortoiseshells by breeding a Red female to a Black or a Blue male; a Cream female to a Black male; a Blue female to a Red male; a Black female to a Red or Cream male; a Blue-cream to a Red or Black male; or a Tortie to a Red, Cream, Black, or Blue male. The addition of a Bicolour lessens the chance of obtaining a tortie but adds the possibility of getting a Calico.

Kittens
Tortoiseshell kittens occasionally look so dark at birth that it is difficult to find red or cream hairs on them, let alone patches. The darker the neonate, many breeders report, the more distinctly patched the adult.

SHOW STANDARD
The coat should be evenly patched with red, cream and black (United Kingdom), or it should be essentially black with unbrindled patches of red and cream (United States). All colours should be clear and brilliant, not commingled. Black areas should not predominate, and over-large patches of any one colour are considered a fault. A red or cream blaze from the forehead to the nose is desirable. The colours should be well broken up on the head and ears, and the fur should be particularly long on the ruff and tail. White hairs and tabby markings are faults. Nose leather and paw pads pink or black. Eyes copper or deep orange.

BLUE-CREAM PERSIAN

The Blue-cream is a female-only variety, genetically a dilute form of the Tortoiseshell, and a most attractive and popular cat. Although relatively slow to gain championship status, achieving official recognition in the United Kingdom only in 1930, Blue-creams had appeared in litters from Blue and Cream matings ever since pedigree cat breeding began, and were first shown in the United States as Blue Tortoiseshells in the early 1900s.

Breeding
If a Blue-cream is mated to a Cream sire, the resulting male kittens can be Blue or Cream, and the females can be Cream or Blue-cream. If a

Blue-cream is mated to a Blue sire, the resulting male kittens can be Blue or Cream, and the females can be Blue or Blue-Cream. Similarly, a Blue female mated to a Cream male will produce Blue-cream female and Blue male kittens, whereas a Blue male mated to a Cream female will produce Blue-cream female and Cream male kittens.

Kittens
The kittens are attractive and colourful. Those with the palest coats will probably develop into the best adults from a competition point of view. Often a very fine Blue-cream will look much like pale blue in the first few weeks, just as the finest Tortoiseshell coats are predominantly black during the same period.

SHOW STANDARD
The British standard dictates that the coat should be evenly coloured in pastel shades of blue and cream, softly intermingled throughout; the American standard requires the coat to be blue, patched with solid cream, clearly defined and well broken on body, legs, tail and face. Nose leather and paw pads blue or pink or a combination. Eyes deep copper or orange.

TORTOISESHELL-AND-WHITE PERSIAN (Calico)

The Tortoiseshell-and-white (Calico) Persian is another female-only variety with a delightfully patched coat of black, red, cream and white.

Although shorthaired tortoiseshell-and-white cats have been known in Europe for centuries, the origin of the longhaired variety is obscure.

The colour is sex-linked genetically to produce females only, and when the rare male occurs, it is invariably sterile. Cats with this coat pattern were known in the past as 'chintz' cats, because of their bright, bold colour patches.

On the show bench, the pedigree variety did not attain championship recognition until the 1950s. More recently, the dilute variety, Blue Tortoiseshell-and-white (Dilute Calico), has also attained recognition in Europe and the United States. Such cats often appear in the same litter as Tortoiseshell-and-whites, and have patched coats of blue and cream with white.

Breeding
Like Tortoiseshells, Tortoiseshell-and-whites also produce kittens in a lovely assortment of colours. Tabbies should not be used in Tortie-and-white breeding programmes as they might introduce bars and markings, which are undesirable.

SHOW STANDARD
Tortoiseshell-and-white (Calico). The cat should be strikingly patched with black, red and cream, interspersed with white. The

Left: A Black Smoke Persian, with the pale undercoat showing through. The tipping gives the effect of a solid-coloured cat.

Persian
(Longhair)

Tortoiseshell-and-white
(Calico) Persian

Tortoiseshell
Persian

Blue-cream Persian (UK)

27

patches should be well distributed, bright and clear without white hairs or tabby markings, and should be evenly spread over the body with white on the legs, feet, chest and face. Too much white is a fault. The American standard requires white to be concentrated on the underparts. A cream or white blaze from the top of the head to the nose is desirable. Nose leather and paw pads pink, black or a combination of the two. Eyes brilliant copper.

Blue Tortoiseshell-and-white
(Dilute Calico). Coat should be patched with blue and cream. Patches should be well distributed over the body, clear and unbrindled, with white concentrated on the legs, feet, chest and face (US). A cream or white blaze on the face is desirable. Nose leather and paw pads pink. Eyes brilliant copper or orange.

CHOCOLATE TORTOISESHELL & LILAC-CREAM PERSIAN

Varieties developed from the Colourpoint (Himalayan) breeding programme.

SHOW STANDARD
Chocolate Tortoiseshell. The coat should be chocolate, patched with red and cream. The colours should be bright and rich, and well broken on the face. Nose leather and paw pads brown. Eyes copper.

Lilac-cream. Throughout the coat shades of lilac and cream should be softly intermingled with no white hairs. Nose leather and paw pads pink. Eyes copper.

TABBY PERSIAN

Many knowledgeable observers believe that the first domestic cats were ticked and mackerel tabbies, and more than a few people claim that if all human 'interference' in feline reproduction were to come to a stop tomorrow, eventually all cats would be tabbies.

The word tabby was originally used to describe the appearance of plain-woven watered silk or taffeta, which was known in England as tabbisilk. This type of weaving produces a striped or ridged effect on the cloth, the appearance of which resembles the striped pattern found on some cats. *Tabbisilk* probably derives from Attabiya, a district in Baghdad (now the capital of Iraq), where this material was made.

Harrison Weir, the father of the British cat fancy, did not believe that tabbies were among the first longhaired cats brought to Europe from Persia. Weir thought instead that tabbies resulted from breedings among resident European stock. Other writers have pointed out that the brown tabby, which is genetically a black cat, was the

original tabby and that all other tabby colours have evolved from some variety of brown tabby, most likely by mutation that was subsequently fixed by selective breeding.

The four tabby patterns are: ticked, mackerel, blotched (or classic) and spotted.

Breeding
Breeding tabbies presents a certain challenge. Several generations of colourbreeding (mating cats of similar colour together) will produce splendid colour and markings, but at the expense of type. Outcrossing to solids or particolours will improve type, but at the expense of clarity of markings. Furthermore, the number of tabbies in an outcross litter is generally fewer than the number of tabbies in a litter from a tabby-to-tabby breeding. Finally, some breeders believe that clarity of detail can be lost in the first generation of kittens produced by two unrelated tabbies.

Kittens
Tabby markings are distinguishable as soon as a new-born kitten begins to dry. As a rule, the darker the stripes at birth, the more dramatically marked the adult coat pattern will be.

SHOW STANDARD
Classic Tabby pattern. All markings should be clearly distinguished from the ground colour. The characteristic head marking is a letter 'M', resembling frown marks on the forehead. Unbroken lines run from the outer corners of the eyes towards the back of the head. There are other pencil-thin lines on the face, especially in the form of swirls on the cheeks. Lines extend back from the top of the head to the shoulder markings, which are shaped in a butterfly pattern. Three unbroken lines run parallel to each other down the spine from the shoulder markings to the base of the tail. A large blotch on each side of the

body is circled by one or more unbroken rings; these markings should be symmetrical on both sides of the body. There should be several unbroken necklaces on the neck and upper chest, and a double row of 'buttons' running from chest to stomach. Legs and tail should be evenly ringed.

Mackerel Tabby pattern. (Rare in the United Kingdom, but recognized in the United States.) Head is marked with the characteristic 'M', and there is an unbroken line running from the outher corner of the eyes towards the back of the head. There are other fine pencil markings on the cheeks. A narrow unbroken line runs from the back of the head to the base of the tail. The rest of the body is marked with narrow unbroken lines running vertically down from the spine line. These lines should be as narrow and numerous as possible and, ideally, they should be clearly distinguished from the ground colour. There should be several unbroken necklaces on the neck and upper chest, and a double row of 'buttons' on the chest and stomach. The legs should be evenly barred with narrow bracelets and the tail evenly ringed.

Brown Tabby. Ground colour rich, tawny sable to coppery brown. Markings jet black. No white hairs. Nose leather brick red. Paw pads black or dark brown, the dark colour extending up the backs of the hind legs from paw to heel. Eyes brilliant copper or hazel.

Red Tabby. Ground colour rich red. Markings dark, rich red. Lips and chin red. No white hairs or patches. Nose leather brick red. Paw pads pink. Eyes brilliant copper or gold.

Silver Tabby. Ground colour silver. Markings jet black and clearly defined. Nose leather brick red. Paw pads black. Eyes green or hazel.

Blue Tabby. Ground colour bluish ivory with a fawn cast. Markings blue. Nose leather deep rose pink. Paw pads rose pink. Eyes brilliant copper.

Cream Tabby. Ground colour, lips and chin very pale cream. Markings buff cream, not too red, but sufficiently dark to afford a contrast with the ground colour. Nose leather and paw pads pink. Eyes brilliant copper.

Cameo Tabby. Ground colour, lips and chin off-white. Markings red. Nose leather and paw pads rose. Eyes brilliant copper to gold.

Patched Tabby (Torbie) pattern. Markings classic or mackerel tabby with red and/or cream patches. Facial blaze preferred.
Brown. Ground colour coppery brown. Markings jet black, with red and/or cream. Nose leather brick red. Paw pads black or brown. Eyes brilliant copper.
Silver. Ground colour pale silver. Markings jet black with red and/or cream. Nose leather and paw pads rose pink. Eyes copper or hazel.
Blue. Ground colour bluish ivory with fawn patina. Markings deep blue with cream patches. Eyes copper.

VAN PERSIANS

White coat with colour confined to head, ears and tail. Up to three tiny colour spots on legs and body allowed. Nose leather and pads pink or coat 'colour'. Eyes copper.
Van Bicolour. Patches of black, blue, red or cream.
Van Calico. Patches of black/red.
Van Blue-cream. Patches of blue and cream.

Below: A very fine example of a US-standard Blue Tortoiseshell-and-white Persian (Calico), with blue and cream patches well distributed over the body.

Brown Classic
(Blotched) Tabby Persian

Silver Classic
Tabby Persian

Persian
(Longhair)

Red Mackerel Tabby Persian

PEKE-FACED PERSIAN

Good points
- *Affectionate*
- *Intelligent*
- *Quiet*

Take heed
- *Needs frequent grooming*
- *May suffer breathing difficulties*
- *May have feeding problems*

From time to time in Red Self and Red Tabby Persian litters there appears spontaneously a different-looking kitten with a face resembling that of a Pekingese dog. Such a cat has an obvious indentation between the eyes, and because of this is known as a Peke-faced Persian. It is just as sweet and companionable as other Persians, but because of its very large jowls and very snub nose, it may suffer from snuffles and other breathing problems, and also from feeding problems if the upper and lower teeth do not meet in an even bite.

The Peke-faced is among the most rare Persian varieties. Between 1958 and 1991 the Cat Fanciers' Association registered only 516 Peke-faced cats: 94 Reds and 422 Red Tabbies. That amounts to 15 new registrations per year, and the trend seems to be going downwards. There were no Peke-faced Reds enrolled in 1990 or 1989, and there were only six new Peke-faced Red Tabby enrolments in 1990 and four the year before.

Grooming
Like all Persians, the Peke-faced requires frequent grooming with brush and comb to remove knots and tangles from the coat. Attention must also be paid to the eyes, as the tear ducts may become blocked. Any mucus that collects in the corners of the eyes should be sponged away with warm water.

Origin and history
The development of the Peke-faced Red has not been as faithfully chronicled as has that of the standard Red. The earliest breeders of Peke-faces in the United States began working with these cats in the 1930s. Barring a reversal of fortunes, it is doubtful that any breeders will be working with Peke-faced cats by the 2030s.

Breeding
The inheritance of the Peke-faced gene has not been clearly defined. Indeed, no one is certain whether the Peke face is inherited monogenically (as a result of the influence of a single gene) or polygenically (as the result of the influence of a configuration of genes). Since breeders have reported that non-Peke kittens can result from Peke-to-Peke breedings, we can at least rule out recessive, monogenic inheritance.

Kittens
Raising Peke-faced kittens is an exercise in frustration. According to one Peke breeder, 'Many Peke-faced females must have their kittens by Caesarean section, and there is a higher mortality rate among Peke kittens than among others — as high as 50 per cent in the first six months. Much of this is due to the formation of the mouth; the hard palate is concave rather than flat, making it difficult for the baby to nurse.'

The kittens themselves are slow to mature and remain kittens for a longer period than the standard Red or Red Tabby.

SHOW STANDARD
The Peke-faced Persian is a solid, cobby cat of Persian type, but with a distinctive face which resembles that of a Pekingese dog.
Coat. Long, flowing, silky and soft with a large ruff around the neck.
Body. Short, cobby and massive. Legs short. Paws large and well tufted.
Tail. Short, well plumed and especially full at the base.
Head. Large and round with a very short snub nose, indented between the eyes, and an obvious nose break. The muzzle is wrinkled and there is a fold of skin running from the inner corner of the eye to the mouth. The forehead bulges out above the nose and eyes. The neck is short and thick. The ears are larger than other Persians'.
Eyes. Very prominent, almost bulging, round and full.

PEKE-FACED COLOURS
Only two colours are recognized for competition at present, although Peke-faced cats also appear in dilute red (cream).

Red. Body colour an even, deep, rich red throughout with no markings or white hairs. Nose leather and paw pads brick red. Eyes brilliant copper.

Red Tabby. Ground colour red. Markings, in either classic or mackerel tabby pattern, deep, rich red. Nose leather and paw pads brick red. Eyes brilliant copper.

RAGDOLL

Good points
- *Gentle and affectionate*
- *Quiet*
- *Playful*
- *Intelligent*

Take heed
- *No known drawbacks*

The Ragdoll is a semi-longhaired cat of generous dimension. It bears something of a resemblance to the Sacred Cat of Burma (Birman), which is reputed to be one of its ancestors.

Grooming
Because the Ragdoll has a very long coat, it will need frequent grooming, if not to remove knots and tangles, then to remove dead hairs. As it moults heavily in the summer, thorough grooming at this time is particularly important. The tangles should be combed out using a wide-toothed comb, then the coat brushed gently but thoroughly using a long-bristled brush.

Origin and history
The Ragdoll originated in California from a series of breedings among mixed foundation stock. The original breedings are said to have involved a white Angora-type cat, a Sacred Cat of Burma, and a Burmese.

Ann Baker, the woman credited with developing the Ragdoll, cites five differences between Ragdolls and other cats. Ragdolls are bigger, more impervious to pain, less endowed with self-preservation instincts, possess non-matting fur and, finally, they go limp when they are held — a tendency that inspired their name.

These attributes first appeared, says Baker, in kittens born to a white, Angora-type cat named Josephine after she had recovered from being hit by a car in the early 1960s.

While there is little (indeed, almost no) evidence supporting most of these claims, some Ragdolls are larger than most cats. Females can weigh from 9lb (4kg) to 12lb (5.4kg), and males can weigh 15lb (6.8kg) to 20lb (9kg). Recognized for competition in the United States in 1965, the breed is now accepted in five of the six North American cat registries.

Breeding
The foundation sire of the Ragdoll breed was a mitted, seal point male named Daddy War Bucks, whose father was a Sacred Cat of Burma (Birman). Ragdolls were developed by crossing a number of Daddy War Bucks' children and grandchildren to other cats.

Within their accepted colours Ragdolls breed true. So there is no need for continued outcrossing.

Kittens
Ragdoll kittens are slow to mature and it may be three years before the full adult coat is developed.

SHOW STANDARD
The Ragdoll is a large, heavily built cat with a semi-long coat and a characteristic limpness when held.
Coat. Semi-long, full and silky. Non-matting. Luxuriant ruff and long fur on the chest and stomach; shorter on the face. The coat is likely to be longer in cold than in warm climates and will moult considerably during the summer months.
Body. Very large and heavy with strong, heavy bones. Males 15-20lb (6.8-9kg); females 9-12lb (4-5.4kg); shorter in body than males. Hindquarters are heavy and there is a furry, loose-muscled stomach pad. As broad across the shoulders as across the rump, with a deep chest. Legs medium in length and fairly heavy with hind legs slightly longer than forelegs. Paws large, round and firm with tufts between the toes.
Tail. Long and furry. Medium thick at the base with a slight taper towards the tip. A short or kinked tail would be a fault.
Head. Medium in size with a modified wedge; wider in the male than in the female. The skull between the ears is flat. The cheeks are full and taper to a full round chin. There is a gentle nose break, which, with the flat head, gives a distinctive profile. Neck is strong, short and thick. Ears are medium in size, broad at the base, tilted forward, rounded at the tips and furnished with ear tufts. Very large, very small or pointed ears are faults.
Eyes. Very large, oval, set wide apart. Round or almond-shaped eyes or squints are faults.

RAGDOLL COLOURS
Ragdolls are bred in three coat patterns — colourpoint, mitted and bicolour — and in seal, chocolate, blue and lilac point colours.

Colourpoint. Body colour should be an even shade down to the roots. Point colour (ears, mask, legs and tail) is darker, providing a contrast with the body colour. Chest, bib and chin a lighter shade of the body colour. Ticking and white spotting not accepted.

Mitted. Body colour should be an even shade down to the roots. Point colour (ears, mask, legs and tail) is darker, providing a distinct contrast with the body colour. Chest, bib and chin white. A white stripe runs from the bib between the forelegs to the base of the tail. White mittens on both front paws should be evenly matched and scalloped. White boots on hind legs should also match. Coloured spots in white areas or ticking on coloured areas are faults.

Bicolour. Body colour should be an even shade down to the roots. The colour of the ears, mask (with the exception of an inverted 'V' down the nose, which is white) and tail is darker and clearly defined. Chest, stomach and legs white. The symmetrical inverted 'V' on the face starts between the ears, covers the nose, whisker pads, neck and bib. It should not extend beyond the outer edge of the eyes. There should be no coloured spots on the white areas. The body areas may have small spots of white.

Seal point. Body colour a pale fawn, shading to pale cream on the underparts. Points dense seal brown. Nose leather dark brown. Paw pads dark brown or black. Eyes deep blue.

Chocolate point. Body colour an even ivory all over. Points warm milk chocolate. Nose leather rose. Paw pads salmon. Eyes deep blue.

Blue point. Body colour an even, platinum grey-blue, shading to lighter blue on the underparts. Points deep blue-grey. Nose leather and paw pads dark blue-grey. Eyes deep blue.

Lilac (Frost) point. Body colour an even milk white all over. Points frosty grey-pink. Inside ears very pale pink. Nose leather lilac. Paw pads coral pink. Eyes deep blue.

Ragdoll

Lilac point Bicolour
Ragdoll kitten

Chocolate point
Bicolour Ragdoll

Peke-faced
Persian

Red Classic Tabby Peke-faced Persian

COLOURPOINT
(Himalayan)

Good points
- *Beautiful*
- *Affectionate*
- *Devoted*
- *Intelligent*

Take heed
- *Needs frequent grooming*

A Colourpoint is essentially a Persian with Siamese (Himalayan) colouring. It is rather more demanding and more enterprising than many Persians, although more docile and less demonstrative than the Siamese. As with all cats, the Colourpoint likes to choose its own activities and will be happiest if given the run of the house.

It would not be advisable to have a Colourpoint as a pet unless you are prepared to devote a lot of time to its grooming. Well cared for, the Colourpoint, or 'Himmy' as it is known, is an extremely beautiful cat and makes a very affectionate and devoted pet.

Grooming
As with all longhaired cats, frequent grooming is essential for the Colourpoint. If neglected, the undercoat will become matted into tight knots. Despite regular attention, mats do sometimes form. In experienced hands a mat cutter, designed for dogs, can be used to cut through a mat and remove it rather than cutting it out and leaving a bare spot.

A wide-toothed comb can be used to remove knots, followed by a medium-toothed comb to remove dead hairs. Finally, the coat should be brushed with a long-handled brush. Repeated frequently, this will ensure a healthy coat.

Origin and history
The Colourpoint or Himalayan is a manufactured breed. It is not a Siamese with long hair, but a Persian with Siamese (Himalayan) colouring. The name Himalayan derives from the coat pattern of the Himalayan rabbit, where the darker colour is confined to the face, legs and tail (as in the Siamese), and not because of any pretensions to a Himalayan origin, geographically. The production of this cat involved complex breeding and took years to perfect into the correct Persian type. Breeders had been crossing Siamese with Persians for many years but had been getting only self-coloured shorthaired kittens as a result. Eventually, in the 1930s and 1940s, a series of experiments was made, crossing Siamese with longhaired Blacks and Blues. The resulting shorthaired self-coloured kittens proved very useful for breeding as they carried the genes required to produce the Colourpoint. They were mated together and back to their parents until Colourpoint kittens were produced. Further selective breeding to longhaired Blacks and Blues to develop Persian type was carried out and the resulting cats, when mated back to Colourpoints,

produced excellent Colourpoints. Eventually, after 10 years of selective breeding, the long noses and large ears of the Siamese were bred out, but the Himalayan coat pattern, blue eyes and Persian type were fixed, and the lovely Colourpoints had arrived. The breed was recognized for competition in 1955 in the United Kingdom, and independently as the Himalayan in the United States in 1957. But by the mid-1980s the Cat Fanciers' Association and the American Cat Association recodified the Himalayan as a divison within the Persian breed, ending the Himmy's status as a separate breed.

Breeding
Colourpoint-to-Colourpoint breeding produces 100 per cent Colourpoint kittens, but to preserve type, outcrosses are still made to Persians and the offspring mated back to the original Colourpoints. With outcrossing to Persians, all point colours are possible. The mixed breeding has rendered the Colourpoint a hardy breed.

Kittens
The kittens are born with creamy white fur. The point coloration develops over the first few weeks.

SHOW STANDARD
The Colourpoint (Himalayan) is essentially a Persian-type cat with the Himalayan coat pattern: the identifying colour is confined to the mask, legs and tail.
Coat. Long, thick, soft and silky, standing well away from the body. The ruff is very full and extends to a frill between the front legs.
Body. Cobby and low on the legs. Deep in the chest. Massive across the shoulders and rump, and short and rounded in between. Long, svelte Siamese lines are a fault. The legs are short and thick, straight and strong. The paws are large, round and firm with long toe tufts.
Tail. Short, very full and carried low. A long or kinked tail is a fault.
Head. Broad and round with width between the ears. The neck is short, and thick. The face is well rounded. The nose is short and broad with a definite nose break in profile. The ears are small, rounded at the tips, tilted forward and not too open at the base. They are set far apart and low on the head, and are well furnished with long tufts.
Eyes. Large, round, brilliant and full, wide apart.

COLOURPOINT COLOURS
Many point colours are possible though not all are recognized everywhere at present.

Coat pattern. Body should be an even pale colour, with the main contrasting colour confined to the points (mask, ears, legs and tail). The mask should cover the whole face, but not the top of the head, and should be connected to the ears by tracings.

Seal point. Body colour an even pale fawn to warm cream shading to a lighter cream on the chest and

stomach. Points deep seal brown. Nose leather and paw pads seal brown. Eyes deep, vivid blue.

Chocolate point. Body colour ivory all over. Points warm milk-chocolate colour. Nose leather and paw pads cinnamon-pink. Eyes deep, vivid blue.

Blue point. Body colour glacial, bluish white, shading to a warmer white on the chest and stomach. Points slate blue. Nose leather and paw pads slate blue. Eyes deep, vivid blue.

Lilac point. Body colour magnolia (UK) or glacial white (US) all over. Points frosty grey with a pinkish tone (lilac). Nose leather and paw pads lavender-pink. Eyes deep, vivid blue.

Red (Flame) point. Body colour creamy white. Points delicate orange to red. Nose leather and paw pads flesh or coral pink. Eyes deep, vivid blue.

Cream point. Body colour creamy white. Points buff cream. Nose leather and paw pads flesh or coral pink. Eyes deep, vivid blue.

Tortie point. Body colour and basic point colour as appropriate to Seal and Chocolate point. Points patched with red and/or cream. A blaze of red or cream on the face is desirable. Nose leather and paw pads in keeping with the basic point colour and/or pink. Eyes deep, vivid blue.

Blue-cream point. Body colour bluish white or creamy white, shading to white on the chest and stomach. Points blue with patches of cream. Nose leather and paw pads slate blue and/or pink. Eyes deep, vivid blue.

Lilac-cream point. Body colour magnolia (UK) or glacial white (US). Points frosty, pinkish grey, patched with pale cream. Nose leather and paw pads lavender-pink and/or pink. Eyes deep, vivid blue.

Tabby (Lynx) point. Body colour as appropriate to the point colour, which can be seal, chocolate, blue, lilac, cream or red. Points should carry characteristic 'M' marking on forehead, bars on face and fainter rings on legs and tail, in the appropriate solid colour, well defined from a paler background. Nose leather and paw pads in keeping with point colour. Eyes deep, vivid blue in colour.

Blue-cream Lynx point. Body colour bluish-white, cold in tone. Points blue with darker blue tabby markings and patches of cream. Nose leather and paw pads slate blue and/or pink. Eyes deep, vivid blue.

Tortie Lynx point. Body creamy white or pale fawn. Points beige-brown with dark brown tabby markings and patches of red. Nose leather and paw pads seal brown with flesh and/or coral pink

mottling. Eyes deep, vivid blue.

TORTIE TABBY POINT COLOURS
In these colours the normal tabby pattern is patched and overlaid with red and cream.

Seal Tortie Tabby point. Seal brown markings, pale brown agouti background, body colour cream, patches in shades of red.

Blue-cream Tabby point. Blue markings, light beige agouti background, body colour creamy white, patches in shades of cream.

Chocolate Tortie Tabby point. Chocolate markings, light bronze agouti background, body ivory to apricot-white, patches in shades of red.

Lilac-cream Tabby point. Lilac markings, pale beige agouti background, body magnolia to creamy white, overlaid with cream shades.

HIMALAYAN HYBRIDS

Outcrossing to Persians to improve type in Colourpoint breeding resulted in the appearance of coloured longhaired kittens. In the United Kingdom some of these cats have now been granted provisional recognition as varieties of Persian (Chocolate Tortie and Lilac-cream: see page 28). In some United States registries, such cats are regarded as Himalayan Hybrids. They are useful for breeding Himalayans as they carry the appropriate genes. Nevertheless, Himalayan Hybrids were not eligible to compete in shows in the US until the mid-1980s. Now, however, US registries have awarded Himalayan Hybrids championship status. Some associations allow them to compete in the Persian division for which their colour qualifies them. Others have established separate classes for non-pointed Himalayan hybrids.

KASHMIR

The self-coloured chocolate and lilac cats that appear in Colourpoint breeding programmes are classed as self-coloured Persians in the United Kingdom and as solid-coloured Himalayans in most North American registries. But these cats are classified as Kashmirs (a separate breed) in two North American registries: The Cat Fanciers' Federation and the Canadian Cat Association. The show standard is the same as for the Colourpoint (Himalayan).

SHOW STANDARD
Chocolate. Coat colour medium to dark chocolate-brown all over. Nose leather and paw pads brown. Eyes deep orange or copper.

Lilac. Coat colour pinkish dove-grey all over. Nose leather pink. Paw pads pale pink. Eyes pale orange.

Lilac Kashmir

Tortie point
Colourpoint

Colourpoint
and Kashmir

Seal point Colourpoint

33

BALINESE
(Javanese)

Good points
- *Quieter than Siamese*
- *Lively*
- *Affectionate*

Take heed
- *Dislikes being left alone*

A Balinese makes an excellent pet; it wants to enjoy fun and games with the family and loves people. In reality a longhaired Siamese, it resembles the Siamese in its graceful beauty, but is quieter in voice and temperament and less boisterous.

The Balinese is becoming increasingly popular because of its delightful personality. A Balinese would be a good choice for the person who likes the Siamese look, but prefers a less overwhelming personality.

Grooming
The Balinese is easy to groom. The coat is silky and non-matting. A few minutes' gentle brushing with a soft brush every few days are sufficient to keep the coat shining.

Origin and history
In the 1930s and 1940s, several breeders tried to produce a long-haired, pointed cat. Among the by-products of their efforts were shorthaired, pointed cats carrying a longhair gene. Most ended up as pets, but some were registered as Siamese and were incorporated into breeding programmes. Whenever two such 'Siamese' carrying the longhair gene were mated, the odds of getting longhaired kittens were one in four.

Other sources of the longhair gene in Siamese lines were the longhaired outcrosses, particularly the Turkish Angora, that were used by Siamese breeders in England who were trying to rejuvenate the breed after World Wars I and II.

Most Siamese breeders treated semi-longhaired kittens as if they did not exist, but the enthusiasm of a few breeders was enough to establish longhaired Siamese as a separate breed.

The breed was named Balinese because the cats' graceful movement reminded one fancier of the dancers on the island of Bali.

Breeding
When two Balinese are mated together, they breed true, producing all Balinese kittens. Outcrossing to Siamese is necessary occasionally to improve type.

Kittens
The kittens are born white, the point markings gradually appearing over the first few weeks.

SHOW STANDARD
The Balinese is a medium-sized, svelte and dainty cat, yet lithe and muscular, with long, tapering Siamese lines and a long silky coat.
Coat. Ermine-like, soft, silky. No downy undercoat and no ruff around the neck.
Body. Medium sized, long and svelte. Fine boned but well muscled. Males may be larger than females. Legs long and slim, hind legs longer than forelegs. Feet dainty, small and oval.
Tail. Long, thin and tapering to a point, but well plumed.
Head. Long, tapering wedge, making a straight-edged triangle from the jaw to the ears. There should be no whisker break. The nose is long and straight with no nose break. Neck long and slender. Ears wide at the base, large and pointed. Not less than the width of an eye between the eyes.
Eyes. Medium sized, almond shaped, slanted towards the nose.

BALINESE COLOURS
In the United Kingdom and in most United States cat federations, Balinese are recognized in solid, parti and tabby pointed colours, as are all Siamese. The exception is the Cat Fanciers' Association, which insists that Siamese — and therefore Balinese — come in only four colours: seal, lilac, chocolate and blue points. The Cat Fanciers' Association calls all other shorthaired pointed cats Colourpoint Shorthairs and all other longhaired pointed cats Javanese.

Coat pattern. Body should be an even, pale colour with main contrasting colour confined to the points (mask, ears, legs and tail). The mask should cover the whole face, but not the top of the head, and be connected to the ears by tracings. Older cats may have darker body colour.

Seal point. Body colour an even pale fawn to warm cream, shading to a lighter cream on the chest and stomach. Points deep seal brown. Nose leather and paw pads seal brown. Eyes deep, vivid blue.

Chocolate point. Body colour ivory all over. Points warm milk-chocolate colour. Nose leather and paw pads cinnamon-pink. Eyes deep, vivid blue.

Blue point. Body glacial white, shading to a warmer white on the chest and stomach. Points slate blue. Nose leather and paw pads slate blue. Eyes deep, vivid blue.

Lilac point. Body colour magnolia (UK) or glacial white (US) all over. Points frosty grey with a pinkish tone (lilac). Nose leather and paw pads lavender-pink. Eyes deep, vivid blue.

Red point. Body colour creamy white. Points delicate orange to red. Nose leather and paw pads flesh or coral pink. Eyes deep, vivid blue.

Cream point. Body colour creamy white. Points buff cream. Nose leather and paw pads flesh or coral pink. Eyes deep, vivid blue.

Tortie point. Body colour and basic point colour as appropriate to Seal and Chocolate point. Points patched with red and/or cream. A blaze of red or cream is desirable.

Nose leather and paw pads in keeping with the basic point colour and/or pink. Eyes deep, vivid blue.

Blue-cream point. Body colour bluish white or creamy white, shading to white on the chest and stomach. Points blue with patches of cream. Nose leather and paw pads slate blue and/or pink. Eyes deep, vivid blue.

Lilac-cream point. Body colour magnolia (UK) or glacial white (US) all over. Points frosty pinkish grey, intermingled (UK) or patched (US) with pale cream. A facial blaze is desirable. Nose leather and paw pads lavender-pink and/or pink. Eyes deep, vivid blue.

Tabby (Lynx) point. Body colour as appropriate to the point colour, which can be seal, chocolate, blue, lilac or red. Points should carry characteristic 'M' marking on forehead, bars on face and fainter rings on legs and tail, in appropriate solid colour, well defined from a paler background. Nose leather and paw pads in keeping with point colour. Eyes deep, vivid blue.

BIRMAN
(Sacred Cat of Burma)

Good points
- *Charming*
- *Intelligent*
- *Quiet*

Take heed
- *No known drawbacks*

Birman cats have a quiet, gentle charm. Intelligent and companionable, a Birman will enjoy being part of the family and will mix well with other animals.

Grooming
Although the Birman's coat is said never to mat, it must be brushed often to remove any dead hairs.

Origin and history
According to legend, the Birman — or Sacred Cat of Burma — was originally an all-white cat that lived in the temple of Lao-Tsun in western Burma. When Mun-Ha, a priest in the temple, was killed by invaders from Siam, a cat named Sinh stood guard on the fallen priest. Before long Sinh's yellow eyes turned a deep, sapphire blue; and his legs turned brown — except for his feet, which remained sparkling white. By the following morning, all the cats in the temple had been transformed just like Sinh.

In reality, the Birman was most likely developed from crosses between Siamese and longhaired, bicoloured Angoras. Perhaps in Burma, perhaps elsewhere. By 1925 the Birman had made its way to France and was established well enough to gain championship status. The first Birmans reached the United States in 1959, and by the mid-1960s the breed was accepted for championship competition in North America. At about the same time Birmans arrived in the United Kingdom.

Breeding
Birmans breed true to type and need not be crossed with any other breed.

Kittens
Birman kittens are large and healthy, and seem to maintain their playful behaviour into adulthood.

SHOW STANDARD
The Birman is a large, longhaired cat with the Himalayan coat pattern, but with four white paws.
Coat. Long and silky with a tendency to wave on the stomach. Non-matting. Thick and heavy ruff around the neck.
Body. Medium long, but stocky and low on the legs. Legs heavy, medium in length; paws round, firm and very large with toes close together.
Tail. Medium in length and bushy.
Head. Strong, broad and rounded. Cheeks full. Roman nose. Ears wide apart, as wide at the base as tall, and rounded at the tips.
Eyes. Almost round.

BIRMAN COLOURS
In the UK, only Blue point and Seal point Birmans compete in championship classes. In most US federations, chocolate point and lilac point are also included and The International Cat Association recognizes even more colours.

Coat pattern. Body should be an even, pale colour with the main contrasting colour confined to the points (mask, ears, legs and tail). The mask should cover the whole face, including the whisker pads, and is connected to the ears by tracings. The white foot markings should be symmetrical. Front paws have white gloves ending in an even line across the paw over the knuckles; in the hind paws the white glove covers the whole paw and extends up the backs of the legs to a point just below the hocks.

Seal point. Body colour an even, pale beige to cream, warm in tone with a characteristic golden glow over the back, especially obvious in adult males. Underparts and chest are slightly paler. Points (except gloves) dark seal-brown. Gloves pure white. Nose leather deep-seal-brown. Paw pads pink. Eyes deep violet blue.

Chocolate point. Body colour even ivory all over. Points (except gloves) warm milk-chocolate colour; gloves pure white. Nose leather cinnamon-pink. Paw pads pink. Eyes deep violet-blue.

Blue point. Body colour bluish-white, cold in tone, becoming less cold on the stomach and chest. Points (except gloves) deep blue; gloves pure white, nose leather slate grey. Paw pads pink. Eyes deep violet-blue.

Lilac point. Body colour cold glacial white, points (except gloves) frosty grey-pink; gloves a pure, unsullied white. Nose leather lavender-pink. Paw pads pink. Eyes deep violet-blue.

Blue point Balinese

Balinese

Seal point Birman

Birman

NORWEGIAN FOREST CAT

Good points
- *Beautiful*
- *Athletic*
- *Water-repellent coat*
- *Playful*

Take heed
- *Moults heavily in spring and summer*

The Norwegian Forest Cat has a robust, hardy disposition. It is affectionate, intelligent and extremely playful.

Grooming
The Norwegian Forest Cat has a double coat: an undercoat that is tight and woolly, and a water-resistant, silky top coat. The coat does not mat, but it needs careful grooming if the cat is destined for showing. To prevent fur balls, even the non-show cat should be groomed frequently with a brush and comb, especially during the early summer months when the undercoat is being shed. After this, less attention is necessary until the full coat is grown again sometime in the autumn.

Origin and history
We cannot be certain how long the Norwegian Forest Cat has existed in Norway or how it got there. The Forest Cat is most often found on the farms and in the woodlands of central Norway, where the harsh winter climate encouraged the development of the Forest Cat's ingenuity, stamina and water-repellent coat.

Until the 1930s no one but the farmers of Norway, who prized the 'Wegie's' hunting ability, paid any attention to the Forest Cat. Indeed, shortly after World War II the Forest Cat nearly became extinct because of continued breeding with free-ranging domestic cats.

In the early 1970s Carl-Fredrik Nordane, a former president of the Norwegian Cat Association, organized a breed club to promote the Forest Cat and to see to its preservation. As a result the Feline International Federation of Europe (FIFe) voted in November 1977 to accept the Forest Cat for championship competition. When Nordane returned to Oslo following the Forest Cat's coronation by FIFe, he was welcomed home by music, flags, and a parade of celebrating Norwegian Forest Cat fanciers.

In 1979 the Norwegian Forest Cat arrived in the United States. The breed has not gained championship status in every association there, partly because of its resemblance to the Maine Coon Cat, but Forest Cat breeders cite these differences between the cats. The Maine Coon is long and rectangular; the Norwegian is boxy. The Maine Coon has a slight curve in its nose; the Norwegian does not. The Maine Coon has a prominent, squared-off muzzle; the Norwegian's muzzle fits smoothly and neatly into its face. The Maine Coon's ears sit upright on top of its head, the Norwegian's ears are widely spaced and tilted forward.

Breeding
Naturally robust, Norwegian Forest Cat queens deliver kittens easily and make attentive mothers.

Kittens
Norwegian Forest kittens are healthy and playful. The first adult coat begins to grow at three to five months of age.

SHOW STANDARD
The Norwegian Forest Cat should give the impression of strength, being well built and muscular, with a long body and long legs. The characteristc feature is the shaggy, weather-resistant coat.
Coat. Very long top coat; guard hairs are smooth and oily, making the coat water-repellent. Tight woolly undercoat. In autumn a ruff grows around the neck and chest, but this is shed the following summer. Coat quality may vary with living conditions.
Body. Long, large and heavily built. Legs long; hind legs longer than forelegs. Feet wide, with heavy paws. Slender type is a fault.
Tail. Long and well furnished.
Head. Triangular in shape, with a long, wide, straight nose without a nose break. Neck long. Cheeks full. Chin heavy. Ears long, set high on the head, upright and pointed, well furnished inside with long ear tufts. Whiskers prominent and long. Faults include a short nose, small or wide-set ears.
Eyes. Large, almond shaped; set at a slight angle with the outer corners a bit higher than the inner corners.

NORWEGIAN FOREST CAT COLOURS
Any coat colour or pattern — except pointed — is permitted, with or without white. Commonly white appears on the chest and paws. Tabby cats generally have heavier coats than the solid and bicoloured varieties. Eye colour should be in keeping with the coat colour.

MAINE COON CAT

Good points
- *Hardy*
- *Active*
- *Fun-loving*
- *Adaptable*
- *Even-tempered*

Take heed
- *No known drawbacks*

The Maine Coon is a large cat, very hardy and active, but sometimes shy. It is good-tempered, easy to groom and to care for. It loves playing and performing tricks, and has a most delightful, quiet, chirping voice.

Requiring little grooming, it makes an ideal pet for the person who likes the beauty of a longhaired cat, but does not have the time to devote to frequent grooming.

Grooming
The Maine Coon's undercoat is slight, so the cat is easy to groom. A gentle brushing and combing every few days or so will be quite sufficient to remove any dead hairs and to keep mats from forming in the coat.

Origin and history
Like many breeds of cats, the Maine Coon's origin is largely unknown. Most likely, it developed from matings between domestic shorthaired cats and longhaired cats brought by traders from Asia Minor to Maine and other parts of New England, long before records of cats were kept. But some accounts of the Maine Coon's origin are more fanciful. There are 'historians' who believe that Maine Coons descended from cats sent to the United States from France by Marie Antoinette, who had hoped to join her cats in the New World but whose plans were cut short by the guillotine. Others contend that a sea captain named Coon brought Persian and Angora cats to North America. Coon's cats, after jumping ship, introduced the longhair gene to the New World.

Persons with little knowledge of feline deportment and reproduction believe that the Maine Coon Cat resulted from matings between cats and racoons. While fertile unions between these species are a genetic impossibility, the cat-meets-racoon theory was probably inspired by a few similarities between Maine Coons and racoons: the first Maine Coons were brown ticked or seal-brown in colour, liked to climb trees (and still do) and had tabby rings on their tails — much like the racoon.

Although no early records were kept, the Maine Coon was well known in the East Coast states by the end of the nineteenth century. Maines were kept as mousers long before they became show cats, but were one of the earliest breeds seen at cat shows. A Maine Coon was best cat in show at a Madison Square Garden show in New York in 1895. After that time, however, interest in the breed almost died out until the formation of the Maine Coon Cat Club in 1953 revived interest, and held regular, one-breed shows for Maine Coons.

The Maine Coon is no longer confined to the state from which it takes its name, but is well known and bred throughout both the US and Europe.

Breeding
Maine Coons usually have no problems breeding, and the females make good mothers.

Kittens
The large, robust kittens mature slowly and may take up to four years to develop their full beauty.

SHOW STANDARD
The Maine Coon is a tough, large and rugged cat, solidly built, with a smooth, shaggy coat.
Coat. Heavy and shaggy, yet silky in texture, lustrous and flowing. Short on the face and shoulders, but longer on the stomach and hind legs, where it forms long breeches.
Body. A long-bodied cat with a broad chest and level back, giving a rectangular appearance. Males 10-12lb (4.5-5.4kg); females smaller, 8-10lb (3.6-4.5kg). Muscular, with strong legs set wide apart. Feet large and round. Paws well tufted.
Tail. Blunt ended, but well furnished with long fur. Wider at the base. No kinks allowed.
Head. Width is medium; length is medium long. Set on a medium-length, powerful neck. Square muzzle. Firm chin, not undershot. High cheekbones. Nose is medium length and may have a slight nose break. Ears large and well tufted, wide at the base and tapering to a point; set high on the head.
Eyes. Slightly slanting, large and set wide apart.

MAINE COON COLOURS
Maine Coons are bred in all coat colours and patterns but pointed. The combinations of colours and patterns include tabby with white. In this case, there should be white on the bib, stomach and all four paws, and preferably on one-third of the body. Eye colour can be green, gold or copper, though white cats may also be blue-eyed or odd-eyed. There is no relationship between eye colour and coat colour or pattern.

Below: Healthy Maine Coon kittens taking an active interest in life. Though tabbies are quite frequently seen, Maines are bred in all coat colours and patterns but pointed.

*Brown Tabby-and-white
Norwegian Forest Cat*

Norwegian
Forest Cat

Maine Coon

*Blue-and-white
Bicolour Maine Coon*

ANGORA
(Turkish Angora)

Good points
- *Graceful*
- *Intelligent*
- *Loyal*
- *Quiet*
- *Adaptable*

Take heed
- *No known drawbacks*

The Angora makes a charming companion and is a very attractive cat with its long lithe body and plumed tail. It is not a talkative cat but is alert, lively, intelligent and loves to play games.

Angoras are bred in many colours and patterns, although white is the most popular. Some of the blue-eyed and odd-eyed whites may be deaf, and it is advisable to make sure before purchase that your chosen kitten is not deaf, unless you feel competent to take care of such an animal and protect it against the dangers that deafness inevitably involves.

Grooming
Although the Angora is easier to groom than a Persian, it needs the occasional grooming session. Use a medium-toothed comb to remove dead hairs. Grooming is important in spring and early summer, when much of the coat is shed.

Origin and history
The Angora, thought by some observers to be the oldest longhaired breed known in Europe, came originally from Ankara in Turkey, where it is known to exist today as a free-roaming domestic cat and in the local zoo.

Angoras arrived in the United Kingdom via France and were known for a time as French cats. In the early days they were mated indiscriminately with other longhaired cats (the original Persians), and in the process the Persian type achieved dominance and the Angora type was lost until quite recently, except of course in Turkey. Apparently the early Persians had long, thick coats, lacking the silkiness of the Angora coat, and it is thought that Angoras may have been used to improve the Persian coat.

In the United States, Persians and Angoras were both registered as 'longhairs' until the mid-1950s. At that time all pedigreed longhairs became *de facto* Persians, and as a result of this ruling, Angoras became virtually extinct.

Despite this change in registration policy, some people were interested in (re-)establishing the Angora as a breed in its own right. In the 1960s a few American cat fanciers obtained Angoras from the Ankara Zoo. These cats were white, but other colours have been bred, and many are now recognized for showing on both sides of the Atlantic, although numbers in the UK remain relatively small.

Since the Angora had not been subject to selective breeding for

Above: A graceful Blue-eyed White Angora. Some Blue-eyed Whites are born deaf; check before buying or you may encounter problems later.

almost 50 years before it was revived in the United States, it remains true to its original type.

Breeding
Many colours are available in this breed, but white is by far the most popular, accounting for roughly three-quarters of all Angora registrations in the Cat Fanciers' Association, North America's registry of record.

The preponderance of vanilla among Turkish Angora flavours is no accident. Indeed, some people claim that the pure-as-the-driven-snow Angora comes only in white. And a few people insist that the pure Angora comes only in odd-eyed white. If this last is true, fewer than 300 of the Turkish Angoras ever registered have been worthy of the name.

Deafness is particularly common among Blue-eyed and Odd-eyed White Angoras, and for obvious reasons it is best not to use a deaf cat for breeding.

Kittens
Angora kittens are charming, fluffy and playful. They mature slowly, and the long, silky coat is not fully developed until two years of age.

SHOW STANDARD
The Angora is a medium-sized cat, solidly built, but graceful and lithe.
Coat. Medium-length, silky hair; slightly wavy on the stomach. No thick woolly undercoat. The hair is long on the underparts and ruff, and shorter along the back and on the face.
Body. Medium in size, long, graceful and lithe. Fine but strong-boned. Long but sturdy legs; hind legs slightly longer than forelegs. Feet small, oval to round and dainty; toes well tufted.
Tail. Long and tapering, wider at the base and well plumed. When the cat is moving, the tail is carried horizontally over the body, sometimes almost touching the head.

Head. Medium sized, wide, gently pointed wedge. Nose straight without a stop. Neck long and slim. Ears set high on head, large and pointed, broad based and tufted.
Eyes. Large, round to oval in shape and slightly slanted.

ANGORA COLOURS
Chalky white is the favourite colour, yet all other longhaired coat colours are accepted. (Chocolate, Lilac and the Himalayan pattern are not accepted in the US.) Eyes are amber in all colours, but Brown and Silver Tabbies may have green or hazel eyes, and Whites may be blue- or odd-eyed (one blue, one amber). Angoras have the same body shape as Balinese.

TURKISH VAN

Good points
- *Distinctive appearance*
- *Elegant*
- *Intelligent*
- *Hardy*
- *Lively*

Take heed
- *No known drawbacks*

The Turkish Van makes an exotically different pet with its beautiful chalk-white coat and striking face and tail markings. This cat is lively and affectionate and makes a charming, intelligent companion.

Although they originated in the same country, there are characteristic differences between the Angora and the Turkish Van. The Angora is a lithe and fine-boned cat. The Van is wide bodied and heavy boned with a distinctive colour pattern. In its purest manifestation, the Van's pattern consists of a spot or two of colour on the cat's head and a fully coloured tail. The rest of the cat is entirely white.

Grooming
The Turkish Van is an easy cat to groom, but twice weekly combing is recommended to remove dead hairs, particularly when the cat is moulting in the spring and summer months.

Origin and history
Though the Turkish Van was named after the Lake Van district in Western Turkey, there is no evidence that the breed originated in this area, nor is it the only place in Turkey where Van cats have been found.

The evolution of the Turkish Van as a breed began in 1955 when Laura Lushington and Sonia Halliday, two British women holidaying in Turkey, brought a pair of Van kittens back to England. When these kittens grew up and reproduced their type, Lushington and Halliday were convinced they were dealing with a distinct breed of cat and began working to secure championship status for it.

They imported two more Turkish Vans in 1959, and by 1969 the breed was recognized in the United Kingdom. The following year the first Turkish Vans arrived in the United States. As of May 1, 1985, the Turkish Van was eligible for championship competition in The International Cat Association, the first — and so far the only — North American registry to recognize this breed.

Breeding
The Turkish Van's unusual pattern is caused by a piebald spotting gene. This dominant gene accounts for the presence of white in bicoloured and tricoloured cats. When the gene governing a trait is dominant, a kitten will exhibit that trait as long as the kitten inherits a copy of that gene from one of its parents.

Kittens
The kittens are born pure chalk white — not pink, like most all-white animals — with the auburn markings already visible.

SHOW STANDARD
The Turkish Van is a medium-sized cat, sturdy and strong in build, with a long, silky coat. Males are rather larger and more muscular than females.
Coat. Very silky, long, straight fur, without a thick woolly undercoat. Coat heavier in winter than in summer.
Body. Long but sturdy, with medium-length legs. Feet small and round, with tufted toes.
Tail. Medium in length and possessing a full brush.
Head. Short and wedge-shaped. Medium-length neck. Nose long, not snub. Ears large, upright, close together, shell pink inside and well tufted.
Eyes. Round, pink-rimmed. Large in size, oval in shape.

TURKISH VAN COLOURS
White with no trace of yellow. Markings — which are limited to cream or auburn in the UK, but include other solid, tortie and torbie colours in the US — are displayed in a blazed head patch and a rump patch extending to the tip of the tail. One or more random spots of colour are permitted on the upper body, flanks and outside of legs to the ankles. Markings may be broken with patches of white. Nose leather and paw pads pink.

Angora
(Outline beneath fur)

Amber-eyed White Angora

Turkish

Turkish

*Turkish
kitten*

CYMRIC
(Longhaired Manx)

Good points
- *Intelligent*
- *Quiet*
- *Loyal*
- *Affectionate*

Take heed
- *Troublesome to breed*

The Cymric's tailless appearance distinguishes it from every other cat save the Manx, and the Cymric's long hair distinguishes it from its tailless, shorthaired relative — the Manx.

The Cymric has the same temperament and personality as the Manx, being loyal and affectionate, intelligent and gentle, courageous and strong. It makes an excellent family pet.

Grooming
Although the Cymric has long hair, the fur does not mat easily, and the cat is therefore easy to groom. A good comb-through occasionally is required to remove dead hairs.

Origin and history
On the Isle of Man, where Manx cats originated, free-roaming longhaired cats often bred with shorthaired, tailless Manx. In addition, starting in the late 1930s and continuing for several decades, Manx breeders used Persians in their breeding programmes, not from any real desire to produce longhaired Manx, but to improve body conformation and coat quality in their shorthairs.

Cat fanciers are inclined to seek recognition for anything new or different that appears in their litters. Just as frequently they will attempt to attribute newness to the occurrence of a rare mutation. This is how some people tried to explain the appearance of longhaired Manx kittens in litters born to shorthaired parents. But such was not the case. The Canadian Cat Association, in the mid-1970s, was the first group to grant championship status to Cymrics. The breed is now accepted in five of the six North American registries.

Breeding
The gene for taillessness is dominant. Therefore, a kitten that inherits one gene for a normal tail and the other for taillessness will be tailless. However, kittens with normal tails can appear in litters born to two tailless parents.

The tailless gene is lethal, thus one-quarter of all Cymric kittens fail to develop in the womb. In addition, a percentage of Cymrics are stricken with spina bifida.

Kittens
Cymric kittens are venturesome and playful, even though frequently denied the built-in toy that other breeds have in the nest, that inviting feature — mother's tail.

SHOW STANDARD
The principal attribute in the show Cymric is the complete absence of a tail. The Cymric should have a round, rabbity look with a short back and long hind legs.
Coat. Medium to long, and double. The undercoat is thick, and cottony. The top coat is silky and glossy.
Body. A solid, rounded cat, with a short back, rounded rump, very deep flanks and muscular thighs. The forelegs are set well apart and are short and heavily boned. The hind legs are longer than the forelegs. The back is arched from shoulder to the rump. The feet are neat and round.
Tail. Absent, with a decided hollow at the end of the spine.
Head. Large and round, with prominent cheekbones. Short, thick neck and strong chin. Nose of medium length with a gentle nose dip. The whisker pads are rounded, and there is a decided whisker break. Ears are large, wide at the base, tapering to slightly pointed tips, set slightly outward with ear tufts at the ends.
Eyes. Large, round and expressive; set at an angle to the nose. Outer corners slightly higher than inner corners.

CYMRIC COLOURS
Most coat colours and patterns and combinations of coat colours and patterns, such as white with tabby, are permitted. However, Chocolate, Lilac and the Himalayan pattern are not accepted.

SOMALI

Good points
- *Easy to groom*
- *Affectionate*
- *Even-tempered*

Take heed
- *Does not like to be caged*

The Somali is a longhaired Abyssinian, similar in temperament and colouring to the Aby, but less active. The Somali makes an interesting pet, as it is playful and lively.

Grooming
The Somali coat does not mat and, therefore, daily grooming is not essential, though a periodic run-through with a medium-toothed comb is advisable.

Origin and history
One day in 1969 a year-old, longhaired Abyssinian cat named George — who had been given away at the age of five weeks by his breeder — was surrendered by his fifth owner to a private shelter in New Jersey. Evelyn Mague, who operated the shelter, found a home for George, but before she did, she traced his pedigree back to his original breeder.

Mague learned that George had been sired by a male she owned and that a female she had recently acquired was George's mother. Outraged that George 'had been no better off than an unpedigreed cat in the street', Mague resolved to breed longhaired Abyssinians and to work towards their recognition. She chose the name Somali for her

breed because Somalia borders on Ethiopia, once called Abyssinia.

Mague's choice of 'Somali' was descriptive as well as ironic. The difference between the breeds, like the borders between Ethiopia and Somalia, are man-made. The longhair gene was introduced into the Abyssinian gene pool by breeders who used cats of unknown origin (or known, longhaired origin) in their breeding programmes during times when pedigreed Abyssinian breeding stock was scarce.

Through an advertisement she ran in *Cats* magazine, Mague met a Canadian breeder who had been working with longhaired Abys for four or five years. Gradually other Aby breeders with longhairs came out of the woodwork, and in 1972 Mague founded the Somali Cat Club of America (SCCA). Registration and championship status soon followed — first by the now defunct National Cat Fanciers' Association, eventually by all registries in North America.

Breeding
Mating two Somalis will produce all-Somali kittens, but they may also appear in Abyssinian litters where both parents carry the gene for long hair. Somalis can also be mated to Abyssinians to improve the Somali type.

Kittens
Somali kittens are slightly larger than Abyssinian kittens, and are slower to develop their full adult coats.

SHOW STANDARD
The Somali is a medium-sized, lithe-bodied cat, firm and muscular with a long coat and distinctive colouring.
Coat. Full, dense, silky and fine-textured. A ruff around the neck and breeches are desirable. The coat is longer on the stomach and shorter over the shoulders.
Body. Medium in length, lithe, graceful and muscular. Rib cage rounded. Back slightly arched. Legs long and slim. Paws small and oval, with tufted toes.
Tail. Full brush; thick at the base and gently tapering.
Head. Rounded, short wedge, all lines gently curving. Wide between the ears, which are large and alert, pointed, wide at the base, set well apart towards the back of the head, and furnished with long ear tufts. Chin rounded, firm and full. No whisker break.

Above: A Sorrel (Red) Somali shows itself to the best advantage.

Eyes. Almond shaped, large, brilliant and expressive.

SOMALI COLOURS
The Somali is recognized for championship competition in the following colours in the United Kingdom and United States:

Ruddy. Coat colour orange-brown, each hair ticked (banded) with black. Double or treble banding is preferred. Darker shading forms a line along the spine and continues along the tail, which ends in a black tip. The ears should be tipped with black or dark brown. The eyes are dark-rimmed and surrounded by a pale area. The underside, insides of the legs and chest should be an even ruddy colour, without ticking or other markings. The toe tufts on all four feet are black or dark brown, with black between the toes extending up the back of the hind legs. White or off-white is allowed only on the upper throat, lips and nostrils. Nose leather brick red. Paw pads black or brown. Eyes gold or green, deeper colours preferred.

Red. Body colour warm, glowing red ticked with chocolate brown. Deeper shades of red preferred. The ears and tail should be tipped with chocolate brown. The underside, insides of the legs and chest are reddish brown without ticking or other markings. The toe tufts are chocolate brown, the colour extending slightly beyond the paws. Nose leather rosy pink. Paw pads pink. Eyes gold or green, deeper colours preferred.

The Somali is recognized for championship competition in the following colours in the US only:

Blue. Coat warm, soft blue-grey, with slate-blue ticking. Ivory undercoat. Tail tipped with slate blue. Undersides and forelegs, warm cream to beige. Nose leather dark pink. Paw pads mauve, with slate blue between toes. Eye colour gold or green.

Fawn. Coat warm rose beige. Coat and tail ticked with light cocoa brown. Underside and insides of the legs harmonize with the main colour. Nose leather salmon. Paw pads dark pink, with light cocoa brown between the toes. Eyes gold or green.

Blue Tortoiseshell-and-white
(Dilute Calico) Cymric

Cymric

Red Somali kitten

Ruddy Somali

Somali

SCOTTISH FOLD LONGHAIR

Good points
● *Comely*
● *Affectionate*
● *Merry dispostion*

Take heed
● *Fold-to-Fold breedings can cause skeletal anomalies*

Although longhaired kittens appeared in Scottish Fold litters from the earliest days of the breed, the Longhaired Fold, also known as the Highland Fold in some associations, did not gain championship status until a decade after its shorthaired counterpart had.

Grooming
Coat length varies among Scottish Fold Longhairs. Some cats can be maintained with brief, twice weekly grooming sessions. Others need more close attention.

Origin and history
All Scottish Folds, regardless of coat length, are descended from a white, fold-eared, shorthaired cat named Susie, who was born near the village of Coupar Angus in east central Scotland in 1961. Since Susie produced only one litter, and it contained two shorthaired kittens, one cannot be certain if she was carrying a gene for long hair. Susie's daughter, Snooks, did produce longhaired kittens; and one may conclude that if the Scottish Fold was not a dual-coated breed at the start, it quickly became one — the longhair gene being supplied by the British shorthaired cats, both pedigree and domestic, to which Folds were originally bred.

The decision to pursue championship status for shorthaired Folds only was a calculated one. William and Mary Ross, the breed's founders, were advised not to promote longhairs because they looked as if they didn't have any ears at all, and cat fanciers involved with Folds in the 1960s already anticipated some difficulty in gaining recognition for their singular-looking breed. They were, of course, correct. The Governing Council of the Cat Fancy eventually banned registration of Scottish Folds in England, though the breed is currently accepted by the Cat Association of Britain.

If Fold breeders were not committed to promoting longhairs, no one seemed committed to stop producing them either, for that would have required neutering or spaying any cat that produced a longhaired kitten. Indeed, Fold breeders continued to add the longhair gene to their breed. Exotic Shorthairs, which frequently carry a longhair gene, were used in some Scottish Fold breeding programmes in the United States up to — and in some cases beyond — the time when the official outcrosses for Scottish Folds were limited to British and American shorthairs. Furthermore, the longhair gene continues to make its way into the Scottish Fold gene pool legitimately via the British Shorthair, for which the Persian is still an approved outcross in the United Kingdom.

By the early 1980s, within five years after shorthaired Folds had been accepted for championship competition in the US, longhaired Folds began appearing in household pet classes in a few shows sanctioned by The International Cat Association. Eventually that group and others accorded the 'new' breed championship status.

Breeding
Breeders recommend that Folds be mated only to straight-eared cats since Fold-to-Fold breedings can give rise to skeletal anomalies. These anomalies — which usually occur in the tail and hindquarters — are found primarily in cats that have inherited two genes for folded ears.

Kittens
Fold kittens' ears look normal — that is, floppy — at birth. At about two to three weeks, when the ears on most kittens begin to straighten, Folds' ears start heading in the opposite way.

SHOW STANDARD
A medium-sized cat, the Scottish Fold Longhair has a well-padded, semi-cobby body with medium bone and a semi-long to long coat.
Coat. Soft and resilient. Stands away from the body. Varies from semi-long to long.
Body. Medium, well rounded, even from shoulder to pelvic girdle. Somewhat cobby.
Tail. Medium to long, tapering, in proportion to the body.
Head. Well rounded with a firm chin and jaw. Cheeks full, muzzle short. Nose short with a gentle curve or a brief stop, but no break.
Eyes. Large and round with a sweet expression.

SCOTTISH FOLD LONGHAIR COLOURS
All colours except chocolate and lilac, all patterns except pointed.

AMERICAN CURL

Good points
● *Sound healh*
● *Easy maintenance*
● *Novel appearance*
● *Balanced temperament*

Take heed
● *No known drawbacks*

A new twist on a hardy domestic-cat theme, the American Curl is as genuine as baseball, hot dogs, apple pie and Chevrolet. Since wandering into the backyard of two California residents in 1981, the Curl has wandered into the hearts of a considerable number of breeders.

Grooming
The Curl's modest-length, flat-lying coat does not pose the same grooming challenges that other longhair coats do.

Origin and history
One fine California day in June 1981, two stray kittens — a longhaired, black female and her shorthaired, black-and-white companion, who was presumed to be her sister — presented themselves at the home of Joe and Grace Ruga. The black-and-white kitten stayed only a week, then resumed her travels; but the black kitten, who was subsequently named Shulamith, liked the accommodation so well that she decided to stay on at the Rugas' and give birth to a new breed of cat.

Subsequent to a meeting with a neighbourhood gentleman, Shulamith had a litter of four kittens in mid-December 1981. Although Shulamith and her sister had curled ears, the Rugas thought this was nothing more than a curiosity — until two of Shulamith's kittens developed curled ears. One of those kittens, a longhaired, brown tabby female named Mercedes, went to live with Grace Ruga's sister, Esther Brimlow, in Orange, California. About a year later Grace sent Esther a second Curl — a longhaired, colourpoint male with blue eyes, who was also Shulamith's offspring.

One day in 1983, about two years after Shulamith had appeared on the Rugas' back doorstep, a woman named Nancy Kiester, who owned a meat market at the time, was making a delivery to Esther Brimlow's home. As soon as she saw Mercedes, Kiester recalls, 'I was hooked'. Two months later Brimlow gave Kiester two Curl kittens. In no time Kiester became 'cat crazy, and what had been a flash of an idea at first became a steady, burning desire to see this new breed established'.

Shortly after she had acquired her kittens, Kiester, who had bred and shown Australian Shepherds, read an article about Scottish Folds in a California newspaper. She called Grace Ruga, and they decided to put Shulamith and her grandchildren on exhibition at a show in Palm Springs, California, on October 23. This would be the first cat show for all concerned.

Despite the fine reception given to the Curls at their first and subsequent shows, Kiester thought that it might be a long time before this new breed would be accepted for championship competition. But early in 1985, barely 16 months after the first American Curl had appeared on exhibition at a show, The International Cat Association accepted Curls for registration. Then, almost as fast as you can say 'What are the outcrosses for this breed?', TICA granted longhaired Curls championship status at its annual meeting in September the following year.

Breeding
The allowable outcrosses for the American Curl are unlimited — as long as they are not pedigree cats. One suspects that this requirement, unique among 'purebred' cats, would make standardization of breed type difficult if not virtually impossible to achieve.

Kittens
The mutation gene responsible for curled ears is a simple dominant. If a kitten inherits one gene for straight ears and one gene for curled ears, that kitten will have curled ears. This means that only one parent has to be a Curl in order for a kitten to develop curled ears.

SHOW STANDARD
The American Curl is a medium-size, semi-foreign cat with a modified wedge-shape head and a silky, flat-lying coat.
Coat. Medium-long with a minimal undercoat and no ruff. Lies flat to the body.
Body. Semi-foreign. Not cobby. Medium bone and moderately developed muscle strength.
Tail. Wide at the base, tapering. In proportion to body length.
Head. Medium, modified wedge-shape. Longer than it is wide. Straight nose, slight rise to the forehead. Muzzle neither pointed nor square.
Eyes. Walnut shaped. Moderately large, set at a slight bias. There should be the width of an eye between the eyes.

AMERICAN CURL COLOURS
American Curls are accepted in all colours and patterns, including pointed.

Below: The gene responsible for the American Curl's ears is a simple dominant: for a kitten to develop them, one parent must be a Curl.

American Curl

American Curl

Scottish Fold

Scottish Fold

SELKIRK REX

Good points
- *Sound health*
- *Unusual appearance*
- *Good disposition*

Take heed
- *As the Selkirk Rex is still young, it is too soon to know whether the breed possesses any drawbacks*

Scarcely a year goes by, it seems, in which someone does not discover a new rex-coated cat somewhere. To date, Rex cats have been discovered in Germany, in the United Kingdom (twice), and in various of the United States of America, including Pennsylvania, California, Oregon, Ohio and Wyoming. The Rex cat discovered in Wyoming, known now as the Selkirk Rex, is the latest Rex to be accepted for registration by a North American cat association. Perhaps one day it will join the established Rex breeds — the Cornish and the Devon — on the show bench.

Grooming
Although the Selkirk Rex's coat is somewhat longer than that of the Cornish and the Devon Rexes, it does not present an exceptional grooming challenge. A careful run through with a wide-toothed comb every few days will maintain the coat in fine condition.

Origin and history
The first Selkirk Rex, a blue-cream-and-white kitten, appeared in the United States in 1987. This kitten, 'discovered' by a humane society worker in Bozeman, Wyoming, had been born in a litter of straight-coated kittens.

Although some people might think it ironic that a cat with humane-society connections would be used eventually in the purposeful breeding of pedigree cats — given the scope of the cat overpopulation problem in the US — the blue-cream-and-white kitten was bred at the age of 14 months to a registered Black Persian. Three of the six kittens in the litter had curly coats like their mother's. Thus, breeders concluded, the gene governing coat type in the Selkirk Rex is inherited in a dominant fashion; that is, if a kitten inherits one gene for a Selkirk Rex coat and one gene for a normal coat, that kitten will have a curly coat. If the Selkirk gene were recessive, all the kittens would have had normal coats because there was virtually no chance that the Black Persian

father of the litter, who was unrelated to the mother cat, also was carrying a Selkirk gene.

Breeding
Because the Selkirk Rex's coat is governed by a dominant gene, this breed differs from the Cornish and the Devon Rexes, whose coats are governed by recessive genes. A number of breeds have been used in the development of the Selkirk Rex, including British, American and Exotic shorthairs. About the only breeds excluded from the allowable-outcrosses list at this point are the established Rex breeds, the Cornish and the Devon.

Kittens
Selkirk Rex kittens are born with curly coats. When kitten coats are shed at around the age of six months, they are replaced for a time by coats that are rather sparse and wiry. Within two to four months, the plush adult coat is in evidence.

SHOW STANDARD
The Selkirk Rex is a medium-to-large cat with a rectangular torso set on long, heavily boned legs. Although females are less massive than are males, both sexes have definite jowls.
Coat. Thick, medium length, arranged in loose individual curls that are particularly prominent around the neck and tail. Guard hairs (the longest kind) are slightly coarse, but the overall effect is soft and plush.
Body. Rectangular torso. Medium-long, heavily boned legs. Large paws. Slight rise from shoulders to the hindquarters.
Tail. Thick, medium long, tapering to a rounded tip.
Head. Round and full cheeked. Top of head is gently rounded, muzzle is short and squared off. Nose has stop that contributes to cat's unique profile. Medium, pointed ears set well apart on head.
Eyes. Round and set far apart.

SELKIRK REX COLOURS
Selkirk Rex are accepted in all colours and patterns, including pointed.

SIBERIAN CAT

Good points
- *Strong and sturdy*
- *Resilient coat*
- *Affectionate*
- *Good conversation starter*

Take heed
- *No known drawbacks*

Longhaired cats from Russia were among the earliest cats shown when the cat fancy was established in the United Kingdom in the late nineteenth century. These cats failed to gain a toehold in the UK fancy, but 100 years later Russian longhairs, known as Siberian Cats, arrived in the United States.

Grooming
Comb every two or three days; bath as needed.

Origin and history
When American journalist Lincoln Steffens returned from a trip to the then Soviet Union in 1919, he declared, 'I have seen the future, and it works'. When American cat fancier David Boehm returned from a trip to Russia in 1990, he, too, believed he had seen the future. That future involved a large, muscular cat with a semilong coat and a short pedigree: it was known as the Siberian Cat. Such was Boehm's belief in these Siberians that he had brought 15 of them back to the US with him.

Boehm first read about Siberian Cats in a magazine article in March 1990. He was impressed by their looks, and was determined to be the first importer of Siberians to the US. He called the woman in Germany who had written the article, but after determining that 'it would be difficult to obtain these cats from the known sources', he decided to plunge into the unknown and began preparing for a trip to Russia.

Boehm left Kennedy airport, New York City, on June 27, 1990, bound for Leningrad, where there was a cat show scheduled for that weekend. But at almost the same time that his plane arrived at Moscow, three Siberian kittens were leaving that city's airport on a flight bound for the US. The kittens — a brown classic tabby-and-white male, a brown mackerel tabby female and a brown mackerel tabby-and-white female — were being shipped to Elizabeth Terrell, a Himalayan breeder in Baton Rouge, Louisiana. They were part of a cultural exhange programme between Terrell and Nellie Sachuk, a member of Leningrad's Kotofei cat club. In return for the Siberians, Terrell had sent two Himalayans to Russia — a male and a pregnant female — and had promised to send another cat in the autumn.

The exchange between Terrell and Sachuk had been inspired by a 1988 article in a Himalayan breed publication that asked if any American breeders would be willing to send Himmies to Russia to help get that breed established there. Terrell obtained the name of a Russian breeder, wrote a letter offering to send cats to Russia and eventually heard from Sachuk, who suggested trading Siberian kittens for Himalayans.

Left: A Black Selkirk Rex. The first Selkirk Rex kitten was 'discovered' among a litter of straight-coated kittens in 1987. The coat-type is governed by a dominant gene.

Although Boehm had spoken with Terrell by phone a week before leaving for Russia, he did not realize when he landed in Moscow that he was already playing for second place in the rush-to-import sweepstakes. He took a flight from Moscow to Leningrad, checked into a hotel and asked where he could find Siberian Cats. He was told there would be many at the show that weekend, and that he also might find some in the markets: all-purpose Soviet institutions similar to the farmers' markets that are held in the US.

Armed with a note — written for him in Russian — that read, 'I am looking for Siberian Cats', he left for the market, about an hour's walk away. There he bought a young red-and-white male, which he carried carefully by hand back to the hotel.

After five days in Leningrad, Boehm left for Moscow with 13 Siberian Cats, a Russian Blue, and a white, good-luck cat that had been given to him by a Russian teacher of English. He bought two more Siberians in Moscow, then was airborne on the 4th of July. He did not find out until he phoned Terrell two days later that his 15 Siberians were in fact numbers four through to 18 on the import list.

So, although history cannot record that Boehm was the first person to import Siberian Cats to the US, he did achieve another milestone. At 6.45 a.m. on Wednesday, October 19, 1990, Boehm and his wife Mildred watched as the first Siberian kitten born in the US was delivered by a black female named Mary, that David Boehm had brought home from Russia.

Breeding
Breeders working with Siberian cats should be careful to use a variety of animals in establishing their bloodlines. This approach will reduce the chances that subsequent breeders will encounter the genetic mishaps that can occur because of a limited gene pool.

Kittens
May be sparsely coated during adolescence.

SHOW STANDARD
The Siberian Cat is a robust animal — large, massive and strong.
Coat. Semilong and lustrous with oily guard hairs. An abundant ruff about the neck. Virtually no undercoat.
Body. Large, rectangular and muscular. Back is long and slightly arched. Hind legs somewhat longer than front legs.
Tail. Long, full and plume-like.
Head. Large, rounded, modified wedge shape. Broad skull narrows slightly to a voluminous, round muzzle. Slight muzzle break. Cheek bones neither high nor prominent. Ears medium in size, rounded at the tips, wide set and low on the head.
Eyes. Large, round, almost oval.

SIBERIAN COLOURS
All colours and patterns are acceptable.

Selkirk Rex

Blue-cream
Selkirk Rex

Brown-spotted Tabby Siberian Cat

Siberian Cat

AMERICAN BOBTAIL

Good points
● *Intriguing disposition*
● *Unusual appearance*
● *Rich-looking coat*

Take heed
● *Tailless kittens may occur, and these may have health problems*

Many breeds have been developed in the United States, but only four boast the Made-in-the-USA label in their names: the American Shorthair, a naturally occurring breed that is one of the oldest in the cat fancy, the American Wirehair and the American Curl, both of which resulted from mutations, and the American Bobtail, which is more difficult to categorize. (See 'Origins and history', below.)

Grooming
Comb or brush carefully every two or three days.

Origin and history
About 22 years ago John and Brenda Sanders of Clinton County, Iowa, visited an Arizona motel near an Indian reservation. There they noticed a tiny, brown spotted tabby, bobtailed kitten, whose principal playmates were several dogs living in the vicinity.

The Sanders were impressed by the tyke's mettle and were piqued by the story that he was the product of a bobcat-domestic cat cross. They asked the motel owner if they might take the little road warrior home. The owner hesitated at first, but fearing for the dogs' mental stability, he told the Sanders, 'The cat's yours'.

On their farm in Iowa, the Sanders had a Seal point Siamese female named Mishi. They had not planned to breed her to the bobtailed newcomer, whom they had named Yodie; but neither of the cats was altered, and consequently Mishi and Yodie produced several litters. Some of their kittens were black, some were tabby. A few had short tails like their father's. The rest had normal tails like their mother.

The kittens that the Sanders

could not place were sent to live in the barn. Eventually a cream point male with white mittens and markings who also lived in the barn bred several of Yodie and Mishi's offspring. Because these offspring carried a recessive gene for colourpoints inherited from Mishi, some of the cream point suitor's kittens developed Siamese overtones on their faces, feet and tails. In addition, a few of these pointed kittens sported white mittens and markings.

The unusual appearance of these latter kittens inspired a few people to think about creating a new breed. Soon a neighbour had written a provisional standard for the breed, then somebody else came up with the name American Bobtail — and the idea seemed close to becoming reality.

The process was not to be that easy, however. For, over the next 10 years the only significant growth the Bobtail exhibited was in coat length, which evolved from plush to semilong as Himalayans were added to the Bobtail equation.

It is possible that another variable was added as well. Some Bobtail breeders allow that rumpies — cats without tails — appear occasionally in Bobtail litters. In the feline genetic lexicon *rumpy* is a synonym for Manx; and some Manx develop tails about one to four inches (2.5-10cm) long, which is close to the prescribed length for the American Bobtail. Moreover, the stumpy tailed Manx, like many Bobtails', has a tail which is frequently bent to one side, or curved like the head of a violin.

Although it is possible that one of Yodie's parents was a bobcat, in most wildcat-domestic cat crosses first-generation males are sterile. Thus, it is more likely that Yodie's short tail was caused by a mutation.

'The Manx locus seems to be very prone to mutations', explains Solveig Pflueger, Ph.D., M.D., and chairperson of the genetics committee of The International Cat

Association (TICA) 'And new mutations to taillessness occur with surprising frequency'.

The important question about a breed is not where it has been, but where it is going. The Bobtail, at last, now appears to be travelling in the right direction. In 1990 TICA and the American Cat Fanciers' Association accepted Bobtails for registration, so the cats can now be shown in new-breed-and-colour classes. Bobtail breeders have also decided to include another American breed, Maine Coon Cats, as allowable outcrosses for Bobtails.

Breeding
Even when a breeder is careful to use cats with the preferred two-to-four-inch-long (2.5-10cm) tails, fully tailed cats and the occasional tailless cat sometimes appear in Bobtail litters.

Kittens
'Bobtail kittens are effervescent, but not rowdy', says one Bobtail fancier. 'They purr all the time. They wrap themselves around your neck. They play with your nose. If you sit down, they want to sit by you. It's difficult for people who haven't had one to imagine a cat behaving this way'.

SHOW STANDARD
The American Bobtail is a short-tailed, cobby-bodied longhaired cat that owes its appeal to the colour point, white spotting and Manx genes.
Coat. Semi-long, between a Birman's and a Somali's in length.
Body. Cobby and substantial. A slight rise in the hindquarters.
Tail. Two to four inches (2.5-10cm) long is the ideal. Often bent to one side, or curved in the manner of a violin head. May have bumps, and a knot on the end.
Head. Rounded, full cheeked. Ears set wide apart.
Eyes. Round, full and alert.

AMERICAN BOBTAIL COLOURS
All colours and patterns allowed.

NEBELUNG

Good points
● *Always breeds true*
● *Hybrid vigour*
● *Easier to care for than some other longhaired breeds*

Take heed
● *No known drawbacks*

Although *Nebelung* is a German word that means 'creature of the mist', this breed is a creature of Denver, Colorado, in the United States, where the first Nebelung was born in 1984.

Grooming
A careful combing every two or three days and the occasional bath will be sufficient to keep the Nebelung's semilong coat in good condition.

Origin and history
Some people look at cat breeds that exist and say, 'Why?' Others dream of breeds that do not exist

and ask, 'Why not?' Such was the reaction of Cora Cobb after two unplanned matings between the same two nonpedigreed, shorthaired cats produced a couple of blue, semilonghaired kittens.

The first kitten, a male, was born in Denver, Colorado, on August 24, 1984. His mother was a black cat that belonged to Cobb's son, and the kitten's father was a neighbourhood dandy 'that looked like a Russian Blue', says Cobb.

As the furry little blue tyke grew up, Cobb felt he was something special. 'Everything about him was bigger than life and more beautiful than the other cats in the litter, or than any other cats I had ever seen', says Cobb, who named the kitten Siegfried and counted herself lucky to have such a wonderful prize.

Five months later luck struck again when Siegfried's parents produced another litter that contained a semilonghaired blue kitten — this one a female.

'I thought Siegfried was a fluke because his parents were shorthairs', says Cobb. 'Then his sister was born, and she was just as beautiful. Without really thinking, I said, ''I'm going to make a new breed out of these cats''.'

Though Cobb later discovered that what she had considered an act of providence was nothing more mysterious than the work of recessive genes, she determined to press on with the idea of creating a new breed. A member of The International Cat Association's genetics committee suggested that Cobb use Russian Blues to preserve colour and to set type in her new breed. Thus, Nebelungs are sometimes called Longhaired Russian Blues.

Breeding
Since their blue colour and longhaired coat are the work of recessive genes, two Nebelungs will always breed true.

Kittens
Kittens' eyes, blue at birth, change to yellow and then to green as the kittens mature.

SHOW STANDARD
The Nebelung is an elegant cat with an angular, modified wedge-shaped head and a tubular body.
Coat. Medium long on the body. Dense undercoat.
Body. Long and fine boned, lithe and slender. No excessive bulk.
Tail. Fluffy.
Head. Modified wedge shape with flat planes. Medium muzzle with no muzzle break. Ears almost as wide as they are tall, set far apart, as much on the sides of the head as on the top
Eyes. Large, green, set far apart. Sufficiently oval shaped to suggest an Oriental slant.

NEBELUNG COLOURS
Must be blue. The precise shade of blue is difficult to determine because one passage in the breed standard describes the Nebelung's coat as 'medium', while a later passage describes it as 'bright'.

Below: An American Bobtail. Both TICA and the ACFA accepted Bobtails for registration in 1990, so the cats can now be shown in new-breed-and-colour classes.

Red-shaded Cameo American Bobtail

American Bobtail

Nebelung

Nebelung

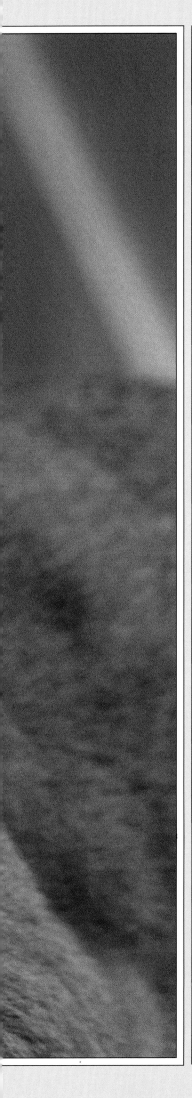

SHORTHAIRED CATS

Cat lovers who do not have a lot of time to groom a pet would do well to select a shorthaired cat. There are many from which to choose, from the plush-coated British Shorthairs to the smooth-coated 'Foreign' cats such as the Siamese and Burmese. For those who like something a little different, the curly-coated Rex cats might be a good choice. In the United States and Canada you might consider a Wirehaired cat or even a completely hairless one, if you find that particular look attractive.

For lovers of the unusual, the Scottish Fold, with its curious 'buttoned-down' ears, may appeal. The tailless Manx and the charming Japanese Bobtail also have a distinct fascination. The Snowshoe, a Siamese with white feet and muzzle, may take your eye. Or you may prefer the lithe elegance of an Oriental Shorthair. The affectionate Tonkinese, a hybrid between the Siamese and Burmese, may be your choice, or perhaps you may favour the sleek Bombay with its glossy black coat and bright, new-penny copper eyes. The quiet Russian Blue or Korat may suit your own temperament, or you may find the active nature of the Abyssinian more in keeping with your lifestyle. Look through the pages of this section and you are likely to find a shorthaired breed that will suit your (and your family's) circumstances and temperament perfectly.

Left: Shorthairs require far less grooming than longhairs.

BRITISH SHORTHAIR

Good points
- *Strong and sturdy*
- *Healthy*
- *Quiet*
- *Easy to groom*

Take heed
- *An even-tempered breed, but some United States lines do not appreciate prolonged handling.*

The British Shorthair is a 'natural breed' that has not been altered too greatly to suit breeders' whims. It is healthy and sound in mind and body and makes an excellent pet for children or old people. The most popular colour is probably Blue, followed by the Silver Tabby and the spotted varieties. Basically, this is a strong, sturdy shorthaired cat; it is active, graceful, intelligent and curious.

Grooming
Regular grooming to remove dead hair is advisable. A weekly combing will probably be sufficient to keep a British Shorthair looking neat and trim.

Some colours require special attention. Blacks, Reds, Tortoiseshells and Tabbies — in addition to being bathed before a show — ought to be rubbed with bay rum to enhance their coats' shine. Blues, Whites, Creams and Blue-creams should be bathed and powdered two or three days before a show. The powder should be brushed out of their coats before show time.

Origin and history
Records of pedigree cats have been kept for a little more than 100 years, but it is evident from history books, literature and art that cats resembling the British Shorthair have been around much longer. They were some of the first to be shown at the end of the nineteenth century, when cat shows started, and they are thought to have descended from shorthaired cats brought to Britain by the Romans.

British shorthaired cats were taken to North America by the early English immigrants, who brought them along as pets and mousers. These cats mated with other shorthaired cats brought to America from other parts of the world and gave rise to the American Shorthair breed. Both the British and American shorthairs are now recognized by the American associations, but fancy-wide acceptance in North America was many years in coming.

Though a pedigree shorthaired cat or two from the UK had been imported by United States breeders not long after 1900, some of these cats were registered in a way that suggested they were domestic instead of imported shorthairs. What's more, American cat fanciers would experience enough trouble gaining the proper respect for their own shorthairs during the first half of this decade without bothering to import any domestic shorthairs from a country that shared the same language. Consequently, there was little interest in shorthaired show cats from the UK in the US until the mid-1960s, and the British Shorthair, at first in blue only, was accepted for championship competition by ACFA in 1970.

Shorthaired cats are bred in Europe and closely resemble the British Shorthair. Often breeding stock is imported from the UK and the European standards set for the breed and its colour varieties are very similar to those in the UK. Only the Chartreuse in France is said to differ because of its distinct history, but in recent years, the British Blue and the Chartreuse have become almost indistinguishable.

SHOW STANDARD
The British Shorthair is a medium to large cat; strong and sturdy on short legs with a short, thick coat. Males are larger than females.
Coat. Short, resilient and dense, without being double or woolly.
Body. Hard and muscular, medium to large, with a full, broad chest built on strong, short legs and with a level back. The straight forelegs are the same length as the hind legs. The paws are neat, well rounded and firm.
Tail. Short, thick at the base, tapering to a round tip.
Head. Broad and rounded, on a short neck. The nose is straight, broad and short without a stop. The ears are set so that the inner ear and the outer eye corners are virtually in line with each other; the ears are small and rounded.
Eyes. Large, round and level. They should be wide awake and full of expression. There should be at least the width of an eye between the eyes.

BRITISH BLACK

Black cats have a long and interesting past. In the Middle Ages they were often persecuted for being the familiars of witches, and were generally regarded with suspicion. At other times in history, they have been considered to be very lucky, at least in the United Kingdom. Black cats are certainly very striking animals, and often have very healthy-looking, glossy coats.

Breeding
Type can be improved by mating Blacks to Blues, or even to Black Persians in the UK, provided that the longhaired kittens resulting from the mating are not used again for breeding, but are neutered and sold as pets. Persians also lend density to Shorthair coats.

Kittens
Black kittens may look rusty coloured when very young, but the reddish tinge disappears as the cat approaches adulthood. The important thing to look for is a coat that is solid black to the roots.

SHOW STANDARD
The dense coat should be a glossy and even jet black from root to tip with no white hairs. Nose leather and paw pads black. Eyes brilliant copper, orange or deep gold.

BRITISH WHITE

There are three types of pedigree shorthaired White cats: those with blue eyes; those with orange eyes; and those with one of each colour (odd-eyed). Non-pedigree white cats usually have green eyes.

Breeding
Blue-eyed White cats are often deaf, which may contribute to their rarity, as deaf cats should not be used for breeding. Orange-eyed Whites are not prone to deafness, but in the process of their development, odd-eyed White cats also appeared; such animals may have perfect hearing or may be deaf.

Kittens
White kittens are born with blue eyes that begin to change to copper — if they are going to change — when a kitten is six to eight weeks old.

SHOW STANDARD
The coat colour should be pure white with no yellow tinge. Nose leather and paw pads pink. Eyes gold, orange or copper; very deep sapphire blue; or one gold or copper and one deep blue.

Below: The highly prized odd-eyed White British Shorthair.

British
Shorthair

Odd-eyed White
British Shorthair

Black British Shorthair

BRITISH BLUE

The British Blue, with its light blue, plush coat, is the most popular of all the British shorthaired varieties in the United Kingdom. Blues are said to prefer a quiet life and are renowned for their calm, well-balanced temperaments.

Although British Blues had always been shown in reasonable numbers, few studs remained after World War II. Thus, frequent outcrosses to other breeds were made, which unfortunately resulted in loss of type. Further outcrosses were made to Blue longhairs. These helped to improve type, as anticipated, but they produced coats that were too long. Selective breeding during the 1950s eventually re-established the shorthaired Blues.

Breeding
It is advisable to outcross to longhaired Blues occasionally to maintain good type. Some of the resulting kittens will have long fur; these are not suitable for the show bench, but, of course, make excellent and charming pets.

Kittens
Blue kittens may be born with faint tabby markings, but these disappear within the first few months as the coat grows.

SHOW STANDARD
The coat colour should be a light to medium blue, sound from root to tip with no white, silver-tipped hairs or tabby markings. Nose leather and paw pads blue. Eyes brilliant copper or orange.

CHARTREUSE
(Chartreux)

Good points
● *Gentle*
● *Healthy*
● *Loyal*

Take heed
● *Females may be difficult breeders*

In the United Kingdom there is virtually no difference between the Chartreuse and the British Blue Shorthair. In Europe and America, however, these cats are considered separate breeds.

Grooming
The Chartreuse coat needs little more than a thorough combing or brushing once a week and the occasional touch-up, when required, in between.

Origin and history
Legend has it that the Carthusian monks developed the Chartreuse in their monastery, known as the Grande Chartreux, near Grenoble. Members of this 900 year old order were known for their steel work and for a potent, green liqueur they created, but there is no evidence that they were cat breeders; or that they obtained cats from monastic knights returning from the Crusades; or that they brought cats back to France from the Cape of Good Hope in the seventeenth century; or that they gave the name Chartreuse to France's all-blue cat. Indeed, Carthusian archives do not mention cats at all.

The first Chartreuse breeders of record were the Leger sisters, who lived on the small Brittany island of Belle-Ile-sur-Mer. In the late 1920s, shortly after they had moved from the mainland to Belle-Ile-sur-Mer, the Legers discovered a large population of blue-grey cats in Le Palais, the island's principal town. No one knows how or when the blue-grey cats migrated from the French mainland to Belle-Ile-sur-Mer, but cat-show records indicate that the first Chartreuse was exhibited in 1931, at a show held in Paris, by a Mlle. Leger.

As with many breeds, the Chartreuse suffered during World Wars I and II. When breeders decided to preserve the Chartreuse in the early 1950s, they resorted to outcrossing to other blue cats — Persians, British Shorthairs, Russian Blues or non-pedigreed cats that resembled Chartreuse. Understandably, breed type was sacrificed in the interests of survival, and by 1970 there was little noticeable difference between the British Blue and the Chartreuse. Thus the Feline International Federation of Europe (FIFe) declared that these two cats had to be judged in the same category. This one-colour-fits-all classification lasted seven years until European breeders insisted that the Chartreuse was a separate breed and deserved to be cultivated and judged as such. In the UK, however, there is still no distinction made between the two cats.

The Chartreux (and this Americanised spelling) came to the United States in 1970. Three of the first ten Chartreux imported by American breeders came from the Leger sisters, who had first begun working with the breed more than 40 years before.

Breeding
Although a number of breeds have contributed to the Chartreuse's development, there are no outcrosses currently allowed.

Kittens
Chartreuse kittens are hearty and robust. Males can be expected to be larger than females.

SHOW STANDARD
The Chartreuse balances a deep-chested, broad-shouldered, well-muscled body on fine-boned, comparatively short legs. Its plentiful torso is connected by a short, stevedore-like neck to a head that is large and broad, but not round.
Coat. Medium-short to medium in length. May be longer than that of other shorthaired cats. Composed of a resilient undercoat and a longer, protective topcoat. A trifle woolly. Should break like a sheepskin at the neck and flanks.
Body. Medium-long physique with broad shoulders and deep chest. Strong bones and solid muscles.
Tail. Moderately long, heavy at the base, tapering to an oval tip. Lively and flexible.
Head. Rounded and broad without being spherical. Powerful jaws, full cheeks, a high, softly contoured forehead and a straight nose of medium length and width. Muzzle comparatively small, narrow and tapered. The contrast between the muzzle and forehead provides the Chartreux with its characteristic smiling expression.
Eyes. Round, open, alert, expressive and set moderately far apart. Colour ranges from copper to gold. A clear, deep, brilliant orange is preferred.

CHARTREUSE COLOURS
Any shade of blue-grey from ash to slate is acceptable. The tips of each hair are lightly brushed with silver. While a bright, unblemished blue with an overall irridescent sheen is the tone preferred, clarity and uniformity of colour are more important than shade.

BRITISH CREAM

The British Cream Shorthair is a very attractive variety. The coat should be a pale, even cream with no tabby markings. Pedigree Cream Shorthairs were not recognized for competition until the late 1920s.

Breeding
The palest Creams are those produced by breeding one dilute — a Cream, Blue or Blue-Cream — to another.

Kittens
Creams are very attractive as kittens, although few possess the desired pale coat; many have tabby markings or are too dark to be shown.

SHOW STANDARD
The coat should be a light even cream all over without white hairs or markings of any kind. Nose leather and paw pads pink. Eyes brilliant copper or orange.

BRITISH BICOLOUR SHORTHAIR

Two-coloured cats have been common for centuries and were seen at the earliest cat shows. The Bicolour is particularly attractive when the standard is met.

Breeding
The amount of white in Bicoloured (or piebald) cats may vary from a dash on the chest to a deluge all over the body. This variability occurs because the gene responsible for white spotting is an incomplete dominant. 'Dominant' means that anyone hoping to produce Bicoloured kittens may begin with only one Bicoloured adult. Dominant also means that two Bicolours can produce solid-coloured kittens. 'Incomplete' means that kittens inheriting two piebald-spotting genes will generally have more white in their coats than kittens that inherit only one copy of that gene.

Kittens
Bicoloured kittens are among the most fetching of all varieties. Their popularity is no mystery because there is no solid colour that cannot be enhanced by the addition of white to the coat.

SHOW STANDARD
The show Bicolour must have a certain percentage of white and colour on the body. The patches must be distinct from the white. The coat pattern should be similar to that of a Dutch rabbit with symmetrical patches of colour (either black, blue, red or cream) evenly distributed on the head, body and tail, and white predominantly on the feet, face, chest and underparts. Not more than two-thirds of the cat should be coloured, and not more than half should be white. A white facial blaze is desirable, and the markings should be as symmetrical as possible on both sides of the body. Tabby markings and white hairs in the colour patches are faults. Nose leather and paw pads according to the 'main' colour or pink. Eyes brilliant copper or orange.

BRITISH TIPPED SHORTHAIR

These cats are the shorthaired equivalents of the longhaired Chinchillas, Cameos, Shaded Silvers and Shaded Cameos. They are one of the most striking varieties with their white undercoats tipped lightly with a contrasting colour.

Breeding
Various breeders have reported that the most unexpected crosses have produced British Shorthair Tipped kittens, crosses such as Siamese to Chinchilla, but the most usual is Silver Tabby Shorthair to Chinchilla Longhair. To develop Chocolate and Lilac Tipped Shorthairs, breed Chocolate and Lilac Longhairs to shorthaired Chinchillas.

Kittens
Because of outcrossing to longhairs, the kittens have rather longer coats at birth but this disappears with the arrival of the adult coat.

SHOW STANDARD
The undercoat should be as white as possible. The top coat should be tipped on the back, flanks, head, ears, legs and tail with a contrasting colour to give a sparkling effect. The chin, stomach, chest and underside of the tail should be white. Tabby markings are faults. Nose leather and paw pads in keeping with the tipping colour. Eyes green in black-tipped cats; rims of eyes, nose and lips outlined in black. Eyes orange or copper in other colours; eye rims and lips deep rose.

Red-and-white
Bicolour British Shorthair

British
Shorthair

Blue British Shorthair

British Tipped
Shorthair (Chinchilla)

Cream
British Shorthair

53

BRITISH SMOKE SHORTHAIR

These cats are the shorthaired equivalents of the Persian Smokes, and have a similar breeding history. The hair for the most part is one colour, but near the roots it is white or silver. Consequently, the coat appears a solid colour until the fur is parted or the cat moves and the undercoat is revealed.

Breeding

The smoke effect is controlled by the 'I' (for inhibitor) gene. This dominant gene suppresses, to varying degrees, the articulation of pigment in the hairs of a cat's coat. Suppression, which occurs to the least extent in Smokes, begins at the root of each hair and drives the colour outwards towards the end (or tip) of the hair shaft, leaving the portion of the hair shaft nearer the body either white or silver in Smokes. The white or silver portion of the hair shaft — which occupies no more than one quarter of the hair shaft in Smokes — is known as the base colour.

Kittens

At birth Smoke kittens look as if they have cigarette ash on their noses and feet, and smoke-tinted goggles around their eyes.

SHOW STANDARD

Coat colour. May be any colour that is accepted in the recognized British breeds. The undercoat should be silver, showing maximum contrast with the top coat. The whole should be free of tabby markings in adult specimens, but kittens should not be penalized too heavily if they exhibit tabby markings in their coats. White or silver guard hairs are considered faults; so, too, is insufficient contrast between the top coat and undercoat. Nose leather and paw pads should be the same colour as the coat colour.
Eye colour. Copper, orange or deep gold. Incorrect eye or rim colour is grounds for disqualification.

BRITISH TORTOISESHELL SHORTHAIR

Cats with the tortoiseshell pattern have been known for centuries and have appeared on the show bench ever since cats were first exhibited. In the British Shorthair, the patches of red and cream on a black base coat are highly attractive and colourful. Tortoiseshell cats are a female-only variety, although the occasional male has occurred and one is even recorded as having sired a litter.

Breeding

Tortoiseshells are usually obtained by breeding a red cat to a black or a blue cat; a cream cat to a black one; a Tortoiseshell to any solid-coloured male; or a Blue-cream to a black or a red male. Some breeders also use Tabbies to produce Tortoiseshells, but Tabbies are apt to produce tabby markings in the red and cream portions of a Tortoiseshell's coat.

Kittens

Tortoiseshell kittens with the fewest red and cream patches usually have the most distinctly marked coats when they grow up.

SHOW STANDARD

A mixture of black, rich red and pale cream evenly intermingled with each colour clearly defined over the whole animal but without any obvious patches of any colour, with the exception of the short, narrow blaze on the face, which is permissible. Nose leather and paw pads are pink and/or black. Eye colour deep orange or copper.

BRITISH BLUE-CREAM SHORTHAIR

A dilute form of the Tortoiseshell, the Blue-cream is also a female-only variety. A relative newcomer to the show scene, this variety was not officially recognized in the United Kingdom until 1956, although Blue-cream kittens had appeared in litters of Blue and Cream matings and in Tortoiseshell litters for many years. The two palest shades of blue and cream are preferred, with no touch of red.

Breeding

Blue-cream kittens are usually produced by breeding a blue cat to a cream one; a Blue-cream to a blue or to a cream male (or to a black or a red male known to carry a gene for dilute colour); or a Tortoiseshell carrying a gene for dilute colour to a blue or cream male (or to a red or a black male carrying a gene for dilute colour).

Kittens

It is not always apparent when kittens are born which is to be a Blue-cream, and some of the best Blue-creams may look more like pale Blues at first.

SHOW STANDARD

Coat colour should be blue and cream softly intermingled over the body. Tabby markings and white hairs or patches are faults. Nose leather and paw pads blue and/or pink. Eyes copper, orange or gold.

BRITISH TORTOISESHELL-AND-WHITE SHORTHAIR
(British Calico Shorthair)

The tortoiseshell-and-white coat pattern, like the tortoiseshell, has been well known for centuries amongst alley cats, and it is always highly prized for its brilliant colouring. Again, this is a female-only variety, and the occasional male is invariably sterile.

Breeding

It was realized only after World War II that the best sires for this variety are the Bicolours. Black-and-white or Red-and-white males are the most likely sires to produce Tortie-and-white kittens when mated with a Tortie-and-white.

Kittens

Kittens may not be very bright at first, only displaying their full glory as the adult coat begins to develop.

SHOW STANDARD

The coat should be boldly patched with black, cream and red on white, the patches equally balanced; white must not predominate. The tricolour patchings should cover the top of the head, ears and cheeks, back, tail, legs and part of the flanks. Patches to be clear and well defined. A facial blaze is desirable. Nose leather and paw pads pink, black or a combination of the two. Eyes brilliant copper or orange.

BLUE TORTOISESHELL-AND-WHITE
(Dilute Calico)
In this dilute form of the Calico or Tortoiseshell-and-white, blue replaces black, and cream replaces red in the coat. Paw pads and nose leather blue or pink or a combination of the two. Eyes copper, orange or gold.

Below: The Tortoiseshell-and-white (Calico) Shorthair has always been prized for its colouring. This is a female-only variety, and the occasional male is invariably sterile.

*Tortoiseshell-and-white
British Shorthair*

British
Shorthair

*Tortoiseshell
British Shorthair*

Blue-cream British Shorthair

BRITISH TABBY SHORTHAIR

The shorthaired tabbies occur in several coat patterns, notably the classic, mackerel and spotted.

'Tabby' was originally used to describe the appearance of plain-woven watered silk or taffeta, which was known in England as tabbisilk. This type of weaving produces a striped or ridged effect on the cloth, whose appearance resembles the striped pattern found on some cats. The word Tabbisilk probably derives from Attabiya, a district in Baghdad (capital of what is now Iraq) where this material was made and where, presumably, tabby cats were in some evidence. They were also known as Cyprus Cats.

The tabby pattern is common among domestic cats. Spotted tabbies were shown at the first cat shows, but at the beginning of this century seemed to have disappeared from the show bench, presumably because the classic tabby pattern had preference in the hearts of the breeders of the time. Fortunately, spotted tabbies made a comeback in the mid-1960s.

It appears that the classic or blotched pattern, the most common in pedigree cats, is a mutation from the striped form.

Of the tabby colours, the Silver Classic Tabby is now, and seems always to have been, the most popular variety.

Breeding
Two Tabbies of the same colour can produce good colour, but breeders sometimes mate tabbies to self-coloured short or longhairs to improve type. Usually this will be to Blues but can also be to other solid colours: Brown Tabby to a Black, Silver Tabby to a Chinchilla, Blue Tabby to a Blue, and Cream Tabby to a Cream.

Kittens
Tabby kittens are born with obvious markings and usually the best marked kittens at birth become the best marked adults.

SHOW STANDARD
Classic Tabby pattern. The head marking is a letter 'M' on the forehead. Unbroken lines run from the outer corners of the eyes towards the back of the head, and there should be other pencillings on the cheeks. Lines extend back from the top of the head to the shoulder markings, which are shaped like a butterfly. Three unbroken lines run parallel to each other down the spine from the shoulder markings to the base of the tail. A large blotch on each side of the cat is circled by one or more unbroken rings; these markings should be symmetrical on either side of the body. There should be several unbroken necklaces on the neck and upper chest, and a double row of 'buttons' running from chest to stomach. The legs should be evenly barred with narrow bracelets, and the tail should, in the best specimens, be evenly ringed.

Mackerel Tabby pattern. The head is marked with the characteristic 'M', and there is an unbroken line running from the outer corner of the eyes towards the back of the head. There are other fine pencillings on the cheeks. An unbroken line runs from the back of the head to the base of the tail. The rest of the body is marked with narrow unbroken lines running perpendicularly to the spine line. These lines should be narrow and clearly defined from the ground colour. There should be several unbroken necklaces on the neck and upper chest and a double row of 'buttons' on the chest and stomach. The legs should be evenly barred with narrow bracelets and the tail evenly ringed.

Spotted Tabby pattern. The head should be marked with the characteristic 'M'. There is an unbroken line running from the outer corner of the eyes towards the back of the head, and there are other fine pencillings on the cheeks. Ideally, all the stripes in the tabby coat are broken up into spots, which may be round, oval or rosette-shaped and should be as numerous and as distinct from the ground colour as possible. A dorsal stripe runs the length of the back, but it should be broken up into spots. There should be a double row of spots on the chest and stomach, and spots or broken rings on the legs and tail.

Brown Tabby. The ground colour should be a rich sable brown or coppery brown. The markings are dense jet black. The hind legs from paw to heel should be black. Nose leather brick red. Paw pads black. Eyes orange or deep yellow.

Red Tabby. The ground colour should be a rich red. The markings, lips, chin and sides of the feet dark red. Nose leather brick red. Paw pads deep red. Eyes deep orange or copper.

Silver Tabby. The ground colour should be silver. The markings should be dense jet black. Nose leather brick red or black. Paw pads black. Eyes green or hazel (United Kingdom); brilliant gold, orange or hazel (United States).

Blue Tabby. Bluish-fawn ground colour with deep blue markings affording a good contrast with the ground colour. Nose leather and paw pads blue or pink. Eyes deep yellow to copper.

Cream Tabby. The ground colour should be pale cream. The markings dark cream, but not too hot. Nose leather and paw pads pink. Eyes gold or copper.

Below: A Silver Classic Tabby shorthair, a most popular variety.

British Shorthair

*Silver Spotted Tabby
British Shorthair*

*Silver Classic Tabby
British Shorthair kitten*

*Brown Mackerel Tabby
British Shorthair*

*Red Classic Tabby
British Shorthair*

AMERICAN SHORTHAIR

Good points
- *Attractive*
- *Hardy*
- *Companionable*
- *Well balanced temperament*
- *Easy to groom*

Take heed
- *No known drawbacks*

This hardy cat makes an excellent pet, not easily affected by ailments or disease. It is typically active and curious; and, being a robust, natural breed, it makes a trouble-free pet with an affectionate, companionable nature.

Grooming
The coat of the American Shorthair is easily maintained. However, it should be combed regularly, and regular attention should also be paid to the ears to make sure they are clean and free from mites.

Origin and history
These cats are reputed to have come to the United States with the original settlers from Europe, who brought them as companions, and as working rodent officers. Every ship had its cat or cats to protect the ship's stores, and many left ship in the New World. These cats mated freely without restriction or regard for pedigree. After years of separation from the parent European stock, they developed characteristics of their own. Although they somewhat resemble the British Shorthair, American Shorthairs have less rounded heads and longer noses.

The first American Shorthair cat to be registered in the US was an orange tabby male with the unlikely name of Belle, who had been imported from the United Kingdom around 1901. The breed in which Belle was enrolled was simply called 'Shorthairs'. Sometime later 'Domestic' was added to that title, an acknowledgment of the presence of native-born sons and daughters — many with 'particulars unknown' — in breeding programmes in the US.

The Domestic Shorthair became the American Shorthair in the mid-1950s, and the breed, which had not been accorded great respect before that, was promoted by breeders who improved its type and social standing.

Breeding
American Shorthairs make good breeders and sensible mothers. They have endless patience.

Kittens
The kittens are confident, courageous and not prone to disease.

SHOW STANDARD
The American Shorthair is a strong, well-built cat, looking for the most part natural rather than contrived. It has the body of an athlete built for an active life. No part of the anatomy should be so exaggerated as to foster weakness. The general effect should suggest power, endurance and agility in a cat of symmetrical proportions.

Coat. Thick, short, even and hard in texture. Not as plush as that of the British Shorthair. Heavier and thicker in winter.

Body. Large to medium in size, lean and hard, athletic and powerful. Well-developed chest and shoulders. Legs sturdy and medium in length, built for jumping and hunting. Paws full, rounded, with heavy pads. Excessive cobbiness or ranginess are faults.

Tail. Medium in length, wide at the base, tapering slightly to a blunt tip. No kinks.

Head. Large and full cheeked. Eyes bright and alert; medium-long, thick, muscular neck, carrying an oval face, only slightly longer than it is wide. Square muzzle, firm chin. Nose medium long and of uniform width. In contour a gentle curve from forehead to nose tip. Ears set wide apart, not unduly wide at the base, with slightly rounded tips.

Eyes. Large. Upper lid shaped like half an almond cut lengthwise. Lower lid shaped in a fully rounded curve. The width of an eye between the eyes. Outer corners a bit higher than inner corners.

AMERICAN SHORTHAIR COLOURS

White. Pure white. Nose leather, paw pads pink. Eyes deep blue or brilliant gold, or one deep blue and one gold in odd-eyed Whites.

Black. Dense coal black, sound throughout with no rusty tinge. Nose leather black. Paw pads black or brown. Eyes brilliant gold.

Blue. One level tone of blue throughout, lighter shades preferred. Nose leather and paw pads blue. Eyes brilliant gold.

Red. Deep, rich clear red without shading or tabby markings. Lips and chin red. Nose leather and paw pads brick red. Eyes brilliant gold.

Cream. One level shade of buff-cream without markings. Lighter shades preferred. Nose leather and paw pads pink. Eyes brilliant gold.

Bicolour. White with unbrindled patches of black, blue, red or cream. Nose leather and paw pads in keeping with solid colour or else pink. Eyes brilliant gold.

Chinchilla. Undercoat pure white. Coat on back, flanks, head and tail sufficiently tipped with black to give a characteristic sparkling silver appearance. Rims of eyes, lips and nose outlined with black. Some tipping allowed on the legs. Chin, ear tufts, stomach and chest pure white. Nose leather brick red. Paw pads black. Eyes green or blue-green.

Shaded Silver. Undercoat white with a mantle of black tipping shading down from the sides, face and tail, from dark on the ridge to white on the chin, chest, stomach and under the tail. Legs to be the same tone as the face. General effect should be much darker than the Chinchilla. Rims of eyes, lips and nose outlined with black. Nose leather brick red. Paw pads black. Eyes green or blue-green.

Shell Cameo. Undercoat white. Coat on the back, flanks, head and tail to be sufficiently tipped with red to give the characteristic sparkling appearance. Face and legs may be slightly shaded with tipping. Chin, ear tufts, stomach and chest white. Rims of eyes rose. Nose leather and paw pads rose. Eyes brilliant gold.

Shaded Cameo (Red Shaded). Undercoat white with a mantle of red tipping shading down the sides, face and tail, from dark on the ridge to white on the chin, chest, stomach and under the tail. Legs to be same tone as the face. General effect to be much redder than Shell Cameo.

Black Smoke. Undercoat white, deeply tipped with black. Cat in repose appears black. Points and mask black with narrow band of white at the base of the hairs, which may be seen only when the fur is parted. Nose leather and paw pads black. Eyes brilliant gold.

Blue Smoke. Undercoat white, tipped with blue. Cat in repose appears blue. Nose leather and paw pads blue. Eyes gold.

Cameo Smoke (Red Smoke). Undercoat white, deeply tipped with red. Cat in repose appears red. Nose leather and paw pads rose. Eyes brilliant gold.

Tortoiseshell Smoke. Undercoat white, deeply tipped with black, with clearly defined patches of red-and cream-tipped hairs in the tortoiseshell pattern. Cat in repose appears tortoiseshell. A facial blaze of red or cream tipping is desirable. Nose leather and paw pads brick red and/or black. Eyes brilliant gold.

Tortoiseshell. Black with patches of red and cream, clearly defined and well broken on body, legs and tail. A facial blaze of red or cream desirable. Nose leather and paw pads brick red and/or black. Eyes gold.

Calico (Tortie-and-white). White with unbrindled patches of black and red. White predominant on the underparts. Nose leather and paw pads pink. Eyes brilliant gold.

Dilute Calico. White with unbrindled patches of blue and cream. White predominant on the underparts. Nose leather and paw pads pink. Eyes brilliant gold.

Blue-cream. Blue with patches of solid cream, clearly defined and well broken on body, legs and tail. Nose leather and paw pads blue and/or pink. Eyes brilliant gold.

Van Bicolours. Mostly white with colour largely confined to the head, legs and tail. Nose leather and paw pads in keeping with the coloured patches or else pink. Eyes should be brilliant gold colour.

Van Calico. Patches of black and red on head, legs and tail, white elsewhere.

Van Blue-cream. Patches of blue and cream on head, legs and tail, white elsewhere.

Classic Tabby pattern. Markings dense and clearly defined from ground colour. Legs evenly barred. Tail evenly ringed. Several unbroken necklaces on neck and upper chest. Frown marks form letter 'M' on forehead. An unbroken line runs back from outer corner of eye. Swirls on cheeks. Vertical lines over back of head extend to shoulder markings that resemble a butterfly. Three parallel lines run down the spine from the butterfly to the tail, the three stripes well separated by the ground colour. Large solid blotch on each side should be encircled by one or more unbroken rings. Side markings symmetrical. Double row of 'buttons' on chest and stomach.

Mackerel Tabby pattern. Markings dense and clearly defined, and all are narrow pencillings. Legs and tail evenly barred. Distinct necklaces on neck and upper chest. Forehead carries characteristic 'M'. Unbroken lines run back from the eyes. Lines run down the head to meet the shoulders. Spine lines run together to form a narrow saddle. Narrow pencillings run around the body.

Brown Tabby. Ground colour coppery brown. Markings dense black. Lips and chin and rings around eyes paler. Backs of legs black from paw to heel. Nose leather brick red. Paw pads black or brown. Eyes brilliant gold.

Red Tabby. Ground colour red. Markings deep, rich red. Lips and chin red. Nose leather and paw pads brick red. Eyes brilliant gold.

Silver Tabby. Ground colour, lips and chin pale, clear silver. Markings dense black. Nose leather brick red. Paw pads black. Eyes green or hazel.

Blue Tabby. Ground colour, lips and chin pale, bluish ivory. Markings deep blue. Warm patina over all. Nose leather old rose. Paw pads rose. Eyes brilliant gold.

Cream Tabby. Ground colour, lips and chin very pale cream. Markings buff-cream, sufficiently darker than ground colour to afford a good contrast, but not too dark. Nose leather and paw pads rose. Eyes brilliant gold.

Cameo Tabby. Ground colour, lips and chin off-white. Markings red. Nose leather and paw pads rose. Eyes brilliant gold.

Patched Tabby (Torbie). A Silver, Brown or Blue classic or mackerel Tabby with patches of red and/or cream.

Shaded Silver American Shorthair

Silver Classic Tabby
American Shorthair

Blue-cream
American Shorthair

American
Shorthair

59

EXOTIC SHORTHAIR

Good points
- *Intelligent*
- *Even-tempered*
- *Playful but not destructive*
- *Sweet and loving*

Take heed
- *No known drawbacks*

If you like the docile nature of the Persian but do not have time to groom a longhaired cat, this may be the breed for you. The Exotic Shorthair is a hybrid produced by crossing Persians with shorthaired cats. An exotic resembles a Persian, with its short, snub nose and wide cheeks, cobby body and short tail, yet has a much more manageable coat. The Exotic combines the best characteristics of its component breeds, having a quiet, gentle nature and an even-tempered, sweet disposition, yet being alert, playful and responsive.

Grooming
The Exotic Shorthair is easy to groom but must be combed frequently to remove dead hairs. The coat is short, but plush, so a medium-toothed comb is best with the occasional use of a rubber or wire spiked brush for massage.

Origin and history
During the mid-1960s the appearance of some American Shorthairs underwent noticeable change. Their eyes grew larger and rounder; their coats grew softer and more plush; and their muzzles grew shorter and more round. The catalyst for this evolution was the Persian cat, furtively employed in some American Shorthair breeding programmes.

Though many breeders and judges preferred to look the other way rather than to look askance at developments among American Shorthairs, one Cat Fanciers' Association judge finally suggested that the CFA create a new breed called the Exotic Shorthair to accommodate these hybrids. The Exotic would consist of crosses between Persians and any shorthaired cats and would be held to the same standard as the Persian, except for coat length.

On May 1, 1967, CFA became the first association to recognize the Exotic Shorthair, which is now recognized in all North American registries. Shortly after the Exotic was accepted for championship competition, the number of allowable outcrosses was reduced to one breed — the American Shorthair.

Breeding
Once Exotic Shorthair breeders had brought the shorthair gene into their breeding programmes, they bred Exotic Shorthairs mainly to Persians. Consequently, many Exotic pedigrees do not reveal the presence of a shorthaired cat — other than an Exotic — for six or seven generations. What's more, few people breed Exotic to Exotic more than once every two or three generations for fear of losing type.

Kittens
It is monumentally challenging to guess at birth which kittens will have short hair and which will have long in an Exotic Shorthair litter. Some breeders claim that the woollier the coat on a newly dried kitten, the more likely it will be to have short hair. Other breeders say they get fooled a great deal of the time.

SHOW STANDARD
The Exotic Shorthair should conform to the Persian standard, but have a short, plush coat.
Coat. Medium in length, dense, soft, glossy and resilient. Not close-lying, but standing out from body.
Body. Medium to large, cobby and low on the legs. Deep in the chest, massive across the shoulders and rump with a short rounded middle. Back level. Legs short, thick and sturdy. Forelegs straight. Paws large, round and firm.
Tail. Short, straight and carried low. Rounded at the tip.
Head. Wide, round and massive with a sweet expression. Short, broad snub nose with a nose break. Cheeks full and chin well developed. Ears small, set wide apart and low on the head, fitting into the curve of the head. The ears have rounded tips and tilt forward on the head. They are not unduly open at the base.
Eyes. Large, round, full and brilliant; set wide apart.

EXOTIC SHORTHAIR COLOURS
All American Shorthair and Persian colours including white with blue, orange or odd eyes; black; blue; red; cream; chinchilla; shaded silver; chinchilla golden; shaded golden; shell cameo; shaded cameo; shell tortoiseshell; shaded tortoiseshell; black smoke; blue smoke; cameo smoke; smoke tortoiseshell; classic and mackerel tabby in silver, red, brown, blue, cream and cameo; patched tabby in brown, blue and silver; tortoiseshell; calico; dilute calico; blue-cream; bicolour; van-bicolour; van-calico; van blue-cream-and-white, lilac and chocolate.

Below: A young Exotic Shorthair in inquisitive mood.

SCOTTISH FOLD

Good points
- *Great personality*
- *Sweet nature*
- *Charming appearance*
- *Hybrid vigour*
- *Quiet demeanour*

Take heed
- *Fold-to-Fold breedings can cause skeletal anomalies*

The Scottish Fold's signature ears are caused by a genetic mutation. Though still unrecognized by the Governing Council of the Cat Fancy (GCCF) in Great Britain, Folds can be shown in the newer Cat Association of Britain, where the shorthaired Folds have gained championship status and the longhaired Folds compete in provisional classes.

Grooming
No special attention to the ears is necessary. A weekly going-over with a brush and comb will keep the coat neat.

Origin and history
All Scottish Folds are descended from a white, fold-eared farm cat named Susie, who was born in the Tayside region of Scotland in 1961. Two years later Susie's owners gave one of the two kittens from her first and only litter — a white, fold-eared female named Snooks — to their neighbours, William and Mary Ross. The Rosses, Patricia Turner (Scintilla cattery) and others worked to establish the Fold as a recognized breed in the United Kingdom, using British Shorthairs as their principal outcrosses.

Efforts on the Folds' behalf came to naught, however, when GCCF banned the further registration of Folds in 1971. The official reason for this excommunication was an alleged difficulty in keeping the Folds' ears free of mites.

At about the same time, three Folds were sent to Neil Todd, Ph.D., a New England geneticist who was studying mutations in cats. Todd soon lost interest in his research, but one of his Folds went to Salle Wolfe Peters, a Manx breeder who lived in south-eastern Pennsylvania. Thanks largely to Peters' dedication, Folds were accepted for registration in the United States in 1973, and by 1978 they were accepted for

Above: The Fold's personality has ensured its popularity in the US.

championship competition. Since then they have become one of the 10 most popular breeds in the US.

Breeding
Breeders recommend that Folds be mated only to straight-eared cats, since Fold-to-Fold breedings can give rise to skeletal anomalies. These anomalies — which usually occur in the tail and hindquarters — are found primarily in cats that have inherited two genes for folded ears.

Kittens
Fold kittens' ears look normal — that is, floppy — at birth. At about two to three weeks, when the ears on most kittens begin to straighten, Folds' ears start heading in the opposite way.

SHOW STANDARD
The Scottish Fold is a cat of British Shorthair type, but with distinctive ears that are folded forwards and downwards.
Coat. Thick, short, dense and soft.
Body. Medium sized, rounded and cobby. The same width across the shoulders and rump. Full, broad chest. Powerful and compact build. Medium-length legs with neat paws.
Tail. Medium in length. Kinked, broad, thick or short tails are faults.
Head. Massive and round. Well-rounded whisker pads. Short, thick neck; cheeks full, chin rounded, jaw broad. Ears wide apart and distinguished by a definite fold line; the front of the ear should cover the ear opening. Small, neat ears are preferred, rounded at the tips. Nose should be short and broad, with a gentle nose break.
Eyes. Large, round, set wide apart.

SCOTTISH FOLD COLOURS
Almost all colours and coat patterns except the Himalayan are recognized, including: solid white, black, blue, red, cream: chinchilla, shaded silver, shell cameo, shaded cameo, black smoke, blue smoke, cameo smoke; tortoiseshell, calico, dilute calico, blue-cream; bicolour; classic, mackerel and patched tabby patterns in red, silver, brown, blue, cream and cameo as appropriate. Eye colour should be in keeping with the coat colour.

*Blue Classic Tabby
Scottish Fold Kitten*

Scottish Fold

*Blue Tortoiseshell-and-white
(Dilute calico) Scottish Fold*

Exotic Shorthair

Shaded Cameo Exotic Shorthair

MANX

Good points
- *Unique appearance*
- *Intelligent and courageous*
- *Affectionate*

Take heed
- *Troublesome to breed*

The Manx, or 'rumpy' as it is sometimes called, is unique in appearance. It has no tail, and because the hind legs are longer than the forelegs and the back is short, it has a rabbity look. Nonetheless, the Manx should be able to stand on all four feet. It should not rest on its hocks as does a rabbit.

The Manx is similar to the American Shorthair, but has a decided hollow where the tail should be; this does not affect its balance, however, and the powerful hind legs are capable of strong, high springs. It also has the ability to run very fast.

The Manx makes a loyal and affectionate pet, as it is curious, intelligent and amusing, and likes to be part of the family. It may resent being left out of things or being on its own.

Grooming
With its short, thick undercoat and soft, medium-length top coat, the Manx will benefit from frequent grooming with a medium-soft brush and a medium-toothed comb to remove the dead hairs and to keep the coat shining and healthy. The ears, eyes and teeth should have regular attention too.

Origin and history
Though tailless cats have appeared in many parts of the world — the British zoologist Charles Darwin, for example, saw them frequently in Malaysia — they are most often associated with the Isle of Man, after which they were named.

Manx cats were observed on the island as early as 1820, but no one knows how they came to be there. Some people believe that Manx swam ashore from a sinking vessel of the Spanish Armada in 1588. Others say that Irish invaders cut the island cats' tails off and used them for helmet plumes. As a result, mother cats began biting their kittens' tails off to prevent this cruel practice occurring again.

The most improbable tale about the Manx is that it resulted from a union between a cat and a rabbit. And the second-most improbable tale blames taillessness on Noah. According to this account, two Manx were the last animals to board the ark. Captain Noah, impatient to beat the weather, slammed the gate on their tails.

Scientists believe that taillessness in the Manx results from nothing more romantic than a mutant gene, which is no small wonder itself. The gene responsible for taillessness was able to grow unimpeded, in a manner of speaking, because the Isle of Man provided the ideal closed environment for incubating a new breed of cat.

The Manx rated its own breed club in England shortly after the turn of the century. King Edward VII is said to have owned Manx when he was Prince of Wales. Manx were first exported to the United States in the 1930s.

Breeding
Manx cats are challenging to breed because like-to-like tailless mating does not necessarily produce tailless kittens. In fact, tailed, tailless and stumpy-tailed kittens may result in the same litter. Furthermore, the tailless gene is a lethal one, and one out of four kittens from Manx-to-Manx breedings fails to survive in the womb. Finally, the tailless gene seems to be connected with other skeletal defects, and results in vertebrae being fused together, giving deformed kittens with spina bifida. Frequent outcrossings to normal-tailed Shorthairs (United Kingdom) or to tailed Manx (US and UK) must be made.

Manx litters may contain the completely tailless Manx or 'rumpy'; a 'riser', which has a very small number of vertebrae, usually immobile; a 'stubby', which has a short tail, often knobbly or kinked; and a 'longy', with a medium-length tail. The show Manx must have a complete absence of tail and, in fact, a hollow where the tail would have been. But many of the 'tailed' Manx make excellent pets and can be used for breeding with rumpies.

Kittens
Many kittens of other breeds seem to regard mother's tail as a built-in toy, but Manx kittens still seem to find plenty with which to play.

SHOW STANDARD
The principal feature of a show-quality Manx is the complete absence of any tail. There should be a hollow in the rump where the tail would have been. Manx should also have the rounded look of a short-backed cat with hind legs longer than forelegs and a deep flank.
Coat. Short, glossy double coat. The undercoat is thick and cottony, the top coat longer, but not too long; soft and open.
Body. A solid cat with rounded rump, strong hindquarters, deep flanks, and a short back. The hind legs are longer than the forelegs, and have muscular thighs. The back arches from shoulder to rump. The feet are neat and round.
Tail. Entirely missing, with a hollow where the tail would have been. A residual tail is a fault.
Head. Large and round with prominent cheeks. Short, thick neck and a strong chin. Nose medium long, with a gentle nose dip (US) or no nose break (UK). There are rounded whisker pads and a definite whisker break. Ears large, wide at base, tapering to slightly pointed tips (UK) or rounded tips (US). Set on top of head.
Eyes. Large, round and expressive. Set at an angle to the nose; outer corners higher than inner corners.
Colour. All colours and coat patterns, or a combination of colours and coat patterns, are permitted, except (in the US) the chocolate, lavender and Himalayan colours and patterns or these colours with white. Colour in a Manx is a secondary consideration in the UK, where all colours except the Siamese pattern are recognized. Eye colour in Manx should be in keeping with the coat colour. White Manx may be blue-eyed, orange-eyed, or odd-eyed (one blue, one orange).

JAPANESE BOBTAIL
(Mi-Ke cat)

Good points
- *Distinctive appearance*
- *Relatively non-shedding coat*
- *Intelligent and friendly*
- *Easy to groom*

Take heed
- *No known drawbacks*

As its name suggests, the Japanese Bobtail is native to Japan, where it is called the Mi-Ke (mee kay) cat. Its most distinctive feature is the short bobbed tail. Bobtails are intelligent, loyal and friendly, vocal without being noisy, and have a large vocabulary of chirps and meows.

Characteristically, the Bobtail will stand with one front paw uplifted in welcome, and in fact the store windows and counters in Japan often display china models of this cat with its paw lifted to welcome shoppers and passers-by. Such cats are called Maneki-neko or welcoming cats.

Grooming
The Japanese Bobtail is easy to maintain in perfectly groomed condition as there is no thick undercoat to get tangled. A light brushing and combing with a medium-toothed comb and pure bristle brush will suffice.

Origin and history
Cats arrived in Japan at least a thousand years ago — most likely from China or Korea. But early records do not reveal whether these cats had bobbed tails or whether the bobtail mutation appeared first in Japan.

Bobtailed cats were valued highly in Japan, but in 1602 the authorities decreed that all cats be set free to contend with the vermin that were then threatening the silk-worm industry. Hence, bobtailed cats took up residence in streets and on farms.

After World War II, United States military personnel stationed in Japan brought their families and their pets to live there. Some of those pets were pedigreed cats, and before long cat shows were organized in Japan. At first, Japanese cat fanciers were interested only in foreign cats, so the bobtailed cats of Japan were not shown; but when American judges began officiating at Japanese shows in the early 1960s, they were impressed with the bobtailed cats of Japan — because these cats were foreign to them.

By the end of the decade there were a handful of bobtails in the US. In 1971 the Cat Fanciers' Association (CFA) awarded the breed provisional status. Five years later Japanese Bobtails became eligible for championship competition in CFA, and they are now recognized in all associations.

The Bobtail gene is recessive, and bobtails, therefore, breed true. Nevertheless, long-coated kittens have appeared occasionally in some Bobtail litters, the result of deliberate or accidental crossing to other shorthaired cats carrying the recessive longhair gene. This demonstrates the truth of one of the oldest maxims in the cat fancy: in breeding cats, what you put in, you get out.

Breeding
Bobtail-to-Bobtail mating produces 100-per cent bobtailed kittens. No outcrossing to other breeds is necessary or permitted.

Kittens
Japanese Bobtail kittens are lively. There is no lethal factor with Bobtails; they are usually very healthy.

SHOW STANDARD
The Japanese Bobtail is a medium-sized cat, slender and shapely, with a distinctive bobbed tail and a decidedly Japanese set to the eyes.
Coat. Very soft and silky, single and not prone to shedding. Medium in length but shorter on the face, ears and paws. Longer and thicker on the tail than elsewhere, camouflaging the tail conformation.
Body. Medium in size; slender, but sturdy and well muscled. Not dainty, like some of the other Orientals, but not cobby either. Same width across the shoulders as the rump. Legs long and slender but not fragile or dainty. Hind legs longer than forelegs. Hind legs bent when relaxed. Paws oval.
Tail. The tail vertebrae are set at angles to each other and the furthest extension of the tail bone from the body should be approximately 2-3in. (5-8cm), even though, if it could be straightened out to its full length, the tail might be 4-5in. (10-12.5cm) long. The tail is normally carried upright when the cat is relaxed. The hair on the tail grows outwards in all directions producing a pompom effect, which camouflages the underlying bone structure.
Head. Forms an equilateral triangle, curving gently at the sides of the face. The high cheekbones give way to a distinct whisker break. The muzzle is broad and rounded, neither square nor pointed. The long nose dips gently at, or slightly below, eye level.
Eyes. Large and oval, slanted and wide apart, with an alert expression.
Colour. The preferred colour is the tricolour: black, red and white, with patches large and distinct and with white predominating. The only colours not allowed are the Himalayan pattern and the unpatterned agouti (Abyssinian). The more brilliant and bizarre the colours, the better.

Red Mackerel Tabby-and-white Manx

Manx

Black Manx kitten

Mi-Ke (Tricolour)
Japanese Bobtail
and kitten

Japanese Bobtail

SIAMESE

Good points
- *Svelte and elegant*
- *Intelligent*
- *Resourceful*
- *Extrovert personality*

Take heed
- *Very demanding*
- *Very active*
- *Dislikes being left alone*
- *Dislikes being caged*
- *Likes to talk*

Judging by the number appearing at British shows, the Siamese is one of the most popular breeds in the United Kingdom. It is loving and lovable, enchanting and delightful, but also exasperating, demanding and very talkative. Some Siamese seem to talk, or rather shout, all day long, and a Siamese queen when calling may be particularly trying. Prospective owners should make sure that everyone in the family is going to enjoy this boisterous temperament before deciding on the Siamese.

A Siamese will enjoy walks on harness and lead. With its very extrovert personality it loves performing tricks and playing games, but dislikes being ignored and is wary and jealous of strangers and other animals.

Because of its terrific personality and affectionate nature, the Siamese has a tremendous following in the UK and becomes more and more popular as a pet with every year that passes.

While still the third most popular breed in the United States, behind Persians and Himalayans, the Siamese suffered a 17 per cent decline in new registrations between 1990 and 1991.

Grooming
Easy to groom, all a Siamese needs is a twice-weekly brushing and a combing with a fine- or medium-toothed comb to remove dead hairs. A polish with a chamois leather and lots of hand stroking will give a shine to the coat.

Origin and history
Siamese cats are believed to have existed in Siam (Thailand) for hundreds of years before they finally made their way to Europe, and then North America, in the nineteenth century. They are certainly of Eastern origin, although their exact early history has been lost. Two of the first to come to the UK were thought to have been a gift to the British Consul from the King of Siam, and they were shown at the Crystal Palace, London, in 1885. The first Siamese had round faces and darker coats than those seen today. Tail kinks and eye squints were also permitted. Such 'faults' have now been bred out, and the modern Siamese does not look much like its ancestors.

For many years the Seal point was the only variety of Siamese shown. When a Blue point was exhibited at an English show in 1896, the judge disqualified the cat (which may have been a self-blue Korat). Blue points were not recognized until the 1930s; Chocolate points and Lilac points in the 1950s.

By the turn of the century interest in the Siamese had spread to the United States, and the breed began to appear at American shows. The progress of the Siamese in the US mimicked its development in the UK — that is, the breed appealed to the well-connected and to persons of some station.

Unfortunately, Siamese in the US do not enjoy the same prosperous outlook as their counterparts in the UK. 'American classes are small,' comments consulting editor Richard H. Gebhardt, 'and although type is generally good, the cats always seem to fall short in one area or another'.

Kittens
Siamese kittens develop early. They have individual personalities very soon after birth and are precocious and self-assured. When born they are all-white, the point colour developing only gradually. In the Seal and Blue points, a blob of colour appears on the nose after about 10 days, but it may be three weeks before the chocolate and lilac points become apparent. In all colours the points are often not fully developed until a year old.

Kittens should not be taken from their mothers until they are at least 12 weeks old. They need to be with their mothers to finish their education, and if left with them for at least part of the day until this age, they always seem to be more balanced as adults.

SHOW STANDARD
The Siamese is a medium-sized cat, long, slim, lithe and muscular, with the characteristic Himalayan coat pattern of pale body colour and darker, contrasting points.

Coat. Short, fine and close lying with a natural sheen.

Body. Medium in size, dainty, long and svelte; fine boned but strong and muscular. Not fat or flabby. Hind legs slightly longer than forelegs. Paws small, neat, oval.

Tail. Whip-like, long, thin and tapering to a point. No kinks.

Head. Long, narrow, tapering wedge with flat width between the ears. Profile straight although there may be a slight change of angle above the nose. No decided nose break. Strong chin, jaws not undershot and no whisker break. Ears very large and pointed, open at the base.

Eyes. Almond shaped, medium in size and slanted towards the nose. There should be the width of an eye between the eyes. No squints.

SIAMESE COLOURS
The first recorded Siamese cat was a Seal point. The Blue, Chocolate and Lilac points followed later. In addition to these solid-pointed colours — which are sometimes called 'traditional' colours — Siamese are now accepted in tabby point and particolour-point patterns in the UK and most North American registries.

Coat pattern. Body should be an even pale colour with the main contrasting colour confined to the points (mask, ears, legs and tail). The mask should cover the whole face, but not the top of the head, and be connected to the ears by tracings (except in kittens). Apparently, paler coats are easier to achieve in warmer climates, and all Siamese coats darken with age.

Seal point. Body colour an even warm cream, slightly darker on the back, lighter on the stomach and chest. Points deep seal brown. Nose leather and paw pads seal brown. Eyes deep, vivid blue.

Chocolate point. Body colour ivory all over. Points warm milk-chocolate colour. Nose leather and paw pads cinnamon pink. Eyes deep, vivid blue.

Blue point. Body colour glacial, bluish-white, shading to a warmer white on the chest and stomach. Points slate blue. Nose leather and paws pads slate blue. Eyes deep, vivid blue.

Lilac point. Body colour magnolia (UK) or glacial white (US) all over. Points frosty grey with a pinkish tone (lilac). Nose leather and paw pads lavender-pink. Eyes deep, vivid blue.

Below: Seal point Siamese kittens. Siamese make extrovert adults, too.

Siamese

Seal point Siamese

Lilac point
Siamese kitten

Blue point
Siamese kitten

Chocolate point Siamese

COLOURPOINT SHORTHAIR

This is a Siamese cat with point colours other than seal, chocolate, blue or lilac. Other colours have been obtained by outcrossing Siamese to British and American Shorthairs.

Although regarded as Siamese in most countries, and having the same temperament and type, because of the crossbreeding involved in their production they are classified as Colorpoint Shorthairs in a few associations in the United States. The colours recognized include red, cream and tortoiseshell points, tabby (lynx) points and tortie points.

SHOW STANDARD

Red point. Body clear white with any shading in the same tone as the points. Points bright apricot to deep red, deeper shades preferred, without barring. Nose leather and paw pads flesh or coral pink. Eyes deep, vivid blue.

Cream point. Body clear white with any shading in the same tone as the points. Points pale buff-cream to light pinkish cream without barring. Nose leather and paw pads flesh to coral. Eyes deep, vivid blue.

Seal Tortie point. Body pale fawn to cream, shading to lighter colour on the stomach and chest. Points seal brown, uniformly mottled with red and cream. A blaze is desirable. Nose leather seal brown or flesh pink where there is a blaze. Paw pads seal brown or flesh pink. Eyes deep, vivid blue.

Chocolate Tortie point. Body ivory. Points warm milk-chocolate uniformly mottled with red and/or cream; a blaze is desirable. Nose leather and paw pads cinnamon or flesh pink. Eyes deep, vivid blue.

Blue-cream point. Body bluish white to platinum grey. Points deep blue-grey mottled with cream. A blaze is desirable. Nose leather and paw pads slate or flesh pink. Eyes deep, vivid blue. (US standard.)

Blue Tortie point. Body white, shading unevenly to pale blue and pale cream on back and sides. Points blue, patched or mingled randomly with varying shades of cream. Nose leather and paw pads blue and/or pink. Eyes intense blue. (United Kingdom standard.)

Lilac-cream point. Body glacial white. Points frosty grey with pinkish tone, uniformly mottled with pale cream; a facial blaze is desirable. Nose leather and paw pads lavender-pink or flesh pink. Eyes deep, vivid blue.

Lilac Tortie point. Body off-white, shading to pale lilac and pale cream on back and sides. Points lilac, patched or mingled with varying shades of cream. Nose leather and paw pads faded lilac and/or pink.

Seal Tabby point. Body cream or pale fawn, shading to lighter colour on the stomach and chest. Body shading may take the form of ghost striping. Points seal brown bars, distinct and separated by lighter background colour. Ears seal brown with paler thumbprint in the centre. Nose leather seal brown or pink edged in seal brown. Paw pads seal brown. Eyes deep, vivid blue.

Chocolate Tabby point. Body ivory, body shading may take the form of ghost striping. Points warm milk-chocolate bars, distinct and separated by lighter background colour. Ears warm milk-chocolate with paler thumbprint in centre. Nose leather cinnamon-pink or pink edged in cinnamon. Paw pads cinnamon. Eyes deep, vivid blue.

Blue Tabby point. Body bluish white to platinum grey, cold in tone, shading to lighter colour on the stomach and chest. Body shading may take the form of ghost striping. Points deep blue-grey bars, distinct and separated by lighter background colour; ears deep blue-grey with paler thumbprint in centre. Nose leather slate or pink edged in slate. Paw pads slate. Eyes deep, vivid blue.

Lilac Tabby point. Body glacial white, body shading may take the form of ghost striping. Points frosty grey with pinkish tone, bars distinct and separated by lighter background colour. Ears frosty grey with pinkish tone. Paler thumbprint in centre.

Below: A fine example of a Seal Tortie point Colourpoint Shorthair.

Nose leather lavender-pink or pink edged in lavender. Paw pads lavender-pink. Eyes deep, vivid blue.

Red Tabby point. Body white, body shading may take the form of ghost striping. Points deep red bars, distinct and separated by lighter background colour. Ears deep red, paler thumbprint in centre. Nose leather and paw pads flesh or coral. Eyes deep, vivid blue.

Cream Tabby point. Body white, shading to palest cream on the back. Points deeper buff-cream bars on white background. Ears cream with paler thumbprint in centre. Nose leather and paw pads pink. Eyes deep, vivid blue.

Blue-cream Lynx point. Body bluish-white to platinum grey. May have ghost stripes and/or cream mottling. Points deep, blue-grey bars. Nose leather pink, edged in slate. Paw pads slate. Eyes deep, vivid blue.

Torbie point. Colours and point markings the same as Blue, Chocolate, Seal and Lilac tabby points but with patches of red and/or cream irregularly distributed over the tabby pattern on the points. Red and/or cream mottling on the ears and tail permissible. Nose leather and paw pads as appropriate to the basic point colour or mottled with pink. Eyes deep, vivid blue.

SNOWSHOE

Good points
● *Striking appearance*
● *Good natured*
● *Easy to groom*

Take heed
● *Vocal*

The Snowshoe is a hybrid breed produced by mating Siamese with bicolour American Shorthairs. It is not usually as noisy as a Siamese, but is not as quiet as most other shorthaired cats.

The Snowshoe has a modified Oriental body, usually larger and heavier than a Siamese with less extreme features. It has a rounder head and a distinct nose break, which distinguishes it from other Siamese-derived breeds.

Grooming
The Snowshoe needs the minimum of grooming with a brush or comb to remove dead hairs.

Origin and history
The Snowshoe — a pointed cat with graceful white markings on its face, chest, belly and feet — was developed in the late 1960s by Dorothy Hinds-Daugherty of Philadelphia, Pennsylvania. Hinds-Daugherty, who also bred Siamese, worked with the Snowshoe for several years, then withdrew from the cat fancy. Yet we can deduce from a consideration of the genetics involved that superimposing a selective ration of the white markings from a bicoloured American Shorthair onto the pointed pattern of a Siamese required at least two breedings.

After creating and christening her new breed, Hinds-Daugherty left its welfare in other hands. Vikki Olander from Norfolk, Virginia, wrote the first breed standard and was instrumental in securing registration status for the Snowshoe, which was conferred by the Cat Fanciers' Federation and the American Cat Association by 1974. Nine years later the Snowshoe was accepted for championship competition by CFF, the only association to do so to date.

Breeding
Producing an excellent Snowshoe — compared to producing a top-show cat in most other breeds — is akin to the difference between chess and draughts.

Kittens
Lively and responsive to affection.

SHOW STANDARD
Coat. Medium coarse in texture, short, glossy and close lying.
Body. Medium to large, well muscled and powerful. Long back; heavy build. Sleek, dainty. Oriental type is a fault. Legs long and solid with well-rounded paws.
Tail. Medium in length, thick at the base, tapering slightly to the tip.
Head. Triangular wedge of medium width and length. Obvious nose break. Round or long Siamese-like head is a fault. Neck medium in length, not thin. Ears large, alert and pointed, broad at the base.
Eyes. Large and almond shaped, slanted upwards from nose to ear.

SNOWSHOE COLOURS
Coat pattern. The mask, ears, legs and tail should be clearly defined from the body colour, and of the same depth of colour. The mask covers the whole face and is connected to the ears by tracings. Slightly darker shading of the body colour is allowed across the shoulders, back and top of the hips. Chest and stomach are paler. Fore feet should be white, symmetrical with the white ending in an even line around the ankle. Hind feet should be white, with symmetrical white markings extending up the leg to the heels. Muzzle should be white; the nose may be white or of the point colour. There should be no other white hairs or patches.

Seal point. Body colour an even fawn, warm in tone, shading gradually to a lighter tone on the stomach and chest. Points, except feet and muzzle, deep seal brown. Nose leather pink if nose is white or black if nose is seal. Paw pads pink or seal or a combination of the two. Eyes deep, vivid blue.

Blue point. Body colour an even bluish white, shading gradually to a lighter colour on the chest and stomach. Points, except feet and muzzle, a deep, greyish blue. Nose leather pink if nose is white, or slate grey if nose is blue. Paw pads pink and/or grey. Eyes vivid blue.

Snowshoe

Blue point Snowshoe

Chocolate Tabby point
Colourpoint (Siamese) Shorthair

Colourpoint
(Siamese)
Shorthair

Chocolate Tortie point Colourpoint
(Siamese) Shorthair kitten

Red point Colourpoint
(Siamese) Shorthair

HAVANA
(Havana Brown)

Good points
- Agile
- Intelligent
- Active
- Affectionate

Take heed
- Since the United States gene pool is limited, finding unrelated cats to breed to is difficult

The Havana, known in the US as the Havana Brown, loves people and needs human companionship and affection. It likes to play and hunt and partake in other activities with the family. It is gentle by nature and makes a hardy, attractive pet.

Grooming
The medium-length hair is easy to groom. A twice-weekly session with a fine-toothed comb and a polish with a chamois leather before a show are all that are required.

Origin and history
The Havana was created in the United Kingdom in the early 1950s from crosses between Seal point Siamese and black domestic shorthairs. (Some people say the breed was named after the rabbit of the same colour. Others say that Havana tobacco was the catalyst.) When the GCCF recognized Havanas for championship competition in 1958, they were called Chestnut Brown Foreigns. A dozen years later the name reverted to Havana.

The first Chestnut Browns arrived in the US in the mid-1950s. The American and British versions of this breed share the same name and origin, but not the same conformation. In the UK the Havana is judged with foreign-bodied cats such as the Siamese. In the US the Havana Brown's conformation is midway between the short-coupled, thickset breeds and the elongated, svelte ones.

Breeding
Havana queens call loudly, clearly and frequently. American breeders do not mate Havanas back to Siamese; they do not wish to perpetuate the Oriental type.

Kittens
Kittens are born the same colour as their parents, but their coats do not have the gloss of the adults'. The white hairs found frequently in the kitten coat disappear when the adult coat is grown.

SHOW STANDARD (US)
The overall impression of the Havana Brown is of a medium-sized cat of rich, solid colour, with firm muscle tone.
Coat. Medium in length, smooth and lustrous.
Body. Medium sized, well muscled; medium length neck. Medium-length legs; oval paws.
Tail. Medium length, tapering to a point; no kinks.
Head. Slightly longer than wide. Distinct nose break and whisker break. Chin strong. Ears large and tilted forward, with rounded tips.
Eyes. Oval; no squints.

HAVANA COLOURS
Brown. Rich, solid mahogany brown all over, solid from tip to root with no tabby markings and no white patches. Nose leather and paw pads rosy pink. Eyes pale to mid-green.

Lavender. Frost grey with a pinkish tone, sound and even throughout, the same shade to the skin. Nose leather and paw pads lavender pink. Eyes green.

ORIENTAL SHORTHAIR

Good points
- Attractive
- Affectionate
- Active and intelligent
- Easy to groom

Take heed
- Great escapologist
- Needs lots of exercise
- Needs companionship

This long-legged, sleek, svelte cat is the great explorer of the feline world. Always into everything with boundless energy, it will take an interest in all the family's activities.

Since this cat may become morose if left alone for long periods, it is a good idea to have more than one, or another domestic pet for companionship. With its need for company met, the Oriental Shorthair makes a charming pet.

Grooming
An occasional comb to remove dead hairs and a rub with a chamois leather or silk cloth are all that are required, plus plenty of hand-stroking to burnish the coat. Check the ears and teeth regularly.

Origin and history
The original Oriental Shorthair cats came from arranged matings between Siamese (for type) and other shorthaired cats (for colour). Later, Siamese were mated to longhaired Chinchillas to produce Oriental cats with tipped coats, and this unusual mating combination opened up the field for all kinds of possibilities in the colour range, including new solid colours (caramel, apricot and beige), tipped tabbies, torbies (patched tabbies) and shaded, tipped and smoke tortoiseshells.

In the United Kingdom, the self or solid-coloured cats are known as Foreign Shorthairs, although 'Foreign' is gradually being replaced by Oriental. The tabby and other varieties are already known as Oriental Shorthairs, and in the United States, all cats of this type are known as Oriental Shorthairs.

Orientals came to the US in 1972 when Peter and Vicky Markstein, two of the United States' better-known Siamese breeders, went to the UK in search of new Siamese lines. To the Marksteins' surprise they found the Siamese type they wanted in the newly emerging Foreign Whites and associated, non-pointed colours.

After returning to the US, the Marksteins decided to seek the acceptance of all Foreign Shorthairs as one breed that would be called the Oriental Shorthair. The foundation for that breed was the Siamese, which provided the type, and American Shorthairs as well as Abyssinians, which provided additional colour and the all-important gene for head-to-toe colour distribution. This formula produced an endless assortment of colourful, attractive cats with hard bodies and superb muscle tone.

By May 1, 1977, the Oriental Shorthair was competing in championship classes in the Cat Fanciers' Association. The breed is now accepted by all US registries.

Breeding
Oriental queens are very prolific.

Kittens
The kittens are born the same colour as they will be when they are adults (unlike the Siamese, whose kittens are paler at birth).

SHOW STANDARD
Oriental Shorthairs are Siamese in type with long, svelte, lithe and muscular bodies, and long, thin tapering tails.
Coat. Short, fine, glossy and close lying.
Body. Medium sized, long, svelte and muscular. Fine boned. Shoulders and hindquarters same width. Legs long and slim; hindlegs longer than forelegs. Paws small, dainty and oval.
Tail. Long and tapering to a point, thin at the base. No kinks.
Head. Long wedge with no whisker break and no nose break. Flat skull; fine muzzle; strong chin. Neck long and slender. Ears large and pointed, wide at the base.
Eyes. Clear, almond shaped, medium in size, slanted towards the nose. No squints.

ORIENTAL SHORTHAIR COLOURS
Selective breeding programmes have produced a varied selection of colours and patterns within this breed. What follows is a representative selection of some of the nearly 50 colours in which Oriental Shorthairs are available.

ORIENTAL SELF BROWN

The first all-brown shorthaired cat, exhibited in the United Kingdom in 1894, was called the Swiss Mountain Cat. It was believed to be a cross between a black Domestic Shorthair and a Seal point Siamese that had resulted from an accidental mating, and the line was not perpetuated. The type, now known in the UK as Havana, was first bred in the 1950s and was the result of a planned mating between a Chocolate point Siamese and a Domestic Shorthair of Oriental type. The name has been subject to much alteration. The variety was first registered as Chestnut Brown Foreign. Exported to the United States, these cats then became Havana Browns, and in 1970 the British and European governing bodies also re-adopted the name Havana. This has caused some confusion, because the variety developed quite differently on each side of the Atlantic. In the UK and Europe the Oriental type was encouraged, and the cats were outcrossed to Siamese. The American Havana Brown is a cat of less extreme type, and outcrossing to Siamese is not permitted. This American version of the Havana Brown is also distinguished by its squared-off, 'corncob' muzzle.

SHOW STANDARD
Coat should be a rich, warm chestnut brown, the same colour from root to tip. Tabby or other markings, white hairs or patches are faults. Nose leather brown. Paw pads pinkish brown. Eyes green.

ORIENTAL LILAC
(Oriental Lavender, Foreign Lilac)

These cats were developed in the United Kingdom in the 1960s, during the Havana breeding programme. Mating two Self-browns (Havanas) will give rise to Lilac kittens if the parents were produced from a cross between a Russian Blue and a Seal point Siamese. Soon, however, there will be sufficient Lilac studs, and outcrosses will be unnecessary.

SHOW STANDARD
Should have a pinkish grey coat, with a frosty grey tone: neither too blue nor too fawn. White hairs or patches or tabby markings are faults. Nose leather and paw pads lavender. Eyes green.

ORIENTAL CINNAMON

Originally developed from a Seal point Siamese carrying a chocolate gene mated to a red Abyssinian, the Oriental Cinnamon should be a warm cinnamon colour to its roots.

Above: Oriental (Foreign) Cinnamons are increasingly popular in the US.

Havana Brown (UK)
and Oriental Shorthair

Lilac Oriental (Foreign) Shorthair

Havana Brown (UK)
Oriental Shorthair

Havana
Brown (US)

Havana Brown (US)

It is a lighter colour than the Havana, but similar, and is becoming even more popular in the United States and Europe.

SHOW STANDARD
Coat colour a warm cinnamon brown throughout, sound from root to tip. No white hairs or tabby markings. Eyes green.

ORIENTAL WHITE
(Foreign White)

One of the most striking varieties, Oriental White cats look like porcelain with their smooth white coats and china blue eyes. They were developed in the 1960s and 1970s by mating white domestic shorthairs to Siamese. As the white coat is dominant genetically to other coat colours, it obscured the Himalayan (point-restricted) coat pattern. Later, the Oriental Whites were outcrossed again to Siamese to improve the eye colour.

In 1964 — after working independently to produce a blue-eyed white cat with foreign type — three United Kingdom cat breeders began pooling their gene pools. They exhibited the first result of their efforts at a cat show in York, England, the next year. Before long, sound-hearing, blue-eyed white cats were the cat's meow in the UK cat fancy.

These cats are sound hearing because they derive their colour from the dominant white gene (not usually associated with deafness).

SHOW STANDARD
Coat should be pure white throughout with no black hairs. Nose leather pale pink. Paw pads dark pink. Eyes brilliant sapphire or china blue (United Kingdom); green or blue (United States); odd eyes not allowed on the show bench.

ORIENTAL EBONY
(Foreign Black)

A dramatic combination of a long, svelte, jet-black cat with emerald green eyes and an alert, intelligent expression.

Interest in the Black Oriental Shorthair began in the 1970s, although previously many had been bred either experimentally or accidentally, but had been sold as pets, as there was no official show standard for them in existence at the time.

They were originally obtained from mating Self-browns (Havanas) to Seal point Siamese, but today as there are sufficient numbers of Oriental Black studs available, back crossing to Siamese is no longer necessary.

SHOW STANDARD
Coat should be jet black all over from root to tip. A rusty tinge to the fur is considered a fault. Nose leather black. Paw pads black or brown. Eyes emerald green.

ORIENTAL BLUE
(Foreign Blue)

Oriental-type blue cats have appeared from time to time in Siamese breeding programmes, but little notice was taken of them because of the other rather similar 'foreign' blue cats already established (Russian Blue and Blue Burmese). However, Oriental Blues appear naturally in litters of Self-browns (Havanas) and Lilacs, and they are now beginning to appear on the show bench.

SHOW STANDARD
Coat should be a light to medium blue all over, sound from root to tip. A lighter shade of blue is preferred in the United States. White hairs or patches, especially on the chin and stomach, are faults. Nose leather and paw pads blue. Eyes green.

ORIENTAL RED
(Foreign Red)

These cats were developed from Red point Siamese breeding programmes, at a time when Red Tabby British Shorthairs were being mated to Siamese to introduce the red colour into the Oriental type. Oriental Reds were a natural product of these matings, but today are obtained by mating Oriental Blacks to Red point Siamese and other Oriental colours. Oriental Reds are difficult to breed without tabby markings, so it is best to use breeding stock without any tabby ancestry, or markings may persist into adulthood. It would now be possible to use Red Burmese as Burmese breeders have succeeded in eradicating the markings in the coat of the Red Burmese. This was accomplished by several generations of careful selective breeding.

SHOW STANDARD
Coat should be a rich, deep, clear and brilliant red without shading or markings. Lips and chin red. Nose leather and paw pads brick red. Eyes copper to green; green preferred.

ORIENTAL CREAM
(Foreign Cream)

The Oriental Creams were a by-product of the breeding programme used to produce Oriental Blue and Lilac Tortoiseshells. In these programmes, Domestic (British) Shorthaired Tortoiseshells were mated to Siamese, and all the solid colours appeared in the mixture. The Cream is genetically a dilute of the Red, and with the Oriental type, makes a very elegant cat.

SHOW STANDARD
Coat should be buff-cream all over without markings, and an even colour from root to tip. Nose leather and paw pads pink. Eyes copper to green; green preferred.

OTHER SELF (SOLID) COLOURS

In order to produce the Shaded Oriental Shorthairs, a Chocolate point Siamese was mated to a Chinchilla Persian female. Their offspring were mated to Red point Siamese to introduce other colours simultaneously. In the process, self-coloured cats were produced, including Oriental (Foreign) Caramel, a cool, bluish-fawn colour, and Oriental (Foreign) Fawn, a warm, rosy mushroom colour.

ORIENTAL TIPPED

A revolution occurred among the Orientals when a Siamese was mated to a Chinchilla Persian in the hope of producing Oriental-type cats with tipped coats. The resulting kittens were originally mated back to Siamese for type, but now Oriental Tipped cats are mated only to Oriental Tipped in order to preserve the coat pattern.

The tipping is similar to that of the British Shorthair Tipped, and such cats look very striking with their sparkling coats. Tipping of any colour is possible, and any colour is allowed in the United Kingdom, including silver, cameo, cameo tabby, blue, chestnut, lilac, and tortoiseshell in brown, blue, chestnut and lilac.

SHOW STANDARD
Undercoat should be pure white. Top coat very lightly tipped on the back, flanks, head and tail with a contrasting colour to give a sparkling sheen to the coat. Chest and underparts should be white. Nose leather and paw pads appropriate to the tipping colour(s). Eyes according to tipping colour but green preferred.

ORIENTAL SHADED

The Shaded Oriental Shorthairs were also developed from the Siamese-Chinchilla Persian mating. The offspring were mated back to Siamese, Oriental Blacks or British Havanas. Thereafter, selective breeding preserved the amount of tipping required. Any colour tipping is possible, and all colours are allowed in the United Kingdom, including silver, cameo, cameo tabby, blue, chestnut, lilac and tortoiseshell in brown, blue, chestnut and lilac.

SHOW STANDARD
Undercoat should be pure white, sufficiently tipped on the back, flanks, head and tail with a contrasting colour or colours, to give the effect of a mantle overlying the white undercoat. Nose leather and paw pads according to tipping colour(s). Colour of eyes according to tipping colour(s) but green preferred.

ORIENTAL SMOKE

Another by-product of the Siamese-Chinchilla Persian mating. The first Oriental Smoke was produced by mating a Shaded Silver to a Red point Siamese. Today the best Oriental Smokes are mated back to Siamese, Oriental Blacks and British Havanas to preserve type. The tipping is heavy, giving the appearance of a solid-coloured cat except when the fur is parted to reveal a narrow band of white hair.

Like the Tipped and Shaded Oriental Shorthairs, any colour Smoke is possible, and most are now allowed for competition. These include black (ebony), blue, cameo (in red and cream), chocolate (chestnut), lilac (lavender) and tortoiseshell in brown, blue, chocolate and lilac.

SHOW STANDARD
Undercoat should be pure white. The top coat should be very heavily tipped with a contrasting colour or colours so that the cat, when in repose, appears to be of that colour(s). Nose leather and paw pads in keeping with tipping colour(s). Eyes green.

ORIENTAL PARTICOLOUR

The Oriental Particolours are all female-only varieties. Originally, Oriental Particolours were produced from the mating of Oriental Blacks with Red point Siamese or Havanas with Red point Siamese, but today Oriental Torties are mated to Siamese or other solid-coloured Oriental Shorthairs.

SHOW STANDARD
Tortie. Coat should be black with patches of red and cream, clearly defined and well broken on body, head, legs and tail. Nose leather and paw pads black and/or pink. Eyes copper to green, green preferred.

Blue Tortie (Blue-cream). Coat should be blue with patches of cream, clearly defined and well broken on body, head, legs and tail. Nose leather and paw pads blue and/or pink. Eyes copper to green, but green preferred.

Chocolate Tortie. Coat should be chestnut brown with patches of red and cream, clearly defined and well broken on body, head, legs and tail. Nose leather and paw pads dark and/or light pink. Eyes copper to green, but green preferred.

Lilac Tortie (Lavender-cream). Coat should be lilac-grey with patches of cream, clearly defined and well broken on body, head, legs and tail. Nose leather and paw pads pink. Eyes copper to green, but green preferred.

White Oriental
(Foreign) Shorthair

Ebony (Black) Oriental
(Foreign) Shorthair

Oriental
Shorthair

Red Tipped
Oriental Shorthair

ORIENTAL TABBY

Tabby Oriental Shorthairs were produced during the breeding programme for Tabby (Lynx) point Siamese, using mongrel tabbies and Siamese, and later, British Havanas mated to Tabby point Siamese.

All colours and tabby patterns have been developed. In the United Kingdom the Spotted Tabbies were formerly called Egyptian Maus, but the name Oriental Spotted Tabby has been adopted to save confusion with the American-bred Egyptian Mau, which is not Siamese-derived.

SHOW STANDARD
Classic Tabby pattern. All markings dense and clearly defined. Frown lines on the forehead form the characteristic letter 'M'. Unbroken lines run from the outer corners of the eyes towards the back of the head. Other pencil-thin lines on the face form swirls on the cheeks. Lines extend from the top of the head to the shoulder markings, which are shaped in a butterfly pattern. Three unbroken lines run parallel to each other down the spine from the shoulder markings to the base of the tail. A large blotch on each side of the cat is circled by one or more unbroken rings; these markings should be symmetrical on either side of the body. There should be several unbroken necklaces on the neck and upper chest, and a double row of 'buttons' running from chest to stomach. Legs and tail should be evenly ringed.

Mackerel Tabby pattern. Head is marked with the characteristic 'M'. An unbroken line runs from the outer corner of the eyes towards the back of the head. There are other fine pencil markings on the cheeks. A narrow unbroken line runs from the back of the head to the base of the tail. The rest of the body is marked with numerous narrow unbroken lines running vertically down from the spine line. There should be several unbroken necklaces on the neck and upper chest and a double row of 'buttons' on the chest and stomach. The legs should be evenly barred with narrow bracelets and the tail should be evenly ringed.

Spotted Tabby pattern (see also Egyptian Mau). Head markings as Classic Tabby. Body markings broken up into spots, which should be as numerous as possible, and may be round, oval or rosette-shaped. Dorsal stripe along the spine should be broken up into spots. There should be a double row of spots on the chest and stomach, and spots or broken rings on the legs and tail.

Ticked Tabby pattern. Body hairs to be ticked with various shades of marking colour and ground colour. Body when viewed from above to be free from noticeable spots,

stripes or blotches except for darker dorsal shading. Lighter underside may show tabby markings. Face, legs and tail must show distinct tabby striping. There must be at least one distinct necklace on neck or upper chest.

Brown Tabby (Ebony Tabby). Ground colour warm coppery brown. Markings dense black. Eyes rimmed with black. Nose leather black or pink rimmed with black. Paw pads black or brown. Green eyes preferred.

Blue Tabby. Ground colour beige. Markings light to medium blue. May have warm fawn highlights over the coat. Eyes rimmed with blue. Nose leather blue or pink rimmed with blue. Paw pads blue. Green eyes preferred.

Chocolate Tabby (Chestnut Tabby). Ground colour warm bronze. Markings rich chocolate-brown. Eyes rimmed with chestnut. Nose leather chocolate or pink rimmed with chocolate. Paw pads chocolate or cinnamon-pink. Green eyes preferred.

Lilac Tabby (Lavender Tabby). Ground colour beige. Markings deep lilac-grey. Eyes rimmed with lilac. Nose leather faded lilac or pink rimmed with lilac-grey. Paw pads faded lilac. Green eyes preferred.

Red Tabby. Ground colour bright apricot. Markings deep rich red. Eyes rimmed with pink or red. Nose leather pink or pink rimmed with red. Green eyes preferred (United States); all shades from copper to green allowed (UK).

Cream Tabby. Ground colour very pale cream. Markings deep cream. Eyes rimmed with pink or cream. Nose leather pink or pink rimmed with cream. Paw pads pink. Green eyes preferred (US); all shades from copper to green allowed in the UK breed standard.

Silver Tabby. Ground colour clear silver. Markings dense black. Eyes rimmed with black. Nose leather black or brick red rimmed with black. Paw pads black. Green eyes.

Cameo Tabby. Ground colour off-white. Markings red. Nose leather and paw pads rose. Green eyes.

EGYPTIAN MAU

Good points
- Beautiful coat
- Agile
- Playful
- Quiet
- Easy to groom

Take heed
- Does not transfer allegiance readily
- Limited gene pool

The Egyptian Mau is the only natural breed of spotted cat and, since it originated in Cairo, it is thought by some to be a

descendant of the cat revered and worshipped by the Ancient Egyptians.

The Mau is shy and loving and is said to have a good memory. It is strong and muscular, can easily be trained to perform tricks, and enjoys walking on a harness and lead. This is the best way to exercise an Egyptian Mau; if allowed out too much on its own, it may be stolen for its beautiful coat.

However, being a highly active cat it should not be too confined. The best solution if you cannot take the cat for walks yourself is to construct a wired-in pen in the garden, complete with roof and some means of access to the owner's house or a shelter to retreat from rain or too much sun. It adores people and should not be shut up on its own for long spells.

Grooming
As with all shorthaired cats, little grooming is required, although the Mau will benefit from — and enjoy — an occasional brushing and combing to remove any dead hairs, which it might otherwise swallow. Before a show, a little bay rum should be used. Do not use powder as this would mar the spots on the coat.

Origin and history
Thought to be the original domestic cats of Ancient Egypt, spotted cats or their descendants are depicted in early Egyptian art and symbolized by the gods Ra and Bast, both of whom were personified as cats. The name 'Mau' is simply the Egyptian word for cat.

The Egyptian Mau gained recognition because of the efforts of Princess Nathalie Troubetskoy. A member of one of the oldest and most distinguished Russian families, the princess was living in Rome when a youngster whom she knew gave her a spotted-silver, female kitten. The kitten, whom the young boy had previously kept in a shoe box, had been given to him by a member of the diplomatic corps of one of the Middle-eastern embassies.

The princess named the kitten Baba and sought to learn more about her background. After talking to a vet and several professors, the princess concluded that Baba was descended from Egyptian stock.

In December 1956 Princess Troubetskoy arrived in the United States with three Egyptian Maus. These were the first and only Egyptian Maus imported to that country. Among them was Baba, now four, a tall, elegant queen. Clear silver in colour, she had black spotting, vivid necklaces and bracelets and large eyes outlined in black. With her was her three-year-old son Giorgio, called Jo-Jo, who was a bigger, stronger-looking bronze cat. The third cat was an eleven-month-old female named Liza, ochre in colour. She was exhibited at the Empire Cat Show in 1957. Eleven years later the Cat Fanciers' Federation granted championship status to the Mau, which is now accepted by all US

registries. (The very first Grand Champion Egyptian Mau in North America was a cat from Princess Troubetskoy's Fatima cattery.)

The breed that Baba produced was the result of domestic crossing and much inbreeding. Temperamentally, the early Maus resembled their mother. They were unpredictable, fiery and wild-natured. They did not tolerate other cats well and were comfortable only in their homes. They would climb the walls in strange surroundings or at shows. Through selective breeding, people working with the Mau in the US have succeeded in producing a more docile cat. Maus today are active, agile and intelligent, and they make fine companion cats.

Breeding
Consulting editor Richard H. Gebhardt, six-term past president of the Cat Fanciers' Association, drafted the first American standard for the Egyptian Mau. Gebhardt observes that, 'Because of the number of outcrosses that had to be made in order to expand the Mau's gene pool when it first arrived in the United States, much of the Mau's original type has unfortunately been lost'.

Kittens
Egyptian Mau kittens are born with obvious spots, and are active and playful from the start.

SHOW STANDARD
The Egyptian Mau is halfway in appearance between the svelte Oriental type and the cobby Domestic Shorthair. Egyptian Maus are alert, well balanced, muscular and colourful.

Coat. The fur is dense, resilient and lustrous, medium long, silky, fine. Coat length is medium. In the smoke colour the hair is silky and fine in texture. In the silver and bronze colours, the hair is dense and resilient in texture and accommodates two or more bands of ticking separated by lighter bands.

Body. A modified Oriental type; medium in length, graceful and muscular, especially the males. Hindlegs are longer than forelegs, and give the appearance that the cat is standing on tip-toe. The paws are small and dainty, round to oval.

Tail. Medium long, wide at the base, tapering slightly. A whip tail is considered a fault.

Head. A modified wedge without flat planes. There is a slight rise from the bridge of the nose to the forehead, but no nose break. Ears large and wide apart, broad at the base, moderately pointed, with or without ear tufts. Small ears are considered a fault.

Eyes. Large, almond shaped. Small, round or Oriental eyes are considered a fault. The adult gooseberry green eye colour may take up to 18 months to develop.

EGYPTIAN MAU COLOURS
Coat pattern. There should be a good contrast between the pale ground colour and the spots. Each

Egyptian Mau

Egyptian
Mau Smoke

Silver Spotted Tabby
Oriental Shorthair

Chocolate (Chestnut) Classic
Tabby Oriental Shorthair

Oriental Shorthair

73

hair carries bands of colour, and the pigmentation of spots and stripes can be seen both in the fur and in the skin.

The forehead is marked with the characteristic 'M', and other marks form lines between the ears. These lines continue down the back of the neck, ideally breaking into elongated spots along the spine. As the spinal lines reach the hind-quarters, the spots merge to form a dorsal stripe which continues along to the tail tip. Two darker lines cross the cheeks; one starts at the outer eye corner and extends to below the ear, the second line starts at the centre of the cheek and curves upwards, almost meeting the first. The upper chest has one or more necklaces, preferably broken in the centre. The shoulder markings may be stripes or spots. The forelegs are heavily barred. Markings on the body should be spotted, the spots varying in size and shape; round, even spots are preferred. The spotting pattern on each side of the body need not be symmetrical, but spots should not run together in a broken, mackerel pattern. The hindquarters and upper hind legs should carry spots and stripes; bars on the thighs and back, spots on the lower leg. There should be 'vest button' spots on the chest and stomach.

Silver. Ground colour light silver, lighter on the undersides. Markings charcoal-grey. Backs of ears greyish pink, tipped in black. Toes black, colour extending up the backs of the hind legs. Nose, lips and eyes rimmed in black. Nose leather brick red. Paw pads black. Eyes gooseberry green.

Bronze. Ground colour warm, coppery brown, shading to pale, creamy ivory on undersides. Markings dark brown. Backs of ears tawny pink edged with dark brown. Paws dark brown with dark colour extending up the backs of the hind legs. Nose, lips and eyes rimmed with black or dark brown. Bridge of the nose brown coloured. Nose leather brick red. Paw pads black or dark brown. Eyes gooseberry green.

Smoke. Ground colour pale, silvery white. Markings jet black. Paws black, with black extending between the toes and up the backs of the hind legs. Nose, lips and eyes rimmed with black. Nose leather and paw pads black. Eyes gooseberry green.

Pewter. Ground colour pale fawn. Each hair on the back and flanks ticked (banded) with silver and beige, tipped with black, shading to pale cream on the undersides. Markings charcoal grey to dark brown. Nose, lips and eyes rimmed with charcoal to dark brown. Nose leather brick red. Paw pads charcoal to dark brown. Eyes gooseberry green.

Disqualify: Lack of spots, blue eyes, kinked tail, incorrect number of toes, a white locket anywhere that white is not permitted.

BURMESE

Good points
- *Great personality*
- *Highly intelligent*
- *Playful*
- *Sweet-natured*

Take heed
- *The US version of this breed is difficult to work with genetically*

The Burmese makes an excellent pet. It has a sleek, shorthaired coat that is very easy to groom, is more intelligent and more affectionate than many cats, but above all has a fantastic personality. It loves peple and is very good with children, but it does not like to be left alone. If you are out all day, then it is better to have two.

The Burmese is buoyant by nature, yet many people consider the smooth shining coat and yellow eyes the height of elegance. This cat will always give a grand, bouncy welcome to the stranger, and time and affection devoted to this breed more than repays the owner in loyalty and companionship.

Grooming
The Burmese is easy to groom. A fine-toothed comb used once or twice a week will remove dead hairs.

Origin and history
Although a cat resembling the Burmese was depicted in a book of poems published during the Ayudha period in Thailand between 1350 and 1767, the Burmese breed as we know it today was developed in the US in 1930, when a brown female cat of Oriental type, named Wong Mau, was imported to the West Coast from Burma. As there were no similar cats for her to mate with, she was bred to a Siamese. All the kittens born were therefore hybrids, but when some were mated together back to their mother, brown kittens resembling the mother were produced.

The progress of the Burmese in the US was not smooth. Siamese breeders complained that Wong Mau was nothing more than a Siamese with poor colour. Indeed, when a Burmese was exhibited at a show in San Francisco in 1938, Siamese breeders raised such a hue and cry that the cat was withdrawn from competition.

The breed's prospects were further diminished when the Cat Fanciers' Association officially de-recognized Burmese in 1947 because most members of the breed could not meet the CFA's requirement that a pure-bred cat be descended from three generations of similar cats. Despite the importation of three Burmese from Rangoon in 1941, breeders were still obliged to outcross to Seal point Siamese in order to keep from in-breeding their Burmese to extinction.

Fortunately, other US registries continued to recognize Burmese, thus ensuring the survival of the breed. By 1956 there were even enough three-generation Burmese

available to merit reinstatement in the CFA register.

No one could question the merit of the Burmese being exhibited in the US today. Yet classes are not large for a breed that is nearly 60 years old. Many observers believe that this is the result of problems that have developed within many Burmese lines. These problems relate to the 'contemporary' look with its extreme head type that became popular during the 1980s. This style has, in some cases, carried with it certain deformities.

The first Brown Burmese were imported into the United Kingdom in 1948, and this breed is now one of the most numerous on the show bench. Of the other colours, the Blue was the first to appear in the UK (1955) and was such an unexpected event that the first kitten was registered as 'Sealcoat Blue Surprise'. Since then, with intensive breeding programmes, Lilac, Cream, Red, Chocolate and Tortie Burmese have been produced, all having the same temperament.

Breeding
Burmese in the UK are hardy, prolific breeders. In the US, however, the typical show Burmese is a cat of another type. During the 1980s the 'contemporary' look — with its extreme head type, short nose and prominent eyes — became popular. Unhappily, this look is associated with cleft palates and other deformities in kittens.

Kittens
Burmese kittens are exceptionally active and playful. They are born with pale coats, and one breeder has observed that when mother and kittens are side by side, they look like plain and milk chocolate respectively.

SHOW STANDARD
The Burmese is a medium-sized cat of modified Oriental type with a muscular frame and heavier build than its looks would suggest. The British Burmese is slightly less rounded and cobby than the American Burmese, with longer, more slender legs.
Coat. Fine, sleek and glossy, short and close lying.
Body. A medium-sized cat, hard and muscular; chest rounded and back straight; legs long and slender, hind legs slightly longer than forelegs; paws neat and oval (UK), round (US).
Tail. Medium in length and tapering slightly to a rounded tip. Not whip-like or kinked.
Head. Slightly rounded on top between the ears, which are wide apart. The high, wide cheekbones taper to a medium-blunt wedge (UK); slight taper to a short, well developed muzzle (US). Chin firm; a jaw pinch is a fault. Ears rounded at the tips and open at the base with a slight forward tilt in profile. The nose is medium in length with a distinct break in profile. Face should have a sweet expression.
Eyes. Oriental in shape along the top line and rounded underneath (UK); rounded (US). Large and lustrous, set well apart.

BURMESE COLOURS
Brown was the first colour to be bred and recognized and is often considered the most attractive. Brown Burmese have been exported to many countries from both the UK and the US, and have immediately become popular everywhere. Although selective breeding in the UK has produced several colour varieties, in the US only Sable (Brown), Blue, Champagne (Chocolate) and Platinum (Lilac) are recognized for competition.

Brown (Sable). Adult colour should be an even, rich, warm or seal brown, shading very slightly to a lighter tone on the underparts. Nose leather and paw pads brown. Eyes deep yellow to gold with no tinge of green.

Blue. Adult colour should be soft silver-grey, shading to a paler tone on the underparts. Ears, face and feet have a silver sheen. Nose leather dark grey. Paw pads pinkish grey. Eyes deep to golden yellow preferred, although a slight greenish tinge is perfectly acceptable.

Chocolate (Champagne). Adult colour should be a warm milk chocolate all over, with slightly darker shading on the points permitted. Nose leather warm chocolate brown. Paw pads brick pink to chocolate brown. Eyes deep to golden yellow.

Lilac (Platinum). Adults should be a delicate dove grey with a pinkish tinge. Ears and mask are slightly darker. Nose leather and paw pads lavender-pink. Eyes deep or golden yellow.

Red. Adults should be light tangerine in colour. Ears are slightly darker. Nose leather and paw pads pink. Eyes deep or golden yellow.

Cream. Adults shoud be a rich cream. Ears only slightly darker. Nose leather and paw pads pink. Eyes deep or golden yellow.

Brown Tortie. Adults should have brown and red patches without any barring. Nose leather and paw pads plain or blotched brown and pink. Eyes should be deep or golden yellow.

Blue Tortie. The adult coat should have patches of blue and cream without any barring. Nose leather and paw pads plain or blotched blue and pink. Eyes deep or golden yellow.

Chocolate Tortie. Adult coat should have chocolate and red blotches without barring. Nose leather and paw pads plain or blotched chocolate and pink. Eyes deep or golden yellow.

Lilac Tortie. Adult coat should have lilac and cream blotches without barring. Nose leather and paw pads plain or blotched lilac and pink. Eyes should be deep or golden yellow.

Brown Burmese
(US type)

Red Burmese

Burmese

Lilac Tortie
Burmese

TONKINESE

Good points
- *Friendly and affectionate*
- *Easy to groom*
- *Active and full of fun*

Take heed
- *No known drawbacks*

The Tonkinese is a hybrid cat, a cross between the Siamese and the Burmese, and — as would be expected — it has some characteristics of each. Indeed, one American fancier has commented, 'On a scale of one to ten, with Burmese characteristics being a "one" and Siamese characteristics being a "ten", the Tonkinese is a perfect "five".'

Grooming
The Tonkinese is an easy cat to groom. All you need is a fine-toothed comb, and perhaps a rubber spiked brush for the occasional massage.

Origin and history
The Tonkinese was developed in the early 1960s by Margaret Conroy, a cat fancier from Ontario, Canada. Conroy bred a Seal point Siamese to a Sable Burmese to produce a cat that would be intermediate in type and temperament between the two.

In developing the Tonkinese, Conroy was reinventing the wheel. In 1930 a female cat named Wong Mau, from whom all Burmese cats are descended, arrived in the United States. Wong Mau was a brown hybrid with dark points. In addition to being the matriarch of the Burmese breed, she was, in retrospect, the precursor of today's Tonkinese.

The Tonkinese was first accepted for championship competition by the Canadian Cat Association in 1965. The breed is now recognized in all US registries, but in the United Kingdom is shown only in the assessment (provisional) classes.

At first Siamese and Burmese breeders made catty remarks about the Tonkinese, yet the public has shown nothing but enthusiasm for the breed. Pointed Tonkinese are especially popular with cat lovers who once owned and still prefer the old, round-headed Siamese.

While the Tonkinese is an intermediate cat by design, there is one exceptional feature about the breed: its dazzling, aqua-coloured eyes. A singular blend of the blue Siamese and gold Burmese eye colours, the Tonkinese's eyes range from aquamarine to turquoise.

Breeding
Tonkinese, or Tonks as they are affectionately known, are bred now only to other Tonks, giving 50 per cent Tonks, 25 per cent Siamese and 25 per cent Burmese. The first cross of Siamese to Burmese gives 100 per cent Tonkinese.

Kittens
Tonkinese kittens are born paler in colour than their parents, the adult colour gradually developing.

SHOW STANDARD
The Tonkinese is an Oriental-type cat, medium in size, lithe and well muscled.
Coat. Soft and close lying with a natural sheen.
Body. Medium sized, well muscled with long legs, the hind legs slightly longer than the forelegs. The slim legs terminate in small, dainty, oval paws.
Tail. Long and tapering from a thick base to a thin tip. No kinks. Proportionate in length to the body.
Head. A modified wedge with a blunt muzzle. In profile there is a slight stop. A medium-long neck, but not as long as that of a Siamese. Ears medium in size, pricked forward and rounded. Oval tips, broad at the base. Set as much on the sides of the head as on top.
Eyes. Almond shaped, set wide apart.

TONKINESE COLOURS
The following colours are accepted in all six North American registries:
Natural Mink. A warm brown with dark chocolate points. Nose leather, paw pads brown. Eyes blue-green.

Champagne Mink. A soft, warm beige with light brown points. Nose leather and paw pads cinnamon-pink. Eyes blue-green.

Blue Mink. A soft blue to blue-grey, with light blue to slate blue points. Nose leather and paw pads blue-grey. Eyes blue-green.

Platinum Mink. A soft silver body with metallic silver points. Nose leather lilac and paw pads pink. Eyes blue-green.

The following colour is accepted by every North American registry except the American Cat Association:
Honey Mink. A warm, ruddy brown with chocolate points. Nose leather and paw pads mid-brown. Eyes blue-green.

The following colours are accepted by the American Cat Association and The International Cat Association only:
Natural Solid, Blue Solid, Champagne Solid and Platinum Solid; Natural Pointed, Blue Pointed, Champagne Pointed and Platinum Pointed.

BOMBAY

Good points
- *Striking appearance*
- *Delightful personality*
- *Even-tempered*
- *Reasonably quiet*
- *Easy to groom*

Take heed
- *Does not like to be ignored*

The Bombay has been described as a 'mini black panther' with a patent-leather coat and copper-penny eyes. It has an ideal temperament and personality. It is hardy, affectionate and contented, seems always to be purring, and loves human company.

Grooming
The close-lying coat needs combing with a very fine-toothed or flea comb to remove dead hairs; the show animal can be polished with a silk cloth or chamois leather.

Origin and history
In the late 1950s and early 1960s, some Burmese breeders in the United States resorted to unauthorized outcrosses to Black American Shorthairs to improve body type and coat colour in their cats. Many kittens from these breedings were shown illegally as Black American Shorthairs or Sable Burmese.

In truth, several top-winning Burmese during the late 1950s and early 1960s sported thick, pliant coats that indicated an American-made influence. The appearance and success of these cats was a matter of some discussion among judges, breeders and exhibitors. The Burmese need for an outcross was obvious, but since US registries did not allow outcrosses for this breed, they created a situation ripe for fraud.

In time, Nikki Horner of the Shawnee Cattery in Kentucky sought recognition for the black hybrid kittens, which she named Bombays, from American Shorthair-Burmese crosses. After the Cat Fanciers' Association accepted the Bombay for championship competition in 1976, the other North American registries followed suit.

Breeding
North American registries permit Bombay fanciers to breed their cats to Sable Burmese to improve type and to Black American Shorthairs to improve colour. Unfortunately, most registries insist that all kittens from such outcrosses, be they black or be they brown, be registered as Bombays. The 'brown Bombays', which can also appear in Bombay-to-Bombay litters, can be used in

Above: A US-standard Champagne Mink Tonkinese, characteristically highly curious about what's going on around it.

Bombay breeding programmes; but they cannot be shown unless their breeders create bogus pedigrees for them, as some breeders do. The only realistic policy in this regard is the one followed by The International Cat Association, which allows black kittens from Bombay-to-Burmese crosses to be shown as Bombays, while allowing brown kittens from those crosses to be shown as Burmese.

Kittens
Bombay coats may be rusty at first, before maturing to pure black.

SHOW STANDARD
More show points are given to the coat condition and colour in this breed than in any other, as the coat is considered to be more important even than the type.
Coat. Very short and close lying with a patent leather sheen or satin finish. It most resembles the Burmese coat.
Body. Medium in size, muscular, neither cobby nor rangy. Males larger than females. Females more dainty. Legs medium-long.
Tail. Medium-long, straight, no kinks.
Head. Rounded without any flat planes. Face wide with a good width between the eyes. Short, well-developed muzzle. Nose broad with a visible nose break. Ears rounded, medium in size and alert. Broad at base, set wide apart on curve of head, tilted forward.
Eyes. Round, and set wide apart.
Colour. Black to the roots without white hairs or patches. Nose leather and paw pads black. Eyes new-penny copper, deep and brilliant. Gold eyes sometimes accepted, but not green.

Tonkinese

Natural Mink
Tonkinese

Bombay

Champagne
Mink Tonkinese
kitten

Bombay

RUSSIAN BLUE

Good points
- *Very sweet natured*
- *Gentle and shy*
- *Companionable*
- *Easy to groom*

Take heed
- *It may be difficult for breeders to tell when the cat is calling because of its very small voice*

The outstanding feature of the Russian Blue is its quiet sweetness. It is shy and gentle, and makes a loving, agreeable companion. It will become very attached to its owner, and is willing to please. Its blue, plush coat is different from that of any other breed and somewhat seal-like in texture. The guard hairs are tipped with silver, which gives a silver sheen to the coat, enhancing the look of this lovely, docile cat.

Grooming
The Russian Blue is easy to groom, as the fur is very short and plush. It needs only an occasional brushing or combing with a fine-toothed comb, and a polish with a chamois leather or an ungreasy hand.

Origin and history
Until 1912 all shorthaired blue cats, regardless of origin, competed in the same class at British shows. Some of those cats were foreign-born blues that were known as Archangel cats, Russian blues, Spanish blues, Chartreuse blues and even American blues. The blues from Archangel, wrote cat fancier Harrison Weir, 'were of a deeper, purer tint than the English cross-breeds'. The Archangel cats, said Weir, had been named after the town of Arkhangelsk, a port on the White Sea 150 miles (240km) south of the Arctic Circle. Weir and other fanciers believed that Archangel cats might have been brought to Western Europe by sailors during the 1860s.

Russian cats were assigned to their own judging category, called the Foreign Blue, in 1912. Their fortunes improved after this, but they fell into decline during World War II. After the war, breeders in the United Kingdom outcrossed to other cats whose colour and type most nearly resembled their Russian Blues. Some UK breeders chose the British Blue for its plush, pale coat, while others selected Blue point Siamese in pursuit of a more extreme body type.

At about the same time, Scandinavian breeders began working to develop a Russian Blue of their own, crossing a blue Finnish cat with a Blue point Siamese. Their cats were known for their magnificent heads, but their colour was rather dark.

Though a few Russian Blues had reached the United States around 1900, serious work with the breed did not begin in that country until the late 1940s.

Breeding
With the recessive blue point gene in the background, a few litters of Russian Blues will still produce what some people call 'White Russians'. Though they are born white — as are all Blue point Siamese — these cats are not truly white. They are nothing more than the natural outcropping of the Blue point Siamese that were used for a time in their breed's post-war redevelopment.

Kittens
Russian Blue kittens are born with fluffy coats and may have faint tabby markings until the adult coat develops.

SHOW STANDARD
The Russian Blue is a medium-to-large cat of Oriental type, lithe and graceful with a short, dense, plush coat.

Coat. Very short and dense. Very plushy, silky and soft, resembling sealskin.

Body. Long, lithe and graceful. Medium-strong bones. Long legs with small oval paws (UK); rounded (US). Hind legs longer than forelegs.

Tail. Long and tapering, thicker at the base.

Head. Wedge shaped, shorter than that of a Siamese, with a receding forehead. Straight nose and forehead with a change of angle above the nose. Flat, narrow skull. Prominent whisker pads. Strong chin. Neck long and slender but appearing shorter because covered with thick, short, plush fur. Ears pointed, large and wide at the base, set vertical on the head. Almost transparent, without ear tufts.

Eyes. Almond in shape and set wide apart, slanting to the nose.

Colour. A clear all-over blue without shading or white hairs but with silver-tipped guard hairs giving the whole coat a silvery sheen. A medium-blue colour is preferred in the UK and a paler blue in the US. Black Russians and White Russians are now being bred, particularly in New Zealand. Nose leather and paw pads slate blue. (Paw pads lavender-pink in the US.) Eyes bright, vivid green.

KORAT

Good points
- *Pretty*
- *Lovely eyes*
- *Quiet*
- *Sweet and gentle*
- *Intelligent*

Take heed
- *No known drawbacks*

The Korat has been described as having 'busy charm'. It loves to be petted, is smart, and likes energetic games.

The Korat prefers quiet, gentle people and gets very attached to its owner. It is not too talkative, except when 'calling', and would make an ideal pet for someone wanting a sweet, loving, quiet companion.

Grooming
The Korat's single coat is very easy to keep in perfect condition. All it needs is combing to remove dead hairs, so that the cat does not swallow them, and a polish with a chamois leather or silk cloth. It will enjoy lots of hand-stroking, which will be good for the coat and make it shine.

Origin and history
The earliest-known portrayal of the cat thought to be the ancestor of the Korat appears in the *Cat-Book Poems*, a manuscript rescued from the Siamese city of Ayudha, which was levelled by Burmese invaders in 1767. This silver-blue cat with the heart-shaped face and glowing green eyes was named after the province of Korat, but it is found in most other provinces of Thailand (Siam) as well.

In 1896, a blue cat was sent down from the Siamese class at the National Cat Club show in the United Kingdom because its body was blue instead of biscuit-coloured. The cat's owner insisted that his cat was, indeed, from Siam from whence he had just returned. He also claimed that he had seen other cats there that looked like his.

We do not know whether this cat was a Korat or a Blue point Siamese, but we do know that blue point kittens appeared in litters born to the earliest Korats sent to the United States.

The first Korats exported from Thailand to the US arrived at Portland, Oregon, in June 1959. These cats — a brother and sister named Nara and Darra — were a gift to Mrs. Jean Johnson of Gresham, Oregon, from a friend in Thailand. Johnson and her husband Robert had lived in Thailand from 1947 to 1953. During their stay, Johnson learned that what American cat fanciers knew as the Siamese was not, in fact, the cat of the Siamese people. That honour was reserved for the Korat or *Si-Sawat* (see-sah-what) cat. In the Thai language the compound *Si-Sawat* means 'a mingled colour, a smooth glossy shell' — a definition no doubt inspired by the silver sheen of the Korat's fur. Among *Sawat*'s various meanings are 'good fortune' and 'prosperity'. Thus, the Korat, which is rare even in its native land, is also known as the good-luck cat.

In September 1964, Korats were exhibited at the Empire Cat Club show in New York, and the following year the Korat Cat Fanciers' Association was formed. Korats were accepted for championship competition in 1966 by the American Cat Association, the now-defunct National Cat Fanciers Association and the United Cat Federation. By the decade's end, the other North American registries had recognized Korats also.

Breeding
Although Korats were outcrossed to a few Blue point Siamese in order to enlarge the Korat's gene pool after it had first been brought to the US, the overriding concern of the members of the Korat breed club has been to keep this cat as pure — and as true to its original look — as possible.

Kittens
Kittens are born the same colour as adults; the beautiful silver-grey coat is present from the start. Kittens often have amber eyes, and the adult eye colour may take from two to four years to develop fully.

SHOW STANDARD
The Korat is a medium-sized, strong and muscular cat. The males are more powerful than the females.

Coat. Single, short, glossy, fine and close lying. Extra short and fine on the back of the ears, nose and paws.

Body. Medium sized, strong and muscular, semi-cobby with a rounded back and low on the legs. The forelegs are slightly shorter than the hind legs. Paws oval.

Tail. Medium long, tapering to a rounded tip.

Head. Heart-shaped head and face with a semi-pointed muzzle, a strong chin and jaw, and a large flat forehead. The nose is short with a downward curve above the tip of the nose. Gentle nose break. Ears alert with rounded tips, medium large, set high on head; open at the base; only slight interior furnishing is present.

Eyes. Prominent, over-large, luminous and set wide apart. Round when open, with slight slant when closed.

Colour. Silver-blue all over, tipped with silver to give a sheen, especially intense on backs of the ears, nose and paws. There should be no white hairs, spots or tabby markings. Nose leather dark blue or lavender. Paw pads dark blue or lavender with a pinkish tinge. Eyes brilliant green; amber tinge permitted in kittens.

Below: A charming Korat kitten. Kittens often have amber eyes, and the adult eye colour may take up to four years to develop.

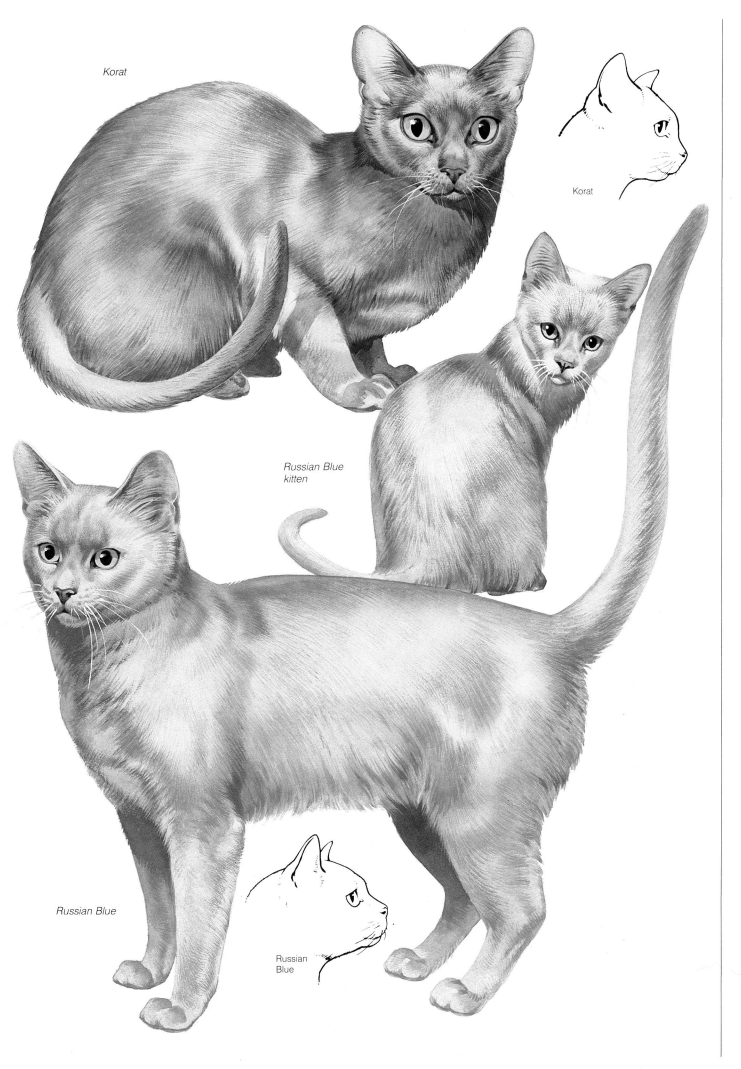

Korat

Korat

Russian Blue
kitten

Russian Blue

Russian
Blue

ABYSSINIAN

Good points
- *Pretty*
- *Playful*
- *Loving*
- *Easy to groom*

Take heed
- *Very active*
- *Amyloidosis, a fatal disease, is present in many Abyssinian lines*

The Abyssinian is a highly intelligent cat. It is responsive to affection and likes to be part of the family. It can easily be trained to do tricks and to retrieve.

An Abyssinian looks like a little wild cat, and this appearance, coupled with its responsive personality, makes the cat particularly appealing.

Grooming
An Abyssinian is very easy to groom. It is advisable to brush frequently to remove dead hairs. A shorthaired soft-bristle brush or rubber brush is ideal, and a very fine-toothed comb with a handle will remove loose hairs and double as a flea comb if necessary. For show cats, a little bay rum and a rub with a chamois leather will show off the coat to advantage.

Origin and history
The early Abyssinian-like cats were known as hare or rabbit cats because of their ticked coats. Rabbit fur, however, has only a single band of colour (ticking) on each hair, whereas a good Abyssinian will have two or three bands of darker colour on each hair (double or treble ticking), with the pale colour located next to the skin and between each layer of the dark bands.

Because the Abyssinian resembles depictions of ancient Egyptian cats, some people believe that the Aby descended from cats worshipped in Egypt more than 4,000 years ago. Other fanciers suggest that Abys originated in North Africa and were brought to the United Kingdom by soldiers returning from the Abyssinian War in the late 1860s. And some people argue that the Abys' most prominent ancestors were nothing more 'foreign' than the ticked domestic cats that had lived in England for many years.

The first Abyssinian to reach the UK was a cat named Zula, who was imported in 1868. Zula and perhaps other imports were bred with similarly marked British cats, and thus, most likely, the Abyssinian breed was born. By 1882 the Aby was listed as a separate breed, but it would remain for a number of years a breed based on type rather than lineage. Indeed, each of the twelve Abyssinians registered in the Stud Book of the National Cat Club in England for 1900-1905 was descended from at least one parent of unknown origin.

The first Abys arrived in the United States shortly after the turn of the century. Since their names were Ch. Aluminum and Salt, these cats were most likely silvers. The next recorded imports arrived in the 1930s. Fortunately, breeders in the US were becoming interested in Abyssinians just as British breeders were forced to interrupt their activities by the onset of World War II. In 1947 the records of the General Council of the Cat Fancy included only four Abyssinians, and two of those were unproven. The US Abyssinian population numbered close to 50 by that time. That the breed was able to rebound from this situation is a tribute to its appeal and to the tremendous dedication of its followers.

Breeding
The Abyssinian is an easy cat with which to work. The development of new Aby colours should add hybrid vigour to the breed.

Kittens
Abyssinian kittens mature early and are fearless and playful. But it may take 18 months before the coats develop their adult beauty.

SHOW STANDARD
The Abyssinian is medium sized, of modified Oriental type, firm, lithe and muscular with a distinctive ticked coat.
Coat. Short, fine and close lying, lustrous and resilient.
Body. Medium sized, slender and lithe, solid and muscular. Oriental in type, though not as extreme as a Siamese. Medium length, slim, fine-boned legs with small oval paws; characteristic stance as if on tip-toe.
Tail. Medium long, broad at the base and tapering. Not whip-like and no kinks.
Head. Medium broad, slightly rounded wedge on an elegant, arched neck. Muzzle not sharply pointed. Ears wide apart, broad at the base, well cupped and tufted. Chin firm; slight nose break in profile.
Eyes. Set wide apart and expressive. Large and somewhat slanted in setting, almond in shape. A squint is a fault.

ABYSSINIAN COLOURS
The following Abyssinian colours are recognized for championship competition in the UK and the US.

Usual (Ruddy). Coat is rich, rufous, ruddy brown, ticked with two or three bands of black or dark brown, with a paler orange-brown undercoat. Darker shading along the spine; tail tipped with black, and without rings. Black between the toes with colour extending up the back of the hind legs. Tips and edges of ears black or dark brown. Nose leather brick red. Paw pads black. Eyes green, yellow or hazel, rimmed with black or brown, encircled by a paler area.

Sorrel (Red). Body colour a rich, copper red, ticked with chocolate brown with apricot undercoat. Darker spine and tail tip. Chocolate colour between the toes extends up the back of the hind legs. Nose leather and paw pads pink. Tips and edges of ears chocolate brown. White allowed only on lips and chin.

Eyes green, yellow or hazel, the more brilliant and deep the colour, the better. Pale eyes are a fault.

Blue. Body colour a soft, warm blue-grey, ticked with a darker steel blue. Base hair is cream or oatmeal. Spine, tail tip and back of hind legs dark steel blue. Tips and edges of ears slate blue. Nose leather dark pink. Paw pads mauve-blue. Eyes green, yellow or hazel. Pale eyes are considered a fault.

Above: A Blue Abyssinian kitten: only five weeks old, but already brimming with confidence.

The following Abyssinian colours are accepted in several US registries for championship competition. They, along with chocolate and additional shades of silver, are shown in preliminary classes in the UK:
Fawn. Coat warm rose-beige, ticked with light cocoa brown, the extreme outer tip is the darkest. Tail tipped with light cocoa brown. The underside and inside of legs should harmonize with the main colour. Nose leather salmon. Paw pads dark pink. Light cocoa brown between the toes.

Lilac. A pale ivory ticked with frosty grey. The extreme outer tip is the darkest. The undersides and forelegs (insides) harmonize with the undercolour. Ears and tail tipped with frosty grey. Paw pads lilac pink with dusky lilac between the toes and extending up the back of the hind legs. Nose leather mauve or pink.

Cream. A pale cream, distinctly ticked with a darker cream. The extreme outer tip is the darkest. The undersides and forelegs (insides) harmonize with the undercolour. Ears and tail tipped with darker cream. Paw pads pink with dark cream between the toes and extending up the back of the hind legs, preferably to the hocks.

SINGAPURA

Good points
- *Pretty*
- *Responsive*
- *Relatively quiet*
- *Easy to groom*

Take heed
- *A severely limited gene pool makes working with this breed difficult*

A small, muscular cat with a sparkling appearance and large eyes, the Singapura has been promoted as the world's smallest breed of cat and as Singapore's national treasure.

Grooming
A Singapura needs little grooming; just the occasional comb-through will keep the cat looking smart.

Origin and history
Until she was obliged to admit otherwise, Tommy Meadow had always maintained that she and her husband, Hal, had discovered three brown-ticked kittens whom they named Tes, Ticle and Pusse on the streets of Singapore in the summer of 1974. After returning to the United States with their 'foundling' cats and two of those cats' offspring the following year, the Meadows began showing these 'Singapuras' in provisional classes; and the rest, as the cliché goes, is cat fancy history.

This history had to be revised after an American travelling in Singapore discovered that import papers filed by the Meadows when they entered Singapore in 1974 contained the singular names of three 'brown Abyssinian' cats: the aforementioned Tes, Ticle and Pusse. When this information was given to Sandra Davie, a Singapore reporter, she phoned Tommy Meadow in August 1990, and Meadow recanted her story about finding cats on the streets of Singapore in 1974. She did the same in front of the Cat Fanciers' Association board of directors — which oddly enough took no disciplinary action against her — in February 1991. On both occasions Meadow insisted that her husband had found three cats in Singapore when he was there on sensitive oil-company business in 1971. He then shipped the cats to Meadow in the US, and the Meadows took three grandchildren of those cats back to Singapore in 1974.

The Meadows fiercely maintain that — despite their fabrication — the Singapura's ancestors did come from the streets of Singapore. But some Americans maintain that the Singapura came instead from a basement in Houston, the city where the Meadows lived in the early 1970s. In support of their contention, Meadows' critics cite the lack of veterinary records showing that Hal Meadow ever sent cats from Singapore to the US in 1971. In addition, the recent death of one Singapura from amyloidosis, an affliction largely confined to Abyssinians, suggests a link between the two breeds.

Singapura

Abyssinian

Singapura

Ruddy Abyssinian
kitten

Sorrel (Red)
Abyssinian

Breeding

Because all Singapuras descend from only four cats — and because Singapura fanciers in most registries have virtually closed the books on subsequent imports — this breed's gene pool is barely large enough for wading, let alone thriving reproductive manoeuvres. Thus, Singapuras are difficult to breed because some are slow to mature sexually, and males may be troubled by infertility as a result of inbreeding.

Kittens

Singapura litters are somewhat smaller than the average breed's.

SHOW STANDARD

The Singapura is a very small cat, but alert and healthy with noticeably large, cupped ears and large eyes.
Coat. Very fine, short, silky and close lying.
Body. Moderately stocky, dense and musuclar body. Back slightly arched, medium-long legs and small, tight paws. Body, legs and floor should form a square. Neck short and thick with high shoulder blades.
Tail. Medium long, tapering to a blunt tip. No kinks.
Head. Rounded, narrowing to a blunt, medium-short muzzle with a definite whisker break. Full chin. In profile, a slight break well down the bridge of the nose. Ears large, slightly pointed, wide open at the base and possessing a deep cup.
Eyes. Large, almond shaped, wide open and slanted.
Colour. Each hair on the back and flanks and top of the head must have at least two bands of dark brown ticking separated by bands of lighter, warm, old-ivory colour. The tip of each hair should be dark and the base light. Legs with some barring allowed. Toes dark brown, the colour extending up the back of the hind legs. Muzzle, chin, chest and stomach should be a warm, pale fawn. Ruddier tones are allowed on the ears and the bridge of the nose. Eyes, nose and lips are rimmed in dark brown. Nose leather red, paw pads dark brown. Eyes hazel, green or gold.

REX

Good points
● *Distinctive curly coat*
● *Intelligent*
● *Quiet*
● *Very easy to groom*

Take heed
● *Spasticity has been detected in some Devon Rex*

The Rex is an unusual-looking cat with a coat of curly hair and curly whiskers and eyebrows. Characteristically, the coat feels warm to the touch because the hair is so fine and short.

There are two types of Rex: the Cornish and the Devon. The latter is particularly playful, and its pixie-like face betrays a devilish sense of mischief. Intelligent and enterprising, both Rexes make excellent pets.

One point to watch, however: the Rex has a tendency to overeat and so can easily ruin its streamlined figure. Overfeeding should be avoided as a fat Rex is particularly unattractive.

Grooming

Rexes are easy to groom. All that is needed is a silk cloth or a chamois leather to polish the coat, and lots of hand grooming to remove any dead hairs. If the cat requires a wet bath, it is advisable to do this a week before a show, as the curl goes limp immediately after a bath.

Origin and history

The first Rex cat born in captivity, a cream male named Kallibunker, arrived with a retinue of four straight haired littermates on July 21, 1950, in Cornwall. Though his father was not known, Kallibunker's mother was a straightcoated domestic cat named Serena. Nina Ennismore, who owned Serena, had formerly bred Rex rabbits. Ennismore knew, therefore, that Kallibunker's wavy coat was most probably caused by a mutated gene.

At the urging of cat fancier Brian Stirling-Webb and geneticist A.C. Jude, Ennismore bred Kallibunker to his mother. This mating produced a normal-coated female and two Rex-coated males.

Ennismore had stopped working with Rex cats by the late 1950s, but Stirling-Webb soldiered on. In 1961 he learned that a male Rex kitten had been born in Devon the preceding year. The dam of this kitten was a tortie-and-white stray which had attached itself to a woman named Beryl Cox. The sire was a feral, Rex-coated male who lived in an abandoned tin mine near Cox's home.

Having heard about Stirling-Webb's interest in Rex, Cox gave him a male kitten named Kirlee. When Kirlee was introduced to a few Rex ladies from Cornwall, however, the kittens that sprang from those matings all had straight hair.

Stirling-Webb concluded that there were two separate mutation genes — and two separate Rex breeds — at work here. Since, as Stirling-Webb knew, the Rex gene is recessive, all kittens born from Cornish Rex females bred to Kirlee would have been wavy coated if the gene responsible for Kirlee's mutation was the same as the one responsible for Kallibunker's. But the strains never met. Instead of Kirlee contributing to the development of Cornish Rex, he wound up contributing to the development of a new breed called the Devon Rex.

Before giving up her cats, Ennismore had sent several Rex to breeders in the United States in the late 1950s. Stock was scarce, but dedication, ingenuity and Siamese outcrosses were not. The latter contributed fine bone, distinctive head type, large ears and a sporty, greyhound look to the Cornish Rex.

The Devon Rex, for its part, looks as if it was on the other end of the line when E.T. phoned home. If unique had a superlative form, the

Devon Rex could claim it. Especially unique are the Devon Rex ears, which are large enough to merit their own postcode.

The Rex breeds are different in several ways. The Cornish Rex has a longer, more plush, more wavy coat. The Cornish Rex has a Roman nose; the Devon has a decided stop to its nose. The Cornish sports a dramatic, tucked-up underbelly; the Devon Rex does not.

Breeding

The year after the first Rex had been born in Cornwall, a wavy-haired, black, female cat living wild in East Germany was adopted by a cat lover named Dr. Rose Sheuer-Karpin. This cat, bred to one of her straight-haired sons, produced curly-coated kittens. In time, the German Rex was found to be compatible with the Cornish Rex but not with the Devon Rex strain.

Kittens

Rex kittens are robust and healthy. They will certainly keep you busy, being highly active, precocious and mischievous.

CORNISH REX

SHOW STANDARD

This cat should be fine boned and elegant with a wedge-shaped face and a long whip tail.
Coat. Short, thin hair, but dense, plush and close lying. No guard hairs. The hair should curl, wave or

Above: A Brown Mackerel Tabby Devon Rex (US standard).

ripple, especially on the back and tail, but preferably all over, even on the paws. Whiskers and eyebrows should also be curly.
Body. Hard, muscular, medium in size but slender, not cobby, standing high on long, straight legs. Back arched. Paws small, dainty and oval.
Tail. Long, thin and tapering.
Head. Modified Foreign type with medium-length wedge, flat skull and straight profile with no nose break. Ears large, set high on the head, wide at the base, rounded at the tips, covered in fine short fur.
Eyes. Oval and medium in size.

DEVON REX

SHOW STANDARD

The Devon Rex has a coarser coat than the Cornish Rex, and a different face. The Devon is a medium-sized cat with a long tail and huge ears.
Coat. Very short, fine, wavy and soft, not shaggy, but coarser than that of the Cornish, due to the presence of minute guard hairs. Short curly whiskers and eyebrows, which tend to be brittle.
Body. Medium in size, slender, hard and muscular. Broad in the chest; carried high on long, slim legs. Hind legs generally longer than forelegs. Feet small and oval.
Tail. Long, fine and tapering, covered with short, curly fur. No kinks.
Head. A rounded wedge with a flat top, set on a slender neck. Rounded cheeks with a whisker break, and a definite nose break in profile. Ears set low on the head, very large, with or without ear tufts; wide at the base, rounded at the tips, and covered in very fine fur.
Eyes. Wide set, large, oval and slightly slanted.

REX COLOURS

All coat colours are acceptable for competition. Assymetrical white marking to be allowed for Cornish Rex. White marking, however, not allowed on Siamese pattern.

Eye colour should be in keeping with the coat colour or pale green, yellow or gold. White Rex may be gold-, blue- or odd-eyed (one gold, one blue); Si-Rex must be blue.

Below: A Tortie-and-white (Calico) Cornish Rex (US standard).

Black Devon Rex
(UK eye colour)

Cornish Rex

Devon Rex

Devon Si-Rex kitten (UK)

Blue-cream
Cornish Rex (UK)

AMERICAN WIREHAIR

Good points
● *Different in appearance*
● *Affectionate*
● *Agile*
● *Intelligent*

Take heed
● *Some lines appear susceptible to respiratory problems*

The American Wirehair is a shorthaired cat with a distinctive wiry coat that is hard and springy to the touch. The Wirehair is bred in all colours.

Grooming
Virtually no grooming is necessary. Brush with a soft brush twice a week to remove loose hairs.

Origin and history
The first known wirehaired kitten appeared in a litter of barn cats born on March 5, 1966, in Verona, New York. Five kittens in that litter had ordinary coats. The sixth, a red-and-white male, had a scant, wiry coat that resulted from a genetic mutation. When Joan O'Shea, a Rex breeder living near Verona, heard about this kitten, she called on the farmer who owned it. The farmer eventually sold the kitten to O'Shea for $50.

O'Shea named the kitten Adam. One day when Adam was 14 months old, O'Shea saw a calico cat wandering in her yard. The cat, who belonged to a neighbour's child, behaved as if she were in season. O'Shea invited the cat in to meet Adam. This meeting produced two kittens with normal coats and two red-and-white, wirehaired females.

O'Shea mailed samples of Adam's coat to British geneticists Roy Robinson and A.G. Searle. Robinson determined that Adam's coat was not related to the Rex mutations. All three types of Adam's hairs — down, awn and guard — were twisted. In addition, the awn (or mid-length hairs) were hooked at the tip. By comparison, the three types of hairs in the Devon Rex are so foreshortened that they resemble down hairs (the shortest kind), while the Cornish Rex lacks guard hairs (the longest type) altogether.

Adam sired three litters before dying of cystitis in 1970. Shortly afterwards O'Shea stopped working with American Wirehairs. Fortunately, other breeders took up the cause, and the breed is now recognized in several North American associations.

Breeding
The Wirehair gene is dominant. Thus, breeding one Wire to another may produce an all-wirehaired litter or some Wires and some straight-coated kittens or all straight coats. Straight-coated cats, when bred to a Wire, will produce Wires 50 per cent of the time.

Consulting editor Richard H. Gebhardt, a Wirehair breeder, observes, 'Breeding Wire to Wire has resulted in many defects.

Outcrossing to American Shorthairs has strengthened the breed, but produces fewer Wirehair kittens, and it will be some time before the coat gene is firmly set'.

Kittens
Wirehair kittens are born with tight, curly coats. They are healthy, playful and robust.

SHOW STANDARD
The wiring, coarseness and resilience of the coat is more important than the crimping of each hair.
Coat. The distinctive feature of this cat is its unique coat, which is medium in length and tightly curled. All the hairs are crimped, even in the ears. The whiskers are crimped or wavy and untidy.
Body. Medium to large, well muscled with shoulders the same width as haunches. Back level. Legs medium long; paws oval.
Tail. Moderately full, tapering to a rounded tip.
Head. Round with prominent cheekbones, well-developed muzzle and chin and a slight whisker break. Nose is concave in profile. Ears medium in size, set wide apart with rounded tips.
Eyes. Large, round, bright and clear, set well apart, at an angle.

AMERICAN WIREHAIR COLOURS
Many colours and patterns are permissible and possible They include solid white, black, blue, red and cream; chinchilla, shaded silver, shell cameo, cameo tabby, shaded cameo, black smoke, blue smoke, cameo smoke; tortoiseshell, calico, dilute calico, blue-cream; bicolour; classic and mackerel tabby patterns in silver, brown, red,

blue and cream; and any other colour or pattern, or combination of colours and patterns with white, with the exception of the Himalayan pattern or chocolate and lilac (lavender). Eye colour appropriate to coat.

SPHYNX

Good points
● *Affectionate*
● *Needs no brushing or combing*
● *Certainly attracts attention*

Take heed
● *Should be sponged regularly*

Across decades and continents the Sphynx has been praised for its demeanour. One anonymous fancier wrote in 1903, 'They are the most intelligent and affectionate family pets I have ever met [and] the smartest cats I have ever seen'.

Grooming
No brushing or combing is required, but Sphynx must be bathed or towel-washed frequently since they have no hair to absorb the oils exuded by a cat's body.

Origin and history
A portrait of a Mexican Hairless cat named Jesuit, 'believed to be the only specimen ever exhibited in England', appears in C.H. Lane's *Rabbits, Cats and Cavies* (London: J.M. Dent and Company, 1903). Lane reported that 'old (two-legged) Jesuit fathers in New Mexico

Below: A Silver Tabby American Wirehair. The hard, springy fur — distinctive and attractive — appeared as a natural mutation.

believed the hairless cats to be "the last of the Aztec race" '.

Writing 36 years later in the *Journal of Heredity*, Ida M. Mellen claimed that New Mexican Hairless cats had been exhibited in the United States in the early 1900s. The immediate ancestor of these cats, said Mellen 'undoubtedly was a scant-haired cat of South America'.

Like others before her, Mellen suggested that the hairless cat 'may be extinct'. Yet other hairless cats appeared in Wilmington, North Carolina, in 1936; in Paris in the 1930s; and in Ontario, Canada, in the 1960s and again in 1978. Except for the Paris cats, whose parents were Siamese, the parents of these hairless cats were non-pedigree domestic shorthairs.

The Sphynx was accepted for championship competition in 1971 by the late CROWN association. The International Cat Association (TICA), founded in 1979, also included the Sphynx among its recognized breeds. Since CROWN no longer sponsors shows, TICA is the only association in North America in which Sphynx enjoy championship status.

Breeding
The Sphynx gene is recessive — at least among cats with normal coats — but some breeders suspect it may be an incomplete dominant in Sphynx-Devon Rex crosses.

Kittens
Sphynx kittens are born with a fine covering of soft, short hair, most of which is lost as they approach adulthood.

SHOW STANDARD
The Sphynx is not truly hairless. Its skin, described by one observer as feeling like a suede-covered hot water bottle, is frequently covered with virtually imperceptible down.
Coat. There is a short, velvet pile covering the face and ears that is longest and heaviest on the nose and sides of the mouth. The paws are also covered with fine hair up to the ankles, as is the end of the tail. There is a ridge of fine hair on the back, and the testicles are covered in close-lying hair.
Body. Long, fine boned and muscular. The skin is taut without wrinkles, except on the head. The legs are long and slim with small round paws; hind legs are slightly longer than forelegs.
Tail. Long, thin and hard. No kinks.
Head. Neither round nor wedge shaped; flat between the eyes. The neck is fairly long, and the chin square. The short nose is covered with velvet-like fur, and there is a decided nose break. The ears are very large, wide at the base and rounded at the tips, sticking out from the head at the lobes.
Eyes. Deep-set and slanted.

SPHYNX COLOURS
All colours and coat patterns are allowed excluding the Himalayan pattern, chocolate, lilac (lavender), or any of these with white.

Eyes gold, green or hazel, or in keeping with the coat colour.

American Wirehair

Black Smoke American Wirehair

Blue Sphynx

Sphynx

OCICAT

Good points
- *Striking appearance*
- *Robust health*
- *Intelligent*
- *Sociable*
- *Playful*

Take heed
- *Does not always breed true*

The Ocicat was created through the artful blending of Siamese, Abyssinians and American Shorthairs. The breed has retained the best qualities of each of its components, says one enthusiast. 'Ocicats are extremely intelligent, social animals. They'll follow you everywhere. If you want to take a shower, you'd best make sure that you shut the door, or you might have a cat in the shower with you'.

Grooming
The Ocicat's coat is user-friendly, demanding little more than an occasional brushing to retain its glorious appearance.

Origin and history
In 1965, the year the first Ocicat was exhibited, astronomers discovered that Venus rotates in a different direction from the other planets. The same might cordially be said of Virginia Daly, the breeder who created the Ocicat.

Besides working with as many as four established breeds at once, Daly experimented with new varieties. This did not always sit well with more conservative breeders, one of whom once said to Daly, 'The next thing you'll be making will be an Abyssinian-pointed Siamese'. And just about the next thing, Daly did, though it took her two generations to do so.

She bred a Seal point Siamese female to a ruddy Abyssinian male. The resulting kittens looked like Abyssinians, but they carried the recessive gene for the Siamese pattern; and when Daly bred one of them — a female named She — to a Siamese, She produced an Aby-pointed Siamese. She also produced a large, ivory cat with bright golden spots and copper eyes, whom Daly named Tonga — and whom her daughter christened the Ocicat because of his resemblance to an Ocelot.

About a week after Tonga had been sold — for $10 with the stipulation that he be neutered — Daly read an article in the erstwhile *Journal of Cat Genetics* wherein the author intimated that somebody ought to try to reincarnate the long-extinct Egyptian spotted fishing cat. Daly wrote to the author saying that she had and that the cat had just been sold.

When a second breeding between Tonga's parents produced a second Ocicat, Daly forgot about Aby-pointed Siamese and began promoting the Ocicat. Her work proceeded very slowly. First, the town that she lived in passed an animal-limitation ordinance, and Daly's cats far surpassed the three-cat limit. Second, Daly's 87-year-old aunt, who had just broken her hip, 'came to stay with us, which made the cats take a back seat for a while'.

As a result, the Ocicat — which Daly had hoped was on the verge of obtaining provisional status in 1966 — did not get off the starting block until February 1986, making it the slowest overnight sensation in the cat world.

And overnight sensation it is. Between 1986 and 1989, annual Ocicat registrations leaped 292 per cent. Indeed, 78 per cent of the 2,254 Ocicats registered by the Cat Fanciers' Association between the mid-1960s and 1990 were registered during the last four years of that span.

Breeding
Ocicat litters born before January 1, 1995, may have an Abyssinian parent. Ocicat litters born before — and most likely after — that date will no doubt continue to accommodate the occasional non-spotted cat, a reflection of the Ocicat's mixed genetic heritage.

Kittens
Ocicat kittens are intelligent like their Siamese forbears, lively like their Abyssinian ancestors and sturdy like their American Shorthair antecedents.

SHOW STANDARD
The Ocicat is a large, spotted, athletic cat with a powerful body and substantial bone. Its compelling expression is the handiwork of large, almond-shaped eyes ringed with mascara markings. Its distinctive appearance is provided by thumbprint-shaped markings composed of dark tones on a lighter background.

Coat. Short, smooth and satiny in texture. Tight, close lying and sleek, yet long enough to accommodate the necessary bands of colour.

Body. Solid and rather long bodied. Some depth of chest with slightly sprung ribs. Not bulky or coarse.

Tail. Farily long with a slight taper and a dark tip.

Head. The skull is a modified wedge with a slight curve from muzzle to cheek. Muzzle is broad and well defined with a suggestion of squareness.

Eyes. Large, almond shaped and angling slightly upwards towards the ears. More than the length of an eye between the eyes.

OCICAT COLOURS
Each hair on the Ocicat's coat, with the exception of the hairs on the tip of the tail, accommodates several alternating bands of colour. At the spots where these bands coalesce, they form distinctive, thumbprint-shaped markings composed of dark tones on a lighter background. These large, well-scattered spots are deployed in the suggestion of a classic tabby pattern across both sides of the torso in the following colours: blue, blue silver, chocolate, chocolate silver, cinnamon, cinnamon silver, fawn, fawn silver, lavender, lavender silver, silver and tawny.

BENGAL

Good points
- *Wildcat appearance*
- *Lively*
- *Intelligent*

Take heed
- *Temperament is still a consideration*

Ernest Hemingway — a celebrated patron of domestic cats (though a frequent despoiler of other species) — was asked one evening in a cafe in Malaga why, since he was such a hunter, he was always photographed with cats instead of dogs. 'Don't you realize', Hemingway responded, 'that the fireside tabby is merely a shrunken lion without a mane?'

This earnest explanation pertains as well to cats that resemble the smaller varieties of wild, spotted felines. Indeed, the desire to get cosy with the beauty — if not the beastliness — of an exotic species is the chief reason why the Bengal was created.

One of the primary differences between Bengals and the two spotted breeds already in championship classes, the Mau and the Ocicat, lies in the way the spots on the three breeds are distributed. The Mau's are deployed in a random fashion; the Ocicat's in a pattern that subtly suggests the classic tabby configuration; and the Bengal's in a horizontal alignment.

Grooming
The thick, luxurious coat of the Bengal, short-to-medium in length, requires a combing or brushing no more than once or twice a week.

Origin and history
The Bengal is the only spotted breed whose relationship with its wild counterparts is more than skin deep. Developed by Jean Mill of Covina, California, the Bengal includes a dash of Asian Leopard Cat blood among its ingredients.

Mill bought an Asian Leopard Cat in the late 1950s when they could still be acquired at some local pet shops in the United States. She first attempted to capture and preserve the wild, spotted phenotype in 1963 by crossing a female Leopard Cat, which she had imported from Malaysia, with a shorthaired, black domestic male adopted from a shelter. She kept a spotted female from that breeding, the first of its kind in her country, and eventually took that female back to its father, which union produced spotted and solid-coloured cats. But after her husband died in 1965, Mill abandoned her breeding programme.

By the late 1970s Mill set out once again to duplicate the pattern, colour and facial characteristics of the Asian Leopard Cat. The bulk of her foundation stock — eight females out of crosses between Leopard Cats and domestic shorthairs (all males from such first-generation crosses are sterile) — was provided by a pediatrician/geneticist working at the University of California at Davis.

Having suddenly become the head-mistress of a feline boarding school, Mill set about finding a suitable escort for her charges. She 'haunted all 32 shelters' in the Greater Los Angeles area for a year in search of a sturdy, sweet-tempered, domestic shorthair male, preferably a brown spotted tabby with no white in his coat.

On a visit to a zoo in Delhi, India, in 1980, Mill spotted a feral, orange domestic cat with deep brown rosettes who lived in the rhinoceros compound and earned his keep as a ratter. Mesmerized by the cat's beauty — and mindful that any youngster that hung out with rhinos would not be intimidated by eight calling females — Mill later wrote to an official at the zoo who agreed to ship the cat to the US. There it was assisted in its new employment by a brown spotted tabby, domestic shorthair male which Mill had later found in a shelter in Los Angeles.

Now, the second time around, the Bengal is becoming, if not yet a dead ringer for the Asian Leopard Cat, the closest thing to it. In addition, the Bengal has gained championship status in The International Cat Association.

Breeding
The International Cat Association rules insist that all Bengals in the show ring must be the products of at least three generations of Bengal-to-Bengal breedings.

Kittens
Many people ask if a genetic recipe containing even some wild blood is a recipe for disaster. The answer is no: the Asian Leopard Cat's influence on the Bengal's personality is an invigorating, but not a threatening, touch.

SHOW STANDARD
The goal of Bengal breeders is to replicate as nearly as possible the appearance of wild leopard cats while maintaining the loving, dependable temperament of domestic cats.

Coat. Short-to-medium. Thick and luxurious in texture. Unusually soft to the touch.

Body. Long and substantial, but not oriental or foreign. Robust and very muscular.

Tail. Thick, medium long, tapered with a rounded tip.

Head. Broad modified wedge with rounded contours. Longer than it is wide. Nose has a slight concave curve.

Eyes. Oval to slightly almond shaped. Large and set wide apart.

BENGAL COLOURS
Dark markings on a complementary ground colour shading to a light underside. Cheeks, chin and throat are white.

Leopard. Black spots on a bright orange background.

Mink. Black spots on a rich mahogany background.

Sorrell. Brown spots on a light orange background.

Ocicat

Ocicat

Bengal

Bengal

BURMILLA

Good points
- *Dense, plush coat*
- *Buoyant, friendly disposition*
- *Hybrid vigour*

Take heed
- *No known drawbacks*

The Burmilla belongs to the Asian Group: cats whose type is Burmese but whose coat colour, pattern or length is not.

Grooming
Comb or brush carefully every two or three days. Be sure to clean the ears and clip the claws as needed.

Origin and history
According to many zoologists, humans played a supporting role in the domestication of cats. The latter, it is theorized, in effect domesticated themselves by finding a vacant evolutionary niche — the position of despoiler of granary-robbing vermin — and exploiting it skilfully.

The same may be said regarding the creation of some cat breeds, the Burmilla being a most recent example. In 1981 in the United Kingdom, a Chinchilla Persian male and a Lilac Burmese female belonging to Baroness Miranda von Kirchberg exploited a niche in their respective breeding programmes. Their resourcefulness produced a litter of hybrid kittens. As they matured, these unexpected ducklings grew into magnificent swans with comely green eyes and handsome black or brown tipping over a shimmering, silver base coat. The Baroness and other cat fanciers conceived of these kittens as the foundation stock of a new breed, which was christened the Burmilla.

Within three years of its baptism, the Burmilla was being promoted for championship recognition by a breed club in the UK. In 1990 the breed advanced to preliminary status in its native land, where it is one of the most popular new breeds.

Breeding
Though longhaired kittens appear occasionally in Burmilla litters, especially if Persians are used as an outcross for this breed, the longhaired kittens may not be shown.

Kittens
At birth, Burmilla kittens are somewhat pale in colour. Their tipping does not develop until they begin to mature.

SHOW STANDARD
The Burmilla is a shorthaired cat with a semi-foreign body and large eyes. It bears the same relationship to the Burmese as the Oriental Shorthair does to the Siamese.
Coat. Short, fine and lying close to the body.
Body. The body and legs should be medium in length and thickness with firm muscle. The back should be straight from shoulder to rump.

The chest should be ample but not disproportionately broad.
Tail. Medium to long, elegant and carried proudly. Medium in thickness, tapering slightly to a rounded tip.
Head. Modified wedge shape. Wide at the jaw-hinge. The wedge should be short, and a distinct nose break should be visible in profile. The head should be gently rounded on top and exhibit good width between the ears. The ears should be medium to large in size, rounded at the tips and set well apart, and inclined slightly forwards. The chin should be firm, and the bite even.
Eyes. Full and expressive and set well apart. Although slightly Oriental in set, they should be neither round nor almond shaped.

BURMILLA COLOURS
The Burmilla is an agouti cat. The coat, in both the shaded and the silver varieties, may be shaded or tipped with black, blue, chocolate, lilac, red, black tortie, cream, blue tortie, chocolate tortie, lilac tortie or with the Burmese expression of any of these colours. The undercoat should be as pale as possible in standard varieties and nearly white in silver varieties. The shading on the body should be as free from tabby markings as possible with a denser concentration of colour along the spine, extending down the tail, dispersing gradually over the flanks and becoming as light as possible on the under parts.

CALIFORNIA SPANGLED CAT

Good points
- *Jungle-cat allure*
- *Graceful*
- *Easy to maintain*

Take heed
- *Purchase price may lower your bank-account balance significantly*

Few breeds are introduced by means of an announcement mailed on their behalf to 2 million prospective buyers, yet such was the happy circumstance under which the California Spangled Cat was presented by the Neiman-Marcus company in 1986.

The Spangled — a spotted, domestic hybrid that had been developed by Hollywood screenwriter Paul Casey — made its debut in the annual Christmas book of the exclusive United States department store Neiman-Marcus. Priced at a daunting £775 ($1,400) — including delivery — the Spangled was the official 'His and Hers' gift for the Christmas of 1986. (Other examples of extravagant Neiman-Marcus Christmas presents included a Sharpei puppy; a pink jeep with a fringed, surrey top and a Chinchilla coat inside; a stuffed tiger draped with costly jewels; and an acrylic mouse ranch.)

Grooming
Twice-weekly brushing and routine attention to the cleaning of ears and the clipping of claws.

Origin and history
The California Spangled Cat was a calculated production, an attempt to create an indoor replica of an outdoor, jungle-dwelling, spotted cat. The idea for the Spangled sprang from a long conversation between Paul Casey and Dr. Louis Leakey at a Beverly Hills, California, party in 1970. Casey got the inspiration for the Spangled when he and Leakey agreed that 'It was too bad house cats don't have the same beautiful spots that wild cats have.'

It took Casey 10 years to produce the cat he and Dr. Leakey had envisioned. Casey began work in 1971 with 'a longhaired, Angora-type, spotted-silver male and an apple-faced Siamese female. I got a nice, silver male in their first litter. He had a block-shaped spot, which was exactly what I wanted.'

In time Casey added a brown, spotted tabby Manx; a yellow-coloured, faintly spotted, part-Abyssinian-part-Egyptian-domestic cat from Egypt; and a shorthaired, spotted, 'ordinary house cat' from Malaya to his breeding programme. By 1981 he was happy with the cats he was producing and with the fact that they were no longer producing solid-coloured or ticked kittens.

At that point the only people who knew about the Spangleds were a few of Casey's friends. 'They thought I was nuts at first,' says Casey, 'but when I started getting the cats I wanted, one of my friends told me that the cats were "definitely Neiman-Marcus"'.

Breeding
As with any developing breed, there is a variety of type and pattern among Spangled cats.

Kittens
Although breeders report that no tabby, solid or marbled kittens appear in Spangled litters, one fancier allows that 'we get a white toe on a kitten once in a while'.

SHOW STANDARD
The California Spangled is an athletic-looking cat with a long, tubular body; almond-shaped eyes; wide, prominent cheekbones; and blocked or rounded spots.
Coat. Soft and short, slightly longer on tail and underbelly. Spots cover the back and the sides of the cat. Spots may be blocked, rounded, square, oval or triangular — but not crescent, eyelet or fish scale in shape.
Body. Long, sturdy and tubular. Well muscled.
Tail. Dark and blunt at the tip, the tail must exhibit from one to three dark rings.
Head. Skull is medium in length and width. Forehead is slightly rounded. Medium-sized ears are set high on the head and well behind the face. Wide, prominent cheekbones; medium-broad muzzle with strong chin and jaw.
Eyes. Medium large, somewhat sloping. Almond shaped, wide set.

SPANGLED COLOURS
Silver, charcoal, bronze, gold, red, blue, brown or black.

MUNCHKIN

The Munchkin is a shorthaired, short-legged cat that reputedly sprang up (or down) from ordinary domestic shorthair cats in Louisiana in the United States. The newest of the new, the Munchkin is not yet recognized, even for registration, by any of the cat federations in the United Kingdom or North America. But not for want of trying.

A few years ago Munchkin supporters applied for registration status with The International Cat Association (TICA), the most progressive cat federation in the US. After careful consideration, permission was denied because TICA board members were not convinced that the Munchkin had been demonstrated to be free of potential genetic difficulties. Board members were also very concerned that the Munchkin's abnormally short legs might compromise its quality of life.

The Dachshund, to which the Munchkin obviously invites comparison, is plagued by a number of structural difficulties that result from its long back and short legs. One vet with an interest in the genetic anomalies that affect purebred dogs estimates that as many as 15 to 20 per cent of all Dachshunds are prone to spinal disc problems because of the breed's unusual conformation. Many cat fanciers fear that if the Munchkin is bred to extremes — as most pedigree animals are — it, too, will be subject to the same difficulties.

The initial rebuff of the Munchkin — there will, no doubt, be subsequent petitions for registration status in TICA and in other associations — may signal an outbreak of commonsense in the cat fancy. So far, most cat breeds have been spared the genetic deterioration that has plagued virtually every breed of dog. More than 300 inherited conditions are known to affect purebred dogs, and new afflictions are added to that list at the frighteningly high rate of ten each year. Cat fanciers, many of whom hold the American Kennel Club in unusually high esteem, would be foolish not to profit from the dog fancy's mistakes in this respect.

The Munchkin may prove to be free of genetic complications — as its adherents somewhat prematurely claim it to be — and its short legs may not be an impediment to living an active cat life. If so, there is no reason it should not be advanced. That some cat fanciers find its looks offensive is of no moment. If that were a criterion for accepting or rejecting cats, it would be easy to name several breeds that would never have had a chance of being accepted.

But if Munchkin fanciers are the cat lovers they claim to be — which they hopefully are — they will not let the thrill of competing in championship classes seduce them into putting their cats at any risk of the agonies that may result from imprudent breeding practices.

Burmilla

California
Spangled Cat

Chocolate Tipped
Burmilla

Brown California Spangled Cat

Munchkin

Black Smoke
Munchkin

89

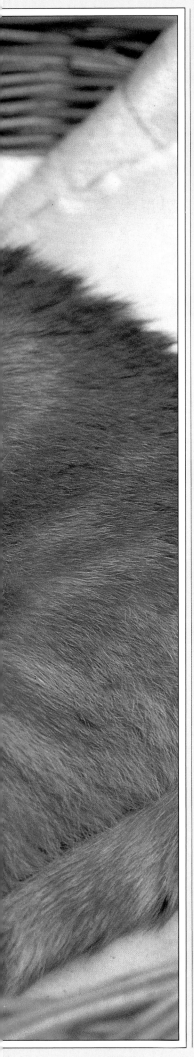

Part Two

PRACTICAL SECTION

*Essential information for everyone who owns a cat
or is thinking of buying one.*

Contrary to their undeserved reputation for being aloof, cats are charming and devoted companions who comfort us with affection and amuse us with their antics. What's more, cats are meticulously clean and supremely self-sufficient. They are content to spend the day indoors when we are away and are pleased to see us when we return. And just as their ancestors have adapted to meet the earth's changing conditions over the last three million years, modern-day cats adapt well to the restrictions of urban living and the cluttered schedules of two-career families or single-parent homes.

While not quite as significant a decision as choosing a mate, selecting a kitten (or an adult cat) to share your house with you is a matter that requires some thought. In the eleven chapters that follow in the Practical Section, we will explain everything you will need to know in order to get off on the right feet with your furry new friend.

Choosing a Cat, in addition to providing tips that make it easy to select a healthy kitten, is intended to evoke an internal dialogue on the readers' part. For the best cat keepers are those who understand their motives for wanting a cat and who choose a cat that is most compatible with their own habits.

The New Kitten supplies a list of the equipment and materials you will need to have ready before you bring your kitten home. This chapter also contains hints on how to make your house kitten-proof and on the best way to introduce your kitten to his new surroundings.

Knowing Your Cat discusses the feline psyche, which is not as mysterious as many writers would have us believe. Indeed, the more we know about the effects of evolution and domestication on feline behaviour, the less we are apt to be confounded by the cat's proclivities.

The chapters on *Feeding, Grooming* and *Basic Health Care* are treatises that discuss what, when and how much you should feed your cat; how often you should groom him and how you should go about doing it; and how to recognize symptoms that indicate your cat is unwell.

Breeding and Rearing measures the responsibilities and rewards of raising cats — and advises straight away that these are activities not to be indulged in lightly.

The History of the Cat explains the circumstances attending the domestication of the cat and discusses how they have affected the cat's development.

Genetics and Pedigrees provides the first words — there has yet to be a text that provides the last words — on setting goals, devising a breeding programme to attain those goals, and selecting the cats to take that programme from the drawing board to the show pen.

Showing Your Cat guides you one step at a time through the processes of locating and entering a cat show, and then preparing yourself and your cat for the royal debut.

The final chapter, *The Law and Your Cat*, informs you of your rights and responsibilities as an owner — and contains some gentle reminders about a cat's rights.

Overall, the chapters in the Practical Section are intended to make everyday life more enjoyable for you and your cat for many years to come.

1

CHOOSING A CAT

Once you have set your heart on owning a cat, do not rush straight out and get one — unless, of course, one has got you already. Instead, ask yourself some questions, such as: do you want a show cat as well as a pet? Will you want to breed it — and why? Do you prefer a male or a female? A longhair or a shorthair? And do you want just one cat, or two?

Show cat or pet?
All cats can be classified into three types: show, breeder and pet. These classifications apply to form as well as function — and, of course, to price. According to form, a show cat is one that hews closely enough to its breed standard that it can be reasonably expected to defeat many, if not most, of the fellow members of its breed in competition. Breeder-quality cats are cats of varying merit. For some reason — either they are almost good enough to be show cats, or their pedigrees read like the royal family's — breeder cats are deemed by their breeders and/or the people who want to buy them to have a contribution to make to the furtherance of their breed. Pet-quality cats — an unfortunate and snobbish-sounding term — are those with sufficient cosmetic liabilities to preclude their success as show cats or breeders. A pet-quality Persian, for example, may have ears that are too large, or a nose that is too long for showing or breeding. Yet it will still be able to hear and smell proficiently, especially around dinner time.

The terms show, breeder and pet denote function as well as form. You may want to buy a beautiful creature that you have seen for sale, but have no intention of showing it. You want it simply because you fell in love with it or, perhaps, because

Above: A Blue Exotic Shorthair. If you do not have the time to groom a longhaired cat, this could be the breed for you.

Left: Tabbies make excellent pets: they are affectionate, good with children and, like all shorthairs, easy to groom.

only the finest is good enough for you. Chances are the owner will not sell you the cat, but if she did, even though it was a show cat and you were buying it at a show price, it would simply be a pet to you. Normally, however, people looking for a cat to function solely as a pet end up buying a pet-quality kitten or cat.

Finally, some people are interested in showing but not in breeding. If you fall into this category, you should look for a show-quality kitten. Many breeders are happy to sell show-quality kittens to people who will have the kittens altered when they are old enough and who will show them when they are adults in classes for altered cats.

Male or female?
Some people, for personal reasons, prefer male or female cats as pets; but either sex — if given love, attention, and someone to cuddle up with at night — will make a charming companion.

Spaying a female cat will cost one third to one half more than neutering a male, and neutered males, as they get older, should not be fed a diet whose mineral composition would produce a base rather than an acid urine. (See Feeding Your Cat, page 97.) Otherwise there is no difference in the cost associated with — or the care required in — housing an altered male or female.

Breeders and vets generally recommend that females be altered when they are six months old, and males when they are seven-to-ten months old. Sexual development is nearly complete at these ages, but undesirable habits such as spraying by male cats have yet to become habitual.

Whole, or unaltered, cats are not so user-friendly to live with as altered cats. Males tend to spray their urine about the house to attract females. Males are also likely to regard any cat — male or female, young or old, in season or out — as a potential mate or sparring partner. Females will come into season periodically, a condition that will be accompanied by frequent caterwauling, restlessness, excessive attachment to their owners, occasional spraying of their urine, and an inclination to bolt out of doors a fraction of a second after these have been opened.

One cat or two?
If you have no other pets and there is no one to keep your cat company during the day while you are away, you should consider getting two

kittens. If buying a second pedigree kitten would break your budget, adopt a kitten — one that's roughly the same age as the pedigree kitten you are purchasing — from a local animal shelter. Not only will you receive double the pleasure by being able to watch two kittens playing instead of one, but a kitten is also less apt to be bored or lonely if it has another kitten to keep it company in your absence.

When you adopt a kitten from an animal shelter, you should follow the same guidelines — presented later in this chapter — that you would follow when purchasing a kitten.

Testing for personality

Kitten personalities range from the vivid to the vapourish. The vivid sort wade right into the scrum of flying bodies at playtime. Kittens that roll and tumble with their mates are likely to be healthy and developing normally. Kittens sitting on the sidelines might just not be feeling well, or they may have that vapourish kind of character that means they will need extra patience and attention.

To test a kitten's personality, wiggle your fingers along the floor about 6in. (15cm) in front of the animal. Or dangle a small toy back and forth about the same distance away. Now watch the kitten's reaction carefully. Does the kitten leap to investigate? Does he shy away in fright? Does he dash off under the sofa?

Well-adjusted kittens are curious about fingers, toys, keys and more-or-less everything else that moves in their domain. Shy kittens are more cautious. Poorly adjusted kittens go to ground beneath the nearest chair.

If you have other pets or children, the inquisitive, pleased-to-meet-you kitten is the best choice. He will probably adjust more quickly and get along better with other family members. The bashful kitten might well make a fine companion, too; but he may take longer to adjust, and is, perhaps, a better choice for someone who has owned a pet before but who hasn't got one just now. And the little pair of eyes under the chair? Shy kittens need love, too. If you do not already have pets and if you have the time and patience required to nurture such a waif, this could be the kitten for you. If not, perhaps the next person who comes along will be the perfect owner for this shy creature.

The healthy kitten

A healthy kitten's eyes are bright. His nose is cool and slightly damp. His gums are neither pale nor inflamed. His ears are free of wax or dirt. His body is soft and smooth, a little lean, perhaps, but not skinny. His coat is shiny and free of bald patches, scabs or tiny specks of black dirt. The area around his tail is free of both dirt and discoloration.

Tearful eyes suggest poor health — especially in concert with a dry, warm nose. Inflamed gums may indicate gingivitis or, if they are pale, anemia. Waxy ears are signs of neglect; caked-on dirt around the ears may indicate ear mites.

Protruding ribs or bellies are signs either of undernourishment or of worms. A dull coat or one that is dotted with scabs, tiny specks of dirt or bald spots, usually means ringworm, fungus or fleas.

When you select a kitten, ask the breeder if the animal is used to being groomed, how frequently it has been groomed, and what sort of comb or brush the breeder uses with the kitten. If you collect the kitten at the breeder's house, ask for a grooming demonstration.

How old is old enough?

New owners are eager to take their kittens home as soon as possible. Nevertheless, responsible breeders do not let kittens go until they are 12 weeks old. A twelve-week-old kitten has been weaned and has been eating solid food for about six weeks. He has begun to make the transition to adulthood. Furthermore, a 12-week-old kitten has had most, if not all, of his inoculations.

While breeders may sometimes let an especially mature kitten go at eleven weeks, kittens much younger than that are still babies. Take them away from their mothers and their siblings at that age, and the stress of adjusting to new surroundings may cause them to become sick, untidy in the use of their litter trays or to 'nurse' on blankets or sofa cushions — a habit they might then keep all their lives.

Unfortunately, some breeders are eager to place kittens as quickly as possible. This applies especially to those breeders who have many kittens underfoot. Do not let an irresponsible breeder persuade you into taking a kitten that is too young.

Buying a pedigree cat

People interested in breeding should buy the best female they can find. They should also remember that quality cannot always be measured by price and that registration papers simply guarantee that a cat is eligible to be registered, not that he is good enough to be shown.

Novices are at some peril when evaluating a kitten's show potential. Most members of a breed look alike to the untrained eye, and, therefore, attributes of the proper size, shape and setting are more difficult for newcomers to identify. Because kittens are still immature, this difficulty is, of course, magnified.

Once you have decided on the breed you want to acquire, visit shows, talk to people working with that breed, watch classes being judged, note carefully what the winning cats look like, mark down the numbers of the cats you like best and see if your selections match those of the judges. If possible, visit several breeders who are willing to spend an afternoon or an evening 'showing' their cats at home.

Most importantly, read your breed's standard until you have memorized it. Take a copy along when you go to look at kittens. Ask breeders to explain where a kitten meets the standard and where he does not. If the breeder does not object, take an experienced breeder with you when you go to look at kittens.

If you are buying a kitten from someone who lives in another part of the country, you may have nothing more on which to base an informed decision than a few pictures, plus the breeder's glowing

---

Below: A girl with her new kitten. It is best to resist the temptation to bring a kitten home until it is about 12 weeks old.

Above: Young kittens at play. If you are away all day, consider buying two cats, not one: they will keep each other happy.

description of the kitten. If the pictures are not of the best quality, request additional ones. If, in the end, you feel you cannot fully trust the breeder, find another breeder.

When you buy a show cat, you are buying an assortment of genes that the cat has inherited from its ancestors. The names and titles of

Below: This Chinchilla revels in the close attention of a devoted and caring human companion.

the first four or five generations of those ancestors are recorded on a cat's pedigree. Study that pedigree to see what titles the members of a cat's family have won. Note especially the parents and grand-parents — for the first two generations exert the greatest influence on a cat's development.

Although some kittens look smashing from birth, the average youngster goes through several stages when growing up — from prince to toad and back again — and sometimes vice versa. Thus, buyers should not purchase a potential show-quality kitten until he is five or six months old. It is difficult to predict how good a 12-week-old kitten will look when he is eight

months old. But clearly, the older the cat, the easier that judgement is to make. A five- or six-month-old kitten is less subject to change without notice, and buyers are wise to wait until a potential show kitten has reached that age, and preferably until he has been shown, before signing the cheque.

Contracts

When buying a kitten, it is best to record the terms of the exchange formally in a written contract. Most contracts are elementary documents that indicate the price of the kitten, the amount of the deposit required to hold the kitten, if any, and precisely when the balance of the payment is due, and so on.

Contracts may also stipulate that if the buyer can no longer keep the kitten (or no longer wishes to keep it), the breeder must be given first opportunity to buy the kitten back at the going rate for kittens or cats. Finally, a contract should allow the new owner three to five working days in which to take a kitten to a vet for an examination. If the vet discovers pre-existing conditions such as leukaemia or feline infectious peritonitis, the buyer should have the right to return the kitten at the seller's expense and to have the purchase price refunded.

Buyers should be given a receipt for any payments made, and they should find out in advance — and in writing if they wish — whether a deposit is refundable if they decide not to take the kitten. Buyers should also remember that once a breeder has accepted money or some other consideration in return for reserving a kitten, he or she has entered into an option contract. The breeder cannot legally revoke the offer if the kitten turns out to be much better than he or she had anticipated.

In addition to the pedigree that records a kitten's ancestors, a new owner may receive 'papers' when he buys a pedigreed cat. These papers usually consist of a registration slip that the new owner fills out and sends, along with the appropriate fee, to the administrative office of the association in which that kitten's litter has been registered. The association then returns a certificate of ownership to the new owner.

Anyone buying a cat or kitten that has been already registered by his breeder will receive an owner's certificate. There is a transfer-of-ownership section on the back of that certificate which must be signed by the breeder and the new owner. The new owner then mails the certificate, with the appropriate transfer fee, to the administrative office of the association in which the cat has been registered. The association will send back a new, amended certificate of ownership to the new owner(s).

Health records

Health records and inoculation certificates should also accompany a kitten to his new home. Do not accept a kitten without them. Some breeders in the United States, especially those that produce large numbers of kittens, like to save money by giving inoculations themselves. Most experienced breeders are competent enough to do this but few, if any, are sufficiently skilled or knowledgeable to examine kittens as thoroughly as a vet can. An examination by a qualified vet prior to a kitten's initial inoculation is important because vaccine given to a sick kitten will do more harm than good. In the UK, vets are the only people qualified to treat animals.

Lastly, all kittens being shipped by air should be accompanied by a health certificate issued by a vet — and by a certificate verifying that a kitten has received his rabies shot if such is required by the country (or state) in which the buyer resides.

2

THE NEW KITTEN

According to a Russian folk tale, a person who brings a new cat home should throw the animal onto the bed at once. If the cat settles down promptly, it will remain with its new owner, and life will be good.

Perhaps this hit-and-miss method works in Russia, but it is certainly true that cats require more from the human-cat relationship than merely being tossed onto a bed. In truth, cats are more inclined to settle into the home if their new owners have laid in some basic supplies in anticipation of their cats' arrival. It is also best to have conducted a meticulous safety check of the home as well.

Feeding dishes and water bowl
Reusable plastic can retain odours even if it is washed carefully after each use. Disposable dishes are, in the long term, expensive and wasteful of resources. Glass, ceramic or metal dishes and bowls are the best choice. Whatever kind you choose, the bowl should be sufficiently heavy so as to prevent it tipping over easily. If the bowl is made of glass, it should be sturdy enough not to break, crack or chip when a cat knocks it over.

Placemats
Whether made of vinyl paper or plain rubber, placemats will protect the floor or carpet where food dishes and water bowls have been placed.

Food
Most speciality shops sell a wide selection of foods that will suit a cat's palate and meet his nutritional needs. In short, you do not need to have taken a correspondence course in feline nutrition in order to be able to feed a cat properly. The owner merely needs to select foods that provide 100-per-cent-complete

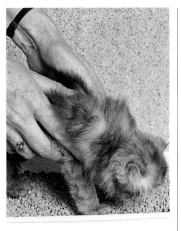

Above: This Persian kitten's owner is introducing her new kitten to the litter tray. Usually, house-training kittens is not difficult.

Left: Every kitten or cat should have its own place to sleep. Later, these Somali kittens should be provided with their own beds.

nutrition for the appropriate stage or for all stages of a cat's life. Making that selection is simple, because cat food labels should tell you whether a food may be fed to all cats, to adult cats only, or to adult cats and kittens, but only on an intermittent or supplemental basis.

Fresh water, of course, should be available to your kitten at all times. Chances are that by the time a kitten is 12 weeks old, he will have virtually outgrown the need for milk. As kittens mature, they lose the enzymes required to process milk. Once this has occurred, in fact, milk actually has an upsetting effect on a kitten's stomach and digestive system. (See Feeding Your Cat, page 115, for a complete discussion of cat nutrition.)

Litter
While most litter is sufficiently absorbent to perform the task requested of it, no litter is entirely dust-free, no matter what the claims of its manufacturer. As a rule, the finer the grains of the litter, the more likely they are to get scattered about on the floor, especially if the tray is not enclosed or fitted with a detachable rim. Deodorant litter, while frequently more expensive than the standard kind, is not always worth the extra cost.

Recently, a new kind of litter has become available. This variety is designed to 'clump up' when wet. And clump it does, making waste removal much easier for the cat owner. The one drawback to this litter is that a light breeze is enough to scatter it across the room. It should, therefore, only be used in an enclosed litter tray.

Litter trays
Like cars, litter trays come in several styles. Some are open, some enclosed and some are equipped with raised, detachable rims. The enclosed and raised-rim models are designed to keep the litter inside the tray when the cat is using it. Whatever the design, however, litter trays should be at least 19in. (48cm) by 15in. (38cm) by 4in. (10cm) deep, and should be made of sturdy, washable material.

Litter tray liners
These are convenient because they allow you to bundle up the contents of the litter tray and discard them in one fell swoop. Tray liners are not always practical, though, because some thoughtless cats have a tendency to poke holes in them; then, when you lift the liner up to carry it across the room to the rubbish bin, you leave clouds of dust along the way. Liners are most

apt to earn their keep in a hotel or motel, where convenience and tidiness are of the essence.

Litter scoop
Litter scoops, like foul-weather shoes, ought to be sturdy and sensible. In fact, the sturdier the better. And always have one or two spares on hand.

Beds
Cats that are presented with elaborate and precious-looking beds frequently disdain them in favour of a comfortable windowsill, a well-worn chair or their owners' pillows. Accordingly, before you buy a bed for your cat, observe carefully where the animal prefers to sleep, then buy a bed that fits neatly into that spot, thereby making the place more comfortable for your cat. And don't be surprised if the cat then removes the bed and sleeps in the spot as it was before.

Grooming implements
Although cats are naturally fastidious creatures, supplemental grooming from their owners should be a part of every cat's routine — a daily routine for longhaired breeds that are being shown, a less frequent routine for other longhairs and for shorthaired cats. Pet shops, many veterinary surgeries and vendors at cat shows sell shampoos, nail clippers, combs, brushes, powders, ointments and sprays for your cat. These items and their use are discussed in Grooming Your Cat, (page 121).

Scratching post
A scratching post can spare the furniture from damage while providing cats with a safe, convenient and healthy outlet for exercising their natural inclination to scratch. The post should be well anchored so that it will not tip over when used, and it should be tall enough so that adult cats can stretch, and thus exercise their muscles, while scratching. The scratching surface should be made of strong, resilient material such as sisal or hemp. Floor-to-ceiling posts with shelves for cats to sit on should be especially well anchored and secure.

Window perches
These are recommended for rooms in which the windows are not deep enough to accommodate a reclining cat. The perch can easily be clamped to the window frame, even by people who do not possess degrees in structural engineering.

Carrying boxes
You will need a safe, sturdy and secure carrier in which to bring your cat home for the first time. You will also require a carrier when taking your cat to the vet for annual check-ups, and for any emergencies. Finally, you may need the carrier to transport your cat to shows or to your holiday home in the country.

A good carrier, as well as having a secure handle and an escape-proof door latch, should be well ventilated and washable. Heavy-moulded plastic carriers are the best choice. They can be bought at pet shops, at cat shows and at some airline cargo offices. One important piece of equipment is a towel or small blanket to place on the floor of the carrier.

Many people cover the outside of their carriers with fitted, quilted covers in cold weather. These bonnets, which resemble toaster covers, are available at shows or from companies that advertise in cat magazines. Alternatively, you can make your own if you wish.

Toys and other diversions
Humans have devoted much thought (and considerable capital) to devising entertainment for cats. Consider the variety of cat toys available at pet shops or cat shows: stuffed toys, bouncing toys, rolling toys, toys infused with catnip or without; peacock feathers and sparkling, multicoloured strips of plastic; shaker toys that look like miniature rubber spaghetti mops; brightly coloured balls that play a tune when they are bounced about the room; toys that, when wound up, scuttle across the carpet; organically grown catnip; clockwork mice; and other diversions too numerous to relate.

The most important element in the design of a toy is its safety. Balls

Above: A covered litter tray allows the cat some privacy — and is more pleasing to the people living in the house.

Below: Cats tend to avoid elaborate or precious-looking beds: a simple basket in a quiet corner will suit most cats down to the ground.

house and numerous shelves for climbing or sitting. Be sure that the run has a roof and that it is completely escape-proof.

Cat-proofing your house

Bringing a kitten into your house is not that much different from adopting a two-year-old child with astonishing athletic ability. All cats, no matter how young, are hunters and explorers by nature. They are keenly territorial as well, inclined to examine new objects and openings and anything else that is new in their domain. If there are rooms you do not want your cat to investigate, keep the doors to them closed. If there are small, delicate objects in the rooms your cat is allowed to visit, move those objects beyond the cat's reach. Make sure all balconies are enclosed, all window screens are secure, and all electrical cables are intact, not frayed or badly connected. Cats — and especially kittens — like to gnaw on electrical cables. It might be sensible to wrap exposed cables in heavy tape, or cover them with plastic tubing, which you can buy in a motor repair or supply shop. Indeed, until you are quite certain your cat does not have a taste for electrical cables, it's a wise precaution to unplug all appliances that are not in use. To prevent your cat from getting a shock from an electricity socket, cover it with a plastic, plug-in socket guard, which you can buy at an ironmonger or electricity showroom.

All kitchen, toilet and bathroom cleansers should be stored in cupboards that can be tightly closed or locked. Keep the lids of all rubbish bins closed. Consider replacing rubbish containers that have swing-open lids that could be dislodged if your cat were to overturn the container. Another lid to keep closed is that of the toilet.

When you shut any door in your house — the front door, back door, refrigerator door, wardrobe doors, the doors on washing machines and dishwashers or driers — be sure that your cat is not on the wrong side of it. Keep the bathroom door closed when you are filling the bath. When you are cleaning, rinse all solutions and chemicals thoroughly from any surfaces on which a cat is likely to walk. What gets on a cat's paws usually winds up in his stomach.

Return sewing needles, thread and the like to their proper storage places after you have finished using them. Do not leave rubber bands, hot irons, cigarettes, plastic bags or pieces of string lying about. As suggested above, learn to think like a cat who is looking for any kind of mischief: the tinsel on a Christmas tree, a dangling tablecloth, a hot burner on the cooker.

To discourage your cat from jumping onto the cooker, put him gently on the floor whenever you find him doing so. Then say 'No!' sharply, and clap your hands or stamp your foot. Use the same technique to discourage him from jumping onto the kitchen table or any other place you do not want his feet to touch.

with tiny bells inside should be sufficiently sturdy to prevent the cat removing the bells and swallowing them. The eyes, noses and other appendages on small, stuffed mice and other such toy animals should be very firmly fixed for the same reason, as should streamers or any attachments on other toys. Before you buy a toy for your cat, imagine yourself in the cat's position and try to think of every possible way in which the animal could injure himself with it. Unless you are certain that the toy is perfectly safe, do not buy it.

High-tech, store-bought toys are, of course, only one of the alternatives when it comes to keeping your pet entertained. Cats will amuse themselves by the hour with a crumpled piece of paper, an empty film canister, a cardboard box (turned upside down and with holes cut at either end) or with a plain paper bag.

The same reservations expressed about store-bought toys apply to the home-made kind. Toys should not have dangling strings, in which cats may get entangled, or which they may even swallow. Similarly, avoid bits or pieces that cats can chew off and eat, or sharp edges on which they may hurt themselves. What's more, cellophane, plastic wrap, aluminium foil, twist ties from sandwich and rubbish bags, rubber bands and cotton swabs should never be left lying about within the curious cat's reach.

Fresh air

An outdoor run is beneficial for cats that cannot be given complete freedom to come and go as they please. If there is plenty of wildlife to be observed in the garden, your cat

Above: A Tonkinese enjoys a deluxe scratching post. The scratching surface should be made of a strong material such as sisal.

Below: A bicolour kitten with a wall-mounted scratching post tall enough to allow a mature cat to stretch and exercise its muscles.

will be happier out of doors than sitting inside.

Outdoor runs can lead off the house or be constructed as stand-alone units in the garden or yard. An outdoor run should include provisions for sunbathing and for getting in out of the sun. The run should contain a small, heated

Finally, keep poisonous plants out of reach. Poinsettia, philodendron, dieffenbachia, caladium, English ivy (in the US only), hydrangea, Jerusalem cherry, mistletoe and holly are some of the plants poisonous to cats. Ask your vet for a complete list.

Welcoming the new cat

You have bought every item on your shopping list. You have washed the litter tray, filled it with 1½ in.(4cm) to 2in. (5cm) of litter, and have put it in a quiet spot away from places where your cat will be eating or sleeping. You have checked the house for the tenth time to make sure that it is 'cat-proof'. At last, it is time to bring your new cat home.

If you work during the week, schedule the welcoming party for the start of a weekend or a holiday, when you will have more time to devote to your cat. And remember that even though you have planned carefully for this day, the event will

Above right: The big outdoors awaits this Black tipped British Shorthair, making its first, tentative, foray into its owner's garden.

Below: If your kitten cannot be given complete freedom, an outdoor run will enable it to enjoy the fresh air in complete safety.

come as something of a surprise to your cat, who is not in the habit of planning any further ahead than his next meal.

Being moved summarily to a new home can be a very disturbing experience for a kitten. He will be leaving his mum, his playmates, his keepers, his favourite things and the only home he has ever known. Some kittens adjust well. After they are taken from their carriers and placed in their new litter trays, they look around as if to say, 'Nice home you've got here. Is there anything to eat?'

Other cats are less self-possessed. So do not be surprised if the new

arrival appears apprehensive at first — or looks around and then scampers under the sofa. Pull up a chair and have a cup of tea. or something more robust. Watch television or read the newspaper. The quiet sounds of everyday life will have a calming effect on your cat. Eventually his curiosity will get the better of him.

If your curiosity about your new pet gets the better of you, a toy or a plate of food might lure the cat from his hiding-place. No cat will wish to spend eternity hidden beneath a sofa. Once he has taken the measure of the underside of the sofa, the cat will be ready to familiarize himself with other parts of your house. His instinct to explore will draw him out.

New cats feel more at home if they have something to remind them of their old home: a favourite toy, a blanket or bed, a familiar food, even a small amount of soiled litter scattered in the new tray. These items all emit well-known smells that are comforting and reassuring to the kitten in his strange, new world.

Litter training

As soon as your new cat is in the house, take him out of his carrier and place him in the litter tray. Virtually all cats have been dependably litter-trained by the time

they are 12 weeks old, and even in new surroundings a cat's instinct for cleanliness will direct him to his tray — as long as he knows where the tray is. Always keep the tray in the same quiet, easy-to-reach place. For the first few days, place your cat in the tray after meals, naps and hearty play to reinforce his instincts. Praise your cat quietly after he has used the tray. Do not allow him to wander far from the room where the tray is unless you are going to be there to supervise him. If you leave your cat alone in the house, confine him to the tray room, and be sure to leave food and water there.

If your cat makes a mistake, clean the spot with a non-ammonia-based, disinfectant cleaner, then sprinkle a bit of white vinegar and salt on the spot to remove odour. Because a cat's attention span is approximately 20 seconds long, you will not be 'teaching him a lesson' if, well after the event, you drag him to the scene of the

Above right: Once your cat has settled in, he will soon find a favourite place to sleep and relax in, both indoors and (if you allow it) outside.

Below: An outdoor run should be as large as you can afford, with shelves at different heights for exercise and amusement and a house for shelter.

accident and scold him. This will only teach your cat that humans behave in strange ways at times. Indeed, the practice of dragging a cat to a spot where he misbehaved hours before and scolding him is an odd one. If you came home and found a wet spot in the litter tray, you wouldn't fetch your cat,

carry him to the tray and say, 'Now that's a good kitty' would you?

If you catch your cat in the act of misbehaving, a stern, disapproving 'No!' will convey your displeasure. When your cat has finished relieving himself, carry him gently to the tray, place him in it, and remind him that this is where business is

conducted. If accidents are repeated, perhaps the litter tray is too remote for your cat's convenience. Or perhaps the tray is located too close to the places where your cat eats or sleeps. There should be at least one tray on every floor of the house to which a cat has access.

Dirty trays also can lead to accidents. All waste should be scooped out of the tray and disposed of each day. Additional litter should be added as required. Once a week — or sooner if your nose suggests — dump all the litter, wash the tray thoroughly with a mild, non-ammonia-based cleaner, rinse well, and put an inch or two of fresh litter in the tray.

If your cat is accustomed to one kind of litter, keep using that brand. Cats are creatures of habit as well as cleanliness. Changing to a new brand of litter might play havoc with your cat's routine, which itself could result in accidents.

Children and other pets

Some children are too young or immature to treat a cat properly. They might constitute a threat to a cat's sense of confidence and safety. If you have young toddlers, you should wait until they are about four years old before buying a cat or a kitten.

Children should not be allowed to interact with pets until the children are mature enough to understand that cats do not like to be disturbed when they are eating or sleeping, that there is a proper way to hold a cat, that cats are not toys to be carted about the house, and that a litter tray is not a sandbox.

Some breeders will not agree to sell a cat to anyone who has children until they (the breeders) have had a chance to meet the youngsters. Conversely, buyers who have children ought to look for breeders whose kittens have been raised in a family atmosphere.

Children must be made to understand that what is fun for them may be painful for their cats. Thus, when you cat-proof your house before bringing a new cat home, schedule a briefing session with the kids. Explain that they have to be careful to watch where they walk and run when the cat is around. Tell them that cats are often frightened by loud, unfamiliar sounds. Ask them to speak and play quietly until the cat gets used to them. Caution them not to pick the cat up until you feel he is comfortable enough in his new surroundings not to be scared by a sudden ride preceded by a dramatic vertical take off. Demonstrate the proper way to hold a cat: one hand under the cat's rib cage just behind the front legs, the other hand under the cat's bottom, with the cat's face pointing away from you. Make your children practise this technique while sitting down, in case they drop the cat or he jumps from their arms. Reinforce your sound advice by setting a good example yourself.

Cats can instil a sense of responsibility in children, but children should never be made to take care of animals in which they have no interest. Even when a child willingly cooperates in taking care of a cat, parents should keep a careful eye on the cat's food dish and water bowl and be aware of the general condition of its litter tray. Parents should also remember that when they buy kittens for their children, they are really buying kittens for themselves. Sooner or later the most cat-responsible adolescents grow up and leave home, and they cannot always be counted on to take their cats with them.

Caution must also be exercised when you introduce a cat to any other four-legged members of the family. The chances of hostilities breaking out depend on the age of the cat which is already in residence and on how long it has lived in the house. If your eight-year-old cat has previously had the house to itself, you should probably not get a new cat or kitten. If your cat is four years old or younger, you should be able to introduce a new cat if you manage the introduction carefully. But remind yourself first how you would feel if a stranger were suddenly brought to your house for an indefinite stay without proper introduction and letters of reference.

Bring the new cat home at a weekend or holiday. Before you do, prepare a room where the newcomer will spend some time in isolation. Do not select the old cat's favourite den or resting place for this purpose. Your aim is to fit the new cat into the old cat's routine — you do not want to make the old cat feel disenfranchised.

Solitary confinement is always recommended for a new cat, no matter how up-to-the-moment the old cat's inoculations are, or how well the new cat fared during its veterinary inspection. Until you are satisfied that the new cat is not incubating any infections that were not identified during the veterinary inspection — that is, for ten days to two weeks — he should have no direct, prolonged contact with the old cat.

The new cat should, of course, have plenty of visits from you. And be sure to disinfect your hands thoroughly after each visit.

For a few days allow the cats to sniff, and perhaps hiss, at one another from either side of a closed door. When you feel the time is right (and after you have clipped both cats' claws), put the new cat into the cat carrier, open the door to his room, and allow the old cat to saunter in for a ten-minute visit. Be sure to remove the new cat's water

Below: Handling a kitten the correct way will stop you being scratched: with its hind end supported by one hand, this kitten feels secure.

bowl, food dish, and litter tray first, just in case he is carrying an infectious disease.

Repeat these daily visits until most of the serious hissing, growling or back-arching has subsided, then allow the cats unrestrained, but supervised, contact. Bring the old cat into the isolation ward for a visit, but do not confine the new cat beforehand. Put the old cat on the floor and retire to a corner. Have a blanket, a broom and a bucket of cold water or a water gun handy. All should go well; but if warfare breaks out, use the bucket of water, the gun, and/or the broom to separate the cats. Then throw the blanket over the nearest combatant. While he is wriggling about furiously underneath the blanket, pick him up carefully but firmly and return him to his original territory.

After you have given peace a chance for a day or so, begin holding the brief introductory sessions again. A few days after that, attempt the free-range introduction once more. Perhaps things will go more smoothly this time. If they do not, you may have a long-term problem on your hands: these cats may never become friends. The best arrangement they may be able to achieve is a cool but mutually tolerant relationship. Reversing the introductory procedure — that is, confining the old cat to one room and allowing the new cat to wander over the house — may sensitize each cat to the other's scent and diffuse the situation. It is worth a try.

To introduce a new cat to a resident dog, you should follow much the same procedure. You have the advantage here, however, of being able to put a lead on the dog before taking him in to meet the cat. The lead will make it easier for you to pull the dog off the cat if they start fighting, though you still may need the water bucket to persuade the cat to leave the dog alone.

Do not allow the dog off the lead until you are certain that the animals will not start fighting. Be especially careful if you own a terrier, a sight hound, a retriever, or any other kind of dog that might consider the cat fair game.

Conclusion

Once your kitten has adjusted to his new home, you and he will settle into a comfortable routine that will constitute one of the more civilized and pleasant aspects of your day. If the kitten has the run of the house — and why should he not? — he will want to sleep near to you. When you are reading, he will want to help turn the pages. When you are cleaning, he will take a keen interest in all you do. There will be few people whose company you will enjoy as much and no one — save the most devoted of spouses — who will enjoy your company more.

3

KNOWING YOUR CAT

The more you understand your cat — the more you learn about its needs, desires, instincts and, perhaps, neuroses — the more you will enjoy its company. First, you should remember that a cat is not a dog and should not be expected to behave like one. Cats can be trained to retrieve objects, walk on a harness, jump through hoops and perform other tricks — if any of that is important to you. But the chances are such activities will not be as important to your cat, nor will they be learned or performed by a cat as readily and as cheerfully as they will be by a dog. If you require that sort of obedience and performance in a pet, perhaps you should have a dog as well as, or instead of, a cat.

Yet for all their renowned independence — and for their talent for doing what they wish while getting what they want — cats are willing to dance attendance on our comings and goings as if they were front-page news. Their dance, however, is a minuet, not a jitterbug. Their song a *chanson*, not an opera. Their poetry a *haiku*, not an epic.

Instincts

Cats are born into this world with a variety of instincts in place. These instincts shape many aspects of the cat's behaviour. Understanding these instincts — and understanding that some behaviour which you might consider unsuitable is completely normal from the cat's point of view — will make your relationship with your cat a more rewarding one, and vice-versa.

Scratching. Because your cat will scratch instinctively, it is better to provide a suitable place for exercising this instinct rather than leaving the choice of a place up to

Above: A cat will chase and jump at moving toys. This should be encouraged to keep your pet amused and well exercised.

Left: Hunting is a natural pursuit for cats. Outdoors they will find plenty of things to stalk and chase, so keeping themselves fit.

your cat. If you have a scratching post on hand before you obtain your cat, he will probably prefer it to most other surfaces most of the time. If accidents occur, this is what to do.

Wave a toy directly in front of the scratching post so that your cat's claws dig into the post as they grab for the toy. Two or three times after realizing how good it feels to sink its claws into the post, the cat will get the idea. Then wave the toy farther up the post so that the cat is encouraged to climb to reach it.

Play this game two or three times a day for a few days. The cat will soon be climbing the post as though a neighbourhood dog were in hot pursuit, and the scratching problem will be over.

Playing. This instinct is associated with hunting. Indeed, the cat is the only animal to play with its prey before killing it. Toys for the indoor cat are, therefore, an important means of keeping your cat exercised, amused and in tune with its nature.

The cat's senses

The cat can be said to have nine senses: touch, smell, taste, sight, hearing, temperature, balance, place and time.

Touch. This sense conveys the sensations of pressure, temperature and pain. A kitten becomes aware of touch through early contact with its mother. The mother washes the young kitten with her tongue and moves the kitten towards her in the nest with her paws. Thus, the kitten learns to associate its mother's tongue with a caring attitude. Later in life the kitten will make the same association with attentive, or even absent-minded, stroking from a human hand. Petting and grooming are said to reduce tension by slowing down the heart rate. This is perhaps the reason why a cat will often start to wash itself in situations that evoke stress.

The importance of a cat's fore-paws as a source of tactile information is suggested by the size of the area of the cat's brain that receives messages from the fore-paws. In fact, all four paw pads are extremely sensitive. They provide information about the texture of objects and about their temperature as well. Some people believe that a cat's paw pads can detect vibrations, which explains why some cats appear to be able to hear through their feet.

The sense of touch is also employed when a cat chooses a place to sleep. Cats like warm, soft fabrics and will often refuse to stay on the lap of someone wearing a cold or slippery dress or one made of synthetic fibre.

Smell. This is another sense that develops early in the nest. If young, neonatal kittens are moved from a familiar nest into a new one, they may begin to cry — the smell of this new nest, different from the one to which they had become accustomed, causes them distress. Often kittens will not settle down in the new nest until their mother rejoins them and reassures them, by her smell, that all is well.

Kittens seem to become attached to one specific nipple when they are breast-feeding. The sense of smell is probably what guides them to the nipple of their choice. In later life their sense of smell is the chosen instrument that cats use to investigate and inspect any new object brought into the house.

The difference in capability between a cat's sense of smell and a human's is considerable. Humans may be able to smell a clove of garlic when it is still attached to the bulb (if we are close enough), but we can only smell it keenly when it has been minced and is being sautéed in olive oil in the frying pan. The cat, it is safe to assume, can smell the garlic at that latter, high-impact level before we even get it out of the shopping bag.

When cats rub up against a piece of furniture or a human leg, they leave a scent mark on that surface. Similarly, two cats rubbing heads will leave their scent on each other so that they will recognize one another the next time they meet. If one cat in a household of several goes off to visit a stud cat to be mated, she may be rejected at first by the others when she returns home because she is carrying the unfamiliar scent of the stud cat.

In the same way, your cat will know when you have been to a house where there are other cats, and the cats in that house will have been more than a little interested in you because you will have been trailing clouds of scent from the cats in your house. The scent of one cat probably tells another cat far more about its age, sex and health than we humans, with our primitive senses of smell, can suspect.

Taste. The sense of taste begins to develop early in cats. One-day-old kittens have demonstrated an ability to distinguish between salted and non-salted liquids.

Taste is linked to smell, and a cat that for some reason cannot smell will often refuse to eat. This association between taste and smell is the reason that you will occasionally see your cat smelling with its mouth open, an activity known as 'flehming'. A cat in full flehmen is trapping airborne molecules of scent on its tongue and then pressing the tongue against the opening of its Jacobson's Organ, a small, cigar-shaped sac with a narrow passage leading from the roof of the mouth. Catnip, a stranger in the house or a female in season in the garden next door may trigger this reaction, which involves both taste and smell.

The cat's tongue is equipped with special detectors that are used to relay information about temperature and taste. From careful study, humans have learned much about taste reactions and preferences in cats. Of the four basic dimensions to taste in mammals — sweet, salt, bitter and acid — sweet is not important to cats. They are virtually alone among mammals in exhibiting no significant reaction to sweets. Yet this does not prevent cats from ingesting sweet substances, such as milk, that may later give them diarrhoea.

Sight. Cats are born blind, and their eyes remain closed for seven to ten days after birth. The retina is incompletely developed during early life, so a kitten's vision is poor. Vision improves gradually over a period of about three months, by the end of which the kitten is able to see as well as an adult cat.

The cat's are a hunter's eyes, set well forward on the head and aimed straight ahead so as to provide the best three-dimensional picture. The ligaments surrounding the lens of the cat's eye enable the lens to bulge out in order to focus on objects close at hand or to flatten in order to focus on objects that are further away. The cat's normal field of vision enables it to see most clearly objects that are 7ft (2.1m) to 20ft (6m) away.

Cats adjust to varying light conditions by narrowing or dilating their pupils. In the brightest sunlight, the cat's pupils are closed completely but for two tiny openings at the top and bottom of the pupil. In dim light the pupil may be as much as ½in. (1.2cm) wide.

Cats cannot see in total darkness. They are able to distinguish some colours from each other — mainly red from blue and both of these colours from white. But researchers believe that green, yellow and white are all the same in the eyes of a cat.

While their eyesight is acute, cats are able to see moving objects better than those which are immobile. This explains why cats often freeze when they are hunting — so their prey will not notice them — and, of course, why their prey often does the same.

Hearing. Cats have acute hearing and can detect sounds too faint and too highly pitched for humans to register. Furthermore, from a distance of 3ft (0.9m) cats are able to distinguish between two sound sources which are only 3in. (8cm) apart. The cat's remarkable hearing abilities enable it to detect the faintest squeaks and rustlings caused by small creatures that are completely hidden from view.

Temperature. Cats sense warmth and cold by means of receptors in their skin. They always seek out warm sleeping spots (the crooks of a reclining human's knees are a favourite spot). As their faces are the most cold-sensitive parts of their bodies, cats are quick to curl up into a ball when they are cold,

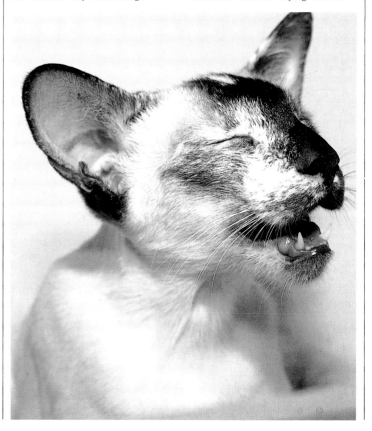

Above: A Blue Persian uses its fine sense of balance to climb high into a tree, where it sits silently hoping that a bird will fly within range.

Below: A Siamese cat complaining vocally about something. Attentive owners soon learn to understand what their cats are saying to them.

immobile until he is rescued by members of the fire brigade or he drops to the ground from exhaustion.

Nature seems to have played a cruel trick on cats — she has equipped them with powerful hindquarters and sharp claws that allow the animals to climb trees rapidly, while leaving them ill-equipped to come back down. Because their claws are curved backwards, they are of no use when descending from a tree: nor are their hindquarters much help. The wise cats reverse their steps, descending backwards from their perch in a tree or on a pole until they are close enough to the ground to drop down safely.

The cat's brain receives information regarding its place and orientation in the universe from its eyes and from a specialized sense organ called the vestibular apparatus. This organ forms part of the inner ear. It ascertains the direction and rate of acceleration of any movement of the head and sends this information to the brain, which constructs an internal 'picture' of the cat's location in space. This process is responsible for the cat's vaunted ability to right itself and land on his feet when he falls (or is dropped) from a low or medium height. This righting reflex is present in cats from the day they are born.

Place. Numerous stories, some well authenticated, are told of cats that have travelled hundreds of miles from their owners' new homes back to the places where they used to live. Like homing pigeons, some cats seem to have a direction-finding ability that enables them to make this sort of journey.

That cats make 'return' journeys over shorter distances could be explained by their ability to follow a scent trail to the former home, but the longer treks must be the result of a different ability. Of course, newspapers never tell stories of cats that leave their new homes only to get lost in the search for their old ones, so we have no way of knowing how powerful or effective this supposed homing instinct really is in cats.

Time. Cats are creatures of routine. They like the same things to happen at the same times every day. They are true conservatives in this, for they do not like anything to happen that has not happened before — to their satisfaction. This preference for a well-ordered life is somewhat surprising in an animal with such a reputation as a supreme individualist.

Body language. The cat's best-known use of body language is the lordosis posture assumed by females in season: front end down, back end up, tail swept recklessly to one side, hind feet paddling up and down in blatant entreaty. But this is not the only way in which cats use their bodies to communicate with each other and with humans. Cats also convey feelings and intentions through movements of the tail, ears,

Above: The aggressive (left) and defensive (right) postures are clearly seen here. The aggressor's tail is at half-mast, the body slung low.

Left: A Burmese in defensive posture: back arched, body turned sideways on, fangs bared and paw raised in warning

using their tails as mufflers for keeping their faces warm.

Cats can tolerate higher temperatures than can humans. Cats do not experience pain from heat until it reaches a temperature of 126°F (52°C), a full 14°F above the point where humans feel discomfort.

Balance. Cats have an extraordinary sense of balance which they employ for climbing to the highest limbs of trees, onto rooftops, out onto narrow ledges and to other high-wire places. Their prowess at climbing, however, often leads cats into trouble, particularly if the ascent has been inspired by a chase — with the cat as the pursuer or the pursued. Suddenly finding himself high above the ground, a cat will freeze and remain

Above: A British Shorthair kitten is not sure how to react to its strange, new world: curiosity just wins over fear of the tortoise.

Below: A Tonkinese surveys its domain from a car. Cats living in the wild have much larger territories than have domesticated cats.

paws, eyes, head or entire body.

The cat speaks eloquently with its tail, which may be held upright to indicate pleasure, or to signal a cheery greeting. It may be carried low in a dispirited slump. It may twitch impatiently from side to side to warn of impending attack.

Cats' ears move as they follow sounds in the environment. They also flatten sideways if a cat feels threatened or angry, or backward and downward if a cat means to extend an invitation to play.

A cat's paws also convey pleasure, through a light, claws-in pat, or annoyance, by means of an imperious whack, which may be delivered with the claws in or out as the occasion requires.

A cat with wide open, attentive eyes is interested, in a positive fashion, by what it sees. Cats peering with narrowed gaze are not sure if what they are seeing is interesting or threatening.

Sometimes cats communicate with their entire heads. A cat that rubs its head against its owner, or against another cat, is signalling affection and acceptance.

A cat's body posture tells us much about the way a cat is thinking and feeling. Arched backs and big tails are obvious signs of fear and displeasure. A low-slung advance with eyes and tail at half mast is a sign of attack. A cat that has been reprimanded will often sit with his back to his owner to signal its indignation.

Basic training. There are two kinds of basic training for cats: aversive/substitution training and performance training. The aim of aversive/substitution training is to teach your cat not to engage in undesirable behaviour, such as jumping on the kitchen or dining room table, conditioning its claws on the sofa, or tipping over the rubbish bin. Performance training, which is based on the principle of positive reinforcement (a reward is given for certain behaviour) is designed to teach the cat to perform particular tasks, such as coming when called, retrieving small objects, or jumping through a hoop.

Cats are never really too young to learn — nor too old to start misbehaving. Indeed, you may find it necessary to impart a few aversive/substitution lessons when the cat is at the stage of development at which you wish to begin teaching it to perform tricks. This is acceptable, so long as you

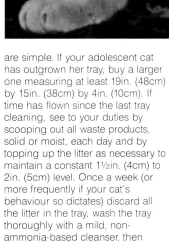

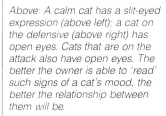

Above: A calm cat has a slit-eyed expression (above left): a cat on the defensive (above right) has open eyes. Cats that are on the attack also have open eyes. The better the owner is able to 'read' such signs of a cat's mood, the better the relationship between them will be.

remember not to mix the two kinds of training. For example, if you have just scolded your cat for jumping onto the dining table and attacking a dried-flower arrangement or eating the remains of a meal, you should not then get out the treats and begin teaching him to jump through a hoop.

Why cats misbehave

In the back alleys of our cities, the gardens of suburbia, and in the countryside feral cats lead singular lives. Low population densities, well-established rituals, limited interaction between adult cats, clearly defined territories and one-tom-per-neighbourhood living arrangements are characteristic of the feral cat's existence.

Cats that live indoors — in exchange for regular meals and climate-controlled lodgings — are asked to adapt to conditions that violate the established patterns of life in the wild. In one British study of cat-population densities, researchers found that feral cats living in East London, where the cat population density was the greatest, had 871sq ft (81m²) to themselves. It is doubtful whether the average two-cat household provides the 1,742sq ft (162m²) that would be needed merely to approximate the space that the cat enjoys in the most dense, urban setting.

Obviously, cats that spend all or part of their time indoors must live in very much smaller 'territories'

than do outdoor cats and, in multicat households, must tolerate greater interaction with other adult cats. These departures from a cat's natural lifestyle can lead to a variety of deviations in behaviour, and other departures from a cat's usual, established routine can have a similar effect.

Remedial litter box training

One of the more dismaying discoveries in life is finding that your (supposedly house-trained) cat has failed to use his litter tray, especially if you make such a discovery with your bare foot at 2 a.m. on your way to the kitchen.

Thankfully, the percentage of house-trained cats that suddenly decide not to use their trays is small — probably in the single digits among cats that are neutered or spayed (as all companion cats should be). A cat can forget her manners for several reasons: she may have outgrown the tray she has been using since kittenhood; maybe her tray has not been cleaned for days; perhaps her tray has been moved to a different spot, which she doesn't like; or it could be that she is playing or sleeping on the second floor, and does not feel like going all the way downstairs to relieve herself; or her owner has changed brands of litter, and she prefers the old brand because the new one does not smell right; she is used to an open tray, and her owner has suddenly switched to an unfamiliar, high-tech, enclosed model; her tray is located in a part of the house where there is too much commotion for her sense of privacy; her tray is situated too close to her dining area or her favourite sleeping spot; she is registering her objection to the new cat or kitten her owner recently brought home.

The solutions to these problems

are simple. If your adolescent cat has outgrown her tray, buy a larger one measuring at least 19in. (48cm) by 15in. (38cm) by 4in. (10cm). If time has flown since the last tray cleaning, see to your duties by scooping out all waste products, solid or moist, each day and by topping up the litter as necessary to maintain a constant 1½in. (4cm) to 2in. (5cm) level. Once a week (or more frequently if your cat's behaviour so dictates) discard all the litter in the tray, wash the tray thoroughly with a mild, non-ammonia-based cleanser, then rinse, dry and refill the tray.

If you must move the litter tray to a new location, put a second tray in the new spot and wait until the cat has begun using that tray before taking up the old one. If your cat is allowed upstairs as well as downstairs, install a litter tray on each level of the house that the cat visits. If you want to change brands of litter, for whatever reasons, make the change gradually. The next time you wash and refill the litter tray, mix two or three cups of the new brand of litter in with the old brand. If your cat does not object, mix two or three additional cups of the new brand in with the old when you clean and refill the tray again. Repeat this gradual infiltration of the new litter until the transition is complete. If your cat stops using the tray at any time before or immediately after the transition, throw the new litter away, wash and rinse the litter tray, and return to the old brand of litter.

If you want to change from an open tray to an enclosed model, do not fill the new tray with fresh litter. Use the litter that was in your cat's former tray instead. This familiar litter, especially if it is a little soiled, will make the new litter tray smell reassuring to your cat. Should your cat refuse to set foot in the covered

tray, resign yourself to keeping the old model.

If your cat's tray is located in a busy, much-used part of the house, move the tray to a more secluded place. Cats are creatures of decorum as well as habit, and most of them prefer to conduct their private affairs in private.

If you suspect that your cat has stopped using her tray because it is too close to her dining or sleeping area, move the tray farther away from that spot. If she begins misbehaving shortly after you have brought a new cat or kitten into the house, provide the more senior resident with a tray of her own at some distance from the old tray's location. If this doesn't work, confine the newcomer to a separate room for a week or two. (You should do this anyway as soon as you acquire a new cat, to make sure that she isn't harbouring any viruses or other contagions.)

These solutions, virtually painless and cleverly manipulative, should serve to rehabilitate your cat if she forgets her manners. Catching her in violation of the house rules and reprimanding her promptly is also effective, but a reprimand is only as effective as it is timely. Remember that as a cat's attention span is scarcely more than 20 seconds long, it serves little purpose to scold her for something she did even 15 minutes, let alone two hours, ago. Should you catch your cat in the act of relieving herself, wait until she has finished, then express your annoyance with a sternly spoken 'No! Bad!' In time, 'Bad!' and 'No!' are words which will be recognized by the cat (see Litter Training, page 100).

Once your cat has left the scene of the accident, clean the soiled spot with a non-ammonia-based disinfectant cleanser. If she has soiled the carpet, sprinkle white,

Above: A cat or kitten pleased to see its owner moves forwards with its tail held high in the air. A tail hung low expresses fear or displeasure.

confine her for a while. A pet shop may carry this kind of cage; if not, cat magazines have advertisements for companies that sell them. The price of such a cage is not prohibitive, and may not be any more than the cost of having a rug or sofa cleaned professionally. It is also far less taxing than the emotional cost of having to give up on a cat that has given up on her tray.

Once you have acquired a cage for your miscreant cat, place her and her tray in it and leave them both there until the cat is using the tray consistently. To aid in her rehabilitation, before you fill the tray with litter, dab a few drops of ammonia cut with water on the bottom. The ammonia's odour is similar enough to the odour of cat urine to inspire the desired conduct in your cat. If for some inexplicable reason she persists in refusing to use the tray, you may have no choice but to place her in a new home in the country where it would be relatively safe for her to roam in and out of doors at will. But in most cases the rehabilitation method should bring her back to her old, house-trained habits again.

While your cat is confined in the cage, make the cage comfortable for her by fitting it with a perch for her to sleep on and a few toys with which to play. Let her out for half-an-hour or so of supervised recess a few times a day, but keep her in the cage at night. Increase her free time gradually until the cat exhibits dependability in her confinement room, then allow her the run of the house. Be sure to leave her old tray in its former location, and her new tray in her confinement room. If she uses both trays consistently without misadventure, the price you pay for her retraining may be an extra litter tray to look after. This is a small price for feline cleanliness. You could try taking up the new tray once order has been restored to your cat's litter habits. If accidents reoccur, restore the new tray to the confinement room at once. It is nearly as easy to clean two trays as it is to clean just one.

The rehabilitation method works with kittens, with housebroken adult cats, and with the stray cat that may have been fine living in your garage over the summer, but which really needs to spend the winter snugly indoors.

Additional aversive training
The best way to teach your cat not to do something you do not want him to is to establish an association between the unwanted conduct and an unpleasant occurrence. If possible, the unpleasant occurrence should be something the cat does not associate with you. This is because, first, you do not want your cat to be afraid of you. And, second, because you do not want him to refrain from unwanted behaviour only when you are in the neighbourhood.

Jumping to conclusions
You are sitting at the kitchen table one morning having breakfast when your cat jumps onto the table to investigate. With a restrained

distilled vinegar and salt on it to expunge the odour. Do not use an ammonia-based cleanser for this job because an ammonia cleanser smells too much like the odour you are trying to remove. If you do use the latter, the cat is likely to return to the spot to repeat the mistake.

Sometimes a cat's misbehaviour has physiological, not psychological, causes. If you find tiny urine spots around the house, much smaller than the volume your cat usually expresses, he or she may be suffering from a urinary infection and should be taken to a vet at once. Older, neutered males are especially prone to this difficulty. Unable to pass urine normally, and uncomfortable from their increasing urinary-tract blockage, they strain to squeeze out a few drops of urine wherever the urge overtakes them.

Rehabilitation litter training
People who breed cats often help a mother cat to litter-train her kittens by placing the kittening box at one end of a large cage and a litter tray at the other end. The cage should be approximately 44in. (112cm) long, 22in. (56cm) wide, and 22in. (56cm) tall. The top of the cage should be left open, allowing the mother cat to jump in and out as she desires. When the mother cat has shown the kittens what the tray is for, and they have begun finding their way to the tray on their own — generally, this should happen by the time they are four to five weeks old — their owner begins leaving the cage door open for short periods of supervised free time. This allows the kittens to explore their immediate surroundings outside the cage, while the owner can test their litter-tray homing instincts.

The kitten who occasionally tries to relieve herself outside the cage can begin to learn what 'No' means at this point. The owner should pick her up gently, say 'No' a little less gently, and place the errant kitten in the litter tray. Surprisingly quickly, the kittens will be sufficiently trustworthy to be allowed longer and longer periods of free time outside the cage. Still, the kittens should remain in their cage at night for a while, but by the time they are 9 or 10 weeks old, they should be ready to have the run of the room in which their tray is located. Generally (but not always), this will be in their owner's bedroom.

This elementary training method often serves to rehabilitate a cat that has failed to respond to less regimented forms of remedial litter-tray instruction. If you haven't switched brands of litter suddenly, changed from an open to an enclosed tray, forgotten to clean your cat's litter tray for a week, had company of whom your cat disapproved, or committed any other transgressions, and your cat still refuses to use her tray consistently, consider borrowing or buying a large cage in which to economy of motion, you rap a knife sharply on the rim of your plate. (If you are using the best china that morning, you could substitute a severe stomping of your foot.) Whatever, if the sound you make is startling enough, the cat should immediately beat a retreat back to lower ground.

You could probably achieve the same response by rattling the newspaper, smacking the underside of the table with your fist, or making any other abrupt, unsettling noise. If you happened to be wearing a whistle that morning, an extended blast or two would work very nicely.

Do not swat at the animal with your hand, leap up gesticulating, or make any other sudden, aggressive motion towards your cat. If you strike him, you may make him hand shy, which could interfere with intermediate and advanced training sessions. If you rise up menacingly from the table, shouting, he will certainly leap off the table and race out of the room — but he may also take to racing out of the room every time he is in the kitchen and sees you getting up from the table, which is not something you want.

Although cats are sensitive enough to cease and desist when they are startled, they are curious enough to return to the scene of a misdemeanour. Do not be discouraged, therefore, if your cat lands in the middle of the breakfast table the morning after he was frightened away by the clang of the fork on china or the stomp of the foot on floor. Be prepared to repeat the measure you took to chase him off the first day, and be prepared to escalate the war of nerves if necessary. You may have to come to the breakfast table armed with a water pistol or an umpire's whistle. A squirt in the face or a very loud blow on the whistle may be the method by which you achieve the response you desire.

It should go without saying that there is a difference between creativity and cruelty in training a cat. If, when your cat had jumped onto the breakfast table, you had grabbed him by the scruff of the neck and dunked his nose into a steaming cup of coffee, he would probably refrain from jumping on

Below: One of the many ways a cat shows affection towards an owner is to lift itself up to the owner's hand in the hope of being stroked.

Above: Outdoor exercise can be enjoyed even in unsafe areas by training your cat to walk on a harness and lead.

Below: As the upright tail shows, a harness and lead need not keep your cat from indulging in enjoyable pursuits such as hunting.

the table again. He would certainly, however, lose faith in you. And he would most probably, after that, be unwilling to come when you called, or respond to any kind of positive training.

Removing the cat from the table once he has already got himself up is quickly accomplished. Training him to refrain from jumping onto the table altogether takes more time. To accomplish this, the well-trained owner anticipates the cat's arrival, sees him skulking around the table and makes a loud noise or shouts, 'No!' as soon as he sees the cat go into a pre-leap crouch.

Though you must make enough noise to frighten your cat, you should keep your corrections impersonal. This is best achieved by remembering not to take your cat's actions personally. He did not jump on the table especially to annoy you. All he wanted was to find out exactly what smelled so good up there, and all you want is a cat-free kitchen table.

Performance training

Cats have long been considered difficult, if not impossible, to train. Difficult they certainly are — but not impossible. If you wish to teach your cat a few tricks, first ask yourself how well trained you want your cat to be — and why. But whether you want your cat to play études on the piano or simply to play dead for company, the elements of performance training are the same.

1. Select a quiet, reasonably well-confined place to begin training. A table in a corner of a room with the door closed is a good place to start. This provides you with working space and your cat with few avenues of escape.

2. Keep training sessions brief: three to five minutes, three to four times a day.

3. Do not use your cat's name to scold him if he makes a mistake. In fact, do not scold your cat at all during training. When he makes a mistake, show him by voice and example what you want him to do. If he jumps off the table, bring him back quietly and try again. Remember: do not call him by his name when you are trying to coax him back to the table, or he might never come again when he is called. And do not let the session end unless you're ready to end it.

4. Reward your cat with praise — and the occasional treat — when he does well. If he associates performance with good feelings, he will be more likely to turn in good performances.

5. Make sure that only one person is designated to train the cat. Different teachers have different methods when it comes to training cats, so it plays havoc with the training experience if more than one teacher is involved.

The Sit. You will probably wish to teach your cat to sit first. People who have spent time training cats will all tell you that you cannot do much with a cat who will not sit still when he is asked.

To teach a cat to sit, place him on the table in front of you and follow this sequence of steps:

1. With one hand, point to the spot where you want the cat to sit. Do not point to his tail, however. A cat speaks with his tail; he does not see with it.

2. While you're pointing to the table with one hand, run the other hand gently down the cat's spine.

3. When you reach his hindquarters, say 'sit' or 'set' or 'down', and exert a slight but authoritative pressure on his rump.

4. If the cat deigns to sit down, praise him quietly once he has been sitting still for a few seconds. If he refuses to move, take a deep breath and repeat the steps above.

5. If five minutes go by and the cat is still standing, pick up his hind legs, set him down gently, praise him, and call off the training session for the meantime.

The hoop trick

This is one of the easiest tricks to teach a cat — especially if the cat is hungry.

1. Put a plate of food on one end of a narrow table.

2. Place the cat at the other end.

3. Place a hoop on the table between the cat and the food. Unless the cat is totally uninterested in eating, he will eventually step through the hoop to get to the food. When he does, let him have a bite or two, then take the plate and put it at the other end of the table.

4. If the food was worth the effort, the cat will walk through the hoop again to get to the plate. Give him a few nibbles and move the plate one more time. After he walks through the hoop to get it, let him take a few bites, praise him generously, and end the training session for the day.

5. The next day raise the hoop an inch or two so that he has to step over the bottom of it to get to his food. Be sure not to raise the hoop so high in any one increment that the cat jumps off the table instead of through the hoop. Before you know it the cat will be leaping through the hoop to get to the food.

You may want to stop at this point. But if you are game — and more important, if your cat is — you can put the cat on one table, the food on another, and the hoop in between. If the cat jumps from the first table to the floor and then to the food table, put him back on the first table and nudge him gently in the chest with the hoop to let him know what you want. If he persists in jumping off the table anyway, put him back on the foodless table one more time, pick him up in one hand and guide him through the hoop with the other. Then put the food and hoop away and try again later.

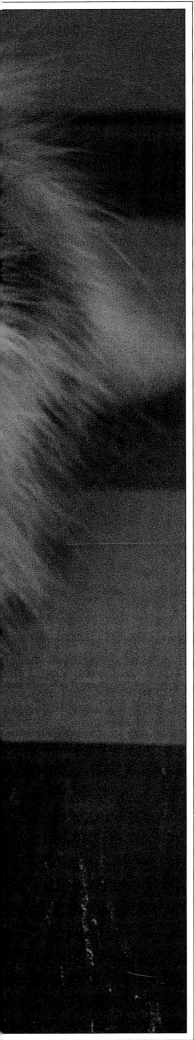

4

FEEDING YOUR CAT

Cat-food manufacturers devote a great deal of time and money trying to create the nutritional equivalent of the mouse. For the mouse provides the critical mixture of protein, vitamins, minerals and essential fatty acids that a cat requires. Indeed, so perfect a source of nutrients is the mouse that one writer has asked — only half in jest — why 'some enterprising company [doesn't] cook some mice, grind the little suckers up, and put 'em in a can?'

The answer, says the Subcommittee on Cat Nutrition of the National Research Council (NRC) in the United States, is that 'cats require specific nutrients, not specific feedstuffs'. So long as those nutrients, about forty altogether, are present in a cat's diet on a regular basis, it doesn't actually matter how they are provided, be it in the form of a mouse, or in a box or a can.

Nutritional requirements

It is important that a cat's diet accommodates his metabolic singularities, which have evolved because of his strict adherence to a carnivorous menu and which have resulted in several unique nutritional requirements.

Protein. Best known among these is the need for protein, which, in growing cats, is roughly four times as great as it is in other mammals.

Protein comprises more than 50 per cent of the dry weight of animals. It helps to build and maintain cells, provide energy (by means of chemical breakdown), inspire muscle contractions and, in the form of genes, transmit hereditary instructions across generations. Furthermore, digestive enzymes, insulin, the antibodies of the immune system and most hormones are made of protein.

Protein is composed of amino

Above: A cat has only small incisors; it tears its food with the large canines at the front and cuts it with the sharp cheek teeth.

Left: A domestic longhair enjoys a bowl of food. Three different categories of cat food can be bought today: dry, semi-moist and canned.

acids, which, in turn, are composed of carbon, hydrogen, oxygen, nitrogen and sometimes sulphur. Amino-acids come in two varieties: dispensable and essential. Dispensable amino-acids are those which the body is able to manufacture for itself. Essential amino-acids are the ones that an animal is not able to make in sufficient quantities. The latter must therefore be present in the feline diet every day.

Fat. No matter the importance of protein, cats do not live by protein alone. Dietary fat — a concentrated energy source, a carrier for fat-soluble vitamins, the source of essential fatty acids and a treat for the palate — is another essential nutrient class.

A cat's unique nutritional requirements are not confined to the protein-amino-acids category. Cats' diets must also contain arachidonic acid, which cats cannot synthesize and which is crucial to the delivery of kittens.

Cats can tolerate and utilize high levels of fat, but research has shown that they have preferences regarding levels of intake. For example, cats have shown a preference for a 25-per cent-fat diet over diets containing as little as 10-per cent-fat and as much as 50-per cent-fat. Cats also prefer animal fats to all other types of fat.

Carbohydrate. Though dry cat food usually contains 40 per cent or more carbohydrate, the NRC reports that 'no known carbohydrate requirement exists for the cat'. In fact, as long as cats obtain the fat and amino-acids necessary for glucose derivation, 'it is probable', the report continues, that they can live healthily with no dietary carbohydrate whatsoever.

This fact is much remarked on by some nutritionists, who point out that the cat was originally domesticated because he would protect grain rather than eat it; but since nutritional science discovered how to make cereal grain palatable to cats about 20 years ago, corn swathed in animal fat and protein has appeared on a growing number of cats' menus.

Though it considers carbohydrate dispensable, the NRC concludes that the starch present in corn and wheat, 'especially when finely ground, is well utilized by the cat'.

Vitamins. No matter how much or what kind of food a cat eats, his body would be unable to process it without the aid of vitamins. For vitamins are the catalysts that combine with protein to create metabolically active enzymes, which

Above: Most domestic cats who are allowed to roam free will instinctively chew grass. In fact, they cannot extract the carbohydrate nutrients from the grass but use it for roughage, and as a source of vitamins. If they vomit up grass, as they often do, it brings with it fur balls, which would otherwise cause a potentially dangerous obstruction.

Digestive system of the cat

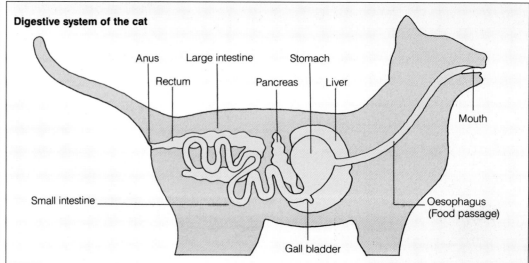

in turn produce hundreds of important chemical reactions throughout the body. Vitamins, in addition to their role in metabolizing food, assist in the formation of hormones, blood cells, nervous system chemicals and genetic material.

Three of the nine vitamins the cat is known to require — vitamins A, D and E — are fat-soluble. Generally found in foods that contain fat, they can be stored in the body's fat reserves. The other essential vitamins — thiamin, riboflavin, pyridoxine, niacin, pantothenic acid and cobalamin — are water-soluble B vitamins. These cannot be stored in the body.

Although cats are mostly affected by the lack of vitamins, an excess of two vitamins — A and D — can also be harmful. Vitamin A toxicity, resulting from excessive amounts of liver in the diet, causes skeletal lesions, while vitamin D toxicity, which occurs when cats are given too much of this vitamin as a supplement, results in calcificiation of the aorta, the carotid arteries and the stomach wall.

Minerals. The following nine minerals are considered essential in the cat's diet: calcium, phosphorus, sodium, potassium, magnesium, iron, copper, zinc and iodine. The need for 12 other minerals is thought to be essential by analogy with other species. These minerals are: chlorine, manganese, sulphur, cobalt, selenium, molybdenum, fluorine, chromium, silicon, tin, nickel and vanadium. Regardless of the species requiring them, minerals are fundamental in maintaining the acid-base balance, tissue structure and osmotic pressure. They are also important constituents of enzyme systems.

Feline Urologic Syndrome

If the words 'acid-base balance' seem familiar, it's probably because articles on FUS (Feline Urologic

Above: A pet drinking concentrated milk. Most cats will drink milk, but many adults do not possess the enzymes required to process it.

Syndrome) have appeared frequently in recent literature on cats. The clinical manifestations of FUS include cystitis and urinary tract obstruction.

The NRC contends that 'inattention' to the effects of diet composition on acid-base balance 'may be a major factor' in the current high incidence of FUS. The 'ingestion of abnormally large quantities of base-forming elements' by the cat — 'an animal that has been . . . adapted to produce acid urine' with a pH of 6.0 to 7.0 — may be responsible for driving a cat's pH above the 7.1 level, where crystallization is apt to occur spontaneously.

The NRC cautions against pinning the blame for FUS on any particular mineral (magnesium is a frequent target). Attention should be directed instead towards 'the mineral composition of cat foods in order to assure the consistent production of cat urine at a pH below 6.6'.

The NRC's advice is reasonable, but it nevertheless leaves the ordinary cat owner with a problem: how does he or she, confronted by a wide choice of different cat foods in the supermarket, determine which foods will produce a urine pH below 6.6? And how much magnesium is too much?

The answer to the first question is: one need not bother. It is impossible to glean this information from a cat food label. Making a phone call to the manufacturer is the only way to satisfy the inquiring mind on this point. As for the second question, the answer is that 0.1 per cent magnesium is the industry standard, but at least one study indicates that as much as 0.5 per cent magnesium is safe.

Water

While we are considering the composition of the cat's feed bowl, we shouldn't neglect the contents of the water bowl next to it. Water, says the NRC, is the single most important nutrient necessary to sustain normal cell function. Mammals can lose nearly all their reserves of glycogen and fat, half their protein stores and 40 per cent of their body-weight and still survive. But they are much less tolerant of the loss of water.

Water intake among cats seems to be affected primarily by diet. The ratio of water to dry matter intake varies from 2.0- to 2.8-to-1 for cats eating dry food and from 3.0- to 5.7-to-1 for cats eating canned food.

Reading cat-food labels

Reading a cat-food label is similar to squinting at the last line of type on an eye-examination chart. You cannot be certain if you are seeing what you think you see, and even when you are certain, you are reading letters not words, letters such as menadione sodium bi-sulfite.

Perhaps one day this problem will be solved when a dictionary of the words found on cat-food labels is published. Until that time, the only vocabulary the purchaser needs to know in order to read a cat-food label is contained in this sentence: 'Moggy Menu provides complete and balanced nutrition for all stages of a cat's life, substantiated by testing performed in accordance with the procedure established by the Association of American Feed Control Officials (AAFCO).'

Different companies, of course, employ different dialects of labelese. Instead of 'complete and balanced', some labels may say '100 per cent complete and balanced'. Or in place of the phase 'all stages of a cat's life', some labels say 'for the growth and maintenance of cats'. And for 'procedure' some labels substitute 'protocol'. Whatever the particular wording, the label should guarantee that the food contained in the package has in fact been tested on a cat.

The purchaser should be aware, however, that not all cat food is suitable for all stages of a cat's life. Some food provides complete and balanced nutrition for adult cats only — or for the maintenance, but not the growth, of cats. Such food is suitable for adult cats, but it would not be appropriate for growing kittens, pregnant or lactating females or for cats with age- or disease-related dietary needs.

Furthermore, do not assume that all the brands of cat food purporting to deliver complete and balanced nutrition have been tested in AAFCO-approved feeding trials. A label stating, for example, that the product 'meets or exceeds the maximum nutritional levels established by the National Research Council (NRC) for all stages of a cat's life' would, in fact, be misleading. For what the label does *not* say is that the food meets or exceeds NRC nutritional levels *before* it is eaten by the cat. And what becomes of that nutrition after the cat eats it is anybody's guess. It is enlightening to remember what the president of a speciality pet food company was once rumoured to have said to a newspaper reporter: 'Give me a tyre, an old leather shoe, and a quart of oil and I can meet the specifications for the NRC diet'.

Obviously, the most reliable nutritional guarantees are those which state that a product has actually been fed to cats, and has passed the AAFCO requirements.

Cat-food labels on products manufactured in the United Kingdom contain similar wording. One brand, for example, states that the food has been 'extensively tested', and that it contains 'all the nutrients known to be necessary for the daily nourishment of cats'.

Dry, semi-moist, or canned?

Three different categories of cat food can be bought today: dry, semi-moist and canned. Dry food is less expensive, easier to store, and more convenient to use than is canned food. Dry food also helps to reduce dental tartar to some extent. Canned food is generally more palatable to cats and, since it is three-quarters moisture, is a better source of water than are other foods. (Dry food contains roughly 10 per cent water, semi-moist food about 35 per cent.)

Semi-moist food, because of its high chemical content and price, occupies an increasingly small section on supermarket shelves.

With three kinds of cat food to choose from, cat owners have no excuse for allowing their pets to

become fussy at meal times. For finicky eaters are made, not born, and two certain ways to transform your cat into a fussy eater are, first, to feed her the same food all the time and, second, to feed her 'people' food.

Be careful to give your cat a refreshing assortment of foods and brands: meat- and poultry-based foods for the most part, fish for occasional variety. The diversity will serve to sharpen your cat's appetite and will help to prevent deficiencies engendered by all-red-meat, all-organ-meat, or all-tuna-fish diets. Have a bowl of dry food available at all times. Change brands every two or three refills. Feed the cat canned food once a day. Change brands or flavours every two or three days. And be sure always to have clean, fresh water available in a clean bowl.

Standard or super-premium?
As well as having three categories of cat food to choose from, the cat owner can usually select from generic (own-brand), standard, or de-luxe brands and prices. The de-luxe brands, generally known as super-premium foods, are more expensive — and, in all likelihood, make a higher profit margin for the companies making and selling them. But does a cat get superior nutrition from such super-premium foods? Some authorities think not: 'Most pet-food companies have gourmet brands, usually with higher-quality ingredients (and higher palatability), but that doesn't make them any better', says Quinton R. Rogers, Ph.D., chairman of the NRC's subcommittee on cat nutrition.

Advocates of super-premium foods claim that their higher digestibility results in lower fecal volume and less fecal odour. What's more, such supporters say, the

price of super-premium brands might be higher than the price of standard foods, but the cost of using super-premium brands is not necessarily greater because the owner feeds less of a super-premium food than of the standard variety.

Snacks and treats
Many cat owners resort to snacks and treats to cajole their cats into eating. When cat owners do this, though, they are feeding their own insecurities as much as they are feeding their cats. For not only are snacks nutritionally deficient (when fed too frequently), but your cat is also going to fall into the habit of demanding them all the time if you offer them too frequently.

You can feed some foods to your cats all of the time, and all foods to your cats some of the time — but the true nutritional wisdom is to know which is which. Again, let the label be your guide. If the label states that the product 'is intended for intermittent or supplemental use

only', then use it intermittently, and sparingly. Do not allow snacks and treats to comprise more than 5 to 10 per cent of your cat's daily nutritional fare.

How much, and when, to feed?
Like people, cats need progressively fewer calories as they grow older. A ten-week-old kitten requires 83 per cent more dry food, 100 per cent more semi-moist food, or 100 per cent more canned food than does a 20-week-old kitten. Compared to an active adult, the hyperactive ten-week-old needs 206 per cent more dry food, 250 per cent more semi-moist food, or 200 per cent more canned food.

A cat with uninterrupted access to food will eat as the spirit moves her, consuming several small meals a day rather than following a precise feeding pattern. Yet even though cats prefer round-the-clock 'grazing' (feral cats, too, eat several small-prey meals each day), adults will adapt to being fed just once every 24 hours.

Above: Spoon-feeding a kitten with a complete liquid diet. When being weaned, kittens should be fed three or four times a day.

Kittens are not as flexible when it comes to feeding as are adult cats. When kittens are being weaned, starting at three to four weeks of age, they should be fed three or four times a day. Reduce feeds gradually to twice a day at six months, and, if you desire, to once per day after a cat's first birthday.

Vitamin and mineral supplements
If the label on a commercial cat food states that it is nutritionally complete for your cat's stage — or for all stages — of life, do not add vitamin or mineral supplements to it. Adding vitamins or minerals will probably upset the nutritional balance present in the food, and may cause vitamin toxicity. The only cats needing vitamin or mineral supplements are those that are not eating properly because of illness, or those which are losing increased amounts of body fluids because of diarrhoea or increased urination.

Keeping your cat trim
Cats gain and lose weight in cycles that may last several months. A cat is overweight if any of the following is the case: if her abdomen begins to droop; if you cannot feel her rib cage when you run your hands along her sides; if she sways when she walks; or if she develops bulges on either side of the point where her tail joins her body. You can prevent these symptoms from developing if you weigh your cat once a month and act accordingly. Whenever she gains a pound, reduce her food by 20 per cent. The easiest way to do this is to feed her twice a day, and to take up her

DAILY FEEDING GUIDELINES*		Dry	Semi-moist	Canned
Kittens:	10 weeks	1.1 oz (31g)	1.4oz (40g)	3.6oz (102g)
	20 weeks	.6 oz (17g)	.7oz (20g)	1.8oz (51g)
	30 weeks	.45oz (13g)	.6oz (17g)	1.4oz (40g)
	40 weeks	.36oz (10g)	.4oz (11g)	1.2oz (34g)
Adults	Inactive	.32oz (9g)	.4oz (11g)	1.0oz (28g)
	Active	.36oz (10g)	.4oz (11g)	1.2oz (34g)
	Pregnant	.45oz (13g)	.6oz (17g)	1.4oz (40g)
	Lactating	1.00oz (28g)	1.3oz (37g)	3.3oz (93g)

(ounces(g) per pound (.45kg) of body weight)

*Adapted from *Nutrient Requirements of Cats*, National Research Council, 1986.
Note: These amounts may be lower than those specified in the feeding instructions on the cat-food label.

food after twenty or thirty minutes. If you have several cats but want to put only one of them on a diet, you may have to feed that cat separately.

Feeding your cat diet (or 'lite') food is another way to reduce her weight. Diet foods contain 20 to 33 per cent fewer calories than normal cat food. Diet and other such special foods should only be fed to overweight, ill, or geriatric cats on a vet's recommendation.

Cooking for Your Cat
For many people, feeding their cats is a labour of love, involving meticulous preparation and adherence to detail. Most owners who cook their cats' food at home insist that their pets would not be as healthy, sparkling, stress-resistant and economical to look after if they were fed a commercially manufactured product. Such owners are certainly correct when it comes to the savings to be made. Ground meat bought from a pet-food supplier is much less expensive than anything that comes pre-packed in a box or can. But

whether raw meat — sometimes cooked and always infused with vitamins, minerals, oils and other supposedly magical ingredients — is superior to commercial brands is questionable.

Cats in the wild eat the whole of their prey, including the contents of the stomach, and so they obtain a complete, and balanced, diet. Anyone feeding cats a diet based on raw meat must add the correct vitamins and minerals in just the right proportions if they wish to provide a balanced diet. This involves more than simply pouring some calcium, a few tablespoons of vitamins and some brewer's yeast into the meat, then mixing it all up. For example, do you know how much calcium you must add to raw meat (which is calcium deficient) to restore the calcium-phosphorus ratio to its optimal 1:1 to 1:2 range? Or how you convert the 10,000 units of vitamin X per pound listed on the label of a jar of cat vitamins into the correct amount to be added to a given quantity of raw meat? Or which vitamin powder is the most balanced and complete? And do

you know if it contains the necessary minerals in the correct amounts and ratios? And do you know if you should cook the meat or feed it to the cat raw?

Unless you have some special intuition or knowledge that cat-food manufacturers, with their huge budgets and battalions of feeding-trial cats have overlooked, you should perhaps leave the nutrition of your cat to the commercial pet food experts.

Foods to avoid
Table scraps are not nutritionally balanced, and they may disturb the nutritional balance of the principal cat food being fed. Scraps also reduce your cat's interest in his own food, may cause stomach problems and may foster obesity.
Raw meat may contain toxoplasma tissue cysts. It may also upset the calcium-phosphorous ratio in commercial foods.
Raw fish may cause thiamine deficiency.
Raw egg whites contain a protein that interacts with biotin, rendering the latter unavailable to the cat.

Above: Kittens eating from twin feeding bowls. Cats need fewer calories as they get older: a ten-week-old kitten requires 83 per cent more dried food and 100 per cent more semi-moist or canned food than a 20-week-old kitten.

Biotin deficiency can lead to scaly skin and dried secretions forming repeatedly around the eyes, nose and mouth.
Raw liver contains too much Vitamin A.
Bones may lodge in a cat's throat or pierce the stomach or intestinal wall.
Dog food does not contain enough protein or taurine for cats.
Canned tuna (intended for human consumption): will, if fed exclusively to cats, cause Vitamin E deficiency.
Chocolate can restrict the flow of blood and cause heart attacks.
Milk may cause diarrhoea in adult cats. Many vets also believe that the high quantities of fat, minerals and sugar contained in milk can be injurious to a cat's continued good health.

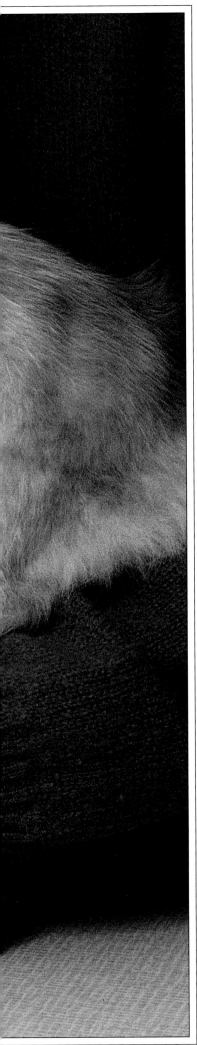

5

GROOMING YOUR CAT

Grooming is the technique of removing dead hair from a cat so that he doesn't have to remove it himself. Like virtue, grooming is its own reward. The more dead hair you remove from your cat(s), the less you will have to remove from your furniture, rugs and clothing.

Most shorthaired cats remain handsome with one or two groomings per week and do not need to be bathed frequently if they are not being shown. Most longhaired cats — even when they are not being shown — require two or three grooming sessions per week and should be bathed with the change of the seasons at least. Longhaired cats being shown will need daily grooming, and they will need to be bathed before each show.

Grooming tools

Before you begin any grooming session, collect the tools you will need for the job. These are:

- comb(s) or brush(es)
- face cloth
- nail clippers
- lukewarm water
- cotton swabs
- mineral oil

Two combs are sufficient for grooming shorthaired cats: a flea comb and a grooming comb with teeth about ⅝in. (1.6cm) long and ¹⁄₁₆in. (2mm) apart. Some combs contain both kinds of teeth: the tight, flea-catching teeth occupy half the comb's length while the all-purpose teeth occupy the other half. When you buy a comb, make sure that the teeth are rounded, not pointed, so that they will not inflict pain on your cat, or injure him in any way.

An adequate all-purpose comb for grooming a longhaired cat has teeth that are ⅞in. (2.2cm) long and are divided into two equal sections.

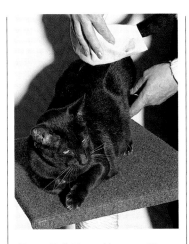

Above: Polishing a Havana with a chamois cloth. This is a simple routine that will keep the coat healthy and shining beautifully.

Left: Grooming removes the dead hair from a cat: the more you remove from your cat, the less will get onto your furniture and clothes.

The teeth occupying one half of the comb are almost ³⁄₁₆in. (5mm) apart. The teeth occupying the other half are a little more than ¹⁄₁₆in. (2mm) apart. A good second comb for a longhair's coat has teeth about ⅝in. (1.6cm) long and roughly ¹⁄₁₆in. (2mm) apart.

Brushes come in a variety of materials and shapes with bristles made of animal hair, plastic, or stainless steel. Many people do not like nylon- or plastic-bristle brushes because they damage the coat and generate static electricity. The same caution regarding the teeth of a comb applies to the bristles in a brush: to avoid inflicting pain on your cat, the tips of the bristles of a brush should be rounded, not sharp.

Combing or brushing your cat

Before you begin grooming, check your cat's claws to see if they need clipping. With the cat facing away from you, lift one of his legs so that the lower part of the leg rests in your upturned fingers. Hold the leg securely between the heel of your thumb and the tips of your middle ring and little fingers, then grasp the cat's foot between your thumb and forefinger. Press down on the top of his foot with your thumb to spread the toes and extend the claws. Check each claw. If the end of the nail is honed to a sharp point, clip it. Be careful not to cut the quick — the pink vein inside the nail (see the diagram on page 123).

After you have seen to your cat's claws, begin combing or brushing. Because many cats do not take to being groomed in some areas (their hindquarters, for example) as well as others, do not begin with one of these sensitive spots. Instead, start at the back of the neck, or at the base of the spine or at some other site that, when touched, usually elicits a purr rather than a snarl from the cat.

Comb or brush with the lie of the coat. Slide the comb into the coat at about a 45-degree angle, then move the comb smoothly across the cat's body. (This same technique works with a brush, the only difference being that the bristles of a brush meet the coat at a 90-degree angle.)

With some cats you will need to comb or brush with one hand while you restrain them with the other. Place your free hand on the cat's chest while you comb his back and sides, or place your free hand, palm up, on his underbelly while you comb his hindquarters.

To comb your cat's underbelly, lift his front legs with one hand and comb him with the other. Place your

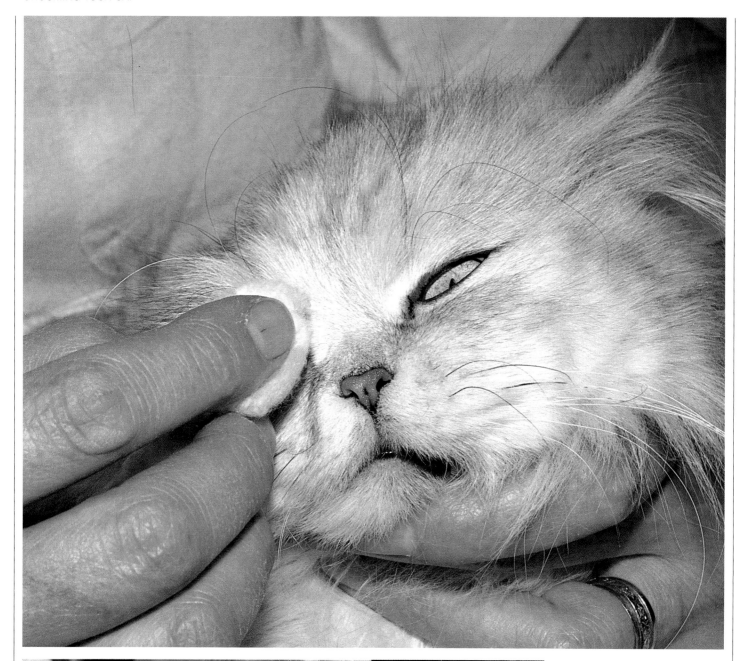

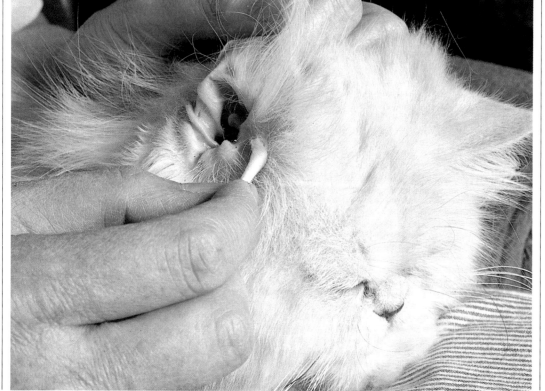

Above: Cleaning a Persian's eyes. Wipe around the eyes with a face cloth that has been dipped in lukewarm water.

Left: The outer parts of the ears can be cleaned with a cotton bud and some rubbing alcohol. Take care to avoid probing too deeply.

free hand, palm up, just behind and above the midpoint of the cat's front legs. Lift his legs gently until the cat is standing on his hind legs with his back at about a 60-degree angle to the table.

Cats should be combed twice per grooming session. With the first combing you are looking for flea dirt, skin rashes or mats in the coat. If you find flea dirt, a flea bath is in order. Skin rashes dictate a visit to the vet.

If you find a small mat, about the size of a marble, do not try to take it out immediately. Instead, grasp the mat in both hands, holding the right half between the thumb and forefinger of your right hand and the left half between the thumb and forefinger of your left hand. Pull gingerly in opposite directions,

Basic Grooming Equipment

1 Dual-purpose bristle and wire brushes for general grooming. Care should be taken when using the wire side, as hard brushing can strip the coat.
2 Pure bristle brush, with short, soft bristles, especially good for shorthaired cats.
3 Rubber brush with short flexible filaments, and rigid plastic type for general grooming.

4 Blunt-edged scissors for cutting through mats (in a longhaired coat).
4 Toothbrush for brushing up the coat of a longhaired cat around the ears and eyes.
6 Cotton-wool buds for cleaning the outer parts of ears.
7 Wide, flat tail comb ensures each hair on the tail of a long-haired cat is separate.

8 Specially shaped scissors for trimming the claws.
9 Fine-toothed comb for short-haired cats — smooths the coat and removes fleas and dirt.
10 Wide-toothed comb for removing tangles in the fur of longhaired cats.
11 Metal comb with wide- and medium-spaced teeth, ideal as general purpose groomer.

12 Non-toxic baby shampoo, safe for cleansing.
13 Bay rum spirit conditioner, removes grease from the coat.
14 Surgical spirit essential for removing stains from pale coats.
15 Cotton wool for cleaning eyes, ears and nose.
16 Non-toxic grooming powder or baby powder for giving body to the coat.

Trimming Nails

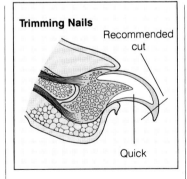

Recommended cut

Quick

Above: Check your cat's claws every month and trim the tips as shown here. Outdoor cats usually wear down their claws naturally.

Right: Grooming a British Blue Shorthair with a rubber brush to remove dead hairs and stimulate the blood circulation in the skin.

being careful to pull parallel with your cat's skin, not away from it. The mat should separate into two, smaller mats. Subdivide these into four mats, which may then be small enough and loose enough to be tugged out gently, one at a time,

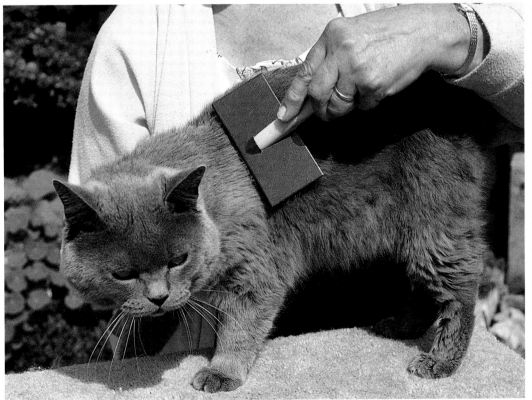

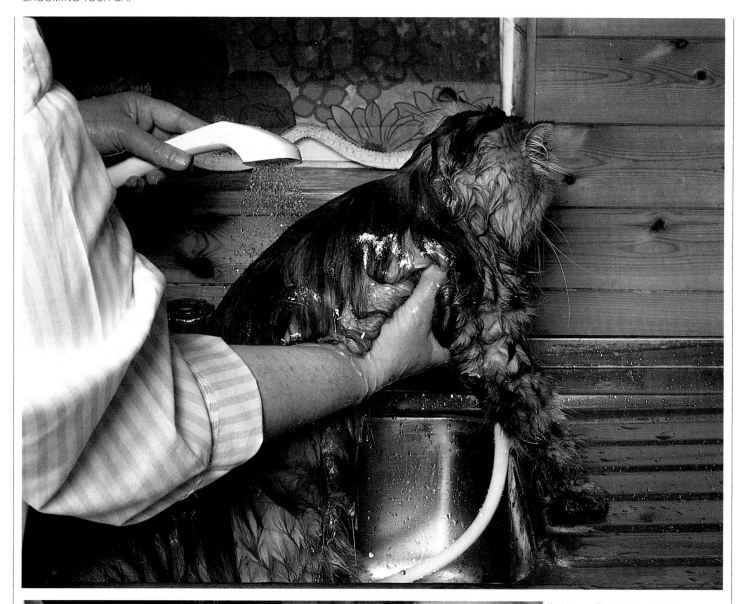

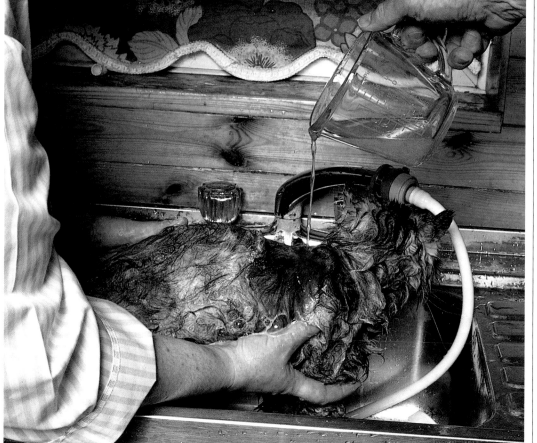

Above: The kitchen sink is the best place to bath your cat. Place the items you need near you, then use a spray attachment to wet the cat.

Left: After wetting the cat's coat, pour on some non-toxic dishwashing-detergent solution; rinse, then apply regular or flea shampoo as necessary.

with the comb. If they are not, separate them once more and then comb them out.

Cats with serious mats that are large enough to make into a hair piece may have to be shaved by a professional groomer or vet.

After a cat has been combed or brushed once, he should be done again. This time, instead of combing in long strokes, employ a lift-and-flip technique to aerate the hairs.

Starting at the base of the cat's tail, slide the comb or brush gently into the coat until you reach the skin. Then flick your wrist lightly in an upward motion, lifting the hair against its natural lie. Continue this backcombing technique until you have reached the cat's head. Then run the comb or brush through the section of coat you have just finished combing to return the coat to its natural lie. Repeat this process down the cat's sides, working from the spine to the ends of the ribs.

This method works on most longhaired and shorthaired breeds.

To backcomb a shorthaired cat's underbelly, lift his front legs as before, but make sure the cat is facing in the same direction as you are. Instead of combing with the lie of the coat, begin combing just in front of the hind legs and work delicately towards the front legs. You need not use the lift-and-flick approach here. Use regular strokes instead.

A longhaired cat's underbelly can be backcombed either front to back, or back to front. The latter method requires that you face the cat when you lift his front legs. Begin combing right in front of his hind legs. Instead of flicking your wrist counter-clockwise (away from your body) as you did when backcombing the cat's back and sides, flick your wrist clockwise (towards yourself). Repeat this stroke, moving the comb or brush an inch or so towards you each time until you reach the cat's front legs.

A cat's legs are easy to comb or brush. With the cat standing up, comb or brush downwards, using short strokes. If you wish, you can also comb or brush the legs upwards to give them a fuller appearance.

To groom a shorthaired cat's tail, cup it on the underside with one hand about midway along the tail. Comb softly along the lie of the coat, moving the comb in 2-inch (5cm) or 3-inch (8cm) increments from the tip to the base of the tail. Then reverse this procedure, holding the tip of the tail this time. To comb the underside of the tail, begin at the tip of the tail and work towards the base, as before.

A longhaired cat's armpits should be combed with care because many cats are sensitive in these areas. Lift the cat's leg gently and comb downwards until the hair has been separated. If the cat will tolerate the extra attention, comb once more, this time in the opposite direction to ensure a finished look.

To groom a longhair's tail, hold it gingerly by its tip. Move the comb or brush through the tail in short strokes from the tip to the base of the tail. Then comb the tail again, but this time use the lift-and-flick technique, flicking your wrist clockwise (that is, towards you) as you work your way down the cat's

Above: Rinse the cat thoroughly, then hold his tail at the base with one hand and coax as much water out of it as you can with the other.

Below: After blotting his legs, tail and body with paper towels, remove the cat from the sink and wrap him in a towel.

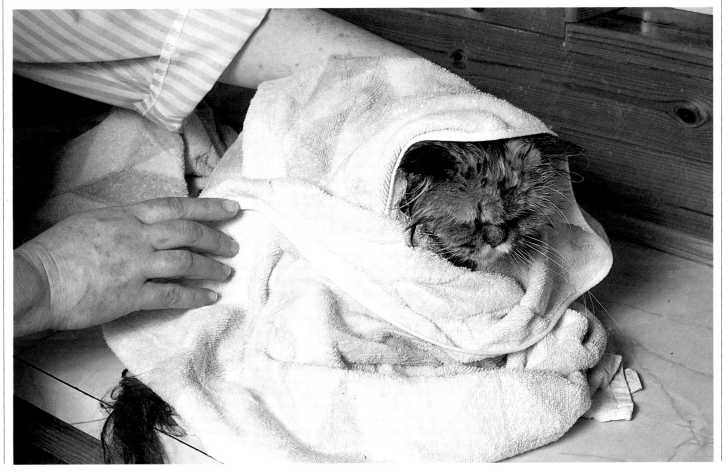

tail from the tip to the base.

If your cat's face needs washing, clean it with lukewarm water and a face cloth. If his face is more than a little dirty, clean it with a weak solution of water and tear-free shampoo. Squirt a few drops of shampoo into a bowl of lukewarm water, stir and, using a face-cloth, rub the solution carefully into the soiled areas of your cat's face.

Rinse by dipping a clean face-cloth into a bowl of clean, lukewarm water and rubbing the shampoo out of the fur.

Routine ear care

A few cotton swabs and some rubbing alcohol in a small container are the only materials you need to clean your cat's ears. Dip the cotton swabs into the alcohol and swab the visible parts of the ear carefully. Do not plunge the swab into the ear canal any farther than you can see, or you may well damage the cat's ear. If you deem it necessary to clean your cat's lower ear canal, buy a cleaning solution from your vet and follow the instructions carefully.

Bathing your cat

The kitchen sink is most people's favoured place to bath their cats. To do the job properly, the sink should be at least 19in. (48cm) wide, 16in. (41cm) long and 6½in. (17cm) deep. Some sinks have built-in spray attachments. If yours does not, buy one at a hardware store, where you can also buy an adaptor that will enable you to fit any spray attachment to any tap.

Bathing a cat is easier if the person masterminding the operation persuades husband, wife, penniless teenage child or friend who has just dropped by for tea to assist. It is also sensible to have a cat carrier nearby, with an absorbent towel covering its floor. The cat carrier is where you deposit the cat if he becomes angry and aggressive during his bath.

Before placing your cat in the sink, gather the implements you will need to bath him. These will include:
- comb(s) and/or brush(es)
- two towelling face cloths
- standard or flea shampoo
- three bath towels

- cotton balls
- paper towels
- blunt-tipped scissors
- toothbrush
- two small bowls of lukewarm water
- mineral oil in a squeeze bottle
- mechanic's-hand-soap solution (optional)
- dishwashing-detergent solution (optional)
- hair drier (optional)

After collecting together the necessary materials and implements, cover the bottom of the sink with a rubber mat or a bath towel to provide secure footing for your cat.

Next, turn on the water and adjust its temperature. Then test the temperature on your wrist. If the water feels uncomfortably warm to you, the likelihood is that it will be to your cat, too. Adjust accordingly. Make sure, too, that the temperature in the house is at least 72°F (22°C).

When you have your cat in hand — but before you put him into the sink — check his claws to see if they need clipping. Put a small wad

of cotton into each of his ears to prevent water from reaching the ear canal (where it might possibly cause an infection). Put a few drops of mineral oil in each of his eyes to protect them from any shampoo that may stray there.

Begin the bath by placing your cat in the sink. If you are going to be using a flea shampoo, wet the cat's neck thoroughly at once and lather it well. This prevents fleas from escaping from the cat's body and seeking refuge on his face.

Next, wet your cat thoroughly,

Right: Shorthaired cats can be allowed to dry naturally, but with longhairs use a hair drier.

Below left: Backcombing a Persian with a brush. To backcomb effectively, flick your wrist upwards, lifting the hair against its natural lie.

Below right: To groom a longhair's tail, hold it by its tip and brush in short strokes from the tip to the base. Then comb again using the lift-and-flick technique.

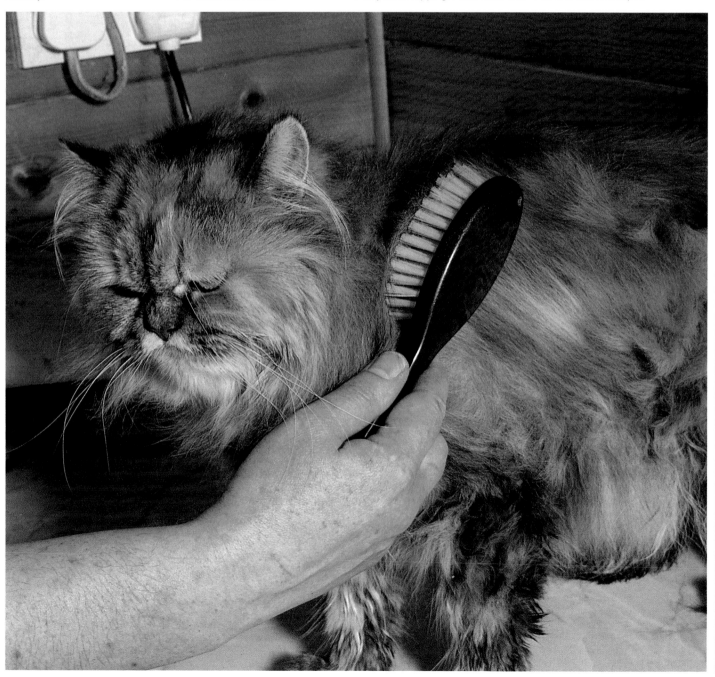

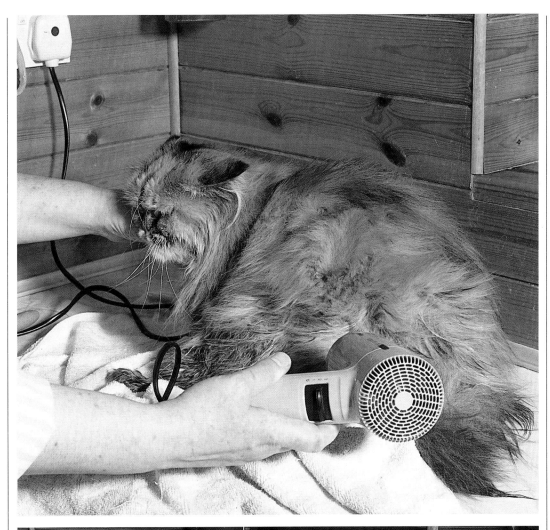

soaking him to his skin. Then apply the dishwashing-detergent solution, lathering the coat generously. Never lather past the cat's neck or you might get shampoo into his eyes. After the cat has been rinsed clean, apply some standard or flea shampoo, again lathering it well. If you are using a standard shampoo, rinse your cat after he has been lathered. If you are using a flea shampoo, check the label before rinsing — the manufacturer may recommend leaving the shampoo on the coat for a while. (A flea bath is only part of the campaign needed to rid your cat, and your house, of fleas. Lack of space precludes giving a full description of how that campaign should be waged. Consult your vet or a summer issue of a cat magazine for advice on how to eliminate fleas.)

After your cat has been rinsed, take hold of his tail at the base with one hand and squeeze gently, coaxing out as much water as you can. Repeat the process from the midpoint to the base of the tail, and on each leg. Blot his legs, tail and body with paper towels to absorb as much additional moisture as possible. Then remove the cat from the sink and wrap him in a towel.

Drying your cat

In a warm house a shorthaired cat can be allowed to dry naturally following a bath. If you don't want a wet cat sitting on the furniture, confine him in the bathroom until he dries. Provide him with water and something with which he can amuse himself. He should be virtually dry within an hour or so.

Longhaired cats can also be allowed to dry naturally — but afterwards they will look straggly and unpresentable. Hair driers are more efficient and produce much better results. If you are going to use a hand-held drier, put two or three drops of a natural-tears solution (or a similar moisturizing agent) into your cat's eyes before you begin.

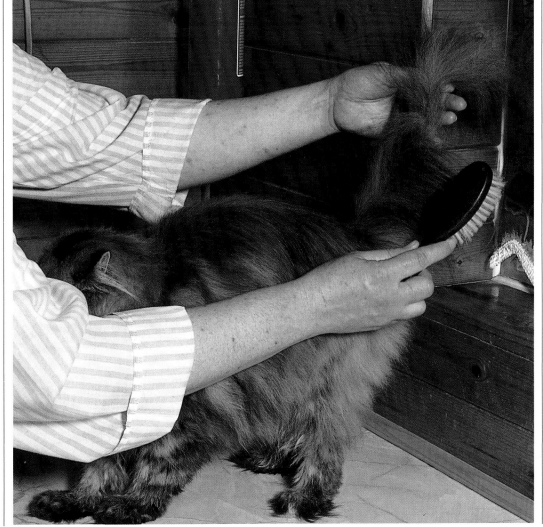

Before using the hair drier on your cat, place a towel on the surface he will be standing on while you dry him. Also test the temperature of the air blowing out of the drier on your wrist before beginning. The air should not be too hot, nor should the current be too strong.

While directing a stream of warm air into the coat, comb carefully. After the hairs in that area have been separated, move to another area of the cat. If you are attempting this job alone, it is best to use a hair drier that has a stand into which you can set the machine. Be sure that the drier stand is resting on a towel; otherwise as soon as you have it adjusted to the correct angle for drying the cat's underbelly, the drier and stand will start moving across the table of their own accord.

When you have gone over the entire cat once with the drier, begin again. The second time around, concentrate on one section of coat at a time, making sure it is virtually dry before moving on to another section of the coat.

6
BASIC HEALTH CARE

To keep a cat in resplendent good health an owner must see that it enjoys a safe, clean, comfortable environment; a balanced, nutritious, invigorating diet; prompt, competent and kindly medical care; and dependable and warmly loving human companionship all the days of its life.

The hazard-free environment
Like charity, a cat owner's obligations begin at home. All cats should live in surroundings that do not constitute a hazard to their continued well-being. The majority of cats, therefore, should spend the majority of their time indoors, where they will be safe from cars, inclement weather and the territorial incursions of other animals spoiling for a fight.

Simply living on the sheltered side of the doorstep does not automatically confer guaranteed safety on a cat. To be sure, a house that contains potentially dangerous toys, frayed electrical cables, poorly screened windows, poisonous plants, or a host of parasites is, for your cat, the environmental equivalent of a minefield. In such a house, the cat is an unsuspecting foot soldier who must navigate his way through these sources of possible injury and disaster.

It is ironic, but true, that people who wouldn't dream of putting their cats at risk will nevertheless provide them with playthings that appear to have been manufactured with no thought of safety in mind.

Before buying what seems to be an attractive toy, cat owners should make certain that there are no loosely sewn eyes, ears, tails, or other embellishments on the toy that an industrious cat could chew off and swallow. If there is a bell in or on the toy, the bell should be large enough — or fastened

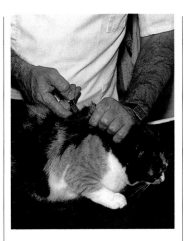

Above: A veterinarian injecting a vaccine as part of a routine series of inoculations recommended for all domestic cats.

Left: A sick cat will usually respond well to human affection — but remember that cats prefer, and seek out, solitude when ill.

securely enough — to prevent a cat removing and consuming it.

Home-made toys should be scrutinized just as carefully. While cats are resourceful enough to make hours of sport out of the most pedestrian object (such as a rolled-up sheet of computer paper), they are heedless enough to swallow string, rubber bands, small pieces of cellophane or aluminium foil and, of course, any tiny objects they can get their jaws around.

Plants, too, can be a fatal attraction for cats. Poinsettia, philodendron, dieffenbachia, English ivy (in the United States), hydrangea, holly and other flora can cause serious illness or death if eaten, in surprisingly minor amounts. (A vet can provide a complete list of

plants that a cat owner should grow — if at all — above climbing range or behind closed doors, where a cat cannot get at them.)

Doors themselves play a key role in keeping cats secure, and safe, in the home. But doors are also a source of potential danger. The door to the clothes drier, the door to the cabinet underneath the sink (where treacherous chemicals disguised as household cleaners lie in wait in tempting, brightly coloured plastic bottles), the door to a room where sewing supplies are left loose, the door to a cupboard sprinkled with moth balls: any door that could lead to grief should be tightly shut to exclude the bewhiskered explorer. And every door, especially the refrigerator's, should be closed cautiously when cats are about.

Cleanliness
Another attribute of a safe environment is cleanliness. A cat should not have to share living space with fleas, mites, dermatophyte spores (ringworm) or other bacterial intruders that can cause skin infections or allergies. The cat's environment is just as important to healthy skin as are food and medical care. One or two flea bites a day can cause rather severe itching and skin disease.

More than a third of the problems that dermatologists treat are related to flea bites. In addition to keeping a cat indoors, an owner can reduce a cat's exposure to other animals and to the retinue of parasites found outside the home by hiring a cat sitter instead of boarding a cat out during holidays.

Regular and diligent vacuuming, scrubbing and disinfecting are also fundamental to a healthful residence. So is immediate, thorough rinsing of any freshly cleaned surfaces that a cat may venture upon; for whatever gets on a cat's paws — or whatever a cat gets its paws on — stands a good chance of winding up in the cat's stomach. This may mean, in turn, that the cat stands a good chance of winding up at the vet's.

Virtually no detail of a cat's environment is too small to be significant to the cat's well-being. Even the method of heating a house can influence a cat's comfort. Forced-air heating systems, for example, can dry out a cat's skin, causing itchiness and scales (dandruff).

The healthy diet

Another obligation cat owners have to their animals is to provide them with a balanced, nutritious and invigorating diet. Some owners feel that they cannot possibly buy a food which is all three, so they decide to cook their cat's food at home. For most other people, feeding their cat is less of a complicated process: it merely involves opening a container and spooning out the contents. The problems of providing the correct nutritional requirements are left to the pet-food companies. Whatever

method you choose, table scraps and occasional treats should be just that — occasional — for they do not provide the balanced regimen a cat needs.

Like table scraps and occasional treats, vegetarian diets do not provide cats with the necessary balanced regimen. Some people who adopt vegetarian diets, whether for moral or medical reasons, presume that what is good for them is good for their cats, too. Unfortunately, this is not the case. Cats are born carnivores: they do not have the nutritional options that are available to their owners. For example, certain essential amino acids required by cats, including taurine, are present only in animal-based foods. (Taurine deficiencies have been linked to blindness and cardiomyopathy in cats).

Such is the vegetarian cat-owners' dilemma: whether to feed the remains of animals they do not choose to eat, to other animals they do not choose to live without.

Supplements

Though cat owners who prepare home-cooked meals for their cats must add vitamins and minerals in the correct proportions, there is no

evidence that a vitamin supplement will do anything for a healthy cat if it is already getting a balanced diet from a commercial product. Nor, in most cases, will adding oil to a cat's diet automatically put a gloss on a cat's coat.

Weight problems

Given that owners now have such a wide choice of balanced, commercial diets, it is the quantity of food eaten by the cat, not its quality, which is more likely to compromise the animal's longevity. Among other impediments, excess weight puts a strain on a cat's heart and musculo-skeletal system. Overweight cats are also prone to diabetes, especially as they get older.

The annual check-up

According to a study conducted by the American Veterinary Medical Association, two out of three cat owners reported that the reason they last took a cat to a vet was for an annual check-up. This procedure — like cars, colleges and stereo equipment — comes in a variety of models and sticker prices. In the basic examination, the vet ruffles a cat's coat to check for

softness, sheen and texture, broken hairs, scales, fleas, flea dirt and ringworm. The vet may also tug a pinch of skin away from the body to see how swiftly the skin returns to its normal position — a rule-of-thumb test for dehydration. Next, the vet looks at the cat's eyes and ears, examines its teeth, listens to its heart and lungs, then palpates its abdomen, kidneys and liver. Unless there is a good reason for the cat not to receive one, the vet then administers a booster shot to inoculate against various upper respiratory conditions and, if required, against rabies.

Young, healthy cats do not need as close (or as costly) an inspection as older cats — or cats with complex medical histories — do. Cats aged ten and above, or cats that have had medical problems in the past, may need additional tests to check for diabetes or to monitor blood chemistry, thyroid level, cholesterol, kidney and liver functions and other conditions.

Below: A vet attends to a patient at the surgery. A large cage is the best place to keep a sick cat, both at home and for journeys to the vet.

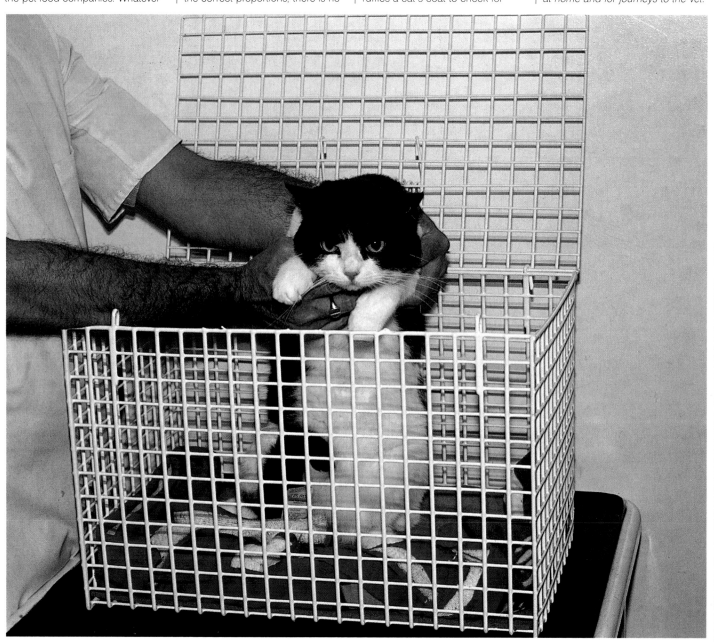

The final component of a cat's annual check-up is the fecal examination, in which a stool sample is analysed for roundworms and hookworms. Tapeworms, which are carried by fleas, cannot be detected by this method. The ancient Egyptian technique of inspecting for tapeworms, which involved lifting a cat's tail and closely examining its anus, has not been bettered since those ancient times. During this procedure, the examiner is looking for small, white segments of tapeworm that look much like rice.

Love and companionship

The last component of the lifestyle of any healthy cat is human companionship. In short, if you genuinely care for your cat, you will give it love and companionship; if you fail to do so, you are merely keeping it, not caring for it. Cats deserve the privilege of lying in their owners' laps for an hour every night (or at some other time) and having their ears scratched. And what would cat owners do without the reciprocal privilege of having a cat to scratch behind the ears when the world has dealt them a few scratches of its own?

When your cat is unwell

Generally, the first sign that a cat is unwell is a persistent lack of interest in food. One missed meal or a half-hearted go at the feeding bowl is no cause for worry; but if a cat misses two consecutive meals, he may be harbouring a condition that warrants a trip to the vet.

Other signs of potential ill health in a cat include, but are not limited to, the following: sneezing or coughing that continues intermittently for more than an hour or two; a wet or runny nose; a parched or warm nose; tearful eyes; a raised third eyelid; bouts of vomiting or diarrhoea that continue over a three- or four-hour period; listlessness lasting for more than a day; and a temperature above 103.5°F (39°C). If your cat displays any of these symptoms, or if he cries in pain when you pick him up, urinates frequently, continually starts to urinate outside his litter tray, or sits with his head hanging over the water bowl, something may be wrong. Call the vet at once, describe your cat's symptoms and make an appointment.

Some signs of illness are so obvious that you immediately know you have to take the cat to the vet.

Before leaping into the car, however, call the vet to describe the problem and to say that you're coming over.

The following is a list of some of the symptoms that suggest you have an emergency on your hands. The list is not exhaustive; nor should it be used in attempts to diagnose your cat's illnesses. Rather, you should use it as if it were a road map (so to speak) indicating where other drivers have encountered potholes and detours with their cats.

See your vet at once if your cat:
● Has been chewing on a plant and suddenly stops breathing.
● Develops a temperature above 105°F (40°C).
● Is constipated and strains at the stool, but fails to defecate.
● Shows any evidence of trauma accompanied by difficult breathing, a temperature of 103.5°F (39°C) or more, pale gums or lethargy.
● Suddenly becomes so weak in the hindquarters that he walks only with great difficulty.
● Develops a red, ulcerated sore on his lips or elsewhere on his body.
● Has a deep wound or a wound that persists in bleeding after you have applied pressure to it.

● Has a runny nose accompanied by a temperature above 103.5°F (39°C), pale gums or weakness.
● Develops an abscess that is warm to your touch and which, when you touch it, causes him pain.
● Vomits and appears lethargic, attempts to urinate often, has a temperature of 103.5°F (39°C) or more and/or bloody stools.
● Has diarrhoea, bloody faeces, raised temperature or is vomiting.
● Has eaten a foreign substance and becomes increasingly drowsy.

Call your vet promptly if your cat:
● Loses interest in food, is coughing, vomiting or has diarrhoea.
● Has diarrhoea accompanied by dehydration. (Check for dehydration by taking a pinch of skin from over the cat's spine and lifting the skin away from his body; then let go of the skin. If it fails to spring back into place immediately, your cat is dehydrated.)

Below: Here, the vet uses a syringe to administer medication in liquid form. Syringes are also useful for feeding liquid food to sick cats.

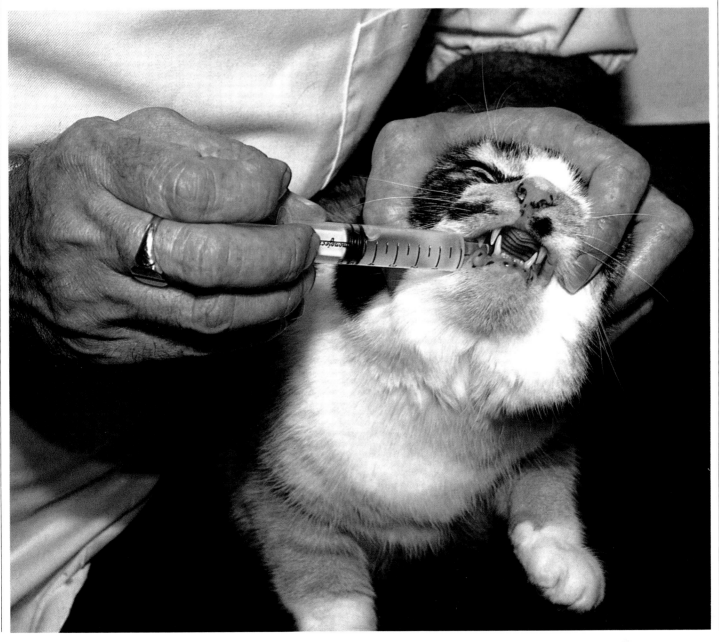

- Has very thin stools and a raised temperature.
- Begins drinking more water than usual and urinates excessively, has diarrhoea, is lethargic or develops a raised temperature.
- Shows signs of general lameness in any leg for more than two days.
- Develops a swelling that is warm and painful to the touch.
- Has a temperature between 103.5°F (39°C) and 105°F (40°C) and other signs of illness.
- Has a cough accompanied by a raised temperature, laboured breathing and lack of energy.
- Has foul-smelling breath, is drinking water excessively, eating frequently, urinating frequently and appears lethargic.
- Has a runny nose accompanied by lethargy, pus in either eye, or rapid breathing.

External parasites

Parasites are living organisms that reside on other living organisms, which are called hosts. Parasites feed on their hosts' blood, lymph cells or tissue. Parasites that live inside their hosts are called internal parasites (or endoparasites). Those that dwell on the surface of their hosts are called external parasites (or ectoparasites).

Fleas, ticks, flies, lice, larvae and mites are the external parasites with which cat owners are most frequently familiar. These marauders — in addition to damaging skin

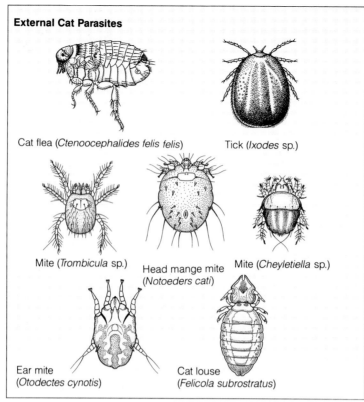

External Cat Parasites

Cat flea (*Ctenoocephalides felis felis*)

Tick (*Ixodes* sp.)

Mite (*Trombicula* sp.)

Head mange mite (*Notoeders cati*)

Mite (*Cheyletiella* sp.)

Ear mite (*Otodectes cynotis*)

Cat louse (*Felicola subrostratus*)

Above: The principal types of external parasites that may be found on cats. The species and severity of infestation vary throughout the world. In some areas, parasites carry diseases.

Below: A vet taking a cat's temperature rectally. If you need to do this at home, get someone to help; one person can then restrain the cat, while the other introduces the thermometer.

tissue — may transmit harmful bacteria and dangerous viruses to their hosts. If they are present in significant quantities, external parasites can leave their hosts sapped of energy and vitality, weaken their resistance to infection and disease and infest them with various kinds of diseases or parasitic worms.

The presence of external parasites is usually revealed by skin lesions, hair loss, itching, redness, dandruff, scaling, growths of thickened skin, or an unpleasant odour. If any of these symptoms appears, take your cat to the vet for a diagnosis. Cats that are infected with external parasites may sometimes have to be isolated from other cats and treated with parasiticidal dips, powders, ointments and shampoos.

Internal parasites

There are four types of internal parasites that infect the cat: protozoa, nematodes, cestodes and trematodes. Protozoa are usually one-celled organisms that may contain specialized structures for feeding and locomotion.

Toxoplasma gondii is the protozoan most familiar to cat owners. It can cause retinal lesions, calcified lesions in the brain, (which are sometimes fatal), or water in the brain cavities of newborn infants whose mothers have been infected by *Toxoplasma* during pregnancy.

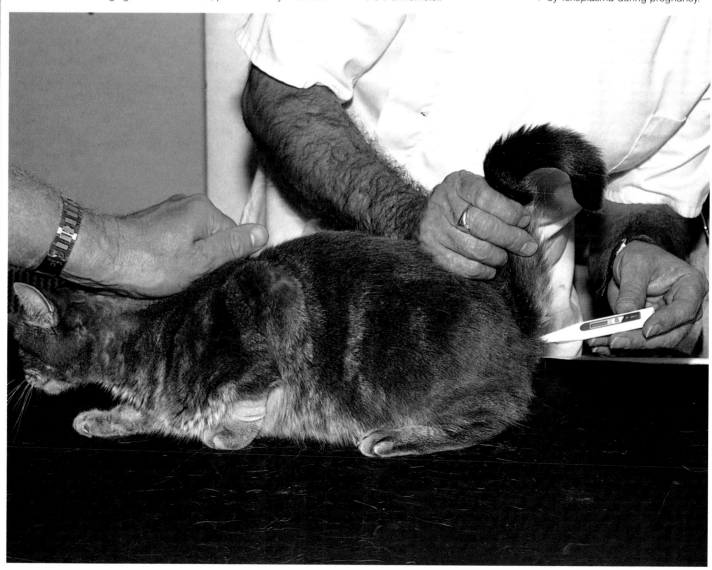

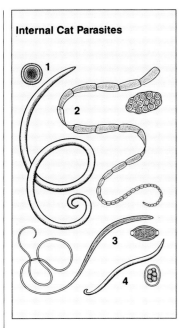

Above: The principal internal parasites that can affect cats. The drawings show the basic shapes of the parasites and are not in scale with each other. The most common species are listed.
1 *Roundworm* (Toxocara canis *and* Toxocara leonina)
2 *Tapeworm* (Dipylidium caninum)
3 *Whipworm* (Trichuris sp.)
4 *Hookworm* (Ancylostoma caninum)

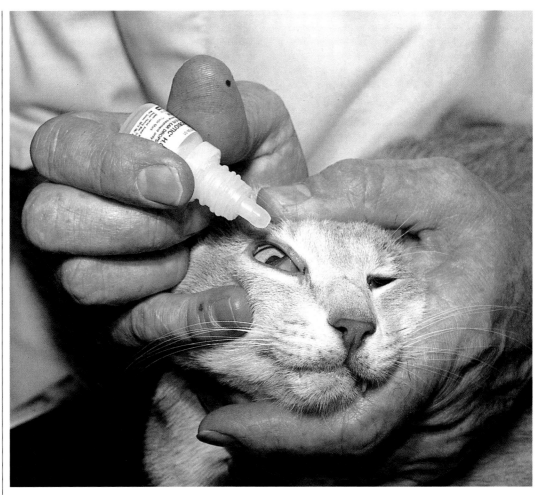

Above: Eye drops can be given at home, but it is important to hold the cat firmly or wrap it in a towel to prevent it struggling.

Children infected by *Toxoplasma* postnatally may develop a rash, flu-like symptoms, heart disease, pneumonia, retinal lesions and an infection of the central nervous system which can be fatal.

To avoid *Toxoplasma* infection, pregnant women should not clean litter trays — or, if they do, they should be sure to wear disposable rubber gloves. Children should be told not to play near litter trays.

Nematodes look something like earthworms. The nematodes that cat owners are most likely to have to contend with in their cats are roundworms and hookworms. Their presence can be detected by means of a stool-sample analysis.

Cestodes (or tapeworms) cannot be identified by stool-sample analysis. These worms, which are carried by fleas, are best identified by means of the anal examination technique described on page 131.

Trematodes are tiny flukes that live in the small intestines of their hosts. Cats generally become infested with trematodes after eating raw fish, frogs or small rodents. Unless such creatures have a way of getting into your house, there is little likelihood that your cat will encounter the trematodes they carry if you keep your cat indoors.

Worms are not difficult to eliminate. If your cat needs to be dewormed, use a product prescribed by your vet, and be sure to use it according to your vet's instructions.

Dental care
A cat's teeth should be clean and white, and its breath should not be offensively smelly. Cats have 30

adult teeth, which usually replace and augment the kitten's 26 deciduous, or milk, teeth by the age of six or seven months. (Milk teeth begin to appear when a cat is approximately four weeks old.)

The gums and tissues of a cat's mouth should be pink, except for the black pigment spots that some cats have on their gums. Firm, pink gums that adhere snugly to a cat's teeth are a sign of good dental health. Pale gums are a warning that a cat may be bleeding internally or suffering from anaemia or any of a number of systemic diseases.

Gingivitis, whose presence is signalled by a raw-looking, red line in the gums just above the teeth, is a frequent and a stubborn problem in cats. Mild gingivitis may be tolerated by a cat without causing any ill effects. More severe gingivitis is accompanied by drooling and bad breath.

Gingivitis is caused by the accumulation of plaque and tartar on a cat's teeth. When plaque spreads beneath the gums, it inflames them, causing redness, swelling and eventual loosening of the teeth. Gingivitis can also be caused by viruses such as feline calicivirus and feline leukaemia virus.

Owners whose cats are tolerant can clean their cats' teeth by rubbing them with a soft cloth that has been soaked in diluted hydrogen peroxide, bicarbonate of soda, or salt water. (As an alternative to the soft cloth, use a cotton wool bud, a clean finger, a child's toothbrush or a soft gauze pad.) Do not use human toothpaste

to clean your cat's teeth. It may cause him to drool, and it may also upset his stomach.

Whether or not your cat allows you to clean his teeth daily, weekly, or once in a blue moon, he should have his teeth cleaned by a vet at least once a year.

Nursing a sick cat
From the cat's point of view, the kindest thing you can do for him when he is sick is to leave him alone. Cats respect and seek out the regenerative properties of solitude, and they prefer that you appreciate and respect these properties as well. Nursing a sick cat, therefore, requires that you strike a balance between respecting his desire for privacy and helping him to recover.

Given cats' fondness for privacy and solitude, it should come as no surprise that they do not make the greatest of patients. Cats resist taking pills as if they were poison. They promptly lick any 'foreign' material — especially medication — from their coats. They object to being force-fed, and since their instincts tell them they ought to hide when they are sick because their condition makes them vulnerable, they must often be caged in order to be readily accessible when it is time for their medication.

For these reasons, the seriously ill or injured cat is better left in the charge of a vet. Your cat is certain to miss you while he is there, and you will miss him, but at least he will not associate you with pills and other intrusive indignities.

Lesser ailments and convalescence should be weathered at home, in

familiar surroundings. This means, of course, that pills and medications must be administered by familiar hands, which will in all likelihood be yours.

The isolation ward
The first precept of home nursing care is that sick or convalescing cats should be isolated from other cats in the house. The second rule is that persons handling sick or convalescing cats should wash their hands thoroughly and change their clothes before handling other cats in the house. Anyone handling a sick cat should wear rubber gloves.

All bedding, food dishes, water bowls and litter trays used by any cat suffering from a contagious disease should be disinfected with an antiseptic that is non-toxic for cats. All leftover food, litter, soiled dressings, excrement and other waste should be sealed in a plastic bag and placed in an outdoor rubbish bin.

The best place to confine a sick cat is in a large cage measuring approximately 22in. (56cm) long, 22in. (56cm) high, and 44in. (112cm) wide. The cage should be located in a warm room that is quiet and free of draughts. Provide the cage with a litter tray, food dish, water bowl and a cosy cat bed. If you are able to hang curtains around three sides and over the top of the cage, this may also make the sick cat feel more secure.

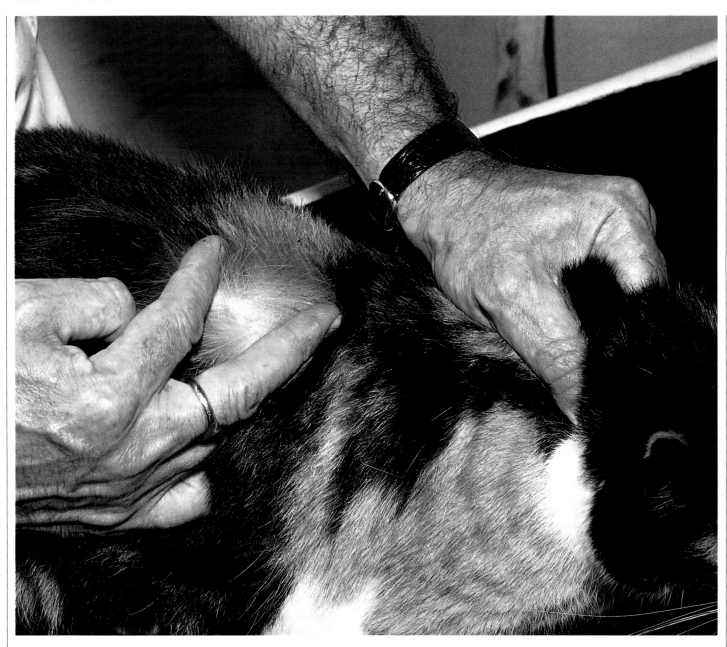

Though a sick or convalescing cat may not feel like playing with toys, a hanging spider or some other device in one corner of the cage may eventually prove diverting. If you are concerned about keeping the patient warm, put a cardboard box — with one side cut down for ease of entry and exit — in one corner of the cage, and place a heating pad covered with a towel in the bottom of the box. Leave a radio, tuned in to a quiet station, playing softly in the room. And if your cat will tolerate it, groom him as usual. Otherwise, just hold him and pet him gently for a few minutes two or three times a day. Don't spend too much time with him. Sleep is the second-best medicine for the majority of cats in most cases.

Feeding the sick cat

Since many sick cats lose interest in their food, you will be challenged to prepare something that your pet will find palatable. Forget about balanced diets for the moment: a good diet for a sick cat is anything he will eat. Cats recovering from upper respiratory infections are a particular challenge because they may not be able to smell their food.

Such patients may respond, however, to strong-smelling items such as sardines, tuna fish, or meat that has been seasoned generously with garlic. Once a cat begins to accept any of these foods, you can begin to add more nutritionally balanced fare.

Sliced turkey breast is a great favourite of sick cats, as are baby foods containing meat. Some cats will eat a high-calorie food substitute that looks similar to molasses and which is available from vets.

To make sure that the patient does not become dehydrated, offer him a variety of fluids until you find one that he will drink. Water, beef or chicken broth, or evaporated milk mixed with baby cereal, egg yolk and corn syrup with a pinch of salt are possible choices. (Be careful that the latter does not upset your cat's stomach or cause diarrhoea.) If your cat is extremely weak, you may have to feed him fluids using an eye dropper or syringe.

Pilling and force-feeding

Administering pills to a cat is always difficult at the best of times, for the majority of cat owners. Having said that, some owners seem to have been born with a knack for pilling. They grasp the top of a cat's head in one hand, and apply pressure to the corners of his mouth with thumb and middle finger or ring finger to force the mouth open. Then, quick as a flash, they drop the pill onto the back of the cat's tongue, jab an index finger against the back of his throat, withdraw the finger, hold the cat's mouth shut and blow quickly into his face to startle him and force him to swallow.

Owners who have failed to master this technique resort to pill guns. Pill guns can be a blessing — and a finger-saver — but, to use one, it is still necessary for someone to pry the cat's mouth open so the gun can be inserted. Gun-shy cat owners may thus prefer to hide ground-up pills in butter or in a piece of meat, such as hamburger. Whichever technique works, praise your cat for taking the pill, and give him a treat afterwards.

Force-feeding is less distressing an experience for your cat than is pilling: his initial resistance may lessen when he realizes that the substance you are inserting into his mouth actually tastes good. The technique for force-feeding is similar to that used to administer pills. Hold

Above: Checking for flea dirt at the annual check-up. Do this regularly at home, too — especially during the summer months.

Below: Pill guns consist of a plastic tube split at the end to hold the pill. A plunger is depressed to push the pill into the back of the cat's throat.

A Pill Gun in Use

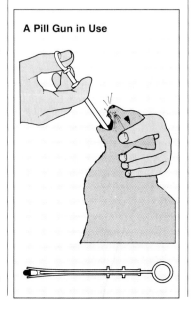

the cat's head from the top. Place a thumb against one corner of the cat's mouth and a middle finger (or ring finger) against the other corner. Squeeze the cat's mouth open. Put a dab of food on the index finger of your free hand and rub it onto the roof of his mouth. Relax the pressure on the sides of his face, allowing his mouth to close; continue to restrain his head to prevent him shaking out the food. Another method of persuading a cat to accept some nourishment is to put a touch of food on his nose — he will promptly lick it and so, again, realize that it tastes good.

If you are feeding the cat liquid food, put it into a syringe, open the cat's mouth as described above, then squeeze some of the liquid into the pocket formed where the cat's upper and lower lips meet. Introduce the liquid slowly, allowing the cat time to swallow.

After applying any skin medication, hold your cat or play with him quietly for a few minutes to distract him so that he will not immediately lick off the medication. If medication must remain on the cat's skin undisturbed for a longer period of time, ask your vet to show you how to fashion an Elizabethan collar that will prevent the cat from licking off the medication.

After you have had to pill, force-feed or medicate your cat, apologize for the intrusion and explain that you are really trying to help. Then sit with him quietly for a while.

Older cats

Everybody loves a kitten. Most people are susceptible to the charms of an adult cat. The true connoisseur of cats, however, knows that the essence of the cat-human bond lies in the bittersweet pleasures of caring for an elderly cat. Your knowledge of one another's character is rich — and stripped of all pretense. The trust, affection and respect you share run deep, furrowed into your relationship by years of living closely together. You have, in many cases, experienced the tribulations of her kittenhood alongside her and have enjoyed the sleekness and agility of her prime. Now it is time to stand by her as she negotiates the final stretch of life's journey.

Every cat has its own personality, with its own unique characteristics. The kind of individual she is will determine her reaction to the experience of ageing.

Not every cat, for example, becomes cranky and captious with age. A warlike cat whom this writer acquired during the cat's middle years has mellowed considerably as she has grown older — a fortunate turn of events for the other cats and the two young puppies with whom she currently shares a home. It is as if the old timer had managed to read this passage from the French writer Camus: 'To grow old is to pass from passion to compassion'.

Just as cats do not all age in the same way, neither do they age at the same rate. A cat's 'biological' age — as opposed to her 'chronological' age — is a function

Right: This commercially produced Elizabethan collar is made of flexible plastic. It is folded into the correct shape then clipped around the cat's neck to prevent it licking medicated or sore areas.

of her genetic background, the quality of her diet, the presence or absence of disease and the quality of the environment in which she lives.

If you are a first-time owner of an elderly or geriatric cat, you would do well to remember that no-one knows your cat as thoroughly as you do. You were the one who found that special spot where she liked to be scratched when she was a kitten. You were the one who discovered that she loved playing in the 'popcorn' in which some mail-order items are packaged. You were the one who was able to comfort her when thunder storms sent her scrambling into the most remote regions of a wardrobe. Now it is time to use all the knowledge you have acquired together to make her life and surroundings as comfortable as possible. To do less would be to neglect an old friend.

The passage of time brings about progressive and irreversible changes in your cat. Sadly, few of the physical changes are for the

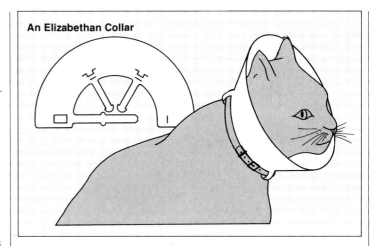

An Elizabethan Collar

better. As your cat's metabolism slows down and her vitality begins to dim, her ability to taste, see, smell and hear all diminish. She is less tolerant of drugs, less able to regulate her body temperature, and her immunity to disease weakens. She requires fewer calories to fuel her body and to maintain her optimum weight. Her thyroid, adrenal and pituitary glands and

Below: The vet examines a pregnant queen. In the majority of pregnancies there is no need to take the mother-to-be to the vet.

her pancreas do not secrete hormones as fluidly as they did when she was younger.

These changes are generally accompanied by other less immediately noticeable physical and behavioural changes. Your cat's eyes may become cloudy, her muzzle may turn grey, her fur may be less luxuriant, her skin may become slack, her muscles flabby and her spine and hips more prominent. She may also experience stiffness in her joints, or lameness. She will most likely become less active, more inclined to sleep, less accepting of

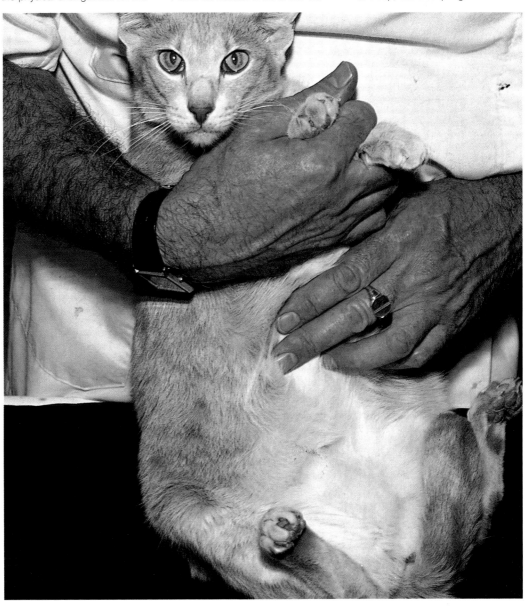

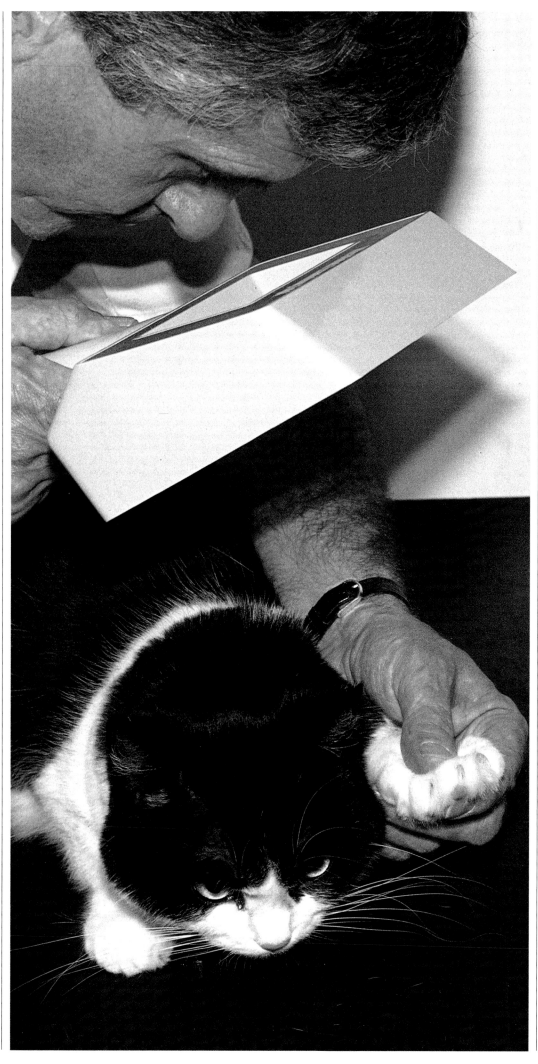

environmental changes, less tolerant of cold temperatures and may, perhaps, grow somewhat irritable as well.

Researchers estimate that old age in cats begins at roughly their eighth or ninth birthdays. According to one estimation, this is the equivalent of between 53 and 57 human years.

With the onset of old age, a cat becomes more susceptible to disease. Therefore, the earlier that conditions are diagnosed, the better her chances of recovery. The annual veterinary inspection becomes more important in old age, and you may consider switching to semi-annual check-ups. Naturally, it is important to ensure that her inoculations are kept up to date in order to protect against panleukopenia, respiratory diseases, feline leukaemia and rabies.

As you and your cat grow old(er) together, you may notice that at least one of you is growing in other ways, too. Older cats often become overweight as a consequence of their reduced activity and metabolic rate. The signs of excess weight are not difficult to detect. If your cat's abdomen begins to droop, if you cannot feel her rib cage when you run your hands along her sides, if she sways noticeably when she walks, or if she develops bulges on either side of the point where her tail joins her body, the chances are that she is carrying too much weight.

To correct these symptoms weigh your cat once every month and adjust the amount you feed her accordingly. If she gains a pound, switch to diet cat food, which contains 20 per cent to 33 per cent fewer calories than does standard cat food. If you are feeding her both wet and dry foods, try a diet dry food for a month. If your cat returns to her optimum weight, return to standard dry food and continue to monitor her weight. If switching to a diet dry food does not bring about the required weight reduction, continue feeding it to her — and switch to a diet canned food also.

As with weight gain, progressive weight loss in older cats is a cause for concern — perhaps even more so. Weight loss may indicate kidney failure, the presence of a tumour, diabetes mellitus, liver disease, or other conditions. If your cat loses weight for two consecutive months, or if she loses more than ½lb (227g) in any month, schedule an early appointment for the cat with your vet.

To make sure that an older cat gets enough food in a multi-cat household, you may have to keep on the look-out for changes in the cats' pecking order. For the cat who formerly ruled the roost may now have passed the mantle of leadership on, if it has not already been jostled from her shoulders. The old pecking order which

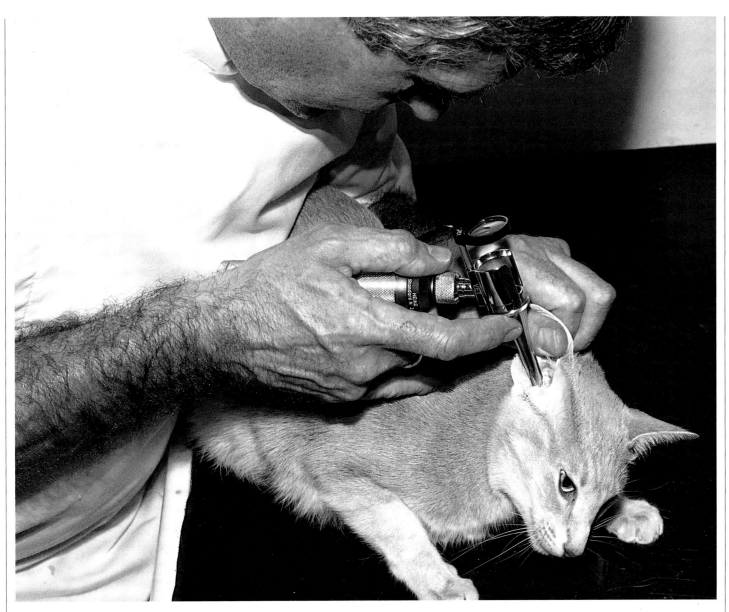

dictated who ate first, who got the choice spot in a sunny window or who had first go on the favourite lap may have been superseded with the physical decline of the older cat. If this occurs, it is important to think of ways to modify procedures so as to ensure the well-being of the senior partner. For example, feeding her alone in a place where her leisurely dining habits can be accommodated, and seeking her out for attention on a routine basis can help her to make a graceful adjustment to her new status as the senior citizen of the house. Your elderly cat may also appreciate a warm nesting-spot near the centre of family activity or, if she has been in the habit of going outdoors, a chaperoned trip outside once or twice a day.

Besides seeing to your older cat's dining and social comforts, you will need to see that she is getting enough exercise. Some older cats' participation in play might be limited by their unwillingness to compete with younger cats in the house, or by arthritis and muscle atrophy. You can help your cat to maintain good muscle tone and suppleness, to increase blood circulation and to improve gastrointestinal motility (the spontaneous movement of the gut) by persuading her to exercise moderately — the feline equivalent

of the window-shopping practised by senior citizens. While you and your cat enjoy her favourite game, be sure to be on the lookout for laboured breathing or the rapid onset of fatigue, which can be symptoms of heart disease.

Frequent grooming — three times a week or so — provides an opportunity to examine your cat for unusual lumps, skin lesions or external parasites. Any lumps or lesions found should be fully examined by a vet. Grooming is an added kindness to the elderly cat. The more dead hair you remove from your cat's coat, the fewer hairballs she will accumulate in her stomach. Hairballs cause more frequent problems for older cats because their reduced gastrointestinal-tract motility aids and abets intestinal impactions. For this reason, bulk-forming agents such as wheat bran or a mild laxative should be given to older cats at the first signs of dry-retching, a reliable indication that your cat is trying to bring up a hairball.

When you groom your older cat, pay closer attention to her nails than you may have done previously. Older cats may not use scratching posts as frequently as do young cats — but the practice is necessary to remove the outer sheaths of claws. Thus, check an

older cat's nails on a weekly basis and trim when necessary.

The digestive tract is usually the last system to show signs of deterioration in the cat. Some researchers believe that rapid cell turnover in the gastrointestinal tract provides a modicum of protection against the degenerative effects of ageing. Nevertheless, older cats are more inclined to constipation than are younger cats. Milk, which is generally not recommended for cats once they emerge from kittenhood, can be beneficial to older cats because it may help them to produce a softer stool. Laxatives and hair-ball medications should not be used more than once a week, however (unless your vet tells you otherwise), because they can interfere with the absorption of vitamins and minerals.

The older that cats become, the more conservative they get. They are less adaptable to, and less happy about, changes in the environment. Consequently, when the family goes on holiday, they should be boarded out only as a last resort. And if there is no alternative to boarding, they should be surrounded with familiar toys and other obejcts from home to help reduce the stress caused by being uprooted. The best option is to arrange to have your older cat

Above: A vet uses an auroscope to examine the deeper recesses of the ear. Such inspection may reveal ear mites, an infection, or a blockage.

cared for at home by neighbours, friends, relatives, or a pet sitter.

Moving to a new house or bringing a new pet into your present house are additional sources of stress for an older cat. Sometimes, moving cannot be avoided — but you can, however, choose not to bring a new cat home. Indeed, once a cat is well settled into middle age (at roughly the age of six), the chances of a new introduction going smoothly and of a lasting friendship developing between the old and young cat are slim.

While the burdens of looking after an old cat are considerable, so too are the rewards of caring for an old-timer. Her measured steps and her treasured attentions will lead you frequently to pleasant reverie: of her life and yours, of eternal concerns such as birth, death, commitment, sadness and joy. What's more, as you muse away an afternoon together, your cat will contentedly nod ascent to all your thoughts and never interrupt to tell you that you are not recalling the details of the story correctly.

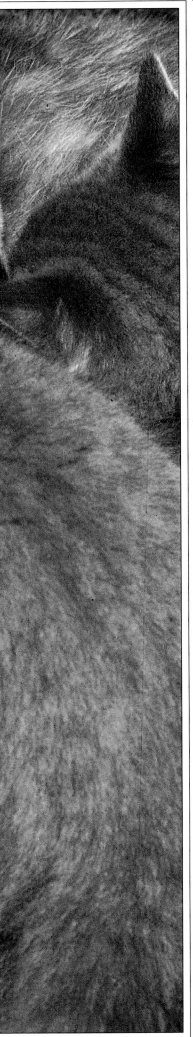

7

BREEDING AND REARING

Few events are so inspiring to cat breeders as the sight of a cat in season. For this is your opportunity to speculate — to roll the genetic dice in hope of making your point.

If cat breeding is a game of chance over which the players have little control, they should, nonetheless, approach the game equipped with certain resources. These include a seriousness of purpose, a clear-cut goal, a scheme for reaching that goal, a sense of responsibility and — let us not forget — a love of cats.

Breeding cats is 20 per cent art, 5 per cent science and 75 per cent luck. It is an art because a breeder must have an eye for cats, for structure, symmetry and harmony, and a plan for achieving them. It is a science because a breeder must gather knowledge about the antecedents of the cats he or she will summon together to create new life. It is an enterprise ruled by luck because even in the absence of points one and two above, a person can stumble onto success.

Though breeding cats is an admirable calling, too many people engage in it on a whim or for the wrong reasons: to gratify their competitive egos, to make a quick profit, or to let their children observe the cycles of pregnancy and birth. If the latter is the case, it would perhaps be more instructive to take the little ones to an animal shelter and let them witness the spectacle of unwanted animals being 'put to sleep'. With so many healthy, non-pedigree cats being destroyed every day for lack of decent homes — and with more and more purebred cats being given to shelters — the decision to create additional kittens should not be made for trivial reasons. For most people, in truth, it should not be made (or even considered) at all.

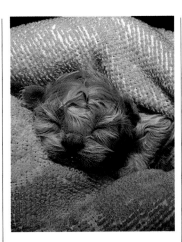

Above: A newborn kitten, still wet from the fluid in the amniotic sac in which it was born. The mother licks the kittens dry after birth.

Left: A Tortie mother with suckling kittens. The kittens are about eight weeks old and weaned, but are returning for a snack.

Competition in the show ring is intense, and few breeders ever become overnight sensations, let alone make a lasting contribution to their breeds. The laws of genetics are as fickle as they are immutable, and few, if any, litters are filled with exclusively show-quality animals. Also, as the day-to-day running of a cattery is labour- and capital-intensive, few people make as much money from raising kittens as they would from working the same number of hours at the minimum wage.

Owners who have read this far and who are still considering making an attempt at breeding should ask themselves the following questions: Will you bring as much to the lives of the kittens your programme will produce as you expect the kittens to add to yours? Would you be willing to trade places with any cat in your cattery? Would you be willing to live with the people to whom you sell your kittens?

The oestrus cycle

Oestrus — commonly known as 'calling', 'being on heat' or 'in season' — is a period of sexual receptivity in female cats. An oestrus cycle comprises a recurring series of such periods, each of which is followed by a period in which the cat lacks any interest in sex.

Most females experience their initial oestrus (from the Greek word for 'mad passion') following the onset of puberty, which is usually between the ages of seven to 12 months. Male cats, which are said to be in perpetual oestrus, generally reach sexual maturity from nine to 12 months of age.

Most cats will, on average, go out of oestrus after six to nine days if they are not bred in the interim. The periods of intermission between one oestrus and another are called metoestrus. Metoestrus periods last as few as three or as many as 30 days, but their average length is nine to 13 days.

Female cats first go into season around January and continue 'cycling' until March. Then, for reasons that are not yet fully understood, many temporarily stop cycling. By June, most unbred females resume cycling. If they have not conceived by mid-September, they remain out of season for about three months or so.

This extended holiday from hormonal influence, called anoestrus, may vary among breeds. In one study reported in the *Journal of Small Animal Practice* in 1977, out of a group of ten longhaired cats observed, nine went into seasonal anoestrus, while only four out of a group of ten shorthaired cats did the same.

How oestrus occurs

During the autumn, when many females are in anoestrus, the days grow increasingly short. Researchers believe that this reduction in daylight hours brings about an increase in the production of the hormones prolactin and melatonin, which are secreted by the anterior pituitary gland and the pineal gland respectively. Once the quantities of these hormones reach a certain level in the cat's bloodstream, ovarian activity, and consequently oestrus, are suppressed.

But once the days begin to lengthen in tiny increments shortly before Christmas, the female cat's eye eventually responds to this increase in light by sending neurochemical messages to the brain via the pineal gland. As a result, production of the oestrus-inhibiting hormones prolactin and melatonin is reduced, and the female soon begins to cycle.

The hypothalamus initiates that process by secreting GnRH (Gonadotropin Releasing Hormone), which stimulates the pituitary gland to release two hormones of its own. One is called Follicle Stimulating Hormone (FSH). This travels through the bloodstream to the ovaries, where it prompts the development of small, sac-like follicles and the eventual maturation of eggs within those follicles.

No-one has measured precisely the time that elapses between the cat's first response to an increase in light and the time she goes into season. But once a sufficient amount of FSH has been released into the bloodstream, an average of two to four follicles swell up and emerge on the surface of each ovary. These follicles approach maturity in ten to 15 days. At that time a small amount of another pituitary hormone is needed to bring about the final maturation of the ovarian follicles. This substance is called Luteinizing Hormone (LH). Like FSH, LH is released from the pituitary on instructions from the hypothalamus.

Soon after their follicles begin developing, the ovaries secrete oestrogen, the hormone that is essentially responsible for the singular behaviour of a cat in season. In fact, behavioural changes begin with the arrival of *pro-oestrus*, which signal a one- or two-day lull before the lightning storm. Females in pro-oestrus act as though they have spring fever. They become fidgety and vocal. They flirt with would-be valentines of either sex. They tread intermittently with their hind feet. They often become cloyingly affectionate towards humans and various pieces of furniture. They even may allow males to mount them during pro-oestrus, but penetration is generally reserved for after the ball.

Pro-oestrus generally gives way to full-blown oestrus after one or two

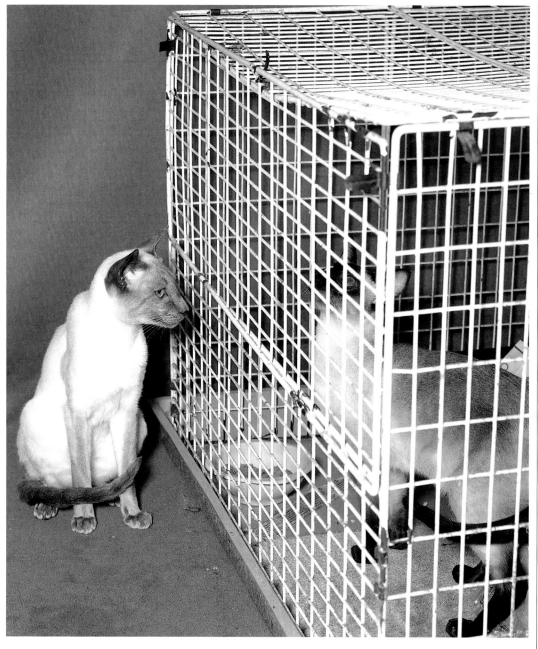

days. The female is then ready for serious courtship, and she will accommodate a male without much in the way of preliminaries. She broadcasts her readiness to mate by howling the whole day and night (or so it seems) and by parading about in the lordosis posture: down in the front, up at the back, tail swept wantonly to the side. She is also apt to fly out of doors the very second any opportunity arrives if she is not properly supervised.

The oestrogen which is responsible for producing this madcap behaviour in cats also acts on the higher centres of the brain to prompt ovulation — the release of eggs by the ovaries. Once the level of oestrogen in the bloodstream rises to a significant level, this hormone is capable of effecting a substantial release of GnRH from the hypothalamus. GnRH, in turn, prompts the release of LH from the pituitary, which eventually instructs the ovaries to release their eggs.

The operative word in this equation is 'capable'. For a large quantity of oestrogen would not be sufficient to trigger this process on its own. Unlike every other mammal (except the rabbit, ferret and mink),

the cat is an induced or reflex ovulator: if she does not copulate, she does not ovulate. Therefore, the oestrogen released by the ovaries as their follicles mature cannot do its job unless the male cat, ultimately, has done his. Only if the male achieves adequate penetration do the nerve endings in the cervix direct a message to the brain. This message, upon arriving at the hypothalamus, tells it to release GnRH as per oestrogen's request.

Normally, the ovarian follicles rupture and release their eggs between 25 and 36 hours after mating has occurred, but this release can occur as many as 50 hours later. Once the eggs have been released, they travel down the fallopian tubes to their rendezvous with the wildly swimming sperm injected by the male cat.

Supervision of breeding

The only females that should be considered for breeding are those that are healthy young animals that have been in season at least once, are older than ten months and that descend from other females who have a history of trouble-free

Above: A Siamese queen (in the cage) and a Siamese stud (left) get acquainted before mating takes place. This familiarization process is essential before mating proceeds: if the queen is not ready for the male, she may reject him.

Right: The Siamese queen and stud in the mating position. The stud mounts the queen from the rear and grasps the back of her neck with his teeth. Immediately after mating the queen will roll about excitedly, and may even attack the stud.

deliveries. The females who make the shortlist should also have pedigrees (and, in most cases, show records) that indicate they may have a contribution to make to their breeds.

Unlike dogs, female cats display little, if any, vulvar swelling or vaginal discharge during oestrus. Accordingly, cat breeders must be aware of other clues that signal the proper time to breed their females. These clues are usually proclaimed in no uncertain terms, as we have seen above, and there is seldom any doubt when it is time to pack

Female reproductive system

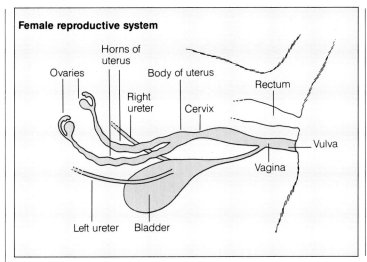

Ovaries
Horns of uterus
Body of uterus
Right ureter
Cervix
Rectum
Vulva
Vagina
Left ureter
Bladder

Male reproductive system

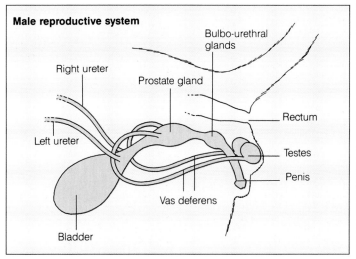

Right ureter
Bulbo-urethral glands
Prostate gland
Left ureter
Rectum
Testes
Penis
Vas deferens
Bladder

your female's overnight bag and take her off to the male that has been selected for her.

However, with some females it is far more difficult to tell when they are ready to be mated. Included in this group are those cats that have what are called 'silent seasons': they neither call nor tread, nor give any other outward sign of their internal physical condition. There is one straightforward solution to solving this problem: arrange for the taciturn bride to cohabit with her intended until their union has been consummated. This solution is only available, however, to breeders who own their own males. For the novice (who is advised not to buy a male at first) it is best to find a reputable, experienced breeder who owns a clever, experienced male and who will accept a shy female for stud service and be willing to keep her for as long as it may take to get her bred.

Once a cat is in season, she will usually accept a male's attentions with little in the way of adverse consequences beyond some ritualistic hissing. But for some females, mating is more than a one-act play. They demand a certain dramatic build-up, occupying several preliminary acts, before the dénouement is reached. Other females, indeed, caper about like strumpets at home but go out of season promptly when they meet their intended mates.

These females — and also those that are more aggressive by nature — frequently can be conditioned to accept a male's advances if they are exposed to an experienced male before they come into season. Some breeders cage a female in the male's quarters and allow the male to greet her through the bars of her cage. Other breeders put the female in a large pen next to a male's or allow her to run loose in the room where his pen is located. This gradual desensitizing process should begin when a female is out of season, so that by the time her hormones come to do their work she will be more friendly when the stud cat comes to do his.

Once a breeder is satisfied that a female is willing to accept a male's attentions, the pair should be left on their own, if possible, for three days. Unlike a female rabbit — which will ovulate faithfully at first breeding — the cat responds to mating stimuli, both single and multiple, in an unpredictable, nerve-wracking fashion; and researchers have yet to decide whether one mating is sufficient to bring about ovulation in all cats. This may be the case for some females, but it probably does not apply for the majority. Furthermore, cats who ovulate after a single mating in one season may not be so predictable the next time around.

Researchers also suspect that the fervour of copulatory motion and the number of copulations per

oestrus wield a significant influence over the dispatch of the message sent from the cervix to the hypothalamus, telling it to release additional quantities of LH, which cooperates with the oestrogen already in the bloodstream to promote ovulation. Cats who do not ovulate after one mating were, perhaps, not sufficiently inspired, and hence the hypothalamus was never told to release additional hormone. Or perhaps the hypothalamus did release LH, but its level in the bloodstream did not remain elevated long enough to trigger ovulation.

In a study conducted in the late 1970s seven groups of 12 females were mated on different days of oestrus and for varying numbers of times on those days. The four groups of females that were allowed to mate only once a day — on the first, second, third or fourth days of oestrus — could do no better than a 33-per cent-ovulation rate. By contrast, in three other groups that were permitted to mate three times a day on either the first, second or third day of oestrus, ten out of 12 females ovulated.

This study suggests that females should be allowed to mate as frequently as they wish for at least

three days. If a male cat — because of his busy schedule or his truculent nature — cannot devote his entire day to one female, the two animals should be allowed to breed three times per day at three- to four-hour intervals during the first three days of oestrus. According to a number of studies, this scheme has produced conception rates of 90 per cent and better because it insures that functioning sperm, which remains functional for only two or three days, will be present in the reproductive tract in sufficient volume when the female begins to ovulate.

Selecting a stud cat
The correct stud for your female is one that will reinforce her good points and repair her bad ones, while not introducing any genetic spanners into the works. The whereabouts of good studs can be determined by visiting shows to study the cats being produced by today's studs; by poring over yearbooks published by the various cat federations; and by looking through advertisements in cat magazines and breed-association newsletters.

A breeder should be guided by three principles in searching for the

proper mate for his or her female. First, the stud cat should live in an antiseptically clean cattery. Second, he should come from a family or a line of cats that has crossed to good advantage with the female's line in the past. And, finally, he should be dependably efficient in producing those qualities the female lacks. If a Persian female has large ears, for example, the male she is bred to should be one who consistently produces kittens with small (or smaller than average) ears. There is little chance of producing small-eared kittens if the male to whom a large-eared female is bred has produced only medium-eared kittens as a rule.

Many breeders prefer to use an older stud cat, that is, one who is already a grandfather, because it is easier to judge a male's reproductive performance by looking at his children and their children in turn than by looking at the honours he has won. Too many people have the mistaken notion that a good breeding programme consists of breeding to the latest winner. While such a cat may have proven himself in the show ring, he has yet to prove himself otherwise. This year's glamour cat may develop into a top producer one

Right: A pregnant Abyssinian queen. The nipples show clearly and the cat is suitably plump. She is glowing with health.

day, but it is more reasonable to assume that his father has already done so.

Terms and contracts

No owner should send a female to a cattery to be bred unless the owner of that cattery is willing to provide a current health certificate for the stud cat in question, and for any other cats with whom the female is likely to come into contact. In addition, owners should be wary about sending their females to catteries that do not request the same certification for incoming females.

The stud-service contract is another document that should accompany all breeding arrangements. The contract does not need to be an extensive document weighed down with legalese. It should, however, state the fee involved, the responsibilities of the stud owner while the female is in his or her care, the length of time the stud owner is willing to keep the female, and the boarding fee (if any) that the stud owner charges for feeding and housing females. The stud-service contract should also specify what will happen if the female is mated but does not conceive; if she conceives

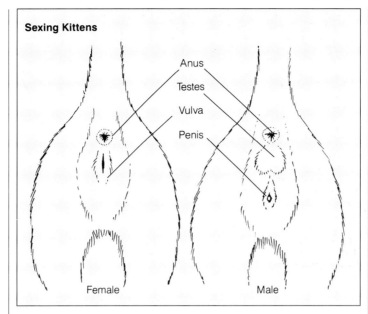

Sexing Kittens

Anus
Testes
Vulva
Penis

Female   Male

Above: The differences in young male and female kittens are easiest to discern in the first few days of life. The vulva and anus are closer together in the female kitten; the anus and developing scrotum are clearly further apart in the male kitten. To sex a kitten, hold it in one hand and lift the tail with the other.

Below: A Black Persian mother licks her newly born kitten to clean the kitten of the amniotic fluid. Once it is clean, the kitten will be drawn close to the mother's body for warmth. The kitten may then start trying to suckle straight away. At this stage, prepare a clean bed for the new family to rest in.

but loses her kittens prematurely after she returns home; if she has only one live kitten; and, indeed, any other eventuality that the parties to the contract consider important enough to put in writing.

How to identify pregnancy

Female cats normally release their eggs 25 to 36 hours following a successful mating — but this has been known to take as long as 50 hours. Therefore, the earliest that a female can conceive following mating is the day after her first successful mating. Generally, a female announces that a mating has been successful by screaming loudly, striking out at her suitor, tumbling about on the floor and grooming herself ardently.

About three weeks after her first succcessful mating, a female's nipples will begin to turn pink and to swell slightly. By that stage, each kitten embryo will measure scarcely ½in. (1.2cm) long.

Embryos and their associated membranes can be detected by means of abdominal palpation between 17 and 25 days after conception. Ultrasonography, which identifies kittens by means of reflected sound waves, can detect the amniotic sac enclosing a

developing embryo 18 days after conception. After 25 days, ultrasound can detect foetal heartbeats as well as the foetus itself. By about the 40th day of pregnancy, the mineralized, opaque foetal skeleton is visible on abdominal radiographs. These enable vets to estimate the number of kittens a female is carrying. In addition, since different bones become visible on radiographs at different stages of pregnancy, X-rays can also help to determine a litter's approximate age and delivery date for those breeders not certain when their females were bred.

Caring for a pregnant queen

Pregnancy effects changes in cat owners as well as their cats. Eager to do something more than mark off days on the calendar, many otherwise prudent owners begin adding vitamins, minerals and all sorts of supposedly beneficial ingredients to their queens' meals. Or they begin heaping prodigious amounts of food into their queens' bowls. The more the queen eats, the happier her owners become. They are now more than mere observers of the mystery; they are active participants in its unfolding drama.

Such behaviour is not only

unnecessary; it may well be counterproductive. Instead, for the first four weeks of your cat's pregnancy, you should groom her as usual, play with her as usual and feed her as usual — so long as you are feeding her a product that is 100 per cent nutritionally complete and balanced for all stages of a cat's life.

Your cat will begin to require additional food in gradual increments about the beginning of the fifth week of pregnancy. According to estimates published by the National Research Council in the United States, pregnant queens

need .5oz (14g) of dry food per lb (453g) of body weight each day, 0.6oz (17g) of semi-moist food, or 1.4oz (40g) of canned food. These amounts represent increases of 41 per cent, 50 per cent and 40 per cent, respectively, over normal requirements for dry, semi-moist and canned food.

Since the queen's abdomen becomes more crowded as her

Below: A Siamese mother nurses her kittens. Suckling continues for three weeks or so, then the kittens are weaned onto other foods.

kittens grow larger, apportion her food over three meals a day soon after you begin increasing her rations. If you notice that the dry-food bowl needs topping up more often than usual, measure the amount you set out there to prevent her from consuming more than the recommended .5oz (14g) per lb (453g) each day. Weight control during pregnancy is important for the health of mother and kittens because queens that gain too much weight often have not only poor muscle tone, but also birth canals that have been narrowed by fatty deposits. As fat queens often have fat kittens, excess weight can be a major problem.

If overfeeding during pregnancy is counterproductive, so are overdoses of vitamins and minerals, unless your queen is ill and your vet has recommended the use of supplements. Excess calcium, phosphorous and vitamin D, for example, can cause bone and kidney damage. Excess vitamin A can cause sterility and coat loss.

Finally, queens should not be exposed to teratogens during pregnancy. A teratogen is any substance that disrupts normal embryonic development.

Griseofulvin, an antidote for ringworm and fungus, is a teratogen in pregnant cats. So are live-virus vaccines, excess doses of vitamin A and some steroids. These and other teratogenic substances are always potentially harmful to the developing embryo.

Preparing for delivery
Gestation, the period between conception and birth, lasts, on average, 63 to 69 days after a female's initial successful mating. Sixty-five or 66 days is the usual length of the gestation period, but viable kittens have been born between 59 and 71 days. Ultimately, the time of delivery is known only by the cat, because breeders do not always witness, or overhear, the first mating; and even if they do, gestation varies according to the individual cat.

Fortunately, the queen provides a number of clues when delivery is nigh. Around the start of her last week of pregnancy, she begins to

---

Left: A newly born Persian kitten suckling. The kitten stimulates the mother's milk supply by using its paws on her nipples.

Below: A Burmilla queen with her Asian litter. After giving birth, the properly attentive queen will hardly move out of the kittening box for the first week.

look for a nesting place, directing her investigation towards open cupboards, open drawers and underneath beds. From this stage on, she should never be allowed out of her owner's sight for more than a few minutes at a time.

Given their choice, most queens would spend the last several nights of pregnancy on their owners' beds. If anyone objects to this arrangement, the queen should be put into a large cage in her owner's bedroom. The bedroom door should be kept closed, and children and other pets should be kept at bay. With the queen close at hand, even the deepest of sleepers should respond to any rattling about in the cage or cries of distress in the night.

Provide the queen's cage with food, water, a litter tray and a nesting box. The top or bottom half of a cat carrier or a modified cardboard box makes a decent nest. If you use a cardboard box, cut the front side down so that only a strip about 4in. (10.2cm) is left at the bottom to prevent newborn kittens from crawling out. Spray the nesting box with a mild, non-ammonia-based disinfectant, then wipe it dry before setting it in the cage. Line the box with cloth towels, newspaper or paper towels.

On the 58th day of pregnancy, many breeders begin taking their females' temperature night and morning using a rectal thermometer.

A cat's temperature is normally 101.5°F (39°C) or thereabouts. If it drops to 98°F (37°C), kittens will most likely arrive within 12 hours. If the temperature rises two or three degrees above normal, call the vet at once.

At about the same time that they begin to monitor a queen's temperature, owners of longhaired cats should clip the hair around their cats' anogenital area for sanitary reasons. Also crop the area around the cats' nipples so as to make them more accessible to the kittens. All owners should clip a queen's claws at this stage, too.

Delivering kittens

In addition to a drop in temperature, other signs of imminent delivery include rapid breathing, deep purring, kneading with the paws, pacing or turning around in circles, frequent attention to the genital area and passing the placental plug. The placental plug is a gelatinous stopper that forms at the cervix early in gestation; it protects the uterus from external sources of infection. The plug is expelled when the cervix begins to relax in anticipation of delivery. The clear, stringy mucous that accompanies the passing of the plug may appear a few hours, or a day or two before delivery.

As long as the queen passes a clear, odourless substance, there is no need worry. Should the discharge turn a dark, greenish colour or smell unpleasant, consult your vet. These may be signs that a placenta has broken away from the wall of the uterus, and that the kittens are in danger of dying from lack of oxygen — if one or more have not died of suffocation already.

Labour begins when a queen starts to have involuntary uterine contractions, which are usually preceded by rapid breathing, deep purring and kneading with the paws. Not long after involuntary contractions have begun, the queen begins to reinforce them by contracting her abdominal muscles to expel her first kitten. The breeder should note the time when abdominal contractions begin. If the first kitten does not appear within an hour, call the vet — and have a clean, towel-lined carrier ready.

As delivery begins, a dark, greyish-coloured bubble emerges from the vagina. Once that bubble of new life appears, the alarm clock should be reset to go off in 30 minutes' time. If the queen cannot give birth to the kitten, either on her own or with help from her owner during that time, call the vet immediately.

Kittens may be born in an anterior position or in a posterior position — that is, they can appear either head first or tail first. If the kitten is born head first, but the queen has not delivered it completely within a few minutes following the appearance of its head from her vaginal opening, remove the amniotic sac (or placental membrane) from around the kitten's face in order to prevent suffocation. The membrane should break and peel away easily if you rub the top of the kitten's skull gently with a clean finger or a small piece of clean cloth. Once the membrane has broken, peel it away from the kitten's face. If the membrane does not break readily, use your thumb and forefinger to pinch it at the base of the kitten's skull, then carefully pull it away from the skull. You may find that you have to push the lips of the vulva back from the kitten's head in order to grasp the membrane at the base of the skull.

If the queen has not delivered the kitten on her own after ten minutes have passed, you may be able to pull it free. If you attempt to wrench it out rather than to ease it out, you are also likely to injure the kitten in the process.

After washing your hands, grasp the kitten between the thumb and

Below: If a kitten fails to nurse adequately, continue supplemental feeding every two hours until the kitten begins nursing on its own.

forefinger of one hand, holding the kitten as far behind the head as possible. If enough of the kitten is protruding, hook it between your index and middle fingers, just behind its front legs. At the same time, support the queen's abdomen in the other hand and push upwards. Then pull the kitten downwards gently. If you and your queen cannot secure the kitten's release after 30 minutes, you will have to call the vet.

In the case of posterior (tail first) births, you are not able to remove the membrane from the kitten's face, and so time becomes precious. If the umbilical cord is pinched inside the birth canal, the maternal blood supply to the kitten will be cut off, and the kitten will suffocate. If a kitten appears tail first and is not delivered within five minutes, begin trying to pull it out. If you are not successful after 10 to 15 minutes, call your vet.

Once a kitten has been born, the queen should begin licking it vigorously to remove the placental membrane. If she does not remove the membrane from the kitten's face at once, do it for her.

Healthy kittens normally move about in search of a nipple and may begin nursing within 15 minutes after being born. Five to 15

minutes after she has delivered the kitten, on average, the queen will pass the placenta; this done, she will begin chewing on the umbilical cord to sever it. Once the placenta has been expelled, the next kitten, if there is one, should appear within 10 to 90 minutes later. However, at this stage the queen's behaviour is more significant than the interval between births. If she strains to deliver a kitten without success for an hour — or if a kitten appears in the vaginal opening and is not fully delivered within 30 minutes (or 10 to 15 minutes in the case of posterior presentations) — you must call the vet at once.

If a newborn kitten is breathing with difficulty or does not appear to be breathing at all, and if the queen has not expelled the placenta, fasten a hemostat to the umbilical cord, about 6in. (15cm) away from the kitten. Grasp the cord on the side of the hemostat which is closer to the mother, and tug gently. If the mother does not expel the placenta at once, cut the cord with sterile scissors on the mother's side of the hemostat, remove the hemostat, dip the severed end of the cord into a bottle of white iodine and try to revive the kitten.

Hold the kitten between your hands in a towel, rub the kitten

briskly to stimulate it and to help it begin breathing. Then hold the kitten in the palm of one hand, face up. Make sure the kitten's head is secure and immobile between your thumb and forefinger. Place your other palm over the kitten's abdomen with your forefinger over the kitten's heart.

Holding the kitten securely in both hands at about eye level, swing your hands downwards abruptly a distance of 3ft (.9m) or 4ft (1.2m), pressing the rib cage over the kitten's heart with your forefinger as you swing. Repeat two or three times. If the kitten fails to begin breathing, hold its mouth open and blow gently into it to resuscitate the kitten. Swing the kitten downwards two or three times more, blow into its mouth, swing, blow into its mouth and swing again until the kitten at last begins breathing or until it is obvious that the kitten is beyond reviving. Do not give up trying to revive the kitten for at least 30 minutes.

Some breeders, if they cannot revive a kitten after five or ten minutes, dip it up to its neck into a bowl of very cool water and then into a bowl of very warm water hoping to shock its heart into beating.

If a weak kitten begins breathing

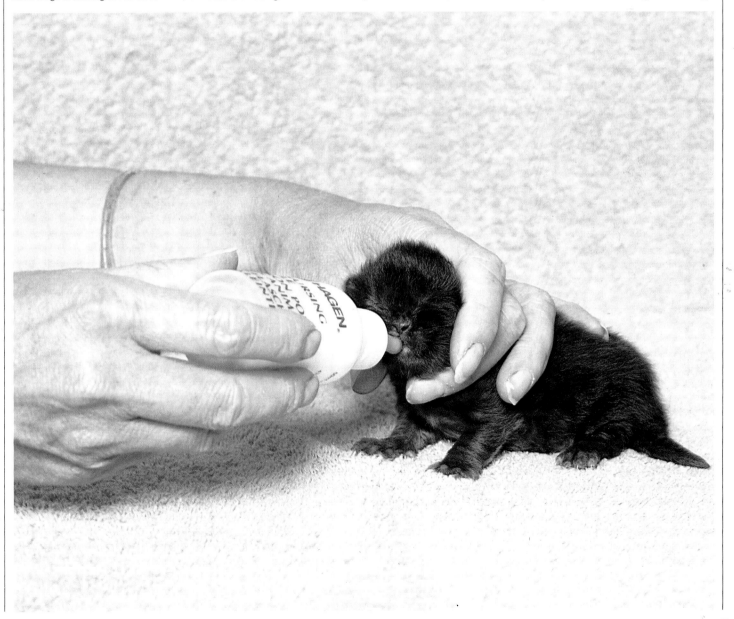

on its own, place it in a small box that has a heating pad covered by a towel on the bottom. The temperature in the box should be maintained at 85°F (29°C). To achieve this you may have to place another towel loosely over the kitten, close the flaps of the box

and place a third towel over the closed flaps. Give the kitten back to its mother when she has finished delivering her litter, but continue to monitor the weak kitten for the next two hours.

Some mothers chew each umbilical cord and eat every

placenta, but after your queen has consumed two placentas, you should dispose of any remaining ones yourself to prevent her developing an upset stomach or diarrhoea. If the queen shows little interest in either the umbilical cords or the placentas, cut the cords five

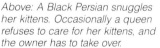

Above: A Black Persian snuggles her kittens. Occasionally a queen refuses to care for her kittens, and the owner has to take over.

minutes or so after the kittens have been born, sterilize the severed ends of the cords and dispose of the afterbirths. Be sure that all placentas are accounted for: a retained placenta can cause serious infection, may have to be removed surgically and could mean that the breeder, instead of the queen, will be raising the litter.

After the last kitten has been delivered, the queen will settle down to nurse her brood. As she does, inspect each kitten in turn for signs of abnormalities such as cleft palates or umbilical hernias.

After the last kitten has been born, continue to monitor the kittens and their mother for two hours to make sure that all the kittens are nursing normally, and the temperature in the kitten box is sufficient to prevent chilling. Kittens should begin nursing no later than two hours after they have been born. If a kitten appears to be too weak to nurse, you may have to feed it by tube (see 'Supplemental feeding' below).

Maintain the temperature in the kittening box at 85°F (29°C) placing a heating pad under the towel in the box if necessary. A kitten's homeostatic mechanism, which regulates its body temperature, is not completely functional at birth. Normally a queen's body heat is

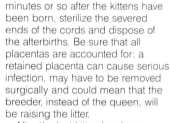

Left: The Black Persian mother lifts her kitten by the neck. Older kittens may be too heavy for the mother to lift in this manner.

enough to maintain the kittens' temperature at the normal 100°F (38°C)-101°F (39°C). After two weeks the temperature in the nesting box can be reduced to 80°F (27°C).

The developing kitten

Kittens nurse almost hourly for the first day or two after birth. On average, they weigh 3.1oz (88g) to 3.9oz (110g) at birth. They may not gain weight during their first 24 hours; indeed, they may even lose a few grams. Following the first 24 hours, though, they should gain ½oz (14g) per day throughout their first week, doubling their weight in that period. If a kitten fails to gain weight during any 48-hour period in its first two weeks of life — or if a kitten begins to lose weight — call your vet. By the time it is a month old, a kitten should weigh 14.1oz (400g) to 15.9oz (450g).

Below: Items to have ready for the delivery (clockwise, from top left): carrying cage; kittening box with heating pad; tissues; measuring jug, milk replacers, evaporated milk; nappies; coffee and pad with vet's number; syringes, scissors, rubber gloves, dropper, petroleum jelly; towels, glucose, Hagen bottle, antiseptic wipes, disinfectant.

Lactating queens require a considerable amount of food: 1oz (28g) of dry food or 1.3oz (37g) of semi-moist food or 3.3oz (94g) of canned food per lb (453g) of body weight each day, depending on the number of kittens they are nursing, the kittens' size, and their age.

Supplemental feeding

If a kitten is not nursing — or if it seems to be crying more than it is nursing — take its temperature with a lubricated rectal thermometer. If the kitten's temperature is below 97°F (36°C), feed it two cc's of warmed (98°F (37°C)) dextrose solution. Below 97°F (36°C), the enzymes in the kitten's stomach are unable to digest milk. If the kitten's temperature is above 97°F (36°C), feed another two cc's of mother's milk replacer. Obtain the dextrose solution, the mother's milk replacer and the syringe with which to administer them from your vet. Keep the dextrose solution in the refrigerator.

The technique for feeding dextrose or milk is the same. Put a towel on your lap, hold the kitten in one hand at a 45-degree angle, slide the end of the syringe gently between the kitten's lips and push the plunger on the syringe a fraction of an inch. Proceed slowly, pushing intermittently on the plunger as the kitten takes in the fluid. (You may find it easier to use a Foster Feeding Bottle rather than a syringe to feed the kitten — it enables you to regulate the flow of milk precisely.)

Kittens whose temperatures are normal can be returned to their mothers following supplemental feeding, but they should be monitored carefully to be sure they are nursing adequately within an hour or so. If they are not, continue supplemental feeding every two hours around the clock until they begin nursing on their own.

Kittens too weak to suck dextrose solution or milk from a syringe may have to be fed by tube. Ask your vet in advance to show you how to measure the length of tube, attached to a syringe, that needs to be inserted into the kitten's stomach. Since tube-feeding, if not carried out correctly, can cause lesions of the pharynx or stomach, it should be attempted only as a last resort.

If a non-nursing kitten with a depressed temperature has to be placed in an incubator to bring its temperature up to normal, check its temperature every two hours. As long as the temperature remains below 97°F (36°C), keep feeding the dextrose solution. When the kitten's temperature rises above 97°F (36°C), feed a milk replacer. When you give the kitten back to its mother, check every hour or so to see that it is nursing properly. If it is not, feed it two cc's of dextrose solution or milk replacer every two hours around the clock until the kitten is able to nurse normally.

Raising orphaned kittens

Occasionally a queen will refuse to care for her kittens — or she will be unable to care for them, for example, because she has contracted an illness, or has not recovered sufficiently from a Cesaran Section to assume her maternal duties. In either case, the owner must raise the litter until the queen recovers or until the litter is old enough to eat on its own.

Orphaned kittens should be kept in an incubator at 85°F (29°C). The kittens' temperatures should be checked every two hours around the clock for the first two or three days, and they should be fed warmed dextrose solution or milk replacer as their temperatures indicate. Feed ½ teaspoon (2-3ml) of dextrose solution or milk replacer at each feeding for the first week.

If the kittens' temperatures are normal for a few days, you need not continue to take their temperatures before feeding. Intervals between feedings may be stretched to two and half hours during the second week, at which time you should increase the kitten's milk ration to ¾ teaspoon (3-4ml). During the third and fourth weeks, feed every three hours and give the kittens all the milk they want. Towards the end of the kittens' third week, you should begin to wean them onto solid food. Begin with a porridge made from baby cereal and milk replacer for a few days, then gradually add dry cat food soaked in milk.

At about four and a half or five weeks, switch to a mixture of soaked dry cat food and canned cat food and finally, at about six weeks, to canned cat food or dry food alone.

For the first two or three weeks, you will have to stimulate the kittens to excrete before feeding them. To do this, form some paper towel into a wad and dip a section of it into a small bowl of warm water. Rub each kitten's anogenital area softly. Wash the area with a clean paper towel once the kitten has excreted, and then pat it dry.

Kittens do not excrete spontaneously until they are three weeks old. When they begin to do so, provide them with a litter tray and show them how to use it. Place the kittens in the tray as soon as they wake up from a nap, or immediately after you have fed them. Take their front paws in each of your hands and scratch the litter gently. They will soon get the idea.

Since hand-raised kittens may not have received antibodies from their mothers, depending on the age at which they were taken from their mothers, take them to your vet when they are three weeks old and have them inoculated with killed vaccine. Your vet will set up a full inoculation schedule for the kittens at that time.

8

THE HISTORY OF THE CAT

Though humans originally recruited cats from the wild to catch rats and mice, a cynic would say that their chief practical value today lies in supporting a hugely profitable cat-supply industry. For cats consume billions of pounds of food annually; their owners spend billions of dollars, pounds, yen and other currencies on veterinary care and millions more on combs, shampoos, flea collars, brushes, cat litter, toys, vitamins and so on. It is even possible to buy a range of exotic accessories for your cat, from spray cologne at £1 ($1.80) per ounce (in scents reminiscent of Chanel, Giorgio, Opium, Obsession or Aramis) to leopard-patterned stud-pants for male cats — who, of course, produce their very own scented spray.

One reason for this modern obsession is that cats fit our two-careers, deferred-child-raising, one-person-household, leisure-oriented times as snugly as a key in a lock. Unlike dogs, whose needs expand to fill all the available space in their owners' lives, cats remain user-friendly even on modest inputs of companionship and care. The average cat-owner rarely (if ever) has to clamber unwillingly out of bed at 5 a.m. in a howling gale to walk the cat. Nor does he or she have to turn down a sudden invitation to go sailing because it is not safe to leave the cat alone in the house overnight. What's more, the medical fees for cats are usually lower than those for dogs. Small wonder, then, that these small wonders in fur appear on so many ties, T-shirts, coffee mugs, Christmas cards, book covers, cushions, curtains, cartoons and movies in the late twentieth century.

Despite their popularity today, cats have not always been the benificiaries of such persistent

Above: A statue sacred to the cat-goddess Bastet, dating from ca. 30 B.C. Bastet was worshipped by the Ancient Egyptians.

Left: The Sorrel (Red) Abyssinian's likeness to Ancient Egyptian cats has led to claims that it is descended from them, but this is unlikely.

idealization. During the 3,600 years that they have been attempting to domesticate the human race, cats have been vilified as well as deified, desecrated as well as elevated, reviled as often as they have been revered. Indeed, no other animal in history has been subject to such violent swings of fortune as the cat, and this turbulent past has surely not been without consequence as regards the development of the cat's character. The truths in these consequences include a quiet independence; an inclination under most circumstances not involving food to greet any summons with indifference; and a social distance that can make Attila the Hun look, in comparison, like a clown from the circus.

Ancestors of today's cat

All cats great and small belong to the mammalian, carnivorous family known as *Felidae*, whose members are supremely specialized hunters, feeding almost entirely on meat and almost exclusively on vertebrates. *Felidae* can be neatly classified into three genera. *Panthera* includes the cats that can roar: the lion, tiger, leopard, snow leopard, clouded leopard and jaguar. *Felis* includes all non-roaring cats except the cheetah, which rates its own genus, *Acinonyx*, because its claws are not fully retractable. The lion is able to roar, whereas the house cat cannot, because the cartilage in the former's hyoid bones — a paired chain of small bones at the base of the tongue connecting the larynx with the skull — renders them flexible. Because the house cat's hyoids consist entirely of bone, on the other hand, they are inflexible.

Felidae (or felids) began to evolve from miacids — small, tree-climbing creatures that resembled today's martens — about 54 million years ago; but the oldest fossils that exhibit close similarities with modern, small cats are roughly 12 million years old. By comparison, the earliest fossils positively identified as belonging to the *Hominidae* family (to which humans belong), are only four million years old; and *Homo sapiens*, the anatomically correct version of our genus and species, did not appear until 30,000 to 35,000 years ago. By then the genus *Felis*, to which domestic cats belong, was well-established in the world.

Domestication of the cat

Cats were the contemporaries of prehistoric people in many places. Despite this, cats were by no means the first animals to be domesticated.

For humans had gentled at least a dozen other species, including dogs, cattle and pigs, before finally coming to terms with the cat.

No records describe that glorious dawn when cats began to associate with humans. Egypt is the most frequently cited precinct for this development, and 'about 3,600 years ago' is as near as anyone can come in pinpointing the date.

The earliest pictorial representations of cats from Egypt date from the third millennium B.C., but no-one can be certain if these animals were wild or domestic. Most researchers agree, however, that cats appearing in Egyptian artwork from about 1600 B.C. onwards were fully domesticated.

The cat most often mentioned as the direct ancestor of the modern-day domestic cat is the African wild cat, variously referred to as *Felis libyca* or *Felis silvestris libyca*. A yellow, mutedly striped, feline which is slightly larger than today's domestic cat, the African wildcat is indigenous to the deserts found throughout Africa, Syria, Arabia and parts of India. There are almost as many reasons as a cat has lives for assuming that the African wild cat is the father of the domestic housecat. Chief among them are correlations between human and feline habitats during the period when domestication is most likely to have occurred; morphological and behavioural adaptations in the domestic cat — a hearing apparatus, for example, that is

Left: Charms were common in Ancient Egypt; this one shows the goddess Bastet and dates from around 1040 B.C.

Below: A Mycenean dagger decorated with cat motifs. Despite such ancient popularity, cats have not always been revered by man.

Above: A scabbard slide in the shape of a cat created during the Han dynasty of China, and dating from the second century B.C.

---

suited to open spaces such as the desert; behavioural evidence — the African wild cat is docile, the European wild cat is not; and etymological grounds. The English word *cat*, the French *chat*, the German *katze*, the Spanish *gato*, the fourth-century Latin *cattus* and the modern Arabic *quttah* can all be assumed to have been derived from the Nubian word *kadiz*, meaning cat.

While particulars regarding the who, where and when of domestication are scanty, the why is not so mysterious. Most researchers declare that cats were domesticated for rat patrol and — to a lesser extent — for companionship. Wild cats, attracted by food refuse and by the large populations of mice and rats that thrived in human settlements in olden times, most likely moved closer to towns and villages over time. Controlling vermin was an urgent necessity in an agrarian society. Thus, as cats demonstrated their skill at protecting grain, farmers began feeding them to encourage them to keep hard at work.

That was as formal as the arrangement ever became. As one zoologist has noted, 'There is no evidence that at any time during its history the cat's way of life and its reception into human homesteads were purposely planned and directed by humans . . . in every sense the cat domesticated himself — if with some unimagined assistance from man'.

The cat's unique lifestyle

If the circumstances of the cat's domestication differed from those of other animals, so did its lifestyle. Other animals that humans have domesticated usually lived in some kind of communal arrangement. They also exhibited several highly significant predictors of domestication: membership in a large social group, an acquaintance with a hierarchial group structure, omnivorous eating habits, adaptability to a wide range of environments, limited agility, the use of movements or posturing to advertise sexual receptivity and a promiscuous lifestyle. The cat scores positively on only three of these traits: sexual posturing, promiscuity and adaptability to a wide range of environments.

This helps to explain why the cat does not regard human beings with the same fawning affection as the dog, or with the same resigned, obedient stoicism as the horse. The horse, for example, follows the lead of the dominant member of the herd, usually the alpha mare. When that mare stops to graze, the rest of the herd also stops to feed; when the mare skips off at a gallop, the herd follows.

It is this centuries-old, follow-the-leader instinct that enables humans to assume the role of the alpha, or dominant, animal in the horse's life once the process of domestication begins. In other words, it is not too difficult for humans to become top of the pecking order in the horse's domain. But the same does not apply in the cat's, who was used to going his own way for thousands of centuries before signing a series of one-generation-only contracts to do light mouse work for humans.

The lionization of the cat

Following their domestication in Egypt, cats became so revered that the law specifically forbade the sinful slaying of a cat. For 'such an evil accident', wrote Diodorus of Sicily, 'a Roman soldier was torn to pieces by the infuriated populace of Thebes'. Herodotus, the father of history, observed in the fifth century B.C. that when an Egyptian's house caught fire, he was more anxious about his cat than his possessions. Upon dying, Egyptian cats were mourned, mummified and buried in a consecrated place.

For all the cat's popularity along the Nile, 'once outside of Egypt, the history of the cat is shrouded in mystery and gloom', wrote Agnes Repplier nearly one hundred years ago in *The Fireside Sphinx*.'There is no proof that [the cat] was domesticated in Babylon or Assyria; and what scanty information we can gather as the centuries roll on is of a dishearteningly fabulous character. As a plaything, as a pretty household toy, she was carried from Africa to Europe a few

---

Below: An illustration from The Mouse and the Cat, *a fable by Aesop Anvers, 1486. Later, cats became the hunted in turn.*

Above: In the Middle Ages, cats were imagined to be the familiars of witches. This woodcut shows two witches and their cats.

Below: Woman with a Cat, *by the French artist Boucher. By the eighteenth century, the cat had returned to favour in Europe.*

hundred years before the Christian era'. In India 'the house cat was known from a very early period', about the time of Christ, and 'her first entrance into the Chinese Empire appears to have been around 400 A.D.'.

Other historians claim that the cat was present in China at least 1500 years earlier. In any case, the Chinese attitude towards cats was somewhat ambivalent. Cats were suspected of bringing poverty into a house, but the only antidote to this affliction was, irony of ironies, a ceramic figure of a cat gazing into the distance. The Chinese also believed that the older and uglier the cat, the greater the fortune that would befall its owner.

'The saddest gap in the chronicles of the cat', said Repplier, was 'her conspicuous absence from "the glory that was Greece", and from "the grandeur that was Rome"'. This absence extended over hundreds of years, and was no doubt caused in part by the existence of the firm of Weasel, Marten and Polecat, which held a monopoly in the vermin concessions in Greece and Rome.

No matter how they behaved when in Rome, the Romans did introduce the domestic cat to all parts of their empire, including England. They also brought the cat to central Europe.

When the domestic cat arrived in Europe, it is very likely that it bred with local wild cats. Known either as *Felis silvestris* or *Felis silvestris silvestris*, the European wild cat was originally found all over the vast region from northern Europe to the

Caucasus and Asia Minor. This forest-dwelling cat, which is adept at tree-climbing and living in dense vegetation and which has never been domesticated, is mainly confined to the Scottish Highlands today. In addition to its trademark wariness, it may have contributed genes for darker tabby markings to the lightly marked African wild cat.

The High Middle Ages

An extraordinary change in the attitude to cats occurred towards the middle of the thirteenth century in the mind of the Christian Church, an institution never fond of cats at the best of times — even when these animals were busy wiping out the plague-bearing horde of black rats that had hitched a ride to Europe on the Crusaders' ships.

The Church had always been suspicious of cats because they were mentioned only once in the Bible. This reference is to be found in the Apocrypha: Letter of Jeremiah, Chapter 6, v.22.

Thus, when a pagan fertility cult that employed cats in its rites and that pledged allegiance to Freyia (the Norse goddess of love and fertility) sprang up in the Rhineland (now in Germany), the Church violently over-reacted. For the next 400 years, open season was declared throughout Europe on the ancestors of today's cats, who were believed to be the familiars of witches or — worse yet — witches in the guise of cats.

Lent was a particularly hard time of year for medieval cats. They were slaughtered in Oldenburg, Westphalia, Belgium, Switzerland

Above: The European wild cat is Europe's counterpart to Felis Lybica, *or the African wild cat. The cat that the Ancient Egyptians worshipped and which became the first domesticated cat was almost certainly derived from* Felis Lybica.

Right: A lithograph showing visitors to the first British National Cat Show at the Crystal Palace, London, 1871.

Below right: Famous cat-lover Louis Wain painted this watercolour, Afternoon at Home, *in 1922.*

and Bohemia; they were thrown into bonfires in the Ardennes, or roasted on the ends of long poles or in wicker baskets on the first Sunday in Lent. They were burnt on Shrove Tuesday in the Vosges in France and at Easter-time in Alsace.

The return to popularity
At the close of the sixteenth century, civilization began to break out in western Europe. 'Life grew softer, sweeter, replete with self-indulgence and self-satisfaction', wrote Repplier. 'All things were working harmoniously for the re-establishment of the cat in popular esteem'.

The first signs of the cat's restoration to popularity began in France. The doors of French country houses built between the middle of the sixteenth and the seventeenth centuries were furnished with specially constructed sections that allowed cats to come and go as they pleased. Eventually, people in other western European countries began making entrance-ways in their lives, if not in their doors, for the cat.

Is the cat domesticated?
The interval since the cat was first domesticated is but a blink in terms of time's steady gaze. And during that interval cats have remained a compelling example of a species that is only in the first stage of domestication, capable of reverting to a feral state and not tremendously different from its ancestors.

Described as the wildest of the tame animals and as the tamest of the wild ones, the domestic cat is, in one crucial sense, not truly domesticated at all. Humans have exercised little control over the cat's reproductive life — save for the occasional bucket of water tossed from a bedroom window in the middle of a night rent by howling. If the conservative standard of domestication is applied to cats —a standard in which natural selection by the domesticated species has no place — then the pedigree cat is the only truly domesticated cat; and it has been domesticated for little more than a hundred years, which is the length of time that people have been keeping close tabs on who begat whom in the sacred realm of the cat.

This view of domestication helps further to explain the differences between cats' behaviour and that of other domesticated animals, dogs especially. Unlike dogs — which were bred in the pursuit of a wide range of skills and temperament for centuries before they were bred for conformation alone — cats have virtually never been bred on purpose; and the specimens that have, have been bred mainly for their physical traits.

Ultimately, such considerations are essentially meaningless to the cat and its advocates. 'The fact that cats associated with humans at all', says American author and cat lover Lloyd Alexander, 'may indicate that they don't consider us such a bad lot. A cat's life can be as difficult as our own. And it may be that we comfort them for being cats as much as they comfort us for being human'.

9

GENETICS AND PEDIGREES

Hereditary transactions are supervised by a group of large molecules called deoxyribonucleic acid (DNA). Molecules of DNA, which govern the manufacture of proteins in the cells of the body, are arranged in tightly coiled strands called chromosomes. Although chromosomes vary in size and shape, they always line up in matched pairs — except for the sex chromosomes. These occur in both matched (XX) or unmatched (XY) pairs. In unmatched pairs the, Y chromosome is smaller than the X chromosome.

The nucleus of the majority of the body cells in the cat contains 38 chromosomes. Thirty six of these, arranged in 18 matched pairs, are called autosomes. The two remaining chromosomes, the sex chromosomes, determine a cat's gender. Cats with two X chromsomes are female. Cats with one X and one Y chromosome are male.

Genes, loci and alleles

Genes, the coding units that deliver genetic instructions from one generation to the next, are arranged, like beads on a string, along the chromosomes. Each gene occupies a specific 'address' (or site) on a chromosome. That address is called the gene's *locus* (plural, *loci*). In addition, the gene for a specific trait always occupies the same locus on both members of a matched autosomal pair.

Although specific genes always occupy the same locus on each member of an autosomal pair, a gene may occur in different forms called alleles. At the locus for coat length in the cat, to give an example, there is an allele that tells the cat to grow a long coat or an allele that tells the coat to grow short and no further.

Above: A Lilac Angora. Genetically, lilac (lavender) is a dilute form of chocolate (brown). The dilution gene is inherited polygenically.

Left: A Brown-patched Mackerel Tabby-and-white Scottish Fold. Traits such as folded ears are governed by a single allele.

Dominant and recessive alleles

All alleles are not created equal. The allele for short hair is dominant over the allele for long hair, which is called, therefore, a recessive allele. Because the shorthair allele is dominant, a cat that inherits an allele for short hair from one parent and an allele for long hair from the other will have a short coat. Only those cats that inherit two alleles for long hair will have long coats.

In genetic notation, dominant alleles are represented by uppercase letters, while recessive alleles are represented by lowercase letters. Thus, to refer to the coat-length example again, the allele for short hair would be a capital *L*, and the allele for long hair would be a lowercase *l*.

Heterozygosity and homozygosity

Cats that inherit similar alleles of the same gene are said to be homozygous for the trait governed by that gene. In such cases the phenotype (or physical appearance) matches the genotype (or genetic makeup) of a cat for that particular trait. Longhaired cats, for example, are always *ll* at the coat-length loci, and their phenotype for coat length (i.e., their long hair) always matches their genotype.

Cats that inherit different alleles of the same gene are said to be heterozygous for the trait governed by that gene. A shorthaired cat that inherits one allele for short hair and another for long hair is heterozygous for coat length. A shorthaired cat that inherits two alleles for short hair is homozygous for coat length. Since shorthaired cats may be either heterozygous or homozygous at the coat-length loci, we cannot know simply by looking at them what their genotype is. Only after breeding a shorthaired cat to longhaired cats several times and getting nothing but shorthaired kittens could we assume, with varying degrees of certainty, that the shorthaired cat is homozygous for coat length. If a shorthaired cat were bred to a longhair and produced five shorthaired kittens — and no longhairs — in her resulting litter(s), we could assume there was close to a 97-per cent chance that the shorthaired cat was homozygous for the shorthair allele at her coat-length loci.

Monogenic and polygenic inheritance

Traits such as coat length that are governed by a single allele are said to be inherited in a monogenic fashion. Folded ears on Scottish Folds, near hairlessness among

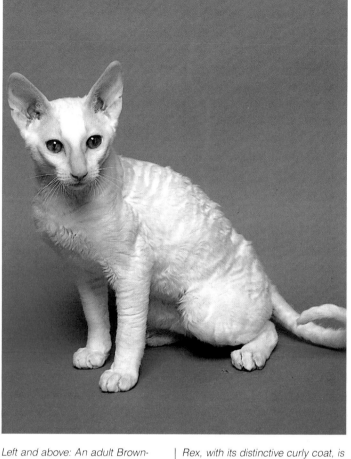

Left and above: An adult Brown-spotted Cornish Rex (above, left) and an Orange-eyed (Golden-eyed) Cornish Rex (above). The Cornish Rex, with its distinctive curly coat, is an excellent example of a breed that has been based around a genetic mutation.

Sphynx and the curly coats on Rex cats are additional examples of monogenic characteristics.

Other traits are governed by committee, by the interaction of a number of genes. Those traits are said to be inherited in a polygenic manner. The intensity (or lack of intensity) of chocolate or brown colouring in the Havana Brown and the head shape and body conformation of all breeds are examples of traits that are inherited polygenically.

Selective breeding
Polygenic traits are not as easy for a breeder to manipulate as are monogenic traits. The effect of polygenes must be modified over generations of selective breeding, a process in which a person chooses cats that are most like the ideal cat he or she wants to produce, then breeds those cats to other cats that come closest to approximating the anticipated ideal. Some individuals from those breedings that are, hopefully, closer to the goal than the preceding generation are then retained and bred to other cats — and so on, and so on, and so on — until the breeder begins to produce cats that are quite close to the vision of the ideal cat that inspired this process. Obviously, the breeder who begins a selective breeding programme with cats that are close to the desired goal in appearance requires fewer generations (and needs to make smaller capital outlays) to approach that goal than

the breeder who begins with cats that are farther from the goal.

Mutations
Nature usually conducts her genetic transactions with all the predictability of a blue-chip-stock investor. Yet every so often she takes a speculative flyer on future developments. In genetics, such flyers are called mutations; and in the cat fancy, mutation is often spelt *new breed.* The Cornish and Devon Rexes, the Manx and the Scottish Fold are four examples of breeds that have been designed around mutations: the curly-coat in the Rexes, the lack of a tail in the Manx and the folded ears in Scottish Folds.

(Readers of a layperson's text such as this, not to mention the writer of the text, are better off thinking of mutations in simple, comparative terms like the investment analogy above than they are by trying to understand the inversions, base changes, translocations, and other cellular events that result in departures from the genetic norm.)

Genetics and breeding
Though it is perhaps too glib to be true, one might argue that a knowledge of genetics has little to do with breeding a good cat. If a breeder did not know beforehand that an Exotic Shorthair might throw longhaired kittens when outcrossed to a Persian, that breeder would find out soon enough anyway; but

that lack of knowledge would have no influence on the quality of the kittens that person produced in the meantime.

In a similar manner, the breeder hoping to produce a tortoiseshell cat would be disappointed if he or she bred a Blue to a Cream in hope of achieving this aim. Blue and cream are both dilute colours. They are recessive to the black and red in the tortoiseshell coat, and two recessives cannot make a dominant. But even though the litter from the blue and the cream cats will contain blue, cream or blue-cream kittens only — and not the desired tortoiseshell — the blue, cream or blue-cream kittens may be excellent in quality, for quality has nothing to do with colour in this example.

While a knowledge of colour genetics is required to produce the colours and patterns that a person fancies, a different language is required for manipulating type and conformation in cats. That language is called pedigree.

Understanding pedigrees
While written in English of sorts, pedigrees are, to many breeders, manuscripts in a foreign, inscrutable tongue, fraught with their own vocabulary and rules of interpretation. Yet breeders who do not learn to speak pedigree fluently might just as well be pondering graffiti on a station wall if they hope to use pedigrees as an aid to producing a good cat.

Quite possibly the scholar who originated the phrase about reading between the lines was poring over a stack of pedigrees when he did so. Virtually all the information needed to understand a pedigree — how the cats on it appear, what their offspring and relatives are about and what families they are most compatible with — is difficult to glean from the surface information on a standard three-, four- or five-generation pedigree. What can be found there (a flurry of names, numbers, titles and colours) merely constitutes a reasonable place to begin reading; and, as any student of language knows, reading ability begins with vocabulary.

Thus, elementary though it may seem, the first step to understanding a pedigree is to become familiar with the names on it so that they mean something to you when you encounter them again on a pedigree. Familiarity, as the old saying goes, breeds good cats.

'In order to evaluate any pedigree', says one Cat Fanciers' Association (CFA) judge, 'you need to study as many pedigrees as you can get your hands on. There's no other way [than by studying pedigrees] that someone just starting out — or even an experienced breeder — can evaluate a line that he's never worked with'.

The study of pedigrees is facilitated by the study of cat association yearbooks and any

Right: A stumpy Manx, showing a vestigial tail. The taillessness of the Manx was the result of the limited gene-pool available on that island.

publications that include show reports and/or pictures of winning cats. Experienced breeders also recommend other vocabulary drills for persons learning to speak pedigree, such as visiting shows and talking to breeders.

People who learn a second language, be it French, the computer language Pascal or pedigree, can be divided into two groups: those who can use the language and those who can merely decipher it. Learning the basic Persian (or Siamese or whatever your chosen breed's) vocabulary, allows you to decipher the information on a pedigree, but to read with understanding and to progress to a standard of fluency, a person has to venture beyond vocabulary into the rules of grammar.

Some principles of breeding

Because of grammatical rules (some would say despite them) there are many ways to express a notion gracefully. Likewise, there are many ways to breed a decent cat. Not all breeders observe precisely the same rules or employ the same style, but their compositions are generally guided by certain fundamental principles.

One is the principle of the good nick, to borrow a term from horse breeders. Indeed, a horse breeder possessed of uncommon horse sense explained once that 'too many people never discover the importance of learning what the compatible crosses are. Certain pairs of families simply don't cross well. Certain other pairs of families are golden crosses. The best way to find this out is by studying the pedigrees of top-quality animals intensely'.

Below: The five-toed paw of a normal cat (left) and the paw of a polydactyl cat (right) showing six toes. The polydactyl gene (the result of a natural mutation) is dominant over the gene for normal toes.

If breeders know the lines of cats with which they wish to work, and if they know what kind of success (or failure) other breeders have had with those lines, it is not difficult to anticipate what sort of cats will result from a particular breeding. But the study of pedigrees is a continuing discipline that's more process than product. The breeder who stops studying pedigrees can become as dated in a few years as the physician who stops reading medical journals.

A second principle of good breeding teaches that the close relatives on a pedigree are the most important: the sire and dam, grandsires and granddams. This is so because each new generation will contribute twice as much, theoretically, to the genetic makeup of a cat as did the preceding generation. It is not wise, therefore,

to place too much emphasis on the characteristics of a great-great-grandparent located a long way back in the family tree. For such a cat provides, in theory, only 6¼ per cent of a kitten's genetic makeup. An ancestor so very far removed from centre stage would have to leapfrog three generations of extras in order to play any kind of leading role in a successful kitten production.

Though the two closest generations on a pedigree are the most influential, it does not always follow that it is the first generation to whom the new generation is tied. There are many examples of top-winning cats that have been produced by average-looking parents, but that turn out to have two, three or four exceptional grandparents. This phenomenon — in which a kitten takes after its

grandparents more than its parents — is known as the skip-a-generation rule. If you keep this rule in mind, it should be easy to answer the following question: which cat is more valuable in a breeding programme, a mediocre cat with a good pedigree or a good cat with a mediocre pedigree? (Hint: there is a wise, old Norwegian proverb that says: 'Marry not the *only* good maid in the Clan.')

Such is the influence of the skip-a-generation rule that many breeders contend that 'You're almost always breeding grandparents when you breed a pair of cats'. For that reason, they will tell you, a great cat from a mediocre pedigree is not going to throw much of anything good because there is nothing much good behind it from which it might throw anything.

The mediocre pedigree usually gives itself away in the second and third generations. Both cats in the first generation could be somewhat less than show quality, and the pedigree might well be worth the price of the cat if the grandparents were for the most part outstanding cats; but if the grandparents and great-grandparents are neither great nor grand, the chances are that the pedigree is not worth the paper on which it is written, no matter how good the fourth and fifth generations look.

The skip-a-generation rule is an equal-opportunity employer: it can be employed with bad traits as well as good. Thus, it can sometimes be turned to a breeder's advantage. A former director of the University of Vermont's Morgan Horse Farm once observed that one of the sires used at the farm — though very strong in most regards — had a conformation fault. As time went by, and the particular stallion was used quite heavily in the breeding shed, it became evident that he was not passing on his fault to many of his get. The more the director analysed this situation, the more he became convinced that the sire in question was not passing on his fault because his dam was exceptionally strong in that trait. Thus, the stallion's offspring tended to look more like their paternal grandmother than their pater familias in that one regard.

The importance of the distaff contribution to a pedigree is one rule of breeding grammar that is frequently overlooked. Unfortunately, a homely granddam to which you did not pay that much attention (because you were dazzled by the national-winning male to whom she was bred) can influence a kitten's type just as easily as the famous male.

While part of the knack of learning to speak pedigree involves the ability to read between the lines, another part involves seeing the cats that are, so to speak, on the lines. A person should try to see as many of the cats as possible that are in the first three generations of a pedigree, even if only in pictures. In addition, the littermates of the cats on the pedigree should not be overlooked in this investigation. This is particularly important if the cat you are considering buying or breeding to is inbred (see below). While the particular cat you are considering may not have an extra ear, it would not be wise to think of breeding from it if one of its littermates showed that deformity.

Three hundred years ago William Penn remarked that 'Men are generally more careful of the breed of their horses and dogs than of their children'. Penn's observation is, perhaps, too cynical to apply to all modern-day cat breeders, but the touchstone of good breeding has remained the same since Penn's day. The idea behind any breeding programme is to raise a kitten with a pedigree that is stronger than that of either of its parents taken individually. The best pedigree is one that will do the most to advance a breeder towards his or her goal.

Of course, the breeder cannot expect progress towards that goal to be entirely straightforward. All genetic influences are a matter of degree, and there is always, somewhere, some deviation from the general rule along the line.

One final precept to keep in mind, therefore, is that the breeder cannot use pedigrees as if they were like the instructions that come with a new bicycle: something the

Above: The attractive butterfly markings on the back are characteristic of the tabby coat pattern, which comes in all colours.

Left: A Seal point Siamese. The slender Oriental type of cat was found in the Far East. Selective breeding has produced the long, racehorse type of head.

owner turns to in desperation at 3 a.m. on Christmas Day after repeated attempts to assemble the machine have failed, and when there are bicycle parts scattered all over the living room.

For using pedigrees is less of a case of following clear instructions, with a clear and guaranteed end in sight; it is more of an intuitive art, whose end-product cannot always be predicted accurately in advance.

Inbreeding and linebreeding
Cat breeders and geneticists define inbreeding in different ways. To most cat breeders, inbreeding includes father-daughter, mother-son, and brother-sister breedings. Linebreeding involves unions between half-brother and sister, granddaughter and grandfather, grandson and grandmother, uncle and niece, aunt and nephew, or any breeding in which the same ancestor appears at least once on the mother's and the father's sides of the pedigree in the first three or four generations.

Geneticists, for their part, do not distinguish between linebreeding and inbreeding. Instead, they use the terms *inbreeding* or *consanguinity* to describe both, and they assign inbreeding co-efficients to various types of breedings. Full-brother-and-sister breedings get the same inbreeding co-efficient as do father-daughter or mother-son breedings. (The inbreeding co-efficient is a numerical measure of the probability that an animal will be homozygous at a given locus for an allele that is passed on to it from some ancestor common to both sire and dam.)

Animals that are homozygous at many loci are more likely to reproduce their own characteristics — good and bad — than are heterozygous animals. Therefore, if the co-efficient of inbreeding for the offspring of a projected mating between two related animals is high, so is the necessity that they conform to their breed standard. 'Never breed fault to fault' is never more important than in breedings between closely related pairs.

Breeding and the law of errors

According to the law of errors, small errors occur more often than large ones; very large errors occur very seldomly; as errors become progressively larger, they become less numerous; and negative errors occur about as often as positive errors (that is, to use a soccer metaphor, the kick will be wide to the left of goal as often as it will be wide to the right).

But what has all this got to do with breeding cats? Simply, that most of the kittens produced by a pair of cats will look rather like that pair of cats. Occasionally (about 5 per cent of the time) a kitten will exhibt significantly better quality in some regard(s) than its parents, but just as very large errors seldom occur, so very large deviations from parental type also occur very seldomly.

Reflections on breeding

The manner in which a trait is inherited can vary from one species to the next. A quality that is transmitted monogenically in one species might be transmitted polygenically in another species. But breeding strategies are constant across species, and since relatively little has been written concerning breeding strategies in cats, a cat breeder can often profit from reading books or magazine articles about dogs or horses and by talking to dog or horse breeders. Not only are these species with which humans had been involved for centuries before they became involved with breeding cats, but they are also species, particularly the horse, in which the top specimens command far greater sums than do the most expensive show cats. And, of course, when there is money riding on the outcome, people tend to give a process considerably more thought than they do when they are engaging in it largely as a hobby.

While browsing through a back issue of one magazine, the author came across a review of a dog book called The Basis of Breeding, which was written nearly 50 years ago. The author of the book was Dr. Leon Whitney, an internationally known and respected breeder of bloodhounds.

'The breeding season, following close on the heels of the shows', wrote Whitney, 'invariably produces fanciers who eagerly book service to the most outstanding stud of the season, and regardless of his family, expect to have winning progeny from this mating'. Often, of course, they are disappointed. Even more frequently disappointed are those breeders who rush out to breed to the top-winning young cats of the season. For the latter are animals who are, genetically speaking, unknown quantities. It makes more sense to breed to the fathers of the current show winners, especially if your female is related to the mothers of current national award winners.

Whitney's breeding programme illustrates the importance of choosing family over flash when acquiring breeding stock. When he was starting out in bloodhounds, Whitney could not afford to buy the bitch that he wanted to use as the foundation of his line. The best he could afford from that bitch's litter was her homeliest litter sister. He could have bought, for about the same price, a handsome bitch from an unknown family, but he chose the well-bred, homely-bitch instead. She became the foundation of Whitney's outstanding line of bloodhounds.

Above: A White Angora displays the finer-boned, lithe, slender body type; the other basic body type has a cobby shape and a round skull.

Below: A Seal point Snowshoe, a Himalayan-patterned shorthair with an added gene for white spotting deliberately introduced.

SACRAMENTO
VALLEY
CAT
FANCIERS

Allbreed

10

SHOWING YOUR CAT

In 1598, the year that Shakespeare published the play *Much Ado About Nothing*, a cat show was held at the St. Giles Fair in England. History does not record whether there was much ado about this event or not, but apparently nothing much came of it, because 273 years would pass before the cat fancy was born in the United Kingdom.

The delivery date was July 13, 1871, and the place of birth was the Crystal Palace in London. The attending 'doctor' was Harrison Weir, a man of varied interests and talents. In addition to organizing the show, Weir wrote the standards by which the entries were appraised, and he also served as one of the show's three judges.

The breeds exhibited at nineteenth-century British cat shows were the Abyssinian; Manx; Royal Cat of Siam (which included both pointed and solid chocolate cats); shorthairs, which were more than likely the descendants of cats that had been brought to Britain by the Romans nine centuries before; and longhairs, which were all judged by the same standard, but which had already begun to be called by separate 'breed' names: Persian and Angora. There were also classes for hybrid cats that had been produced by crossing wild and domestic cats, classes for the heaviest cats, classes for gelded cats, and classes for 'Cats Belonging to Working Men'. The entrance fee for the working men's classes was only one third as much as the fee for the other classes — but the prize money offered to the top three finishers in the working men's groups was also reduced.

Cat shows soon attracted so many followers in the UK that a group of fanciers started the National Cat Club (NCC) in 1887.

Above: The moment of truth. A hopeful — and confident — exhibitor carries two Birmans to the ring at a show in the United States.

Left: A (US-standard) Chinchilla posing proudly with its awards following a show held by a branch of the Cat Fanciers' Association.

Harrison Weir, who would later come to be known as the father of the cat fancy, was the club's first president. The NCC operated under the inspiring motto, 'Beauty Lives by Kindness'. In addition to serving as a forum where cat fanciers could gather to exchange news and information, the club functioned as a governing body, establishing a national stud book and register to keep records of the pedigrees of 'purebred' cats.

The Cat Club, a challenger to the sovereignty of the NCC, was founded in 1898 by Lady Marcus Beresford. Its members, one writer has noted, included 'some of the most important people in the land'.

Like its rival, the Cat Club kept its own stud book and register of pedigree cats; and anyone who entered cats in its shows was obliged to enrol them in the association, too.

For five years The Cat Club and the National Cat Club existed as rivals for the affections and registrations of cat lovers, but then The Cat Club disbanded.

Unity was not entirely restored to the cat fancy in the UK until March, 1910, however — when the various clubs then in existence agreed to join forces. They united under the rubric the Governing Council of the Cat Fancy (GCCF), which remains the oldest and the largest cat association in the UK today.

Yet the GCCF's are not the only shows in town. A second registry, now known as the Cat Association of Britain (CAB), was formed in 1983. This group, which is associated with the Fédération Internationale Féline d'Europe (FIFe), maintains a separate registry from the GCCF's and conducts its shows in accordance with the FIFe rules.

The cat fancy in the US
The cat fancy in the United States was 'officially' born on May 8, 1895, when an Englishman named James T. Hyde organized a cat show in Madison Square Garden in New York City. This show was the first to attract widespread attention in the US, but there had been other cat shows in America before this.

In 1896 a group of cat fanciers created the American Cat Club, the first registry in the US. Its functions included verifying pedigrees, maintaining a stud book, sponsoring shows and promoting the welfare of cats. Half a dozen or so registries —including the American Cat Club — have been started and then disbanded in the US in the meantime. The duties

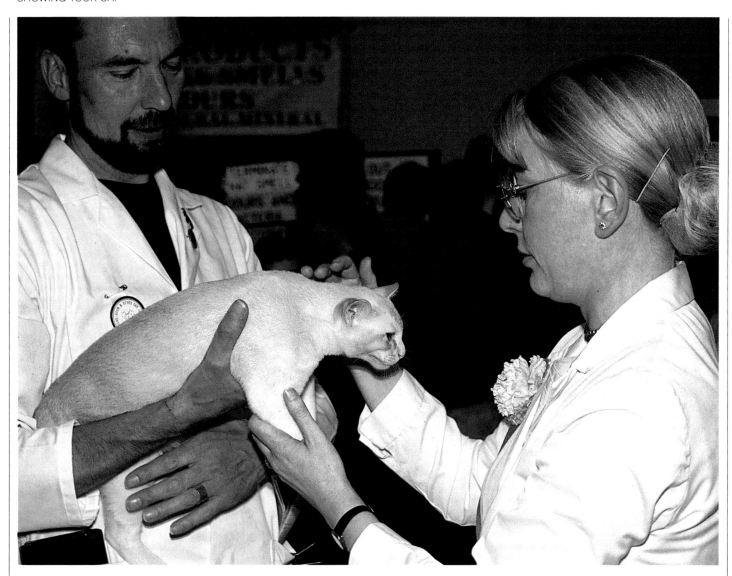

Above: A steward holds an entrant at a GCCF show in the UK while the judge assesses body shape, and coat texture and colour.

assumed by the American Cat Club are currently met by six different registries in North America. The largest of those is the Cat Fanciers' Association (CFA), which was founded in 1906.

Showing in the UK
The first step in entering a show is to obtain a list of shows for the coming season from the GCCF. Forthcoming shows are also listed in *Cats* magazine, along with details such as the show manager and the closing date for entries. Write for a schedule of the chosen show about four months in advance and return the entry form promptly, correctly filled in and with the correct entry money.

The schedule gives particulars of all the classes in the show, the venue, names of judges, club and show officials and officiating vet, together with the name and address of the person to whom entries should be sent and the date by which all entries must be posted. At the front of the schedule is a list of rules and regulations.

GCCF shows are usually (but not always) divided into seven groupings: Longhair (Persian type); Semi-longhair; British shorthair;

Foreign; Oriental; Burmese; Siamese. There is also a separate section for Household Pets if they are included in the show. The classes are split into Open classes, Miscellaneous or Side classes, and Club classes. Sometimes all the classes for one section are grouped together, at other times all the Open classes are first, followed by the Miscellaneous classes for all breeds, and finally the Club classes.

The schedule will tell you what it costs to enter each class and what prize money is given. At many shows rosettes or medals are given instead of prize money for the Open classes and these awards will be placed on the pen at the show.

At the back of the schedule you will usually find a list of cups and trophies offered by the club holding the show and by supporting clubs. Some are points cups awarded at the end of the show season for the cat gaining the most points in the category covered by the cup, points being won for first, second and third places, etc. Other cups are awarded for specific wins or good points in a cat at the show.

Early application is necessary because some shows are over-subscribed, and entries are taken strictly in rotation.

Filling in the entry form
The classes you may enter may not be very clear for your first show and it will help you if you consult the

breeder from whom you bought the kitten, or an experienced cat show friend or cat club member.

Most usually there is one form for pedigrees and one for non-pedigrees. The National and Bedfordshire shows have different forms for different sections. Household Pets always have a separate entry form. Study the form very carefully; the following notes may be helpful.

1 Before you start to fill in the form get out your cat's registration or transfer certificate. The cat's name, sire, dam, sex, date of birth, breed number, registration number and breeder's name must be filled in on the form exactly as they appear on the certificate. Failure to do this may mean your cat is disqualified after the show when the catalogue is checked. In the case of the experimental breeds, these may only be shown in the Assessment classes. Fill in the cat's details on the form, and enclose details of the preliminary standard on a separate card to be displayed on the pen. Cats of unrecognized breeds can only enter on Exhibition.

2 Now select your classes, checking your cat's eligibility for each, and write them in the correct space on the form. There is sometimes a separate space for the open class number, and if so, make sure you write it in there. Put all the class numbers on the same line, not

in a column down the form. At most GCCF shows you must enter the open class and at least three side classes, although some shows of other registration bodies reduce either or both of these numbers. As you fill in the class numbers mark them on the schedule so that you can remember which ones you have entered — and do not forget to make a note of which cat you have entered if you intend to show more than one.

3 Check the entry fees you need to pay. Usually, the entry form will include, for each cat entered, a set fee for benching and for entering the open class and three side classes. Extra fees are paid for additional classes. Some shows include the exhibitor's entry pass for the inclusive fee, and sometimes a catalogue, too, with the first cat entered. Make sure that you enter the correct amounts in the spaces provided.

4 If you are putting a cat on exhibition look up the fee for this and enter it on the form. All details of the cat must be filled in as above. Double pens are available for cats on exhibition; if you wish to book one, fill in the amount on the form. (Double pens are not available for cats entered for competition, except at the Supreme Show.)

5 There may be additional spaces for entrance tickets, club subscriptions, etc., so if you wish, fill these in also.

Above: At British shows, exhibitors must leave the hall while judging is carried out. Here, they can watch the action from a separate gallery.

Below: Best in Show pens at a British all-breed show. The best cat, kitten and neuter will be placed in the appropriate BIS pen.

6 Now add up the various fees, etc., and check your arithmetic. Write a cheque for the correct amount and make sure that it is payable to the right account.

7 On the back of the form fill in the names of clubs of which you are a member.

8 Fill in your name, address and telephone number. If you wish to help at the show, fill in the appropriate space, but if you have never helped before do say so.

9 Before signing the form, check everything again and see that your cat complies with all the rules and regulations.

10 Sign the form and date it.

11 Send the form off as quickly as possible, and certainly by the closing date, or your entry will not be accepted. Many shows do not have room for all the entries they receive and many have to be returned, so the earlier you can send your form in, the less risk there is of yours being one of the unlucky ones. Make a note of the date you post your entry in case there is any query.

12 Remember to enclose your cheque with the completed form; no entry will be accepted unless it is accompanied by the correct entry fee.

13 Enclose a stamped postcard addressed to yourself on which you have written 'your entry has been accepted.' If you do not do this, you may not know whether or not your entry has reached the show manager until you receive your tally just before the show.

14 Also enclose a stamped, self-addressed envelope marked 'tally' in the top left corner. This is for the show manager to send you the following items; a tally (a small disc, usually white, with your cat's show entry number on it), vetting-in and pass-out cards, and entrance ticket (if paid for). At some shows these items are handed out at the entrance to the show, and if so this will be stated in the schedule. In the latter case there is obviously no need to send a tally envelope. The entry number cannot be allocated to the cat until the show catalogue has been compiled, so your tally and cards will not arrive until a few days before the show.

If, for any reason, you have entered your cat and find that it will be unable to go to the show, inform the show manager if possible. If the cat is unable to attend due to illness and you send a veterinary certificate stating this, to reach the show manager at least seven days prior to the show, your entry fees or part of them may be refunded.

Never enter a cat that is unwell or pregnant, and make sure your cat is inoculated well in advance of the show. Once your application is accepted, groom your cat daily until show day, and acquire the show equipment you will need. Preparing a cat for a show career involves handling it regularly from kittenhood. If several people handle it, the animal should grow up used to strangers and remain calm when scrutinized by judges. Groom daily and feed correctly so that your exhibit will be in prime condition for each show. (For grooming information, see page 121).

Show equipment

You will need a white show blanket or 'vetbed', white litter tray, white feeding dish and white water bowl. This uniformity is designed to help the judges judge cats only on their merits, uninfluenced by those of the cats' surroundings. You will also need a length of white ribbon or hat elastic (tally elastic) to tie the cat's number around its neck. All these items can be purchased at some shows or from specialist mail-order firms. A bottle for carrying water is also worth including, and in cold climates a hot water bottle (this must be concealed under the blanket) will keep the cat cosy, but it will have to be changed every four hours or so.

The exception to the rule about anonymous show pens in the UK is the Supreme Cat Show. This was inaugurated in 1976 as an attempt to give an opportunity for winners at Championship shows to compete against one another in their own breed divisions. The awards in this show are Supreme Cat, Kitten and Neuter. A Supreme Exhibit award is also now made. Judging at this show is in the show rings, and the cats may be exhibited during the day in decorated pens.

If you are exhibiting at this show you will want to make the most of your show pen to show the cat off to the public. You will choose curtains and a cushion to match or contrast well with your cat's coat or eyes. Some pens carry other ornaments, too — but note that the cat itself must only have white ribbon or tally elastic around its neck — anything else would be construed as a 'distinguishing factor'. Tastefully done, all these enhance the show scene for the visitor. Exhibition pens — pens containing cats not entered for competition — may be decorated in all countries. Such pens contain cats (but not kittens) for sale, cats as advertisements of breeders' stock, or new varieties.

Last-minute preparations
Have everything ready the night before the show. This means collecting all the show equipment just itemized; cat food and litter; and travelling container labelled with your name and address on one side only, so that it can be left anonymously under the show bench. Make sure that the cat is confined indoors so that it is not missing when you are ready to leave. Don't forget your own clothes.

Choose comfortable shoes for show day; there will be a great deal of standing and walking about. Do not put the show blanket in the carrier for the journey: there may be accidents. Keep the white blanket for the pen itself and use an old, familiar one for travelling. Finally, never take a cat that is off-colour;

Above: This Cream Colourpoint Exotic Shorthair, proud winner of the Open Class, is completely at home amidst the show scene.

Below: Two children display their Norwegian Forest Cat. Such responsible young exhibitors are always welcome at shows.

you may well spread an infection.

If the show is a long way from home, you may have to stay in a hotel for the night. First of all make sure that the hotel of your choice will accept cats. In this case, take a room with a private bathroom and put the cat litter tray in the bathroom. If the cat normally sleeps with you, it can still do so. If you leave the room, you should either put a notice on the door saying, 'Please do not enter, live cat at large' or, if you have room, take along a wire cage with a roof to it, measuring approximately 36in. x 24in. x 24in. (91cm x 61cm x 61cm). Place the cat in the cage with a litter tray, while you are out of the room. This will be for its own protection as well as for your peace of mind. These cat cages can be purchased; they fold flat for storage and travelling.

Remember to take along enough food for your cat for the whole trip. Canned or semi-moist foods are ideal for these occasions. I remember staying in a deluxe hotel once in an English county town. In our rush to pack everything, we had forgotten the cat's food. We asked for the restaurant to send up four ounces of lean, finely chopped raw steak on a flat dish. The meal arrived on a silver salver with great ceremony and when we finally received the bill, we found that the cost of 'chopped fillet steak' from that restaurant was astronomical!

The next day, the hire car which had been booked to take us on to the show broke down and the owner of the car company kindly sent along his own Rolls-Royce. After all this star treatment, the cat just had to win, and in fact the Brown Burmese male in question obtained his third Challenge Certificate on that occasion, making him a full Champion!

Helpful hints for show day
On show day get up and set off early because 'vetting in' usually starts about 8 a.m. This is a medical check to make sure every cat admitted to the hall is healthy. If for some reason your cat does not pass the vetting in, it must go home again, or be confined to isolation quarters for the rest of the day. (Depending on the reason for rejection, the exclusion order could include any other cats from the same household, and even cats which have travelled together in the same car.) Once past the vet your cat can be penned. You can then feed and water it to make the pen ready for the judging. About 9.30 a.m. remove all food from the pen and tidy it, changing the litter if necessary. Place your cat's travelling container under its show bench so that your name and address cannot be seen by the judges.

Exhibitors must now leave the hall so that judging can begin, although many show halls have galleries from

---

Right: Winning is exhilarating for the owner, but don't forget that your cat will be tired. Take it straight home after the show and allow it to rest.

which it is possible to view the judging and to see how your cat handles. During the judging you may take the opportunity to see something of the town and eat your picnic or take a meal in a local restaurant. Usually you will be readmitted with the public at about midday. You can then see how your cat has fared.

Catalogues for the show are usually sold when the hall is cleared, and you may then buy one to check the details of your cat and the classes you have entered in. If there

is any mistake ask to see the show manager quickly. If your cat has been missed out of a class, or is in the wrong one, it may be possible to rectify this before judging has finished in this class.

The classes in the catalogue are in the same order as in the schedule and the cats generally have consecutive numbers in their Open class order.

The first time a cat is mentioned all the details of sire, dam, date of birth etc, are given, and there is a list of other classes in which it is

Above: Flat ribbons and reusable plastic flats laid out ready to be awarded at a show in California. In the United States, exhibitors bring their cats to the judging rings.

Types of Classes (UK)

Open classes

Unless on exhibition, all cats in competition must enter their appropriate breed in the open class; the exception is in the case of full champions and premiers/grand champions and grand premiers who do not have to enter their open class and can just enter their appropriate grand and/or open class. Adults are cats nine months of age or more on the day of the show.

Kittens over four and under nine months old have separate Open classes for all breeds. Kitten classes for popular breeds may be split into males and females or be divided by age.

Neuters, which are castrated males or spayed females, have their own separate Open classes.

Prior to being granted championship status, new breeds go through two basic categories. Briefly, preliminary status affords the cat a breed number, and allows the cats of this breed to be judged individually against the required standard of points; those thought to be a sufficiently good example of the breed are awarded a Merit Certificate. They are not in competition with each other, but are given awards on their own merit. The next stage is provisional status; here the cats have their own breed open class, and are in competition with each other. The cat which the judge feels to be the best in the class may be awarded an Intermediate Certificate. As with a CC, this may be withheld if the cat is adjudged not to be of a suitable standard.

Miscellaneous or Side classes

Open to all exhibits but without the importance of Open classes, they are generally split into categories for cats which have won a certain amount, have been bred by the exhibitor or otherwise, or come from specific areas, and are again divided into sections and into cats, kittens and neuters, for example:

Debutante: For cats (kittens,

neuters) which have never been exhibited before.
Maiden: For cats (kittens, neuters) which have never won a first, second or third prize.
Novice: For cats (kittens, neuters) which have never won a first prize.
Special Limit: For cats (kittens, neuters) which have not won more than two first prizes.
Limit: For cats (kittens, neuters) which have not won more than four first prizes.
Adolescent: For cats between 9 and 15 months of age.
Junior: For cats (neuters) under two years old on the day of the show.
Senior: For cats (neuters) two years and over on the day of the show.
Veteran: For cats (neuters) seven years and over on the day of the show.
Radius: For cats (kittens, neuters) residing within a certain distance of the show.
Visitors: For cats (kittens, neuters) residing more than a certain distance from the show.
Breeders: For cats (kittens, neuters) bred by the exhibitor.
Novice Exhibitor: An owner who has never won a money prize.
Aristocrat: A cat with one or more Challenge Certificates but not a full Champion.
Charity classes: All cats and owners are eligible but entry fees are donated to a cat charity.

Club classes

Put on both by the club holding the show and other cat clubs, to be entered only by members of the club sponsoring the class.

Household Pet classes

For unregistered cats of unknown pedigree, split into Open, Miscellaneous and Club classes. At a small show the Open classes may only be split into Longhaired cats and kittens and Shorthaired cats and kittens, whereas at a large show they may be divided into several colour categories. Household Pets are expected to be neutered when they are old enough, so there are no separate classes for neuters.

entered. In subsequent classes no details are given beyond its number, name and owner, and sometimes a reference to its Open class number.

Sometimes classes are split if there are many entries. Two or more may be amalgamated if there are very few entries, except Open Championship classes.

There may have been a change of judges since the publication of the schedule. These must be published in *Cats* magazine. All judges' changes must be displayed on a board just inside the hall.

At the back of the catalogue, after the classes, will be a full list of cups and specials offered by the club holding the show and supporting clubs. At the very end there is a list of exhibitors' names and addresses in alphabetical order, usually with the pen numbers of the cats they are showing.

While you are still restricted to the side of the hall or gallery overlooking the hall read through the catalogue and make a note of any cats you wish to look at in particular. You may be thinking about a stud for your queen or considering buying a kitten from a particular breeder. It is most annoying to get home, read the catalogue, and then wish you had thought of looking at a certain cat at the show but omitted to do so.

As the slips go up on the results board, mark the results of your classes in the catalogue. You may also wish to mark up the other Open classes in your section, and possibly Side classes too. As you get to know other cats and their owners you will probably wish to study their progress as well as your own.

The cats' numbers on the results slips are usually in the same order as in the catalogue, but occasionally they are not, so check this before writing the results down.

The judging

Judging is done by unpaid judges with the help of one or more stewards. The stewards find the cats which have to be judged in each

class and let the judge examine each one, usually on a movable table, which is taken from pen to pen. The table is disinfected before each competitor is placed on it, as are the hands of the stewards and judge. The judge makes notes in his or her book after examining each exhibit. He or she judges against a standard of points as laid down by the governing body for each breed. Body shape, coat texture, coat colour, eye colour, etc., have a number of points allotted to them, adding up to 100. Most judges do not actually award points but put remarks in their judging books which enable them to assess the cat's standard. If they feel it is not high enough, the Challenge Certificate may be withheld.

The results will appear on an awards board showing each class with the cats entered marked 1st, 2nd, 3rd, etc. The letters CC mean Challenge Certificate, an award granted to the best cat in an Open class. Winning three Challenge Certificates at three shows under three different judges makes a cat eligible to apply for recognition as a Full Champion. Premier Certificates are awarded to the winners of the Open neuter classes for championship status breeds only if the judge deems the cat to be of sufficient merit. Three certificates must be won under three judges for a cat to be awarded Premier status.

Each judge nominates a best cat, kitten and neuter from the exhibits he or she has judged. A panel of judges, usually five of the most senior judges, sees all the nominations, provided they have won their open class, and votes secretly for the Best Cat, Best Kitten and Best Neuter. If the show is divided into sections, there will be a different panel for each section. They may ultimately, if there is such

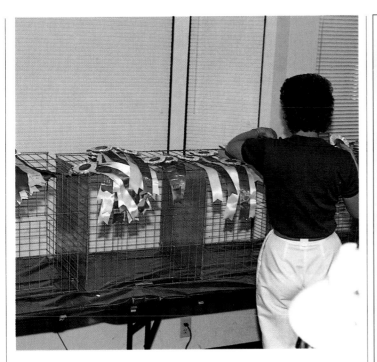

Above: A clerk sorts through rosettes ready for the next day's judging. To obtain a licence in the United States, prospective judges must be prepared to serve as a clerk at shows first.

Below: Two Blue point Birman cats in their benching cage. At American shows, every cat entered may compete (and usually does) in each individual show or ring. A two-day show may hold 12 different 'rings'.

Types of Cat Show (UK)

1 Championship This is run under the strict rules of the GCCF, and Challenge Certificates are awarded. Open classes are provided for all breeds; in the case of breeds with Championship and Provisional status separate classes are provided for male and female adults.

2 Sanction Conducted under the same rules as a Championship Show with the same classes provided, but no Challenge Certificates are awarded. It is a dress rehearsal for a Championship Show.

Some Championship and Sanction Shows cater only for a particular breed or group of breeds; these are called Specialist Breed Shows.

3 Exemption Held under the same basic conditions as the above shows, but many of the rules are relaxed. For instance, the classes do not have to be split up as they are at Championship and Sanction Shows, so that all the Siamese adults of different colours might be put in the same Open class at a small show. Exemption Shows are often run as part of an agricultural show.

In addition to the three types of show described above, special exhibitions of pedigree cats are held, often in conjunction with a cat club meeting. These cats are on display and no judging takes place.

Pet cat shows are often held at agricultural shows or similar events. Household pets may be exhibited at these, but no cat which is registered with the GCCF may compete at anything other than a Championship, Sanction or Exemption Show licensed by the GCCF. Non-pedigree cats are not registered with the GCCF. Where GCCF shows have a non-pedigree section, non-pedigrees may be shown. Non-pedigrees may also be shown at other shows. Note that all non-pedigrees older than nine months must be neutered.

an award, choose the Best Exhibit in Show from the Best Cat and Best Kitten. Neuters may compete against full cats in Best in Show and a Best Neuter will be chosen from other neuters nominated. Where these awards are not made, Best of Breed awards are given.

After the results are pinned up, the award cards are placed on the pens and sometimes the winners' rosettes as well. If your cat has won something, this is a very exciting time. It is a good idea to keep records of each cat's show wins, prize cards, dates of becoming a Champion and any other relevant information.

If judging has not finished when you are allowed to re-enter the hall, you must not talk to the judges while they are judging, and you must not hang around your pen, indirectly telling a judge that the cat is your exhibit. Nor must you obstruct the aisles while the judges are circulating. You must leave your cat on view to the public until the show closes, but for security reasons do not leave your cat alone towards the end of the day, and don't wait until people start dismantling the cages before you put your cat in its carrier: the animal

Below: An exhibitor at an American show with his Red Persian kitten — which clearly is not sure whether it likes all the activity or not.

could be upset by the noise. Lastly, do not leave your prize cards behind on the show cage!

After the show
After the show you and your cat will be tired. It is best to go straight home and rest. If several cats are at home, isolate the show cat for two weeks if you can, in case it has caught and spreads an infection. All the show equipment must be disinfected. Your own clothes and shoes should also be sterilized.

There is a 13-day rule in the UK which means that a cat cannot enter two shows in under 13 days. This helps to curb infection and also prevents the cat being shown too often.

If you have won a cup or other prize, you may have to wait some weeks to receive it. Prize money is paid out on the day at UK shows and must be collected on the day. It is refundable if later the exhibit is disqualified for some reason. If this is not done disciplinary action may be taken. If you have won cards or rosettes you can bring them home on show day, and proudly display them at once. If you have not won a prize, do not get upset: somebody has to lose, and next time could be your lucky day.

If you and your cat have enjoyed your day, by all means go on exhibiting. Many cats plainly revel in show conditions. But if yours has displayed nervous or bad-tempered

behaviour, then it is kinder to leave it at home next time and go just for fun, or take another exhibit.

Perhaps you will come to enjoy shows enough to want to help with the organization. There are many jobs you could probably do — for example, stewarding for a judge, helping to enter results, fixing cards on the pens and placing result slips on the awards boards.

Becoming a steward
To become a steward, you must ask a judge of the breed that interests you if you can act as his or her steward. If two stewards are required, you will probably first get the job as a second steward. In this capacity you would gain a great deal of experience. Some stewards

do this work in order to qualify as probationer judges.

It is the steward's job to make sure everything is ready for the judge to commence the judging, such as seeing that he or she has a judge's book, a Nomination for Best in Show form; a spray bottle containing diluted disinfectant, paper towels and a cloth for wiping the table; a small table or trolley on which the judge can examine each cat; luncheon, coffee and tea vouchers, for both judge and stewards, badges for judge and stewards, which should be worn, and a pencil with a rubber on the end. All of these items are supplied by the club running the show but it is the steward's job to make sure the judge has everything that is

---

UK Official Breed Numbers
(Courtesy of the Governing Council of the Cat Fancy)

Breed number

Longhair

1	Black	22	Tortoiseshell-and-White
2	White (Blue-eyed)	22a	Blue Tortie-and-White
2a	White (Orange-eyed)	25	Manx
2b	White (Odd-eyed)	28	Blue-Cream
3	Blue	30	Brown Spotted
4	Red Self	30d	Red Spotted
5	Cream	30s	Silver Spotted
6	Black Smoke	30+	A.O.C. Spotted
6a	Blue Smoke	31+	Bicoloured
6d or 6f	Red or Cream Smoke, Male	36+	Smoke
6d-6g	Red, Cream, Tortie or Blue-Cream Smoke, Female	39+	Tipped
		40+	Colourpointed British SH
7	Silver Tabby		
8	Brown Tabby	**Foreign**	
9	Red Tabby	16a	Russian Blue
10	Chinchilla	23	Usual Abyssinian
11	Tortoiseshell	23a	Sorrel Abyssinian
12 1	Tortoiseshell and White	23c	Blue Abyssinian
12 2	Blue Tortoiseshell-and-White	63	Usual Somali
		63a	Sorrel Somali
12a1-12a7	Bicoloured	33+	Cornish Red
13	Blue-Cream	33a+	Devon Rex
13b1	Seal Colourpoint	34	Korat
13b2	Blue Colourpoint	68+,72+	Asian-Burmilla Group
13b6,8,9&10	Tortoiseshell Colourpoint	74+	Tonkinese
13b3,4,5&7	A.O.C. Colourpoint		
13b11-13b20	Tabby Colourpoint	**Burmese**	
50b	Chocolate	27	Brown Burmese
50c	Lilac	27a	Blue Burmese
51 1 or 2	Red Cameo, Male	27b	Chocolate Burmese
51 1,2, or 4	Red or Tortie Cameo, Female	27c	Lilac Burmese
		27d	Red Burmese
52 1 or 2	Cream Cameo, Male	27f	Cream Burmese
52 1, 2 or 4	Cream or Blue-Cream Cameo, Female	27e,g,h or j	A.C. Tortoiseshell Burmese
53	Pewter		
54	Golden Persian	**Oriental**	
		29	Havana
Semi-longhair		29c	Oriental Lilac
13c1	Seal Point Birman	35	Foreign White
13c2	Blue Point Birman	37	Oriental Black
13c 3/4	Chocolate series Birman	37a	Oriental Blue
13c 5/10	Red series Birman	37e,g,h or j	Oriental Tortoiseshell
13c 11/20	Tabby series Birman	38-38d, 38f	Oriental Spotted
13d	Turkish Van	41+	Oriental Classic tabby
64+	Maine Coon	42+	Oriental Smoke
66+	Ragdoll	43+	Oriental Shaded/Tipped
67+	Norwegian Forest Cat	44+	Oriental Mackerel tabby
		45+	Oriental Ticked tabby
British shorthair		62+	Angora
14	White (Blue-eyed)		
14a	White (Orange-eyed)	**Siamese**	
14b	White (Odd-eyed)	24	Seal point
15	Black	24a	Blue point
16	Blue	24b	Chocolate point
17	Cream	24c	Lilac point
18	Silver Tabby	32 1-6& 32t 1-4	Tabby point
19	Red Tabby	32a	Red point
20	Brown Tabby	32b 1-4	Tortie point
21	Tortoiseshell	32c	Cream point
		61+	A.C. Balinese

required. It is also the steward's job to get the cat out of the pen and to replace it in the pen once the judging has finished. Consequently, it will be helpful if you are an expert cat handler, for cats are sometimes nervous at shows and take it out on the steward! It is important for everyone to clean his or her hands before handling another cat, or the scent of one cat could upset the next, with dire results. Perhaps more important, this also stops the spread of infection.

Once all the cats in one class have been judged, it is the steward's job to take the award slips to the awards table, having made sure that they are made out correctly. (Make sure that your judge has signed all three copies of the results slip!) When all the classes have been judged, the steward takes all the equipment back to the show manager. Then comes the Best in Show judging and it is once again the steward who takes up to the table the cats that the judge has nominated for

Below: A judge checks the shape of a cat's head at a show in California to see how closely it conforms to the written standard for its breed.

Best in Show. These are collected in their own carriers as there is often a long wait on the platform until each is called for. After judging, it is the steward's job to see that the cat is either placed in the Best in Show pen in front of the stage or taken back to its own pen.

Not all shows have a Best in Show; and some shows allow the judges to judge for the award in pens, which saves cats from the stress of being passed over the top table at the end of what has usually been a long and tiring day.

Stewards are unpaid but the rewards for the true cat lover, or for young people aspiring to be a judge, are manifold. You can learn a great deal. (The GCCF rules state that stewards must be 16 years of age or over.) Stewards are not expected to offer their opinions on judging the various cats unless asked to do so by their judge. Otherwise, listen carefully and learn all you can!

After many years of breeding and showing you may even consider becoming a judge or a show manager. (Stewarding is considered to be a pre-requisite for becoming a judge. The GCCF also runs a Judges Scheme for those aspiring to be judges.) Many famous judges are asked to judge at shows in other countries. Showing could open up for you a whole new exciting field with an international flavour. You may also have the opportunity to export cats with your prefix worldwide.

Showing in the US

The newcomer making his or her way through a show hall will notice judges earnestly examining cats and hanging ribbons on their cages. The visitor may also notice people gathered around a judging area — like youngsters cheering for their favourites in a marbles tournament — while a judge takes one cat after another out of its cage and holds it up for spectators to admire and applaud.

Anybody who is unfamiliar with cat-show protocol may find such activities a bit puzzling, and may feel as though he or she has tuned into a two-hour mystery on television one hour after it has started. If you've never been to a show before, or if you have attended one but have been unable to figure out precisely what was going on, pull up a chair. I will explain what goes on in the rectangular judging area known as a 'ring'. I will also explain what the ribbons mean and what all the cheering is about.

In the United States a cat show is composed of a number of separate, individual shows that are conducted at the same time and in the same location. Each individual show is presided over by a different judge in a separate judging area or ring. The judges make their decisions independently. Hence, a cat which is chosen best in show by the judge in Ring 1 in the morning may not receive the same award — or any award at all — from the judge in Ring 2 that afternoon.

Each judge in the show hall evaluates cats according to a schedule, and the schedule differs from one judge to the next. This arrangement helps to keep cats moving into the judging rings smoothly because, unlike the British system wherein judges move about and cats remain in their benching areas, exhibitors at American shows bring their cats to the judging rings.

The judge in Ring 1 may begin with kittens, then go on to household pets, then proceed through the other competitive categories (which are explained below). The judge in Ring 2 may begin with new breeds and colours, then progress to altered cats, then kittens, and so forth. But no matter what the sequence in a ring might be, the judging schedule is composed of some arrangement of the six categories of competition offered at a show.

Every cat entered in a show may compete — and virtually always does — in each individual show or ring. The number of individual shows held at the typical two-day American show ranges from six to 12. Thus, the expression 'We're going to an eight-ring show in Pittsburgh next weekend' means that the speaker and his or her cat(s) are going to a show at which eight judges will preside over eight different rings (or shows) and will confer eight best in show awards to as many as eight cats.

Types of shows

Individual shows are classified as either all-breed or speciality. In an all-breed show all cats, regardless of coat length or body type, compete against each other for various awards. Speciality shows are conducted by different rules in different associations. In most registries cats of similar coat length compete in speciality shows that are divided into longhair and shorthair specialities. In the Cat Fanciers' Association (CFA), cats of similar type compete for speciality prizes. This means that Exotic Shorthairs, which are identical to Persians in everything but coat length, compete in longhair speciality rings in CFA.

Categories of competition

Whether an individual show is all-breed, longhair speciality or shorthair speciality, competition is held in the following categories: championship, premiership (or altered), kitten, provisional (or new breed and colour), and household pet. If one were drawing a grid to represent the layout of American cat shows, the all-breed, longhair speciality and shorthair speciality rings would constitute vertical distinctions, while the categories of competition would be horizontal distinctions that cut across vertical lines.

Championship competition is for unaltered, pedigree cats at least eight months old. Premiership competition, which is called by the more straightforward term 'altered competition' in all associations except the CFA, is for neutered or spayed pedigree cats that are eight months of age or more. Kitten competition is for pedigree youngsters between the ages of four and eight months. Provisional competition, which is known as new breed and colour competition in most associations, is for those breeds or colours that have achieved registration but not championship status. Household pet competition is held primarily for cats of unknown or unregistered parentage, but many people are now showing pet-quality pedigree cats as household pets. Household pets older than eight months must be altered in order to be eligible for shows.

Judging procedures

The judging format in all North American cat shows — except for those sanctioned by The International Cat Association (TICA) — is similar to the following model, which is used by the CFA. (The TICA method will be explained presently.)

Every cat competing in the championship category begins in the open class. In breeds with large

Below: Spectators watch intently as a judge assesses a Turkish Van at a show. Others watch the action at a different ring (top).

entries, such as the Persian, a cat initially competes for a first-place blue ribbon against other cats of the same sex and colour. (Red second-place ribbons and yellow third-place ribbons are also awarded in open classes.) The male and the female opens that win the first-place ribbons also receive a red-white-and-blue winners' ribbon.

The judge awards ribbons on the basis of how closely each cat conforms to the written standard for its breed. After placing ribbons on the appropriate cages, the judge records his or her decisions in a judges' book, while the ring clerk does the same in a show catalogue.

The judge next appraises the opens in the remaining colour classes of the breed division (there are, for example, six divisions of Persians and two of Burmese). Awards given are the same as those described above.

In breeds with smaller entries, colour distinctions may not be observed. All males, regardless of colour, will compete for the first-place blue ribbon and the accompanying winner's ribbon; and all females, regardless of colour, will compete for their first-place and winner's ribbons.

Once a cat has earned six winners' ribbons, it becomes a champion. At its next show it is eligible to compete against other champions for points towards the grand champion title. (In some associations cats competing in the open class can earn points towards their grand championship, but the CFA requires that a cat become a champion first before it can earn

any grand championship points.)

After a judge has handled the open cats in a breed or a division of a breed, he or she judges the champions in that breed or division. The judge then awards first-, second- and third-place ribbons to the three best male and to the three best female champions. Next, the judge evaluates the grand champions, if there are any present, and awards ribbons for best and second-best grand champion.

The judge then awards best of colour class (black) and second-best of colour class (white) ribbons. These go to the cats in the breed, division or colour class that come closest to meeting the standard. Sometimes, if there are grand champions of sufficient merit at a show, the best and second-best of colour awards will be won by them. But it is not unheard of for a particularly good younger cat, say a champion or even an open, to be judged best of colour class.

Once all the colour classes in a breed or division of a breed have been evaluated, the judge awards the following ribbons: best of breed or division (brown), second-best of breed or division (orange), and best champion of breed or division (purple). The best champion of breed or division receives one point towards its grand championship title for each champion it has defeated in that breed or division. Once a cat accumulates 200 points, it becomes a grand champion.

Finals
Once a judge has examined all the cats in championship competition

— or all the cats of similar coat length (or type) if he or she is doing a speciality show — it is time for the finals, when the judge presents the top ten cats in show.

As an anxious silence falls over the crowd gathered about the ring, the judge introduces the top ten cats in ascending order of merit until the best cat in the show has been held aloft to enthusiastic applause. This is the thrill that every cat breeder lives for: a matchless, singular moment of exaltation and triumph that renders worthwhile all those countless hours spent cleaning litter trays and nursing sick kittens through the night.

Premiership (altered) competition
Altered cats (neutered males and spayed females) are judged by the same standards used for judging whole cats. Altered cats need six winners' ribbons to earn the premier title. Since there are fewer cats in premiership than there are in championship competition, only 75 points are needed to become a grand premier. Cats in premiership competition are also presented in top-ten finals.

Kitten competition
Kittens compete with other kittens of the same breed, sex and colour for first-, second-, and third-place ribbons. Best and second-best of colour class are also awarded to deserving kittens, as are awards for best of division and best of breed. When all the kittens have been judged, the best kittens are called back for finals.

Above: Owner Donna Isenberg poses with her prize-winning White Persian, whose cage has been decorated with its rosettes.

Household pet competition
In CFA shows, household pets are judged in one group regardless of sex, coat length, age or colour. (In other associations household pet judging more closely mimics the structural divisions of championship judging.)

There are no conventional standards for household pets. They are judged solely for their uniqueness, pleasing appearance, unusual markings, sweet dispositions and loud purring.

The TICA method
Suppose you have decided to watch Persians being judged in the championship category in an all-breed ring at a TICA show. As you observed at the CFA show described above, the cats are called to the ring by breed, division and colour class.

Whites are usually the first Persian colour class judged. If there are two white Persians in the show, the judge examines both, then awards a first-place ribbon (blue) to one cat and a second-place ribbon (red) to the other. Depending on the size of the class, the judge may award ribbons to the third-best (yellow), fourth-best (green), and fifth-best (white) cats as well.

After finishing with the white Persians, the judge proceeds to each of the other solid colours, awarding from best through fifth-best of colour as the class size requires. Then, having evaluated all the solid-coloured Persians, the judge reviews these cats and awards three additional ribbons: best of division (black), second-best of division (purple) and third-best of division (orange).

When the solid-coloured Persians have been assessed, the judge advances to the other divisions in the breed: tabby, particolour, and so on, until all Persians have been appraised. At that point, the judge may announce which cats are the best, second-best and third-best of breed, but no additional ribbons are presented for these awards.

At the end of the all-breed championship category, when every breed — from Abyssinian through to Turkish Van — has been examined, the judge has the ten best cats in show called back to the ring for finals. After the cats are settled in the judging cages, the judge introduces the top ten cats individually until the best cat in show has been presented.

TICA titles
All TICA-registered cats in the championship, altered and household pet-adult categories earn points toward titles at shows. Points are awarded for best through to fifth-best of colour (25 through five points), best through to third-best of division (25 through 15 points), and best through to tenth-best cat in show (200 through 110 points in an all-breed ring, 150 through 60 points in a speciality ring.)

A cat may earn as many as six titles in competition. Those titles — described below — that contain the word 'champion' are earned by championship cats and alters. Those titles containing the word 'master' are earned by household pet adults. The requirements for the titles are as follows:
Champion/master, a total of 300 points, from at least four different judges, and one top-ten final win.
Grand champion/master, a total of 1,000 points and six final wins, from at least four different judges (a minimum of three final wins must be top-ten all-breed or top-five speciality wins).
Double grand, triple grand and quadruple grand champion/ master, an additional 1,000 points and one top-ten all-breed win or top-five speciality win for each title.
Supreme grand champion/ master, an additional 2,000 points and one best cat win earned as a quadruple grand champion in either an all-breed or a speciality ring.

National and regional awards
All cats, kittens and premiers (and, in some associations, household pets and even the new breeds and colours) that make finals at the end of a show receive points, on the basis of the number of cats defeated in that show, towards the national titles that are awarded at the end of each show season. (A show season runs from May 1 to April 30.) National titles are awarded to the 20 or 25 highest-scoring championship cats (depending on

the association); to the top 20 or 25 premiership cats, and to the top ten or 20 kittens. In most associations, each region also honours its highest-scoring cats, kittens and so forth at the end of the season. Finally, national honours are awarded to the best and second-best cats in each of the many breeds and divisions recognized by the various associations. It is a very rare cat that cannot lay claim to some title or other once the dust kicked up by the show season has finally settled.

Judges
The men and women officiating at North American cat shows have been licensed by the associations that sanction shows. Judges have been thoroughly trained in the art and science of cat-judging. School teachers, executives, 'blue collar' workers, doctors, lawyers, nurses and such during the week, judges are masters of their second craft on show weekends.

In order to obtain a licence, a judge must demonstrate skill at breeding cats, success in exhibiting them, and a willingness to work for the good of the association. Prospective judges, who must be at

least 21 years old and have five years' active breeding experience (or more, depending on the association) before they apply to join the judging programme, are required to serve on show committees in several capacities, including show manager and entry clerk. They must acquire a facility with show-ring mechanics by serving as ring clerks and master clerks at shows. And, finally, they must of course demonstrate ethical behaviour and good conduct in the cat fancy.

Once accepted into the judging programme, trainee judges must pass examinations on breed standards and show-ring mechanics, and they must serve an apprenticeship alongside a certified judge at a specified number of shows. Upon obtaining a licence, judges must perform satisfactorily at a requisite number of shows before they are advanced from probationary to approved status. This progress through the ranks usually takes several years. Therefore, the judge who is handling cats in the show ring has a minimum of eight to ten years' experience in the cat fancy and, in most cases, many years more.

Above: Owners retrieve their cats after the judging has finished at a show in California. 'Flats' are hung on cages to indicate winners.

Showing in other countries
Show procedure varies from country to country. Standards of points for different breeds also vary and vetting-in regulations in each country depend on the endemic diseases there. In New Zealand, Australia and South Africa it is basically similar to the British pattern.

New Zealand In New Zealand there is only one Cat Fancy comprising many clubs, each running shows. Judges must have bred cats of their section (Longhair or Shorthair) for at least five years in order to be eligible. Foreign judges are often invited to judge at the larger shows. Only Championship shows are held, but there are usually classes for Household Pets.

The shows last one day only, and

Below: Proud winners of the Household Pet section, held mainly for cats of unregistered parentage.

as in the UK the cats are penned anonymously, grouped according to breed. In addition to the Open classes there are various Side classes, including 'type classes' in which the cat is judged on type alone, coat colour and pattern being disregarded.

Sweepstake classes are also held, the winners each getting a percentage of the entry money. Challenge Certificates are awarded to Open class winners of sufficient merit and, as in the UK, three Certificates under three different judges give the cat his Championship.

The hall is cleared for judging, which takes place from the pens. Stewards get the cats out for the judge and make notes for him. Judging usually finishes by 1 p.m., and the exhibitors are allowed back into the hall to see what their cats have won and to decorate their pens in order to make a splendid show for the public.

Below: Two girls with their Siamese and the rosette it has won. Winning is a team effort, requiring much commitment on all sides.

Australia There are seven states in Australia, each with at least one Cat Fancy, but these all cooperate with each other. They use judges from other fancies, recognize each others' registrations and exhibit at shows run by clubs belonging to other fancies.

Judges have to train hard and are not simply accepted on breeding and stewarding experience. As in the UK they are not paid and receive only their expenses.

All judging, including Best in Show, is done by the judge going to the cats in their pens. In all classes cats are judged only against others of their own breed, unless they are nominated for Best in Show, when they will compete against other breeds.

South Africa Shows are run similarly to those in the UK, the judge going from pen to pen. Two stewards get the cats out for the judge, who dictates his remarks on the cats to a note-taker or scribe.

There is a sheet of paper for each cat, giving details of breed, sex, age, etc. (with the name to be filled in later by the judge), on which the judge makes a written report. These reports are later circulated to the exhibitors.

All the classes a cat may be entered in at any one show will be judged by the same person, but Best of Breed or Best in Show is determined by a panel of judges. The panel sits in a roped-off area to which the cats are brought by stewards.

Training to become a judge is very rigorous: clubs nominate suitable people, who then go through a course of lectures and demonstrations, at the end of which there is an examination. Judges are unpaid, receiving only their expenses.

Europe In continental Europe there are many Cat Fancies, some of which are linked together under the Fédération Internationale Féline d'Europe (FIFe), which has member organizations in 12 European countries. FIFe does not recognize registrations with other bodies in Europe, nor may a cat be registered with FIFe members as well as with others. FIFe members may not buy kittens from non-members, nor use their studs.

FIFe shows are all Championship shows and may last one, two or three days. Cats are judged on a point scale as follows:
Excellent 88 to 100 points
Very Good 76 to 87 points
Good 61 to 75 points
Fair 46 to 60 points
The major classes are:
International Champion for Longhair/Shorthair full International Champions.
International Premier for Longhair/Shorthair full International Premiers.
Champion for Full Champions, with classes for both sexes of each breed. A CACIB (Certificat d'Aptitude au Championnat International de Beauté) is awarded to the winner of each class if it gains at least 95 points.
Premier for full Premiers, with classes for each breed. A CAPIB (Certificat d'Aptitude de Premier International de Beauté) is awarded in the same way.
Open for cats 10 months and over, but not including Champions or International Champions with separate classes as before. A CAC (Certificat d'Aptitude au Championnat) is awarded to each class winner if it gains at least 93 points.
Neuter for neuters 10 months and over of each breed. A CAP (Certificat d'Aptitude de Premier) is awarded to winners gaining at least 93 points.
Kitten classes for three- to six-month kittens and 6- to 10-month kittens of each sex and breed.
Neuter Kitten classes as above.
Litters, eight weeks to three months with at least three in each litter.

Four places are given in each class, first, second, third and mentioned, and the judges' reports on each cat are given to the exhibitors at the show.

To become a Champion a cat must win three CACs under three different judges, and to gain its International Championship it must be awarded three CACIBs under three judges, at least one of these being won in a different European country.

In addition to the major classes there are classes for imported cats, progeny classes and novice classes in which unregistered cats may be entered. If the latter gain sufficient points they are registered.

The cats are penned in decorated pens with all the cats belonging to one owner grouped together. The hall itself is also beautifully decorated. Judging usually takes place in a separate room, to which the cats for each class are carried by stewards. They are then penned anonymously in plain pens. The International classes are judged first, followed by all the Champions, then Premiers, Opens, etc. Afterwards all the judges form a panel to select the Best Longhair cat, kitten and neuter, and Best Shorthair cat, kitten and neuter, and finally the Best in Show.

In addition to the shows run by members of FIFe there are also independent shows in most European countries.

175

11

THE LAW AND YOUR CAT

The law in the United Kingdom makes a significant distinction between dogs and cats, in that cats are considered to be untrainable, and so owners cannot usually be held legally responsible for their actions. This applies particularly to cat behaviour. A cat cannot trespass on a neighbour's property for example, but if it is injured there, you are unlikely to be able to claim damages either, provided that the neighbour did not set out intentionally to injure your pet. For example, if the cat gains access to a garage, and drinks anti-freeze containing ethylene glycol (which is converted in the body to deadly oxelic acid), you will have no redress, unless you can prove that the neighbour left the anti-freeze with the intention of poisoning the cat.

In the United Kingdom, there has never been an Act of Parliament which specifically seeks to protect cats but, nevertheless, cats do have legal protection against acts of deliberate cruelty. *The Protection of Animals Act*, which became law in 1911, sought to define what constituted cruelty, making it an offence to cause unnecessary suffering to a cat or any animal, either by deliberate action or as a result of neglecting its needs.

Under this Act, it is also an offence to carry or otherwise move a cat in such a way that it is subjected to unnecessary suffering. No-one may wilfully administer poisonous, injurious substances or drugs, or perform an operation without an anaesthetic. Not only can a court order the removal of a cat from an owner who has been found guilty of a breach of this Act, but it can also order the destruction of an animal under these circumstances, if further suffering would result from the cat being kept alive. In practice, a court will

Above: A cat easily panics in strange surroundings, so keep your pet in an escape-proof container when away from home.

Left: Few cats will enjoy being kept in a cattery, but this may be the best option if the owner has to go away for a long period.

normally take into account veterinary advice before reaching this decision.

Moving cats

Cats are not protected by the *Road Traffic Act*, and there is no legal obligation to report an accident involving a cat, although it is an offence not to inform the police if a dog is involved. Should the cat be injured as a result of the collision, however, then the person responsible for the injury must do something to relieve the animal's suffering, or he or she could subsequently be accused of cruelty. The legal situation may be different in other countries, though in Australia, for example, any collision with a cat must be reported either

to the police or to the RSPCA.

When it comes to travelling in a vehicle, cats are required to be properly constrained before being taken on board public transport. It is an offence to have a cat loose in a car if the driver is alone. As a cat easily panics in strange surroundings, it is as much in your interests as in those of other people to keep your cat secure in an escape-proof container at all times when it is away from home.

Normally, you would not take a cat into shops, but some cats are walked on a leash and harness in city areas. Although securely restrained, they may well become frightened in these surroundings, so take care to exercise your cat in areas in which it is safe to do so. Failure to do this may give rise to charges of cruelty. Similarly, cats should always be taken to a vet in a secure carrier, because the close proximity of other animals (particularly dogs) in a vet's surgery is likely to upset cats.

There are times when cats are moved on their own, without their owners and, again, a suitable carrier is essential. For the purposes of air transportation, standards are laid down in the International Air Transportation Association's (IATA's) *Live Animals Regulations*. These are subject to regular review, and are also likely to form the basis of transport requirements for cats and other animals by other means in Europe. Carriers are also legally bound to feed and water animals in their care at regular, stipulated intervals. They are likely to be held liable for any death or injury which arises as a result of any neglect or default on their part, in not complying with the regulations in force, once having accepted a cat or other creature for transportation purposes.

Disappearing cats

Cats are not licensed in the UK, partly because ownership is difficult to prove. Feeding a cat on your premises could be defined as constituting ownership, even if you have not purchased or acquired the cat directly from another person. This can happen with strays. You can then be held legally responsible for the cat if you go on holiday or move house without making proper provision for it in your absence. Ownership continues to apply until another owner takes over, so once you have accepted the responsibility, you cannot simply opt out of it. It is an offence to cause suffering by neglect.

Under *The Theft Act (1968)* a cat is accepted as having an owner, and so is considered to be a chattel. It is against the law to steal a cat known to belong to someone else, or to receive a cat which has been stolen. The fact that a cat has strayed does not alter the animal's ownership. Only in the case of feral cats, which are deemed to have reverted back to the wild, is there no question of ownership.

There is considerable fear among cat-lovers that their pets may be stolen and sold either for their fur or to laboratories. In reality, cats may disappear for a number of reasons apart from being stolen. They could be killed on the road some distance from their homes, and if they are not wearing an identification disc, then there is little likelihood that their owners will be traced.

Similarly, it is possible that some die away from their home range, through natural causes, or because they have been poisoned. There is also the hazard of urban foxes. Although they do not prey extensively on cats, foxes have been known to kill cats occasionally.

Evidence of gangs roaming the streets and snatching cats into the backs of vans and then vanishing into the night is largely anecdotal. A recent change in legislation has also made it less likely that cats will be stolen for experimental purposes in the UK.

For many years, such experiments were regulated under the *Cruelty to Animals Act (1876)*. This outlawed procedures which caused pain, unless these were carried out with the animal properly anaesthetized. Premises where experiments were carried out had to be registered and required a licence from the Home Office.

This Act has now been replaced by the *Animals Scientific Procedures Act (1986)* which licenses individuals engaged in such work, as well as the premises. Implementation of this legislation is monitored by inspectors. For the first time the Act specifies that cats used for experimental purposes must have been bred or acquired from certified breeding establishments. This should help to remove the fears of pet-lovers about cats being stolen and meeting an unhappy end in a laboratory.

In fact, laboratories prefer cats which have a fully documented history, especially those bred specifically for research and known to be free of pathogens which could compromise test results. Such animals are costly to replace and this, as much as any legislation, should help to ensure that they are reasonably treated under the circumstances, although some experiments are certainly cruel.

Unwanted cats and kittens

While there has been much focus recently on the problems posed by stray dogs, relatively little attention has been given to the increasing number of discarded cats. This may be partly a matter of profile. Stray

Below: Unwanted cats at an animal shelter in London. There are huge numbers of unwanted cats in the United Kingdom and the United States: most will be destroyed, as shelters cannot keep them for long.

cats are not necessarily as conspicuous as homeless dogs, unless they are in poor health. They also prove more adaptable, hunting and scavenging in urban areas. Only when these cats associate in colonies, typically close to railway lines, in vegetation, or in abandoned homes, are they likely to arouse much public concern.

Indiscriminate breeding involving both pedigree and non-pedigree cats means that there are too many unwanted cats. While certain moralists may take the view that all animals should have a legal right to live, others would argue that uncontrolled breeding results in so much suffering that some sort of population control is essential. The

Below: Another unclaimed inmate at a cat shelter. Indiscriminate breeding is the main reason for the excessive size of the cat population: owners should have their cats neutered to help solve the problem.

options are either to lower the birth rate or to raise the death rate.

Most people would prefer the first option, but greater education about neutering (possibly backed by legislation) is required worldwide to make this kind of population control effective. Cat owners should be prepared to do their best to prevent adding to the large numbers of unwanted kittens born each year, but many still shirk this responsibility.

The Abandonment of Animals Act (1969) makes it an offence to discard any animal, including kittens, in circumstances which are likely to give rise to unnecessary suffering. Even so, this legislation is very difficult to enforce, although the abandonment of the kittens need not be permanent for this Act to be broken. Leaving a box of young kittens on the doorstep of a pet shop on a cold night is a typical example of a likely offence, but one which very rarely results in prosecution by the authorities.

In areas of the world where rabies is endemic, the risks associated with stray and feral cat populations are even higher than in the UK today. Health, fire, police and other local services may all lose valuable time attending to problems created by stray animals. Cats which are feral prove almost impossible to tame, although kittens can prove more tractable.

Strays which are caught wandering the streets are taken to an animal shelter and kept for a relatively short period in the often forlorn hope that someone will offer them a home. Sadly, most are destroyed, for their numbers far exceed the available homes.

Most cat-lovers would be horrified to know that as many as 10 million cats are put down in the US alone each year: while most are quite healthy, they remain unwanted. In the United Kingdom, the Cats' Protection League alone takes in up to 40,000 homeless cats each year, and countless tens of thousands

are handled by other welfare organizations.

A well-organized and successful education programme would not only stress the need to neuter cats, but would also provide funds to cover the costs of owners who cannot afford to pay for this surgery themselves. Some British animal charities will organize such surgery free of charge in certain circumstances. Ideally, in due course, every cat born should have a loving owner ready and waiting to care for it.

Cat charities
Cat charities were established to combat cruelty to cats, whether due to deliberate neglect or simple ignorance of the animals' requirements. They remain as necessary today as when they were first founded. The oldest charity for cats in the British Isles is the Dublin Home for Starving and Forsaken Cats, founded in 1885. There are now many national and local cat charities, some with a membership fee, which helps cover expenses.

Such charities often produce a regular magazine or newsletter giving information about the cats in their care, fund-raising events and related areas of interest. Such organizations are usually represented at cat shows, selling a range of goods to assist with their work, which is typically carried out on a very limited budget in the case of small local organizations.

Making purchases or donating gifts for sale will help to raise funds, but if you have cash to spare, donations are invariably welcome, as are any bequests. Some cat charities have been left veritable fortunes by grateful supporters, and even individual cats have received quite large sums of money to assure their comfort after the death of their owners.

If you need to contact a welfare group for any reason, you will be able to find addresses in cat magazines or, locally, from veterinary surgeries or the library. National organizations are usually listed in the telephone directory, if you require their help in an emergency situation, or wish to help at branch level.

Obtaining a cat
Once you have decided to get a cat, you can either contact a local rescue organization to see if they have any suitable animals which need a good home, or you could turn to a breeder. There is currently no requirement for breeders to be licensed in any way, either for breeding purposes or the sale of kittens produced by their cats, unless this is a commercial enterprise.

Under the *Pet Animals Act (1951)*, however, all pet shops selling cats or kittens must be licensed by their local authority. A regular inspection is carried out, usually by a vet, and a number of aspects are considered before the licence is granted or renewed.

The premises must be suitable for the sale of livestock, covering environmental aspects such as

Above: A quarantine cattery. If you are moving to a different country, you may be required to place your cat in quarantine for a defined period before it is allowed entry.

Left: As many as 10 million strays — such as these — are put down in the United States alone each year.

lighting and ventilation, as well as size. Fire precautions are also assessed, and the means of preventing the spread of any disease must also be considered. The maximum number of animals the shop can hold will be stipulated, and their feeding and drinking requirements must be adequately met, with due regard also being given to proper management. Licences are granted for one year and must be renewed annually.

In the case of cats, they must not be kept in a cellar, or near mice or other animals which would normally form their prey. They should not be subjected to unnecessary disturbance from the public. Kittens must not be sold until the age that they are naturally fully weaned, and although this is usually taken to be at eight weeks, the Governing Council of the Cat Fancy recommends that 12 weeks should elapse before kittens are moved to new surroundings.

Above: A cat run at a cattery. In the United Kingdom, it is a legal requirement that all such establishments be licensed.

If you are concerned about conditions under which cats or kittens are being kept in a pet shop, then you should contact the Environmental Health Department of your local authority. It is also not permitted for animals, including cats, to be sold to children under 12 years old.

When a pet shop sells a non-pedigree cat, the responsibility lies with the buyer to select the type of kitten that he or she wants and to be assured about its health. However, if the purchaser is given a warranty of any kind, then there may be redress under the *Sale of Goods Act (1983)*, should this undertaking prove to be false. Certification in writing is always to be recommended; do not be persuaded into accepting a simple verbal undertaking.

If a cat purchased for stud purposes proves infertile, for example, then this may give rise to a claim for damages should the purchaser have given an understanding that it was suitable for this purpose.

Should a cat or kitten fall ill soon after being purchased, then clearly you must seek veterinary advice without delay. You should also notify the vendor in writing, following a preliminary phone call. Obtain a written veterinary report, and be sure to get a receipt for the cost of the treatment, if you wish to pursue the matter further with the vendor concerned.

Where a cat is of pedigree origin, then it may also be worthwhile referring the matter to the governing body which is responsible for registering kittens. In the UK the GCCF investigates all complaints of sick kittens being sold as a matter of policy and does not hesitate to take disciplinary action against breeders which it considers to have broken its rules and procedures by knowingly supplying a kitten in ill-health to an unsuspecting new owner.

In law, however, there is a considerable onus on the purchaser to ensure that the kitten or cat is healthy at the time it was acquired. If it appeared to be in good health you will have little likelihood of redress should it be ill the next day, even though the kitten may have been incubating the disease at the time of purchase. You would need to prove that the vendor knew or had reasonable grounds for suspecting that the animal was sick at the time that it was being offered to your for sale,

if any claim was to succeed.

When selling a pedigree cat, however, it is the vendor's responsibility under the *Trade Descriptions Act (1968)* to ensure that the paperwork is correct for the cat in question. This legislation applies only to businesses such as pet shops, however, and not to private individuals — but again, a feline governing body would doubtless not hesitate to act against a breeder who was suspected of providing false pedigrees. Enforcement of the Trade Descriptions Act itself is a matter for the Trading Standards Department of your local authority. They will prosecute if there are adequate grounds so to do.

Different regulations apply in other countries. For example in some Australian states a licence is required for the sale of cats but, in New Zealand, pet shops only need a licence if stipulated by a local authority by-law. Australian and New Zealand pet shops are visited and checked regularly by RSPCA and SPCA Inspectors, who will inspect the accommodation for the animals, cleanliness, and the supply of food and water, as well as looking for any evidence of overstocking or disease. All pet shops in these countries are required to take precautions against disease, fire and other emergencies.

Cats and property
It is forbidden to keep pets, including cats, in certain types of homes, notably flats and apartments. People who own their own houses usually have no trouble in this respect. But under the *Animals Act (1971)*, the law stipulates that the keeper of a cat is liable for damage caused by the animal, unless this is the fault of the person concerned or that the person has voluntarily accepted the risk. The keeper of the cat, who is responsible for it under the terms of this legislation, is deemed to be either the person who owns it, or the head of household if the actual owner is a household member under the age of 16.

Yet, as mentioned previously, a cat's keeper cannot be held responsible for acts which are ordinarily committed by a cat. These include fighting (unless there is a known history of fighting with vicious intent), and watching or catching birds of any type, including domesticated species such as poultry and pigeons.

The general lack of liability for trespass extends to damage caused by the cat following its instincts, such as digging up a neighbour's seed bed when carrying out its natural functions. Cats cannot be shot merely for trespass. They must also be proved

to have caused considerable commercial damage.

The introduction of the *Pests Act (1954)* helped to prevent cats from being severely or fatally injured by spring traps set for other creatures, such as rabbits. But in some countries, such as France, it can be illegal to allow cats to roam free in any event.

There is no statutory requirement in the UK, Australia or New Zealand for cats to carry any individual identification, but if your cat goes missing, an identification disc may help you to recover it. Have the disc engraved with your name, address and telephone number, and attach it to an expandable elastic collar placed around the cat's neck. If the collar then snags on a branch when the cat is climbing a tree, the animal will be able to slip out of the collar instead of being hanged by it. Do not include your cat's pet name on the disc, however — a would-be thief could easily entice the cat away by using it.

Boarding catteries
In the United Kingdom, boarding catteries must be licensed under the *Animal Boarding Establishments Act (1963)* by their local authority. They are obliged to provide suitable accommodation, food, drink, light and heat, and will be inspected annually by a vet acting for the licensing authority, who may then renew or revoke the licence. It is left to each local authority to decide the precise meaning of terms such as 'adequate' space or ventilation or what constitutes 'suitable' accommodation, so some variations in requirements may exist in different parts of the country. When starting out, planning permission is likely to be required for a boarding cattery, and again this is a local authority matter, at least in the first instance.

Licences are also required in some states of Australia for boarding other people's cats. They are not required in New Zealand, but in both countries the local authority's permission is necessary for the operation of a cattery, and it must comply with town planning specifications. Boarding catteries are also inspected by RSPCA and SPCA inspectors.

Quarantine catteries operate under a much more stringent set of criteria. Animals that could transmit rabies must under current regulations go into a quarantine establishment for six months on entering the UK. This situation may change as a result of the open market policy being pursued in the European community. While this requirement is almost certain to remain in force for cats being imported from outside the EC, it may be relaxed somewhat for cats which originate from other EC countries, if they have appropriate veterinary certification stating they are free from rabies. At the time of writing, the precise details are unclear, and the current position should always be ascertained in advance from the Ministry of Agriculture, Fisheries and Food (MAFF), who oversee UK quarantine arrangements.

Rabies is such a terrible disease that anyone bringing in undeclared cats or other mammals is liable to a large fine and imprisonment, with the animal likely to be destroyed. It is only by strict enforcement of its quarantine laws that the UK has remained free of this disease, which is endemic in continental Europe. Strict quarantine measures have also kept Australia and New Zealand free of rabies.

Some other countries have quarantine laws, but most will accept cats from the UK as being free from rabies, since the disease

does not currently occur on these islands, provided that the cats' owners have a valid health certificate to this effect.

Health certificates are the responsibility of a vet. In the UK vets are the only people qualified to diagnose and treat animals, with a few minor exceptions. Today, most vets are members of the Royal College of Veterinary Surgeons; if the initials 'MRCVS' follow your vet's academic qualifications (which are given after his or her name), this indicates that he or she is a member of this body, and is thus subject to its disciplinary code.

The law in the United States
Various federal, state and municipal laws protect and regulate the lives of cats in the United States. These laws fall into three categories: those that forbid certain actions or the omission of certain actions regarding cats, those that proscribe

Above: It is best to equip your pet with an identification tag, even if this is not required by law as in some parts of the United States.

certain feline behaviours, and those that require specific responsibilities of cat owners.

Cat-protection laws
The federal *Animal Welfare Act (AWA)*, as well as state and municipal anti-cruelty statutes, are the principal laws that forbid certain actions or the omission of certain actions regarding cats. The AWA — passed in 1966 and amended four times thereafter — mandates humane care and treatment for all animals, including cats, in research facilities, exhibition settings, or private houses.

Among its many provisions relating to the humane handling, housing and care of animals, the

---

Principal Animal Charities

In the United Kingdom
Royal Society for the Prevention
  of Cruelty to Animals (RSPCA)
People's Dispensary for Sick
  Animals (PDSA)
Cats' Protection League
Feline Advisory Bureau
Blue Cross
Wood Green Animal Shelter

In the United States
American Society for the
  Prevention of Cruelty to Animals
  (ASPCA)
American Humane Association
  (AHA)
Animal Protection Institute
  (API)
American Anti-Vivisection Society
Friends of Animals (FoA)

Fund for Animals
Humane Society of the
  United States (HSUS)
Morris Animal Foundation
National Anti-Vivisection Society
Society for Animal Rights
United Action for Animals

In Australia
Royal Society for the Prevention
  of Cruelty to Animals (RSPCA)
Animal Welfare League (AWL)
Cat Protection Society

In New Zealand
Society for the Prevention of
  Cruelty to Animals (SPCA)
New Zealand Humane Society
Feline Cat Protection Society

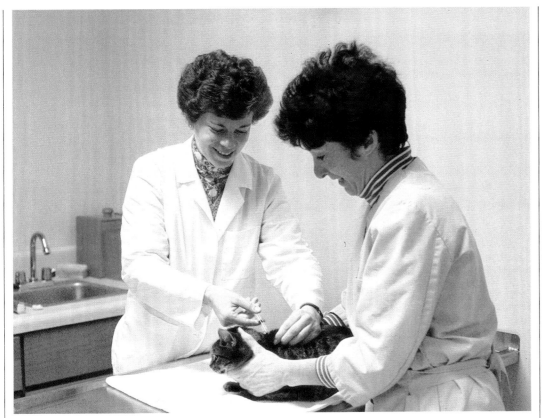

AWA forbids the 'transportation in commerce' of kittens and puppies younger than eight weeks of age. It also forbids dealers and exhibitors from selling or otherwise disposing of any animal for five days after they have acquired it. Finally, the AWA obliges dealers and exhibitors to maintain records of the origin and destination of the animals they obtain. But like many other animal-protection laws, the AWA is not as effective as it might be because adequate funding is not always available to enforce the law.

Anti-cruelty ordinances vary from one state or municipality to another, but they generally provide cats with protection against cruel treatment, abandonment and poisoning. State laws also require that persons keeping cats provide them with food, water and shelter. Obtaining convictions against violators of these laws is not always easy, and it becomes more difficult when the law stipulates — as nearly half the state anti-cruelty laws do — that mistreatment of animals must have been committed wilfully, maliciously, or negligently in order to be actionable. In addition, more than half the state anti-cruelty statutes that specifically require shelter for an animal say that failure to provide shelter also must be proven to have been intentional or cruel.

Laws controlling cat behaviour

Cats' lives are improved by laws that proscribe certain feline behaviours, but most laws of this type apply only to dogs. For example, the state of Maine has specific laws that prohibit owners from allowing their dogs to run at large, that regulate the disposition of dogs caught running at large, that mandate a procedure for handling sick or abandoned dogs and that regulate the purchase and sale of dogs. Maine, as do many other

states, also requires dog licences, regulates the issuance of those licences, sets licence fees and specifies penalties for violating dog laws. Moreover, Maine laws contain regulations regarding dangerous dogs and damage caused by dogs.

When state laws regulate animal behaviour, they often beget bureaux charged with their enforcement. Thus, Pennsylvania has a Bureau of Dog Law, and Connecticut has a Canine Division, which is a unit of the state Department of Agriculture. Such bureaux work for the betterment of the species whose actions they seek to control. If a noise-abatement statute applies to barking dogs but not to howling cats, the latter may suffer. A person who rings up animal control because his or her sleep was interrupted by feline courtship rituals may decide to act unilaterally and inhumanely if animal control replies that it is outside their remit to take action. This is but one example of the way in which the absence of laws dealing with noisy or destructive cats often creates a situation where offended parties take matters, and dangerous implements, into their hands — even if their first impulse was to seek a civilized solution to the problem.

Laws promoting responsible cat ownership

Laws designed to promote responsible cat ownership include licensing, leash laws, pet limitation, mandatory neutering or spaying and breeding restrictions. Although few municipalities in the US have passed such laws, they will become more prevalent as people continue struggling to reduce the surplus cat population.

As they already do for dogs, licence requirements compel cat owners to prove that their cats have been vaccinated properly. More

important, licensing is a life-and-death matter in some states. Wyoming pet owners have no property rights in unlicensed cats or dogs, nor do owners have any rights or actions against a person for the destruction of an unlicensed cat or dog.

Pounds in many states will not hold an unlicensed cat for as long a period as they will hold a cat that is wearing a tag. In some cities, pounds are not required to hold a cat at all, and stray cats that are not wearing any identification are euthanized on the spot. To a degree licensing gives animals legal recognition and, also to some degree, licensing gives pet owners the right to demand certain services because it generates revenue for the community.

Although few states mandate cat licensing — Arkansas, Maryland, Michigan, Oklahoma and Washington among them — municipalities may require licensing even if the state does not. In municipalities that do, the cost of a licence for an unaltered cat is generally higher than the cost for an altered one. That difference is greatest in King County, Washington, where licences for unaltered animals cost $55 while licences for altered pets cost $10. In many municipalities, however, the difference between the two kinds of licences — for altered and unaltered animals — is not significant enough to discourage people from keeping intact animals. Hence, differential licensing fails to make a truly significant impact on the cat overpopulation problem in many communities.

Leash laws for cats are even less prevalent than are licensing requirements, but many people believe that cats, like dogs, should not be allowed to run loose — unsupervized and uncontrolled.

This is not to say that cats ought never to go outisde, but when they do, they should be in the company and/or control of their owners, whose duty it is to make sure that their cats are properly protected and that other people are safe from being hurt or inconvenienced by those cats.

Perhaps the oldest ordinances aimed at inducing responsible pet ownership are laws that limit the numbers of pets an individual or a family may own. Numerous cities and counties across the US have laws restricting a household to three, four, five or six animals. Some of these laws have been in effect for decades (and have been ignored just as long).

Mandatory neutering and spaying is a more recent idea. A number of municipalities have passed or are considering passing laws similar to the San Mateo County, California, ordinance which stipulates that residents may not own or harbour an unaltered cat or dog of more than six months of age without obtaining a licence to do so.

Another provision of this and similar ordinances requires people who want to breed cats or dogs to purchase a licence before they do so. Licence fees range from $25 per litter to a flat fee of $100 for the privilege of breeding as many litters in a year as the owner desires.

Breeders' responsibilities

Whenever legislation that would affect the activities of dog and cat breeders has been proposed as a means of reducing pet overpopulation or making life more pleasant for cats, breeders have responded with snarling attacks against that legislation. Those attacks have so frequently been wrongheaded, self-serving and transparently illogical as to make a body wonder if there ought to be a leash law applied to some people, not just to animals.

For breeders' complaints about their 'rights' being abrogated by pet-limitation or breeding-restrictive ordinances are unwarranted. When one thinks of the rights for which people have struggled and suffered — civil rights, women's rights, gay and lesbian rights, animal rights, the rights of the handicapped — one is hard put not to laugh at people who wax stentorian about their 'rights' to keep dogs in narrow runs in the backyard or to stuff cats into perhaps unsuitable cages in a spare room off the garage.

Keeping a companion animal is a privilege, not a right. Causing animals to reproduce is also a privilege, one that ought to be regulated for the sake of animals and for the good of society. The only people worthy of these privileges are those who enrich an animal's life as much as that animal enriches theirs, and who would willingly trade places with any of the animals in their care.

GLOSSARY

Words in *italics* refer to separate entries within the glossary

A

Agouti The colour between the stripes on a ticked or tabby cat; for example, the warm red tone between the chocolate-brown stripes on a red Abyssinian.

Allele One of two or more genes — each one governing a different physical trait — that can occupy a particular locus (position) on a chromosome; for example, the genes determining coat length — either long or short — are alleles.

Alter 1) A cat that has been sterilized surgically; 2) to sterilize a cat by surgical means.

Anoestrus A period during which a female cat is not in oestrus (heat or season).

Any Other Colour (AOC) Any potential colour that might occur in a breed, excepting those colours or patterns prohibited by the breed standard.

Any Other Variety (AOV) Any cat that is the offspring of two registered parents but is not eligible for championship competition because it does not meet the requirements for coat length, coat colour, eye colour, etc.

Awn hair The coarser of the two kinds of secondary hairs; normally longer than down hair, but shorter than guard hair.

B

Benching cage The enclosure in which a cat remains in the show hall when it is not being judged.

Blaze 1) In blue creams and tortoiseshells, a vertical division of two colours extending down the centre of the forehead and nose; 2) in bicolours, a splash of white on the forehead and/or nose.

Bloodline (or line) The ancestors of a cat; also used, loosely, to refer to any cat produced by a particular cattery.

Break A distinct, unquestionable indentation in the bridge of the nose, occurring between — or at a short distance below a point in between — the eyes.

Breed Cats with similar physical characteristics and, usually, some ancestors in common.

Brindling The random mixture of hairs of different colours in a cat's coat.

Brush The tail on a longhaired cat.

C

Carry 1) To possess a recessive gene (see below) or genes governing a physical characteristic not apparent to the eye; a shorthaired cat, for example, may carry a longhair gene; 2) to harbour a virus or bacteria that could transmit a disease; 3) to be pregnant with kittens.

Cat fancy The general association of cat-registering bodies, breeders and exhibitors dedicated to the welfare, promotion, care and exhibition of all cats.

Cattery A place where cats are bred and/or boarded.

Cattery name The registered name of a place where cats are bred.

Chromosomes Minute, rod-shaped elements in the nucleus of a cell that control the inheritance of characteristics in the cell and in the entire cat.

Cobby Close coupled; that is, short in the body and low on the legs.

Colour breeding Mating cats of the same colour and breed for at least three to five generations.

Condition The state of a cat's health; includes weight, muscle tone, cleanliness and grooming.

Conformation The arrangement of a cat's torso, legs and tail.

Congenital Present at birth but not acquired by heredity.

Cross 1) A mating between cats; 2) to mate or breed one cat with another.

D

Dam The female parent.

Dilute A paler version of a basic colour. For example, blue is the dilute of black, cream is the dilute of red.

Doctoring 1) A synonym for neutering in the United Kingdom; 2) in the United States, a term used to describe the illegal alteration of a cat's colour.

Domestic A nonpedigree cat indigenous to a particular country.

Dominant Prevailing over another. For example, the gene for folded ears is dominant over the gene for straight ears. Thus, a cat inheriting one gene for folded ears and one gene for straight ears will have folded ears.

Double coat A coat in which the awn hairs are as long as the guard hairs. Usually, the awn hairs are intermediate in length between the longer guard hairs (see below) and the shorter down hairs (see immediately below).

Down hair The shorter hair of the two types of secondary hairs, that is, the shortest hair in a cat's coat.

E

Euthanasia The act of ending humanely a cat's life.

F

Feral A formerly domesticated cat — or the descendants of formerly domesticated cats — now living in the wild. Often used to denote a free-roaming cat that does not appear to belong to anyone.

Follicle 1) The indentation in the skin from which hair grows; 2) the sac on the female's ovary in which an egg develops.

Foreign A moderately tubular body conformation as found, for example, in the Abyssinian.

G

Gene pool The total of all the genes that exist in the cats of a breed.

Genes Units of heredity that control the growth, development, function and physical characteristics of a cat.

Genotype The genes an individual inherits from its parents.

Gestation The period between conception and birth; normally lasts from 63 to 69 days in cats.

Ground colour The colour occupying the part of the hair shaft nearest the body.

Guard hairs The outer — and longest — hairs in a cat's coat; also called the primary hairs.

H

Heat A period (usually six to nine days long) in which a female cat is sexually receptive.

Heterozygous Possessing a pair of different alleles (see above) that govern a particular trait.

Hormone A chemical messenger sent into the bloodstream by a gland to affect development or function in another part of the body.

Hybrid 1) A cat produced from a mating between cats of different breeds; 2) a breed developed by combining two or more other breeds.

I

Inbreeding A union between two cats that does not result in the introduction of any new genetic material to the offspring of those cats. Mother-son, father-daughter, and brother-sister matings are examples of inbreeding.

L

Line breeding A mating between cats that have one or more common ancestor(s) among the first three generations of each of those cats' ancestors.

M

Mutation A genetic misadventure — usually caused by environmental conditions or a miscue in the replication process — that alters the normal inheritance of a characteristic.

N

Neuter 1) A castrated male; 2) to remove the testicles from a male cat.

O

Oriental The most slim and elongated of the tubular body styles.

Outcross 1) A breeding between two cats that do not have any ancestors in common for at least three generations; 2) a breed used in the production of another breed of kittens. The British Shorthair, for example, is an outcross for the Scottish Fold.

P

Papers Registration documents issued for a cat.

Pedigree A document containing the known names, titles, colours and registration numbers of the first three to five generations of a cat's ancestors.

Phenotype A cat's physical appearance.

Piebald A pattern in which areas of white surround areas of colour.

Pigment Coloration (or colouring matter) in a cat.

Pointed A pattern in which a pale body colour contrasts with darker colour(s) that are confined to a cat's face, ears, legs and tail.

Points 1) The face, ears, legs and tail of a pointed cat.

Purebred A cat whose ancestors are all of the same breed or allowable combination of breeds; sometimes used as a synonym for *pedigreed*.

Q

Quarantine A period during which a cat is isolated from other cats in order to prevent the spread of disease.

Queen A female cat of breeding age.

Quick The vein in a cat's claw.

R

Recessive 1) A characteristic, such as a long coat, that is not expressed in a cat's physical appearance unless that cat possesses two genes governing that characteristic; 2) a gene governing a recessive trait.

Registry An association that records the lineage of cats, issues registration numbers, licenses shows, etc.

Ring An area, usually oblong in shape, in which cats are judged at a show.

Roman nose A nose characterized by low-slung nostrils and a concave profile.

Rufous A genetic factor that alters (and generally improves) a colour. The rufous influence makes a ruddy Abyssinian out of a cat that otherwise would be a black agouti tabby.

S

Selective breeding The purposeful mating of two cats to achieve desired traits or to eliminate undesired ones.

Self Solid; as in, 'The mother is a self-red cat'.

Sire The male parent of a cat.

Solid All of one colour (see *self*).

Spay A female cat that has been sterilized surgically; 2) to render a female cat sterile by surgical means.

Spotting 1) White areas in a cat's coat; 2) the discharge of fluid by a pregnant cat.

Standard A document that describes the ideal specimen in a breed.

Stop A slight indentation in the bridge of the nose occurring between — or at a moderate distance below a point in between — the eyes (see *break*).

Stud A siring male cat.

Stud book A volume containing the name, sexes, registration numbers and colours of cats and (when known) their ages and dates of birth; also contains similar information (when known) about the cats' parents.

T

Type The arrangements of the parts of a cat.

U

Undercoat The woolly down hairs on a cat; also used to denote the down and the longer awn hairs together.

Right: Two Maine Coon Cats enjoy the sun on a beautiful spring day.

FURTHER READING

Behrend & Wegler, K. & M. 1991. *The Complete Book of Cat Care.* Hauppauge, N.Y.: Barron's.

Edney, Andrew. 1992. *ASPCA Complete Cat Care Manual.* Dorling Kindersley.

Fogle, Bruce. 1991. *Know Your Cat.* Dorling Kindersley.

Gebhardt, Richard H. 1991. *The Complete Cat Book.* New York, N.Y.: Howell Book House.

Gerstenfeld, Sheldon L. 1979. *Taking Care of Your Cat.* New York, N.Y.: Addison-Wesley.

Gerstenfeld, Sheldon L. 1989. *The Cat Care Book.* New York, N.Y.: Addison-Wesley.

Hawcroft, Tim. 1991. *The Howell Book of Cat Care.* New York, N.Y.: Howell Book House.

Kaplan, E. & A. 1985. *The Complete Guide to Cat Training.* New York, N.Y.: Putnam.

Levy, Juliette D. 1991. *Complete Herbal Handbook for the Dog and Cat.* Winchester, MA.: Faber & Faber.

Malone, John. 1992. *One Hundred and Twenty-Five Most Asked Questions about Cats, and the Answer.* New York, N.Y.: William Morrow and Company.

Martyn & Taylor, E. & D. 1991. *The Little Cat Care Book.* Dorling Kindersley.

Muller, Ulrike. 1984. *New Cat Handbook: Everything about the Care, Nutrition, Diseases, & Breeding of Cats.* Hauppauge, N.Y.: Barron's.

Natoli, Eugenia. 1987. *Cats of the World.* New York, N.Y.: Crescent Books.

Neville, Peter. 1991. *Do Cats Need Shrinks? Cat Behavior Explained.* Chicago, IL.: Contemporary Books.

Pyles, Mary. 1990. *Everyday Cat: The Complete Guide to Owning, Understanding & Enjoying Your Pet Cat.* New York, N.Y.: Howell Book House.

Richards, Dorothy S. 1982. *How to Choose and Care for Your Cat.* Los Angeles, CA.: Price, Stern, Sloane.

Sayer, Angela. 1988. *Complete Book of the Cat.* Avenel, N.J.: Outlet Book Company.

Siegal, Mordecai, Ed. 1990. *The Cornell Book of Cats.* New York, N.Y.: Villard Books.

Stephens, Gloria. 1990. *Legacy of the Cat.* San Francisco, CA.: Chronicle Books.

Turner & Bateson, D. &. P. 1988. *The Domestic Cat: The Biology of its Behaviour.* Cambridge: Cambridge University Press.

Vine, Louis L. 1992. *Commonsense Book of Complete Cat Care.* New York, N.Y.: William Morrow and Company.

Viner, Bradley. 1986. *The Cat Care Manual.* Hauppaugue, N.Y.: Barron's.

Wood, Philip, Ed. 1980. *A Passion for Cats.* London: Trafalgar Square.

Below: A black-and-white shorthair stalking prey in the garden.

GENERAL INDEX

Page references to illustrations are in *italics*.

CREDITS

Artists
Copyright of the artwork illustrations on the pages following the artists' names is the property of Salamander Books Ltd.

Colour artwork
John Francis: Pages 12-89

Line artwork
John Francis: Pages 12-89
Alan Hollingberry: 135
Keller-Cross 116; 123 (T); 123 (T); 134.
Gordon Riley: 132; 133.
Clive Spong: 141 (TL); 141 (TR); 143.

Photographs
The Publishers would like to thank the photographers who have supplied photographs for this book. The photographs are credited by page number and position on the page as follows: (B) Bottom; (T) Top; (BL) Bottom left, etc.
Animal Graphics: 80;
The Bridgeman Art Library: 155 (B);
Bruce Coleman: 155 (TL);
Creszentia: 38; 64; 66; 84.
Anne Cumbers/Spectrum: 68.
Mary Evans: 154 (T); 155 (TR);
Marc Henrie: Endpapers; 1; 2/3; 6/7; 8/9; 10/11; 18/19; 48/49; 50; 54 56; 90/91; 92; 104/105; 114/115; 120/121; 145 (B); 150/151; 159 (T); 176/177; 177; 178; 179; 180 (T); 180 (B); 181; 185; 186.
Richard Katris (Chanan Photography): 22; 24; 26; 28; 36; 40; 42; 60 (T); 60 (B); 76; 78; 82 (T); 82 (B); 156/157; 162/163; 163; 168; 169 (T); 169 (B); 170; 171 (T); 171 (B); 172; 173; 174 (T); 174 (B); 175.
Cyril Laubscher: 4/5; 93 (T); 94; 95 (T); 95 (B); 96; 97; 98 (T); 98 (B); 99 (T); 99 (B); 100 (T); 100 (B); 101 (T); 101 (B); 102; 103; 105; 106 (T); 106 (B); 107 (L); 107 (R); 108 (T); 108 (B); 109 (T); 109 (B); 110; 111; 112 (T); 112 (B); 113; 115; 116; 117; 118; 119; 121; 122 (T); 122 (B); 123; 124 (T); 124 (B); 125 (T); 125 (B); 126; 127 (T); 127 (B); 128/129; 129; 130; 131; 132; 133; 134; 135; 136; 137; 138/139; 139; 140; 141; 142; 143; 144; 145 (T); 146; 147; 148 (T); 148 (B); 159 (BR); 160 (T); 160 (B); 161 (T); 161 (B); 164; 165 (T); 165 (B); 166 (T); 166 (B); 167.
Phil Maggitti: 182; 183.
Ronald Sheridan (The Ancient Art & Architecture Collection): 151; 152 (L); 152 (R); 153 (T); 153 (B); 154 (B).
Rob Waugh: 46.

Acknowledgements
The Publishers would like to thank the following individuals and organizations for their help in the preparation of this book: Mrs. Lesley Pring of the GCCF; Jackie and Alasdair Caldwell; Doug Chase; Michele Codd; Gill Cornish; Rosemary Dowdy; Dennis and Irene Duncan; Alan Edwards; Roslyn Elliot; Peter and Margaret Frayne; Nora Gardner; Neil and Michaela Giles; Myra Goggins; Ursula Graves; Helena Haywood; Alan Jones; Hannah Money; Susannah and Rachel Money; Averil Moon; Gloria and Emma Neale; Rebecca and Samantha Prescott; Beryl Reece; Caroline and Francis Roberts; Rohese Cattery; Dennis and Sally Sale; Kathryn Sanders; Lynn Stradling; Maureen Trompetto; Diana Waters.